The Japanese Financial System

The Japanese Financial System

Edited by

YOSHIO SUZUKI

*The Institute for Monetary and Economic Studies
of the Bank of Japan*

CLARENDON PRESS · OXFORD

Oxford University Press, Walton Street, Oxford OX2 6DP
Oxford New York Toronto
Delhi Bombay Calcutta Madras Karachi
Petaling Jaya Singapore Hong Kong Tokyo
Nairobi Dar es Salaam Cape Town
Melbourne Auckland
and associated companies in
Berlin Ibadan

Oxford is a trade mark of Oxford University Press

Published in the United States
by Oxford University Press, New York

British Library Cataloguing in Publication Data
The Japanese financial system.
1. Finance—Japan
I. Suzuki, Yoshio II. Institute for
Monetary and Economic Studies III. Waga
kuni no kinyu seido. English
332'.0952 HG187.J3
ISBN 0–19–828596–5

Library of Congress Cataloging in Publication Data
Waga kuni no kin'yū seido. English.
The Japanese financial system.
Translation of: Waga kuni no kin'yū seido.
Bibliography: p. Includes index.
1. Finance—Japan. 2. Financial institutions—Japan.
I. Suzuki, Yoshio, 1931– .
HG187.J3W3513 1987 332.1'0952 87–24824
ISBN 0–19–828596–5

Set by Butler and Tanner Ltd, Frome, Somerset
and
Printed and bound
in Great Britain by Biddles Ltd,
Guildford and King's Lynn

PREFACE TO THE ENGLISH EDITION

THIS book is an English edition of *Waga Kuni no Kinyu Seido* (The Japanese Financial System), which was written by the staff of my Institute and published in Tokyo in 1986, and which superseded earlier editions of the same title. This English edition is an edited version of the Japanese, with a special reference list added.

The reason for the new English edition was the need for a comprehensive, up-to-date book in English on the Japanese financial system, which has undergone such liberalization and internationalization in recent years. This new English edition is our response to that need, and is intended for a broad audience: foreign business firms, foreign financial institutions, their Japanese counterparts, our fellow central banks, other public authorities, and academics.

I would like to express my gratitude to Dr Robert Alan Feldman of the International Monetary Fund, who was very prominent in the process of translation. I am also grateful to the staff of Oxford University Press for valuable advice. All errors, of course, are my own responsibility.

I sincerely hope that this new English edition will help the foreign community to understand more fully both the Japanese financial system itself and the issues that it faces.

Yoshio Suzuki
Director
Institute for Monetary and
Economic Studies
The Bank of Japan

CONTENTS

LIST OF FIGURES

LIST OF TABLES

PART I

Overview: The Financial Structure and the Financial System

1

Development of the Economy and Change of the Financial Structure

GREAT changes are now occurring in the state of financial transactions in Japan, concerning regulations, customs, and the behaviour of sectors. These changes in the financial structure reflect changes in the real economy, and include changes in all aspects of the financial system—financial assets, financial markets, and financial institutions. Although Part II of this book will explain the details of these changes, Part I will first give an overview of the direction of change in financial structure, and of how the financial system is adapting. This overview will be made by contrasting the current state of affairs with that during the high growth period; that is, Part I is a general overview of the Japanese financial system.

I. Finance and the fluctuations of the Japanese economy

1. OVERVIEW

From 1955 until about 1970, the Japanese economy achieved a high rate of economic growth, supported by flourishing investment in plant and equipment and by expanding exports. Although there were cyclical fluctuations, the economy simultaneously achieved equilibrium in the balance of payments and stability of prices. (The stability of prices, however, was particularly evident in wholesale prices, while consumer prices began to accelerate slowly in the second half of the 1950s.) But the Nixon shocks of 1971 brought suspension of convertibility of the dollar to gold and the large-scale revaluation of the yen. After these events the so-called period of excess liquidity occurred, and inflation pressure mounted. In 1973 there was a considerable expansion of public investment, leading to an overheating of economy and a burst of inflation. The first oil crisis in the autumn of the same year acted to spur inflation even further.

Reacting to these events, the Bank of Japan tightened monetary policy by raising the reserve requirements on deposits at the start of 1973, and by raising the discount rate five times (to 9 per cent) during the year. Prices, however, continued to soar through 1974, and the balance of payments went into substantial deficit, reflecting the large increase in oil prices. Real economic growth was negative for the first time during the post-war period.

3

Japan, along with the other major oil-consuming countries of the world, faced the triple problem of inflation, recession, and balance of payments deficits. Also during this period, specifically in February and March of 1973, the yen moved to the floating rate system along with other major currencies, implying the final destruction of the Bretton Woods system of the post-war period.

The effects that this inflation and the oil crisis had on all sectors of the economy was huge. In 1974, the inflation rate exceeded 20 per cent, and fell to single figures only by the end of 1975. The balance of payments eventually returned to surplus, and the real economic growth rate became positive again only in 1975. And real growth was only about 5 per cent per year between 1976 and 1980, far below the trend rate in the high growth period before 1973. In 1978, a cyclical recovery based on domestic demand finally became clear, and then in 1979 this recovery lost steam due to the outbreak of the second oil crisis. Once again the Japanese economy could not avoid inflation, deterioration of the balance of payments, and recession.

The management of monetary policy during the second oil crisis focused on control of the money supply, as it had begun to do only in the monetary loosening period after 1975, and speculation by corporations and individuals did not occur. Thus, during the second oil crisis, the impact of oil price increases was absorbed relatively smoothly without inducing home-made inflation. As a result, the Japanese economy performed well in comparison with those of other major industrial countries. On the inflation front, the rises in gross profits and wages per unit of output were held at a low level, and the GNP deflator hardly rose at all. Hence the transmission of oil price increases into final goods prices in the domestic economy was held to a minimum, and, in contrast to many advanced countries, a second outbreak of double-figure inflation of consumer prices was avoided. Moreover, balance of payments equilibrium was restored by the end of 1980. Real growth, however, was somewhat slower to recover, and averaged only about 3 per cent between 1981 and 1983, due to the effects of the world-wide recession that accompanied late adjustment in various countries. Growth only resumed its trend level of about 5 per cent in 1984, as plant and equipment based on high technology and exports supported autonomous expansion.

As described above, the Japanese economy ended its high growth period and moved into a new era at the time of the first oil crisis and the shift to floating exchange rates [47]. Reflecting this new era, both the real and the financial sides of the Japanese economy saw major structural changes around 1973–4, which forced a broad-based reconsideration of the state of the financial system.

On the real side, corporations reacted to low growth with austerity, that is, with caution about investment, employment, and borrowing, while households reacted to the decline in the growth of income by paying hitherto unknown levels of attention to the formation and management of savings.

These reactions of the private non-financial sectors of the economy caused them to behave differently in financial markets, to expand the level of surplus savings, and to strengthen their preference for high-interest earnings. In contrast, the public sector expanded fiscal expenditure aggressively, even though tax revenue stagnated. As a result, the fiscal deficit expanded tremendously from 1975 onwards.

The mounting surplus in the private sector and deepening deficit in the public sector expressed themselves—as will be described from the financial side below—in the major change in the structure of the flow of funds in the economy. In particular, the deepening deficits in the public sector required large-scale issues of Governments bonds; as a result, the open market in Government bonds expanded tremendously. At the same time, internationalization of finance was promoted by internationalization of the real economy and by increased activity of cross-border fund flows. These trends were accelerated further in the early 1980s by the strengthening of demands for opening of financial and capital markets.

Such structural changes on the real and financial sides of the economy could not necessarily coexist within the financial framework of the high growth period, with its interest rate regulations and financial market segmentation. This is why financial innovations began to sprout and why movement toward financial liberalization was born. During the high growth period, market participants and interest rates were restricted by law, by administrative guidance, and by custom, in an effort to allocate funds to particular users. With the end of the high growth period, changes in the financial structure would be demanded as a result of diversification of financial needs. Now, when there exist no clear priorities (even tacit ones) for allocation of funds, it is appropriate to ease or to abolish the restrictions that limit competition in order to guarantee the opportunity for diverse financial transactions and to leave financial choices to the market-place.

The decade from 1975 to 1985 saw a gradual process of financial liberalization. This occurred by virtue of the recondiseration, easing, and abolition of controls. Three simple points should be made in this regard.

First, the secondary market for Government bonds expanded at an extremely rapid pace. This expansion was based on the large flotations of Government bonds after 1975, and was spurred in particular by the easing of regulations on banks concerning the sales of such bonds in 1977. The expansion of the secondary market in Government bonds meant an expansion of an open market in long-term instruments with free interest rates, and also promoted expansion of short-term open markets and the relaxation or abolition of interest rate controls.

Secondly, short-term open markets developed considerably after 1975. An example is the market for repurchases (also known as *gensaki*). The *gensaki* market had existed on a small scale since around 1950, but it expanded along with the growth of the secondary market in Government bonds. There was a strong shift of surplus corporate funds from three- or six-month fixed-term deposits into the *gensaki* market, because such transactions offered high rates just as corporations became more sensitive to interest rates as economic growth slowed. A market for negotiable certificates of deposits (CDs) was established, in May of 1979, partly as a reaction to the growth of the *gensaki* market. With the revision of the Foreign Exchange and Foreign Trade Control Law that took effect in December, 1980, cross-border movement of funds became more active. Yen deposits by non-residents and foreign currency deposits by residents also increased. These developments not only caused a reconsideration of interest rate controls but also contributed to reducing the thorough segmentation that had characterized the Japanese financial system.

Thirdly, interest rate arbitrage rose substantially, not only among markets within Japan but also between Japanese and foreign markets. The growth of arbitrage occurred after 1978, with the adoption of a series of liberalization measures that expanded and diversified the open markets in both long- and short-term assets, and abolished controls on who might participate in the markets. Before 1975 the various types of markets were to a large extent insulated from each other through interest rate controls and participation controls. But after 1975 the organic connection among markets strengthened.

These three major trends occurred as a reflection of the new historical era which the Japanese economy entered, and they were irreversible. It is quite likely that the various controls, such as interest rate controls, will continue to weaken, and that the Japanese financial system will undergo yet further evolution in the decade after 1985.

2. ECONOMIC ACTIVITY AND THE FLOW OF FUNDS

a. The savings–investment balance

(i) Overview

The most dramatic indicator of the changes in Japanese financial structure after the first oil crisis was the large change in the structure of the flow of funds. A numerical expression of this indicator may be found in the flow of funds accounts by using the 'net surplus position' of the various sectors.

Figure 1.1 shows the net surplus or deficit of each economic sector as a proportion of nominal GNP. The figure shows that the personal sector had a continuous, stable, and large surplus of about 10 per cent of nominal GNP. This ratio reached a peak in 1972, as investment by the personal sector in housing, for example, increased. But the ratio rose again after the first oil crisis because inflation had reduced the real value of financial assets and had caused households to wish to save more in order to make up for the loss. In contrast, both the corporate and the public sectors had deficits of funds. But the behaviour of the two deficit sectors contrasted markedly, with 1974 as the major turning-point. In the high growth period before 1974, the corporate sector's high level of plant and equipment investment caused it to have the largest deficit of funds. Until about 1971, this deficit was of the order of about 7 per cent of nominal GNP, but rose to more than 10 per cent between 1972 and 1974. The demand for plant and equipment investment fell tremendously after the first oil crisis, and this fall, combined with the trend of cost-cutting, greatly reduced the deficits of the corporate sector. In 1978

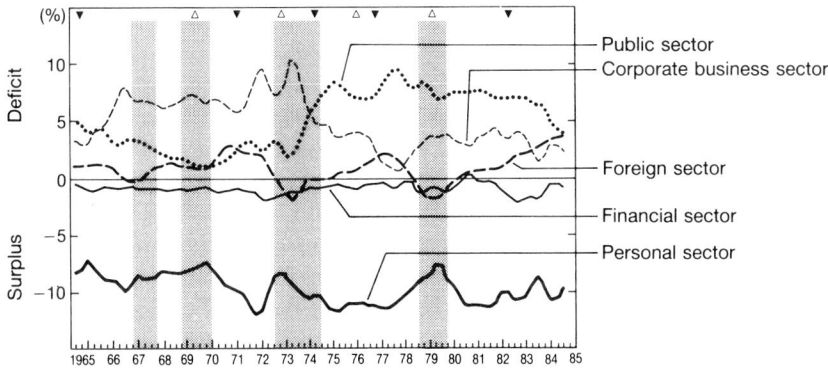

Figure 1.1 *Sectoral Deficits and Surpluses (in percent of nominal GNP)*
Notes:
Three-period moving average of seasonally adjusted figures, with weights of 1: 2: 1.
Shaded areas denote time of monetary tightness.
△ denotes cyclical peak, ▼ cyclical trough.

Sources: BOJ, *Shikin Junkan Kanjo* (Flow of Funds Accounts); and Economic Planning Agency, *Kokumin Keizai Keisan Nempo* (Annual Report on National Income Accounts.

the corporate sector had almost no deficit, a virtually unique situation. Thereafter, the deficit of funds re-emerged for the corporate sector but amounted to only about 3 per cent of nominal GNP. The public sector, on the other hand, had a very small deficit in the early 1970s, but this deficit expanded tremendously after 1974 and became greater than that of the corporate sector by 1975. Thereafter, deficits of about 7 per cent of GNP continued. A slight decline to about 6 per cent occurred in 1984 under the influence of severe fiscal retrenchment.

The net position of the foreign sector is simply the current account position of Japan viewed from the standpoint of foreign countries, and is the inverse of the net position of all domestic sectors put together. The foreign sector showed a surplus on two occasions in the 1970–85 period, that is, around the times of the first and second oil crises of 1973–4 and 1979–80. In other periods the foreign sector had deficits (that is, Japan ran current account surpluses), particularly in 1971–2, 1977–8, and after 1983.

Let us now consider the savings–investment balances of the various domestic economic sectors in some detail.

(ii) The corporate sector

The share of investment (gross domestic fixed capital formation plus inventory accumulation) in Japanese GNP is about 30 per cent, rather higher than those in other industrial countries. (On average between 1976 and 1983, investment as a share of nominal GNP was 31 per cent in Japan compared with 18 per cent in the United States, 20 per cent in the United Kingdom, 22 per cent in West Germany, and 22 per cent in France.) This is somewhat lower than the level of 37 per cent which characterized the Japanese economy just before the oil crisis. The corporate sector had accounted for about half of total real investment, and the decline in the share of investment in GNP was largely the result of the stagnation of investment in the corporate sector. That is, the ratio of investment by the corporate sector to GNP fell from about 20 per cent in the early 1970s to about 16 per cent in the late 1970s where it has remained in the early part of the 1980s (Table 1.1). The reason for this decline was that corporations were cautious about expanding total production capacity and did not invest actively in high technology that would improve the technological level of existing capacity.

Gross saving of the corporate sector is the sum of provisions for capital consumption (depreciation) and retained profits (net saving). Capital consumption has increased year by year due to expansion of depreciable assets. Retained profits, however, have fluctuated with the business cycle; profits fell sharply after the first oil crisis in 1974–5, and recovered only slowly thereafter. As a result of these two trends, the gross savings of corporations fluctuated within a narrow band around 11 per cent of nominal GNP.

Reflecting these trends in investment and saving, the corporate sector's net deficit of funds fell from about 7 per cent of GNP in the early 1970s to slightly less than 3 per cent in the second half of the 1970s. Though this net deficit expanded slightly in the early 1980s, it remained at the low level of just above 3 per cent.

(iii) The public sector

In the public sector, investment exceeded savings by a small amount in the decade from 1965 to 1975, but a major increase in the need for funds occurred

TABLE 1.1   *Composition of Gross National Expenditure (%)*[a,b]

	Composition of GNE in nominal terms					Composition of GNE in real terms				
	1965	1970	1975	1980	1984	1965	1970	1975	1980	1984
Private consumption expenditure	58·9	52·5	57·2	58·5	58·8	63·5	57·7	60·6	58·4	56·6
Private housing investment	5·6	6·4	7·3	6·2	4·7	6·6	7·8	8·2	6·2	4·9
Private plant and equipment investment	15·1	20·8	16·0	15·7	15·4	11·5	18·8	15·3	15·8	16·8
Private corporate inventory increase	1·8	3·4	0·1	0·8	0·5	1·5	3·1	0·2	0·9	0·7
Government expenditure	17·3	15·6	19·4	19·3	17·5	21·3	18·6	20·0	19·3	17·5
Current (goods and services)	8·2	7·5	10·0	9·8	9·8	12·4	9·7	10·1	9·8	9·5
Fixed capital formation	9·1	8·1	9·4	9·5	7·7	8·9	8·9	9·9	9·5	8·0
Surplus of the nation on current account	1·3	1·2	0·1	Δ0·5[c]	3·1	Δ4·4	Δ6·0	Δ4·3	Δ0·6	3·6
Exports of goods and services and factor income receipts	*11·0*	*11·5*	*13·7*	*14·9*	*17·0*	*7·4*	*9·3*	*12·1*	*15·2*	*19·1*
(less) Imports of goods and services and factor income payments	*9·7*	*10·3*	*13·6*	*15·4*	*13·9*	*11·8*	*15·3*	*16·4*	*15·7*	*15·5*
GROSS NATIONAL EXPENDITURE	100·0	100·0	100·0	100·0	100·0	100·0	100·0	100·0	100·0	100·0

[a] In nominal terms, fiscal years (April–March).
[b] Gross domestic fixed capital formation + increase in inventories = private housing investment + private plant and equipment + increase in private corporate inventory investment + public fixed capital formation.
[c] Δ denotes a deficit.

Source: (Economic Planning Agency (EPA), *Kokumin Keizai Keisan Nempo* (Annual Report on National Income Accounts (*ARNA*)).

after 1975. Since then, the deficit of the public sector has exceeded that of the corporate sector.

Table 1.2 gives the savings–investment balance for general Government (that is, a consolidation of central Government and local public bodies), which comprises the largest part of the public sector. As is clear from the table, there was a fairly steady rise in current expenditure (centring on personnel and consumption expenditures) during the first half of the 1970s, but current receipts (centring on tax revenue) also rose steadily and supported the savings side of the balance. In the last half of the 1970s, however, tax revenue stagnated, while social expenditure rose substantially after the major expansion of welfare programmes that had occurred in 1973. As a result, net savings by the public sector fell precipitously. In the first half of the 1980s tax revenue and other current receipts recovered to an extent, but current expenditure also continued to rise quickly, not only because of social expenditure but also because of rising interest costs on debt. As a result, the recovery of savings was limited.

Public investment, on the other hand, continued its high rate of increase throughout the decade to 1975. Even after the first oil crisis, and particularly in 1977–8, fiscal spending filled a gap caused by the fall in private domestic demand; a policy of increasing public works was adopted intentionally. In the first half of the 1980s, however, a policy of fiscal retrenchment was adopted, and the growth rate of public investment was considerably restrained, along with the growth of current expenditures.

Even though public investment is not currently rising particularly quickly, the low growth of tax revenue has meant a substantial reduction in savings. As a result, the net investment of general Government has been very large since 1975 and has continued into the first half of the 1980s. Large flotations of Government bonds have been necessary to finance this net investment.

(iv) The personal sector

The personal sector, especially households, has continuously been the largest net saver in the economy. Personal savings are defined as the difference between personal disposable income and consumption; the absolute amount of such savings has risen steadily since 1965. As a share of GNP, household savings rose from 13 per cent in the first half of the 1970s to 15 per cent in the second, before falling to about 11 per cent in the first half of the 1980s (Table 1.3). These changes were brought about by the movements of the labour share in income and in the personal savings rate. In the second half of the 1970s, after the first oil crisis, high rates of wage increase raised the share of labour income in total national income and thus raised personal disposable income. After 1980, however, with the second oil crisis, economic adjustment was sought through reduction of the labour share of income, and the growth of disposable income stagnated. As a result, the personal savings rate (the ratio of personal savings to personal disposable income) rose some-

TABLE 1.2 *Savings and Investment of General Government, Averages by Financial Years (1965–1981)*

	1965–9			1970–4			1975–9			1980–1		
	¥ (100m.)	% of GNP	% of total	¥ (100m.)	% of GNP	% of total	¥ (100m.)	% of GNP	% of total	¥ (100m.)	% of GNP	% of total
Current revenue (A)	94,197	19·7		235,069	23·1		475,795	25·1		809,259	29·7	
tax receipts	70,139	14·7		170,931	16·8		257,123	13·6		523,819	19·2	
Current expenditure (B)	66,465	13·9	100·0	166,101	16·3	100·0	430,005	22·7	100·0	727,239	26·6	100·0
personnel, goods, etc.	36,378		54·7	85,810		51·7	185,663		43·2	270,396		37·2
social security payments	15,552		23·4	41,170		24·8	132,115		30·7	239,323		32·9
interest costs	2,565		3·9	8,195		4·9	38,533		9·0	107,670		14·8
Savings (C = A − B)	27,732	5·8		68,968	6·8		45,790	2·4		82,020	3·0	
Gross savings[a]	n.a.			70,023	6·9		48,385	2·6		92,910	3·4	
Gross investment + land purchase (gross fixed capital formation)	n.a.			61,673	6·1		125,236	6·6		179,223	6·6	
Financial balance[b]	786	0·1		9,046	0·9		Δ75,491[b]	Δ4·0		Δ99,571	Δ3·6	

[a] Gross saving is the sum of financial saving, depreciation, and capital transfers.
[b] Δ denotes a deficit. The financial balance is that for the central government listed in the flow of funds accounts.

Sources: EPA, *ARNA*; BOJ; *SJK*.

TABLE 1.3   *Savings and Investment of the Personal Sector, Averages by Financial Years 1970–1984*

	1970–4		1975–9		1980–4	
	¥ (100m.)	% of nominal GNP	¥ (100m.)	% of nominal GNP	¥ (100m.)	% of nominal GNP
Disposable income (A)	686,046	67.3	1,384,918	73.1	1,953,503	70.9
Consumption expenditure (B)	550,393	54.0	1,098,005	57.9	1,610,363	59.0
Savings C = A − B	135,653	13.3	286,913	15.1	325,140	11.9
Savings rate (%)		19.8		20.7		16.8
Total savings[a]	167,904	16.5	362,170	19.1	438,666	16.1
Total investment + land pur-						
chase	70,134	6.9	179,596	9.5	190,480	7.0
(gross fixed capital for-						
mation) *of which* housing	65,123	6.4	124,379	6.6	137,448	5.0
Financial balance[b]	95,838	9.4	193,100	10.2	272,409	10.0

[a] *See table 1.2*, note *a*.
[b] The financial balance is that for the personal sector in the flow of funds accounts.

Sources: EPA, *ARNA*; BOJ, *SJK*.

what in the second half of the 1970s but declined in the first half of the 1980s. (The personal savings rate went from 19.8 per cent in the first half of the 1970s to 20.7 per cent in the second, and then back down to 16.8 per cent in the first half of the 1980s.) None the less, the absolute level of this ratio was substantially higher than those in industrial countries, because the propensity to save in Japan was much higher [39]. For example, in 1983 the savings rate in the United States was 5 per cent; in the United Kingdom, 7 per cent; in West Germany, 11 per cent; and in France, 12 per cent.

In contrast with savings, investment by the personal sector, as represented by its largest component (housing investment), rose substantially around 1975; but it hit a ceiling as a proportion of nominal GNP in the second half of the 1970s because of uncertainties about the future growth of income. In the early 1980s a small decline of this investment ratio occurred.

The fluctuations of personal savings were larger than those of investment, and thus the net savings of the personal sector as a proportion of nominal GNP rose from the first half of the 1970s into the second half, but declined slightly thereafter. Nevertheless, the net savings rate of the personal sector remained at the very high level of about 10 per cent [19].

b. The flow of funds

(i) Overview

The imbalances of net investment and net savings of the various sectors have been absorbed through the give and take of financial markets. Figure 1.2 gives an overview of how funds flowed from savings sectors to financial markets and then to investing sectors during the first half of the 1980s.

The figure shows five important facts. First, the personal sector was the largest provider of gross savings in the economy, accounting for 53 per cent. Following the personal sector were the corporate sector with 36 per cent and

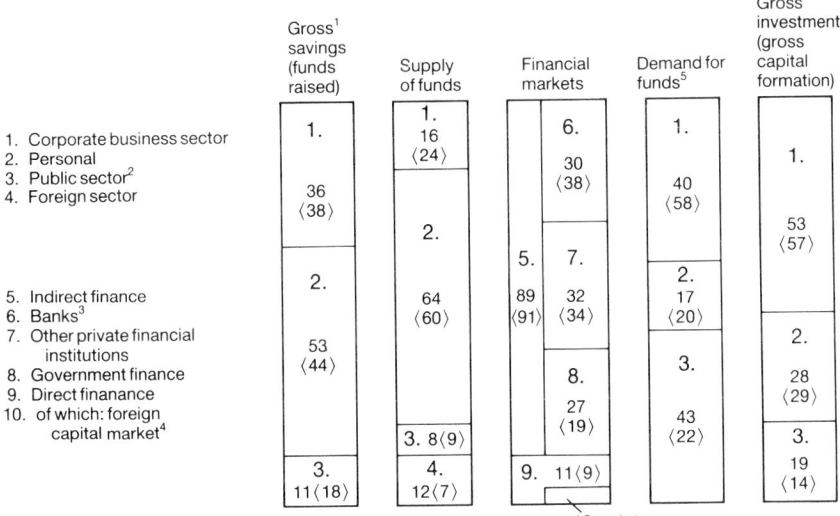

Figure 1.2 *Flow of Funds from Savings to Investment Average for 1980–84 (in percent of total; < > indicate figures for 1970–74)*

[1] Gross savings of business corporations includes investment by public entities such as the Japanese National Railway (JNR) and the Government Printing Office. General government includes central and local government, and public co-operations. The same holds for gross investment.

[2] For gross savings and investment, general government; for funds supply and demand, public sector, which includes general government and public corporations.

[3] Including the Bank of Japan.

[4] The foreign component includes underwriting of securities by financial intermediaries, due to data constraints.

[5] This column shows demand for funds by final domestic borrower, including funds raised abroad. As a memorandum item, the following data show how total fund supply by final domestic suppliers was broken down by demanding sector, including the foreign sector:

Business corporations	Personal	Public	Foreign
34	14	36	16
<53>	<18>	<20>	< 9>

Sources: BOJ, *SJK, Shikin Junkan Kanjo Oyo Hyo* (Application Tables from the Flow of Funds Accounts); EPA, *ARNA*, for gross savings and investment.

the public sector (that is, general Government) with 11 per cent. The personal sector provided a much larger share than it did during the high growth period, and the public sector provided a much smaller share. Secondly, the personal sector also provided the largest share of funds that flowed into financial markets, 64 per cent. The corporate sector provided only 16 per cent, and the public sector only 8 per cent. Thirdly, the largest share of these savings, 89 per cent, continued to be intermediated through indirect finance by financial institutions, while only a much smaller share, 11 per cent, was intermediated through direct finance, such as through the domestic capital market or foreign capital markets. Still, the share of indirect finance declined slowly after the high growth period. Fourthly, the major borrowing sector in the economy changed from the corporate sector to the public sector. The latter accounted for 43 per cent of total borrowing, the corporate sector a much reduced 40 per cent, and the personal sector only about 17 per cent. The rise of borrowing by the public sector reflected its reduced savings owing to the increase of current expenditure. Fifthly, the sectoral shares have not changed for that portion of funds that are used for fixed capital investment. The share of the corporate sector remains highest at 53 per cent, while that of the personal sector is 28 per cent and that of the public sector (general Government) 19 per cent.

(ii) Fund-raising and asset composition of domestic economic sectors

A further breakdown of fund flows reveals more interesting facts. Let us consider the demand and supply of funds by the various economic sectors in some detail.

Trends in fund-raising, that is the demand for funds, are given in Table 1.4. Total fund-raising in the domestic economy are exhibited cyclical movements under the influence of the real economy and financial conditions. In the second half of the 1960s and the first half of the 1970s, both the demand for liquidity and the demand for investment rose substantially. Because this period was also one of relative ease in financial conditions, the pace of fund-raising was extremely rapid. But in 1973–4, the level of fund-raising stagnated, owing to the major decline in corporate investment that accompanied the first oil crisis and to the tightening of monetary policy. From 1975 onwards, fund-raising grew only slowly, reflecting the more stable growth of the economy and improved efficiency in the management of funds.

These trends were reflected in the ratio of total funds raised by domestic economic sectors to nominal GNP. This ratio was between 21–3 per cent in the second half of the 1970s and peaked at 34 per cent in 1972, but then declined to only 23 per cent in 1974. With the pick-up in real growth in the last half of the 1970s, this ratio rose slightly to about 25 per cent but then declined once again to about 20 per cent in the first half of the 1980s.

A sectoral decomposition of these trends shows the major structural change noted above concerning the shift of major borrowing activity from the

TABLE 1.4 Funds Raised by Domestic Economic Sectors, Averages by Financial Years 1965–1984

	1965–9		1970–4		1975–9		1980–4	
	¥100m.	%	¥100m.	%	¥100m.	%	¥100m.	%
By sector								
Corporate business	62,320	60·4	158,804	58·4	149,767	33·1	227,955	39·9
Personal	18,994	18·4	54,668	20·1	92,388	20·5	99,254	17·3
Public[a]	21,942	21·3	58,336	21·5	209,683	46·4	244,613	42·8
of which government	6,129	5·9	18,572	6·8	126,810	28·1	154,222	27·0
By form								
Borrowings	78,992	76·5	215,007	79·1	278,745	61·7	364,067	63·7
from private institutions	65,094	63·0	174,281	64·1	181,394	40·1	253,533	44·4
from public institutions	13,898	13·5	40,726	15·0	97,352	21·6	110,534	19·3
Securities[a]	22,908	22·2	50,118	18·4	170,340	37·7	209,194	36·6
of which bonds	16,169	15·7	38,286	14·1	140,992	31·2	171,661	30·0
Foreign borrowings, etc.	1,356	1·3	6,683	2·5	2,753	0·6	Δ1,439[b]	Δ0·3
TOTAL (A)	103,256		271,808		451,838		571,822	
(Percentage of nominal GNP)	(21·6)		(26·7)		(23·8)		(21·0)	

[a] Excludes the net increases in foreign exchange fund securities of the Government.
[b] Δ denotes a deficit.

Sources: BOJ, SJK; and SKJ Application Tables.

public sector to the corporate sector. Until about 1975, the corporate sector borrowed roughly 60 per cent of total funds raised. But after the first oil crisis and the advent of corporate cost-cutting, fund-raising by the corporate sector fell substantially, for example between 1974–5 and 1977–8. There was an increase in corporate fund-raising in the first half of the 1980s due to recovery of plant and equipment investment, but the tempo of this increase was slow because of the improvements in techniques of money management by corporations. Developments in public-sector fund-raising were in stark contrast to those of the corporate sector. The public sector took a relatively stable share of about 20 per cent of total fund-raising during the second half of the 1960s and the first half of the 1970s. After 1975, however, fund-raising by the public sector grew substantially by means of large-scale issues of Government bonds. Fund-raising by the public sector rose to the neighbourhood of 50 per cent of the total. Since around 1980, the policy of fiscal retrenchment has continued, with the aim of reducing Government deficits and bond issues. Nevertheless, fund-raising by the public sector continued to exceed that of the corporate sector. Fund-raising by the personal sector, in the forms of borrowing for housing loan and consumer credit, rose in the 1950s and 1960s, but has been stable since the early 1970s at about 20 per cent of total funds raised.

The fund-raising of domestic economic sectors continues to be carried out primarily through borrowing. Though still predominant, however, the share of borrowing has fallen from just under 80 per cent in the early 1970s to somewhat over 60 per cent in the late 1970s and early 1980s. The fall in borrowing has hit different financial institutions differently. Public-sector financial institutions have been gaining in share from about 15 per cent to about 20 per cent, while private-sector financial institutions, by contrast, have seen their share decline from about 64 per cent to about 40 per cent.

The decline in the share of borrowing in total fund-raising had its counterpart in the rise in the share of fund-raising through issues of securities. In the early 1970s, issues of securities accounted for about 18 per cent of total fund-raising, but this share rose to almost 40 per cent after 1975 due to the large-scale issues of Government bonds. The foreign sector has also played an important role in providing funds, though the extent of this role has reflected financial conditions both at home and abroad. When international monetary conditions were disturbed between 1971 and 1974, speculative inflows of short-term capital were extremely large. Thereafter, however, such inflows were reduced, and, in the first half of the 1980s, there were even large outflows of funds, on account particularly of the high interest rates that were continuing in the United States.

The supply of funds was the mirror image of the demand for funds. Table 1.5 shows that the supply of funds measured on a flow basis rose quickly at first, from under ¥ 10bn. in the last half of the 1960s to ¥ 32bn. around 1972, and more steadily thereafter to around ¥ 60bn. in recent years. In

TABLE 1.5 *Funds Invested by Domestic Economic Sectors, Averages by Financial Years 1965–1984*

	1965–9		1970–4		1975–9		1980–4	
	¥100m.	%	¥100m.	%	¥100m.	%	¥100m.	%
By sector								
Corporate business	26,289	26·3	70,180	26·7	80,028	18·2	133,032	23·0
Personal	64,335	64·4	168,796	64·3	305,315	69·6	397,675	68·6
Public	9,265	9·3	23,673	9·0	53,707	12·2	48,665	8·4
By form								
Money (cash, demand deposits)	21,011	21·0	57,984	22·1	61,698	14·1	36,722	6·3
demand deposits	16,746	16·8	47,218	18·0	50,328	11·5	28,001	4·8
Time deposits (including CDs and postal savings)	46,310	46·4	117,676	44·8	208,380	47·5	252,526	43·6
Postal savings	8,174	8·2	26,229	10·0	64,961	14·8	84,250	14·5
Trusts	5,509	5·5	13,851	5·3	25,883	5·9	39,957	6·9
Insurance	9,400	9·4	22,354	8·5	43,533	9·9	78,313	13·5
Securities	8,079	8·1	24,906	9·5	55,209	12·6	81,613	14·1
Bonds	5,864	5·9	13,546	5·2	38,474	8·8	50,988	8·8
Foreign claims	1,993	2·0	6,518	2·5	7,028	1·6	33,220	5·7
TOTAL (A)	99,889		262,649		439,050		579,372	
(Percentage of nominal GNP)	(20·9)		(25·8)		(23·2)		(21·2)	

Sources: BOJ, *SJK*; *SJK* Application Tables; EPA, *ARNA*.

1983, supply of funds was ¥ 60bn. and in 1984, ¥ 67bn. These trends in the supply of funds of course reflect economic trends over these years and are inflated by price increases. But expressed as a percentage of nominal GNP, the supply of funds rose from about 21 per cent in the late 1960s to about 26 per cent during the period of excess liquidity in the early 1970s. This ratio declined to 23 per cent in the second half of the 1970s and declined further to 21 per cent in the first half of the 1980s.

By economic sector, personal sector accounted for the overwhelming share of the supply of funds, while the corporate and public sectors provided much smaller shares. This composition became even more extreme over the years as the share of personal sector rose from 64–5 per cent in the 1960s to just under 70 per cent in the 1970s. In contrast, the corporate sector showed substantial cyclical fluctuations during the economic changes of the high growth period. But after 1975, the share of the corporate sector fell to around 20 per cent from the figure of somewhat below 27 per cent before 1975. This fall was due to the reduction of liquidity demands by firms because of cost-cutting and the simplification and diversification of methods of raising funds. The public-sector share in supply of funds remained low, at about 10 per cent.

About half of the supply of funds was in the form of time deposits including certificates of deposits (CDs) and postal savings deposits. After 1975, the share of trusts, insurance, and securities also rose, while that of monetary assets such as cash and demand deposits fell sharply from the 21–2 per cent of the years before 1975 to about 6 per cent in the early 1980s. Within time deposits, the rise was due largely to an increase in postal savings deposits, while the share of private financial institutions fell. The latter reacted to this situation by strengthening their demands for financial innovation. They introduced CDs and money market certificates (MMC) with interest rates tied to open-market rates. In addition, they liberalized interest rates on large-denomination time deposits over ¥ 100 m., (April 1987). Though the share of such instruments in the markets remains quite small, there have been very large increases.

The decline in the share of monetary assets was largely a result of lower holdings of deposit money or demand deposits by the corporate and personal sectors. For the corporate sectors, a major reason for the reduction of monetary assets was the declining proportion of compensating balances held against borrowings that accompanied the cost-cutting associated with lower growth. In addition, development of markets with free interest rates, such as *gensaki* and CD markets, brought an expansion of opportunities to manage short-term funds at high interest rates. Thus, there were high-opportunity costs of holding deposits with interest rates that were controlled at low levels. For the personal sector, the decline in holdings of monetary assets occurred because of a strengthened desire for high-interest earnings. The economization of ordinary monetary deposit balances occurred through the use of so-called 'general accounts' (*sogo koza*).

(iii) Accumulation and diversification of financial assets

The demands for and supplies of funds by domestic sectors were also reflected in movements of the stocks of financial assets. It is interesting to note the trends for the personal sector and the corporate sector individually, as well as that for the total of the two (that is, for the private non-financial sector). Both gross financial assets and net financial assets (gross assets minus financial liabilities) are of interest. Figure 1.3 shows these indicators expressed as ratios to nominal GNP.

Most interesting is the extraordinary jump in both indicators that occurred in 1971–2. This extraordinary rise was due to the combination of the large surpluses in the balance of payments that were associated with the last period of the Bretton Woods system and the large deficits of the public sector that were associated with expansionary fiscal policy. For the corporate sector, the jump in the gross asset ratio was particularly large when compared to that of the net asset ratio. This difference occurred because corporations were keeping an increasing share of offsetting balances in financial assets against loans that were made by financial institutions in this period of monetary ease.

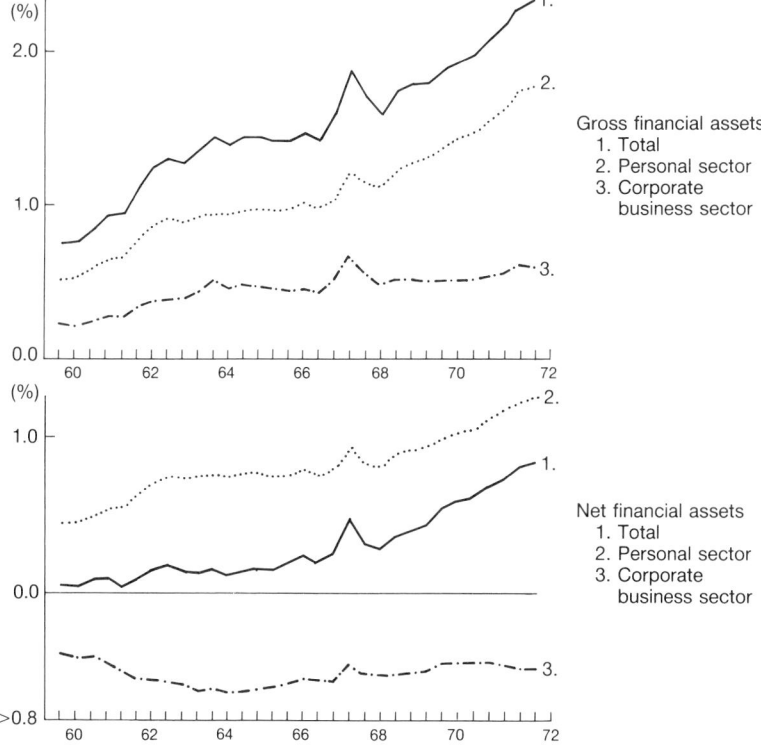

Figure 1.3 *Accumulation of Financial Assets*[1] *(in percent of nominal GNP)*

[1] *Assets as of year-end.*
Sources: as for Fig. 1.1.

With the exception of this extraordinary period, the accumulation of gross financial assets by the private non-financial sector exceeded the growth rate of nominal income throughout the period from the 1950s into the 1960s and even through the 1970s. In the 1950s and 1960s, the personal sector raised its savings rate and added to its financial assets. The corporate sector was increasing its investment activity but also relied to a larger extent on external funding. In order to secure good customer relationships with banks, the corporations held larger levels of financial assets as compensating balances against higher borrowings [52]. This is why the gross financial asset ratio for the corporate sector was rising while the net financial asset rate was falling.

At the end of the 1960s, the flotation of long-term Government bonds began, and the balance of payments turned toward the surplus. These changes in the economic environment meant the first signs of alleviation of the chronic problem of illiquidity, and hence financial asset accumulation slowed to about the tempo of nominal GNP growth. In 1971–2, however, accumulation of financial assets accelerated because of the occurrence of excess liquidity.

After this excess liquidity was extinguished, the net financial asset ratio began to rise rapidly, particularly after 1975. The net financial asset ratio is, of course, only the accumulation of year-to-year financial surpluses of a given sector, so that the rapid rise of the gross financial asset ratio was only the result of addition of investment of funds raised to the net ratio. The increases in these ratios were, therefore, the result of expansion of the savings surplus of the private non-financial sector at the time. As seen above, the deficit of the public sector also expanded at this time; at the same time, the deficit of the corporate sector diminished, and the surplus of the personal sector increased. As a result, the net financial surplus of the latter two sectors combined: that is, the surplus of the private non-financial sector as a whole rose substantially. Meanwhile, the rise in deposits of the corporate sector, which had continued steadily since the 1950s, disappeared with the reduction of the financial deficit of the corporate sector. In short, gross financial assets were accumulated in a way almost precisely parallel with the movements of net financial assets.

The rapid accumulation of both net and gross financial assets in a period of lower growth of income brought a higher interest sensitivity to the private non-financial sector, and caused a diversification of financial needs. In this process, the same trends were seen on a stock basis as were noted above on a flow basis. That is, the share of monetary assets fell, while the share of time deposits was largely unchanged, even though share of postal savings rose and that of deposits in private financial institutions fell. In addition, the total share of deposits fell while those of trusts, insurance, and securities rose.

Thus, the accumulation and diversification of financial assets was one of the main reasons for the changes in the Japanese financial system and for the development of Japanese financial markets. Let us now turn to a step-by-step explanation of the direction of these changes in financial structure.

II. The financial structure of the high growth period

1. THE PROCESS OF CHANGE IN THE FINANCIAL STRUCTURE

The major changes in the Japanese financial structure represented the beginning of a new historical era. But these changes can only be understood in the context of the previous historical era, that is, the period of high growth.

The financial structure of the high growth period has come to be viewed as one fettered by controls, particularly when seen from the viewpoint of the 1980s with its lower growth rates, floating exchange rates, computers, rapid telecommunications systems and, new economic and technological conditions. The controls of the high growth period focused on interest rates, particularly those of deposit-taking banks and the private sector. Such controls led to incentives for the private sector to circumvent regulation, and the authorities realized that the controls did not fill the financial needs of the country and were even becoming barriers to efficiency and fairness. As a result, the controls were loosened and gradually abolished. The process of change in the financial structure of Japan has been an interaction of the innovative financial behaviour in the form of liberalization and internationalization of finance [13]. In order to understand these changes in the financial structure, a brief description of the characteristics of the financial structure during the high growth period is necessary.

2. THE FINANCIAL STRUCTURE DURING THE HIGH GROWTH PERIOD

a. Overview

The characteristics of the financial structure during the high growth period were the result of conditions facing the real economy. In the immediate post-war years, economic growth was constrained by scarcities of capital and raw materials even though there was a surplus of labour. As a result, the road to economic autonomy for Japan lay in giving first priority to investment and exports which allowed the import of raw materials. Given this background, it was quite appropriate for the economic policy of the post-war years to give priority to investment and exports. Fortunately, the goals of this policy were realized as hoped [39].

Various types of policy were implemented to achieve these goals. For example, important roles in the encouragement of investment and exports were played by protectionist industrial policies and by tax policies that promoted savings and investment. At the same time, an important role was played by financial structure policies. These financial policies allocated funds to the investment and export sectors through the use of various types of control, most particularly interest rate controls. Policies that insulated domestic markets from foreign influences were also adopted.

During the high growth period, it was often emphasized that investment and exports could be encouraged by reducing financing costs, particularly through keeping the level of interest rates as low as possible by means of interest rate controls. There is, however, a point of view which doubts that the so-called 'artificial' low interest rate policy was in fact able to reduce financing costs to corporations and thus encourage investment and exports [46]. With the exception of the long-term prime rate, the interest rate on loans in fact fluctuated freely to some extent, and there is some doubt whether the effective rate of interest on loans (which is calculated with an adjustment for compensating balances) was low enough actually to encourage investment or exports. On loans from Government financial institutions, however, there were no compensating balances, and hence the stated loan rate and the effective loan rate were identical. Thus Government financial institutions were able to supply long-term funds at lending rates considerably below those of private financial institutions, and so these institutions did play a role in encouraging investment and exports. In addition, the Bank of Japan's preferential export financing system did in fact lower the financing costs of exporting.

But the more important point for the financial system was that interest rate controls—and particularly controls on deposit interest rates—prevented destructive competition. The absence of destructive competition had an important role in stabilizing the business atmosphere for the financial intermediaries that carried the burden of indirect finance [38]. This was called a 'convoy system' of management. Controls that separated long- and short-term financial business, played a role in restricting competition among financial institutions by separating long-term loan supply from short-term loan supply. As a result of this stable business atmosphere, financial institutions were able to respond to the flourishing demand for funds by corporations. As high growth proceeded, the expected rate of profit of corporations was high enough in comparison with effective loan rates to render firms willing to embark on investments as long as sufficient liquidity was available. In such a world of indirect finance, small firms with high growth potential were able to raise funds through loans, in contrast with a world of direct finance, in which only large firms with established reputations were able to float securities [20]. It is not unreasonable to say that interest rate controls encouraged growth in the sense that they allowed indirect finance to flourish (this theme is developed further in Chapter 2). In addition, the isolation of domestic financial markets from foreign ones played the role of preventing foreign influences from disrupting the various financial controls in the domestic markets. The maintenance of controls on international transactions thus helped to support the overall framework of the high growth period.

Thus the economic framework of the high growth period was one in which economic growth was based on investment and exports, and which relied on a control-oriented financial system. From the viewpoint of the economic units who were conducting financial transactions, this control-oriented financial system had four important characteristics: the predominance of indirect finance, over-borrowing, over-loan, and maldistribution of funds. Let us consider these four characteristics in some detail [36], [46].

b. The four characteristics of the financial structure

The predominance of indirect finance was best illustrated by its overwhelming share in the supply of funds, almost always above 90 per cent throughout the high growth period up to the early 1970s. The background to this phenomenon had historical roots in the early attempts of Japan to become a modern industrial nation through encouragement of the banking system. But there were also three contemporary reasons for the predominance of indirect finance during the high growth period. First was the use of various types of controls; these controls stablilized the business environment of the financial institutions which were the essence of indirect finance and encouraged the development of these institutions. Second was the low level of flotation of public bonds; because such bonds had low risk and were floated in large lots, they would have encouraged market transactions, so that the lack of such bonds made the development of open markets difficult and protected the structure of indirect finance. Third was the use of interest rate controls and controls on foreign transactions; these controls hindered the development of bond markets.

Over-borrowing denotes a state of affairs in which the raising of funds by the corporate sector relies to an extremely high degree on borrowing from banks. Over-borrowing occurred during the high growth period in Japan, from the middle of the 1950s onward. With growth based on investment and exports, the ratio of investment to GNP was extremely high, and thus a mechanism was at work that greatly expanded the funding requirements of the corporate sector. With insufficient accumulation of liquidity of their own, firms had no choice but to rely on outside funding, and most were forced to rely on borrowing from banks, given the priority accorded to indirect finance. (It is interesting to note that the reliance on own capital in the manufacturing industries was about 30 per cent at the beginning of the high growth period but declined steadily to about 17 per cent by 1975.) Moreover, over-borrowing could not be avoided through introduction of capital inflows from abroad. Controls that separated the domestic and foreign financial markets meant that corporations were regulated in their ability to float foreign bonds and to introduce impact loans. In addition, the purchase of equities by non-residents was inhibited.

Over-loan denoted a condition in the private banking sector in which banks chronically extended more credit, either by lending and or by purchase of securities, than they acquired from deposits or own capital. The gap was filled primarily by relying on borrowings from the Bank of Japan. The history of over-loan in Japan goes back to the Meiji period (1868–1912); over-loan first emerged around the turn of the century but was temporarily reduced through the distribution of fiscal funds. It re-emerged, however, during the Second World War and intensified during the 1950s as the counterpart to over-borrowing [4].

Over-loan was retained during the high growth period for two major reasons. First was the concentration of demand for funds on banks as the most important sources of funds for the corporations, who in turn intensified over-borrowing as they relied on investment and exports for growth; secondly, the banks found it profitable to rely on low-interest loans from the Bank of Japan and were able to continue their own excess credit provision in the stable business environment that interest rate controls helped to maintain. It cannot be denied, however, that the policies of allowing over-loan also reduced the banks' consciousness of their own funding position; that is, there was a diminution of self-reliance by banks because they were not forced to adjust total credit granted so long as reserves were available from the Bank of Japan without market borrowing.

The Bank of Japan filled the funding gap of the banking sector through direct lending because better means did not exist. Both long- and short-term financial markets were undeveloped, and therefore the Bank of Japan was unable to conduct open-market operations in a flexible manner. Moreover, given the framework of the artificial low interest rate policy, there was continuous, latent excess demand for Bank of Japan credit and no way to satisfy this demand other than credit rationing [37]. It was quite convenient to transmit guidance of the day-to-day fund-raising of banks through direct lending [11].

The fourth characteristic of the financial structure in the high growth period, the maldistribution of funds, related to the structure within the private banking sector. City banks were chronically in need of funds while regional banks, *sogo* banks (mutual savings banks), *shinkin* banks (credit co-operatives) and other financial institutions usually had surplus funds. As a result of the imbalance, an interbank market developed. The city banks were chronic borrowers and the regional banks and other institutions were chronic lenders in this one-way relationship of fund flows.

The maldistribution of funds emerged during the Second World War but intensified during the high growth period. There were basically two reasons why the city banks became chronically dependent not only on borrowing from the Bank of Japan but also on borrowing from the market. First, the demand for loans was concentrated on the city banks, because the customers of these banks were the chief agents of investment and exports. Secondly, the city banks were put at something of a disadvantage in procedures for flotation of industrial bonds. Such bonds were floated, not on an open market, but rather through an allocation system and at yields that were below market rates. The share of the city banks in this allocation was quite large. The need to find funds with which to buy these bonds forced the banks to borrow from other sources.

These four characteristics of the financial structure during the high growth period were interrelated, For example, over-borrowing reflected the predominance of indirect finance. Also, over-borrowing and over-loan were merely two sides of the same coin. Over-loan only occurred because of the Bank of Japan was more or less forced into granting credit due to the underdevelopment of long- and short-term financial markets, which in turn was a result of the same predominance of indirect finance that caused over-borrowing. In addition, over-loan could be maintained only because the Bank of Japan engaged in direct lending primarily to city banks, and thus underpinned both the maldistribution of funds and over-borrowing by corporations [37].

III. Changes in the financial structure after 1975

1. NEW HISTORICAL CONDITIONS

a. Financial aspects of the shift to lower growth

The financial structure of the high growth era was able to function stably because of the close connection between the characteristics of that financial structure and the financial framework during the high growth period. But two major historical incidents made a change of direction inevitable. These were the shift to floating exchange rates and the first oil crisis of 1973. The Japanese economy was no longer in an environment in which investment- and export-led high growth could be supported as an economic goal. The realities of low growth and internationalization had to be accepted.

The major changes in the economic structure between the high growth period and the second half of the 1970s had a major impact on the financial structure. The resulting changes in the financial structure meant the emergence of contradictions between the financial framework that had functioned during the high growth era and a satisfactory financial framework for the new era. As a result, there was a gradual reconsideration of the financial controls within the financial system, with the purpose of stabilizing the financial structure. Let us consider this process of give-and-take in some detail.

The first noticeable trend under the lower growth economy is the changes in the flow of funds. The expansion of the public-sector deficit brought large-scale flotations of Government and other public bonds in order to finance these deficits. Within the public sector, the deficit of the central Government was the largest. The so-called 'bond-financing ratio', that is, central Government bond flotations as a proportion of expenditure in the Government's general account, peaked at 34·7 per cent in fiscal year 1979. Attempts at retrenchment thereafter sought to reduce the flotation of Government bonds. Even in 1985, however, the bond-financing ratio remained at a relatively high level of 23·4 per cent. The large-scale flotations of Government bonds were the impetus for the development of direct finance through the securities market. The development of the large secondary market was the most important contributor to ensuring that the bond issues were absorbed smoothly. There were also adjustments in the primary market through such methods as diversifying the types and methods of flotation, for example through tender issue of medium-term coupon bonds.

The relatively underdeveloped state of open financial markets in Japan prior to 1975 was due to several factors. First, trading on open financial markets requires assets to be traded, and the most appropriate assets for such trading, Government bonds, were available in only limited supplies. Not only were supplies limited, but banks and other financial institutions had underwritten the largest portion of the available bonds, and faced constraints in selling the bonds. Secondly, even direct finance was not so direct. Under the artificial low interest rate policy, the firms that were able to float bonds were those that had close connections with financial institutions, and it was these financial institutions that bought the bonds. In a sense, corporate bonds were really just another form of bank loan. Neither corporations nor households could become accustomed to holding bonds, with the exception of the financial debentures issued by long-term credit banks. Third, interest rate controls kept the subscriber yields on bonds at low levels, which meant that selling bonds before maturity caused losses. This factor also restrained growth of the secondary bond market [50].

But the large-scale issues of Government bonds had a major impact on all three factors. Along with the expansion of the secondary government bond market, there was a major increase in short-term open-market transactions such as *gensaki*s. Because the interest rates in these open financial markets were determined freely by market forces, the open markets had a major impact on the financial structure after the high growth era.

One of the most important effects of lower growth on financial structure has been a strengthening of the preference for high interest rate assets by the private non-financial sector, and particularly by households. From the 1950s until the mid-1970s, with only temporary interruptions, accumulation of financial assets by the private non-financial sector rose at a rate which exceeded the growth rate of nominal GNP, the reason for this being— particularly in the case of the personal sector—the double-figure wage increases which occurred nearly every year. But with the advent of lower economic growth after 1975, wage increases fell to single-figure levels, and meanwhile a considerable amount of financial assets had already been accumulated. It was only natural for households to become more sensitive to interest rates, and in particular to real interest rates [5]. The corporate sector also took great pains in managing its assets, because it had gained more liquidity after the reduction of its deficit of funds.

The major trends may be described numerically by examination of the personal sector, which held the largest portion (about 70 per cent in 1984) of total financial assets. Table 1.6 shows that the gross financial asset holdings of the personal sector rose more rapidly than personal disposable income after 1965. By 1985 gross assets of personal sector were ¥ 572 bn., eighteen times the level at the end of 1965. A look at the composition of these assets shows that currency and securities grew more slowly than the average, and that time deposits, trusts, and insurance grew more rapidly and thus gained share. The subcategories also show some interesting developments, in particular that the share of currency was more than 18 per cent in 1965 and 1970 but fell to only 10 per cent by the end of 1985. The total weight of securities in gross assets of the personal sector fell slightly over the period, but the weight of equities alone rose very slightly, while the share of Government bonds grew substantially. The rise in the share of Government bonds occurred because such bonds earned high interest, compared to the controlled interest rates available on bank deposits. The rise in the share of time deposits from 42 per cent in 1965 to 49 per cent in 1985 appears somewhat strange at first glance, but the largest part of this rise was accounted for fixed-amount postal savings deposits of ten-year maturity. Such deposits had high fixed interest rates but were also relatively liquid, and thus combined high liquidity with interest rates that were attractive to households. In addition, the tax-free limits for postal accounts were raised in steps over the period, so that total postal deposits outstanding at the end of 1985 stood at over ¥ 100 bn., equivalent to 18 per cent of total financial assets held by the personal sector, and up from 8 per cent at the end of 1965. In contrast, the share of time deposits in total personal sector financial assets fell from 33 per cent in 1965 to 31 per cent in 1985. These facts illustrate the increased preference for high-interest earnings on the part of households. The higher shares of trusts and insurance in personal sector assets were traceable to similar factors.

b. Financial internationalization

Another historical change of equal importance was internationalization, both of the economy and of finance. As a result of Japan's achievements in the high growth era, the nation became the second largest economy in the free world, measured in terms of GNP, and came to account for a major share of goods and services transactions as well as financial transactions. If a country as large as Japan were to allow high barriers to foreign entry to continue, then surely damage would be done to the development of international transactions in general.

The beginning of internationalization of the Japanese economy in the first half of the 1970s was in large measure due to these circumstances. On the financial side, this meant a substantial increase in foreign lending, which centred on the foreign affiliates of Japanese financial institutions, and also meant a noticeable increase in the number of foreign banks that entered the

TABLE 1.6 *Financial Assets of the Personal Sector, 1965–1985[a]*

	1965		1970		1975		1980		1985		Average annual percentage change			
	¥100m.	%	¥100m.	%	¥100m.	%	¥100m.	%	¥100m.	%	1965–70	1970–5	1975–80	1980–5
Money	57,683	18·4	130,186	18·2	297,204	16·6	432,964	12·6	561,109	9·8	17·7	18·0	7·8	5·3
Cash	19,241		44,697		100,627		151,875		202,877		18·4	17·6	8·6	6·0
Demand deposits	38,442		85,489		196,577		281,089		358,232		17·3	18·1	7·4	5·0
Time deposits	130,345	41·7	318,346	44·4	850,734	47·7	1,780,811	51·8	2,781,189	48·6	19·6	21·7	15·9	9·3
Private	104,386		244,296		616,659		1,178,507		1,773,955		18·5	20·3	13·8	8·5
Postal savings	25,959		74,050		234,075		602,304		1,007,234		23·3	25·9	20·8	10·8
Trusts	14,410	4·6	39,937	5·6	103,761	5·8	206,695	6·0	394,422	6·9	22·6	21·0	14·8	13·8
Insurance	36,156	11·6	90,488	12·6	213,746	12·0	452,561	13·2	886,622	15·5	20·1	18·8	16·2	14·4
Securities	74,040	23·7	137,643	19·2	319,192	17·9	567,248	16·5	1,093,690	19·1	13·2	18·3	12·2	14·0
Bonds	11,864		40,952		112,846		260,775		437,414		28·1	22·5	18·2	10·9
Government	705		3,727		9,108		87,201		164,128		39·5	19·6	57·1	13·5
Equities at market price	51,491		84,497		176,708		254,512		485,873		10·4	15·9	7·6	13·8
Investment trusts	10,685		12,194		29,638		51,961		170,403		2·7	19·4	11·9	26·8
TOTAL (T)	312,634		716,600		1,784,637		3,440,324		5,717,532		18·0	20·0	14·0	10·7
Personal disposable income (I)	220,871		460,307		1,087,126		1,699,326		2,072,147[b]		15·8	18·8	9·3	5·1[b]
T as percentage of I	141·5		155·7		164·2		202·5		254·1[b]		—	—	—	—
Savings rate (%)	15·1		17·9		22·8		17·9		16·1[b]		—	—	—	—

[a] As of year-end.
[b] Figures for end of 1984.

Source: BOJ, *SJK.*

Japanese market (there were fifteen foreign banks in Japan in 1965, eighteen in 1970, fifty in 1975, and seventy-seven in 1985). The capital market also became internationalized. Investment in the Japanese stock market was already substantial in the last half of the 1960s, but fund raising by non-residents within the Japanese market began in 1970 with the approval of yen-denominated foreign bond issues. The first such bond was that issued by the Asian Development Bank in December of 1970. Residents' investment in foreign securities markets was liberalized in 1972.

Internationalization of finance accelerated in the second half of the 1970s. For one thing, the floating rate system itself encouraged the internationalization of finance. Under the floating rate system, foreign exchange swap (spot-forward) transactions are important as a means of hedging exchange risks. If the interest rates and business practices in domestic financial markets are inconsistent with those of foreign markets, then the interest rate arbitrage transactions which link the financial and foreign exchange markets both at home and abroad will not occur smoothly, and the floating rate system cannot function effectively. Moreover, there has been a strengthening of international demand for the yen as a store of value, that is as a reserve currency, and of demands that the domestic financial markets, which are the main focus for investing yen, be further opened to foreign transactions. (An example was the foreign demand for the establishment of the treasury bill market.)

Internationalization of financial markets has also been furthered by the structural changes of the flow of funds. Japanese private-sector financial institutions reacted to the decline in loan demand by domestic corporations in part by a considerable expansion of syndicated loans abroad, particularly yen-denominated syndicated loans. In order to strengthen the basis for such business, city banks opened foreign branches in the major capitals of the world, and long-term credit banks and trust banks have also established offices in London, New York, and other money centres. In addition these institutions have founded affiliate companies incorporated abroad in order to deal with securities and leasing businesses. There have even been purchases of local financial institutions in foreign countries. Foreign banks in Japan have also seen the scope of their business activities grow and diversify through such activities as joining the Government bond underwriting syndicate and beginning both over-the-counter sales and dealing in Government bonds (1984).

As internationalization of financial institutions business progressed, the flows of funds across borders became increasingly active, and the legal framework was updated. In 1980, for example, the Foreign Exchange and Foreign Trade Control Law was completely revised. Cross-border transactions became completely liberalized in principle, and this liberalization both recognized and further encouraged the rapid growth of cross-border flows of funds. There were many examples of such growth. In the loan market, yen-denominated loans by Japanese to non-residents grew alongside the growth of impact loans by foreigners to Japanese residents. These trans-actions were liberalized in December of 1980. In the short-term money market, non-residents transactions in the *gensaki* market increased after liberalization in May 1979, while resident holdings of foreign currency deposits increased after the liberalization of these transactions in December 1980. In the bond market, there were large increases in turnover by non-residents along with large increases in issues of yen-denominated foreign bonds. Other actions included the abolition of regulations on yen convertion in June 1984 and liberalization of certain Euro-yen transactions. Short-term Euro-yen lending to non-residents was liberalized in June 1983, and such lending to residents in June 1984. The issue of Euro-yen CDs in maturities of up to six months was liberalized in December 1984, and provision of long-term Euro-yen loans to non-residents was liberalized in April 1985.

The presence of Japanese financial institutions on world financial markets also grew considerably, and active cross-border fund flows became common-place. It was unavoidable that discrepancies would emerge between financial practices in Japan and financial practices abroad. A series of exchanges of opinion were held from 1983, including the US–Japan Yen/Dollar Committee, the UK–Japan Financial Consultations, and the Germany–Japan Financial Consultations. These exchanges reflected foreign demands that Japanese financial practices be changed in order to conform with practices in Europe and the United States. The issues considered in these consultations were very broad and included regulation of interest rates, segmentation of businesses (for example, the entry of foreign banks into trust business in Japan), and regulation of financial activity across borders (for example, relaxation of Euro-yen controls). The foreign demands did not in general stop with seeking national treatment for non-resident agents, but rather sought relaxation of controls from the viewpoint of reciprocity.

The internationalization of finance thus helped to ignite financial liber-alization in the domestic economy. But the more basic causes of financial liberalization within Japan were to be found in internal factors such as the shift to lower economic growth and the new historical conditions which accompanied this shift [13].

2. CHANGES IN FINANCIAL STRUCTURE

Just how the new historical conditions affected the Japanese financial struc-ture may be seen by referring to the four characteristics of the financial system during the high growth period, which were noted above [43].

a. Over-borrowing and indirect finance

The most striking change has been the decline of over-borrowing. As the net funds deficit of the corporate sector declined in the second half of the 1970s, that sector's reliance on outside financing also declined. The share of outside financing in total funds raised by major manufacturing firms declined markedly from 58 per cent in 1968–72 to 36 per cent in 1977–80 before recovering somewhat to 40 per cent in 1981–4. (These figures come from the Bank of Japan's study, *Financial Statements of Principal Enterprises* [58].) Within this environment of reduced dependence on outside funding, firms sought to raise funds at lower interest rates, and contributed to the trend of financial internationalization while also expanding such financing routes as international bond flotations.

The clearest reduction in outside funding was in bank borrowings. The percentage of outside financing in bank borrowing declined from 37 per cent in 1968–72 to 7 per cent in 1977–80 and to 3 per cent in 1981–4. In this sense, over-borrowing was clearly reduced. The major reason for this decline in reliance on bank borrowings was—apart from the increase in corporate liquidity that accompanied the change in the flow of funds structure—the feeling on the part of firms that no particular ill consequences would follow if they reduced the level of compensating balances that had been held in order to maintain relationships with banks. This was a typical example of the cost-cutting management that firms implemented after 1975.

But another characteristic of the high-growth financial system remains. This is the predominance of indirect finance, which remains despite the prediction that the large-scale flotation of Government bonds would increase the ratio of direct finance. Table 1.7 demonstrates that the reduction of indirect finance has not been particularly noticeable. There has, however, been a slight trend of decrease in indirect finance, seen in the decline in the indirect financing ratio from 93 per cent at the end of the 1970s to 89 per cent in the early 1980s. Reflecting this decline, there has been a gradual increase in the weight of direct finance through the securities markets. The share of securities markets in fund supply was only 5 per cent in the second half of the 1960s but rose to 7·5 per cent in the early 1980s or even to 11 per cent if one includes foreign capital markets as well. Though these are only gradual trends, they nevertheless show that the predominance of indirect finance is being reduced gradually.

There has, however, been a major change in the composition of indirect finance; the share of public financial institutions has risen considerably while that of private financial institutions (particularly the share of banks) has fallen considerably. The reason for this change was that interest rates at banks were strictly controlled, so that the banks have not been able to respond to the increased preference for high-yielding assets on the part of corporations and individuals. In the case of personal deposits, this inflexibility caused a major shift into postal savings around 1980. The shift was due to the provision by the postal savings system of ten-year, high-yielding, fixed-interest deposits that could be withdrawn after only six months without penalties. Banks faced conditions that were unknown during the high growth period, and all were forced to introduce financial assets that could compete with other institutions

TABLE 1.7 Supply of Funds through Financial Markets, Broadly Defined, Averages by Financial Years 1965–1984

	1965–9		1970–4		1975–9		1980–4	
	¥100m.	%	¥100m.	%	¥100m.	%	¥100m.	%
Financial intermediaries	97,748	92·7	255,751	91·7	415,852	89·5	533,863	89·3
(Lending)	78,992	74·9	215,007	77·1	278,472	59·9	360,005	60·2
(Securities)	18,756	17·8	40,744	14·6	137,380	29·6	173,858	29·1
Banks and other institutions	66,591	63·1	169,347	60·7	244,956	52·7	271,421	45·4
Banks	42,716	40·5	106,102	38·0	149,742	32·2	176,620	29·5
Other	23,875	22·6	63,245	22·7	95,214	20·5	94,801	15·9
Trusts and insurance[a]	12,635	12·1	34,372	12·3	52,382	11·3	99,081	16·6
Public sector	18,521	17·6	52,032	18·7	118,514	25·5	163,361	27·3
Securities markets	5,315	5·0	14,989	5·4	37,430	8·1	45,051	7·5
Foreign markets	2,419	2·3	8,193	2·9	11,560	2·5	18,977	3·2
TOTAL	105,481		278,933		464,841		597,891	

[a] Including investment trusts.

Sources: BOJ, SJK; SJK Application Tables.

such as securities companies and the postal savings system [55].

Moreover, even among the personal sector institutions, changes in market shares were substantial. That is, banks lost shares after the high growth period, while trusts, insurance, and investment trusts saw large increases in market share. These changes were the result of the increased interest sensitivity of households which had accumulated financial assets, and the higher weight given to yield as opposed to liquidity in their choice of assets.

A third change in the nature of indirect finance has been the decline in the proportion of lending from 74–8 per cent in the decade from 1965 to about 60 per cent in the decade since 1975. Corresponding to this decline has been a rise in the share of securities holdings. The rise in securities holding is what has kept the proportion of indirect finance high. The reason for the rise in securities holdings is that the largest part of Government bond flotations are absorbed by financial intermediaries through the Government bond underwriting syndicate. This underwriting syndicate started around 1966, and was focused on the city banks. During the high growth period about three-quarters of the bonds underwritten were sold to the Bank of Japan after having been outstanding for a year. The funds provided by the Bank of Japan were not inflationary because they constituted the money necessary to accommodate economic growth. As a result of these purchases by the Bank of Japan, the share of Government bonds in total assets of private-sector financial intermediaties remained very small. After 1975, however, the situation changed. Large-scale issues of Government bonds began, and the shift to lower economic growth reduced the purchase of bonds by the Bank of Japan to provide money for economic growth. As a result, the institutions which constituted the underwriting syndicate accumulated very large amounts of Government bonds. Not only did this put pressure on the fund management of the institutions, but it was also a heavy burden on the earning side when the interest rates on Government bonds were low and inflexible [13].

b. Over-loan and maldistribution of funds

The other two characteristics of the financial framework of the high growth era, over-loan and the maldistribution of funds, were characteristics within the banking sector, and also changed over time.

First let us consider over-loan, which was so closely connected with over-borrowing. The chronic and excess dependence of banks on borrowing from the Bank of Japan has been eliminated gradually. This has been because lending by the Bank of Japan to the city banks has not increased very much, owing to the application of a credit ceiling system, and also because the relationship of such borrowings to total credit outstanding weakened. Moreover, Bank of Japan lending has become a tool used primarily for very short-term adjustments in the financial markets. When the Bank of Japan wished to make a large adjustment in total central bank credit outstanding, it generally used operations in the bill market, which became possible at the very end of the high growth period. In addition, the Bank of Japan was also able to use Government bond operations more frequently, and flexibly, because of the development of computer technology.

The nature of the maldistribution of the funds changed as well. For one thing, the major customers of banks were the very large corporations, which had seen such a large increase in their own liquidity and therefore needed banks less. Moreover, banks may now raise funds through the CD market. In addition, local banks have seen a deterioration in their funds position due to their share of the large Government bond flotations. There has been an increase in frequency with which city banks temporarily lend money in the call market and local banks borrow. Foreign banks in Japan also rely to a considerable extent on the interbank market to fund their operations, and securities companies were again permitted to borrow in the call market after 1980, in order to finance their inventories of securities. Thus the interbank markets now have a rather diversified set of borrowers, in contrast to the situation during the high growth period, in which only city banks were the borrowers.

As participation in the interbank markets has diversified, the function of those markets has changed. During the high growth period, the interbank markets were a place which adjusted for the maldistribution of reserves among domestic banks, all of which engaged in retail banking. But after 1975, the city banks, long-term credit banks, trust banks, foreign banks, and securities companies alike became either borrowers or lenders in response to new financial conditions, so that the interbank markets became a locus of wholesale banking.

3. SUMMARY AND CONCLUSION

The changes in historical conditions described above and the effects of these changes on financial structure inevitably influenced the financial transactions themselves and the framework within which these transactions occurred. After 1975 the control-oriented monetary framework at the high growth period came into conflict with the changing needs and developing technologies of finance. The financial structure as a whole became less stable. In order to reconstruct and to stabilize the financial system, it was necessary to reconsider the controls and systems of yesteryear in the light of the needs of the new era.

The reconsiderations were thoroughgoing. This chapter has touched upon such reconsiderations, but the next chapter discusses them, and the direction of their development, in a more organized fashion.

2

Functions and Traits of the Financial System

ONE particular financial structure, the one which functioned smoothly throughout Japan's high growth period, was the subject of the previous chapter, along with the changes in that financial structure brought by changes in the economic environment after the high growth period. The current chapter examines what sort of changes the current financial system in Japan is undergoing now.

1. Fundamental traits of the Japanese financial system

1. FUNCTIONAL SEGMENTATION OF PRIVATE FINANCIAL INSTITUTIONS

a. Overview

A large role for the banking system within the financial structure is a phenomenon also seen in some industrial countries other than Japan. What is special about Japan in this regard is the strict controls on functional segmentation among the banks. That is, even among the financial intermediaries which comprise the indirect finance system, some institutions rely primarily on deposits for gathering funds (such as ordinary banks, *sogo* banks, and *shinkin* banks), while others rely on financial debentures and trust accounts for raising funds and concentrate on long-term finance on the lending side (long-term credit banks and trust banks). Among the former, there are several types of institution which differ according to the controls that are placed on their uses of funds. For example, trade and foreign exchange financing is carried out by the Bank of Tokyo. Financing for small- and medium-sized enterprises is carried out by *sogo* banks, *shinkin* banks, credit co-operatives, and the *Shokochukin* Bank. Agricultural finance is carried out by agricultural co-operatives, fishery co-operatives, and the *Norinchukin* Bank. These financial intermediaries are, in principle, forbidden to engage in the securities business except for public bonds. That is, they are prohibited from underwriting and dealing in securities because there exist special securities companies to handle such business.

This system is similar to those of many other countries in that there are special financial institutions to provide credit to small businesses and to the agricultural sector. But there are not many countries which also enforce triple segmentation among private financial institutions as is done in Japan. The three types of segmentation are those between long- and short-term finance, deposit banking and trust business, and financial intermediation (banking) and securities business.

b. Segmentation of long- and short-term finance

The segmentation of long- and short-term finance in Japan is based on a philosophy of commercial banking similar to that of the United Kingdom. The philosophy was introduced to Japan in 1882 in the establishment of the Bank of Japan. Supporting documents to the Bank of Japan charter emphasize a very clear distinction between commercial funds used in the sale of commodities on one hand and agricultural or manufacturing funds used in promoting production on the other:

The purpose of our central bank and the national banks that are hereby established is to be commercial banks. The purposes of aiding agriculture and encouraging industry are to belong to a different type of banking corporation, and the central bank is not to engage directly in such business.

The Government promulgated the Banking Act of 1890 based on this philosophy. This was a period of great prosperity for 'ordinary banks', which were the commercial banks of the period. In 1897 the so-called 'special' banks were established, including the Hypothec Bank and the Industrial Bank of Japan. The Banking Act did not establish particular controls on the use or raising of funds by ordinary banks; however, commercial banking philosophy gave great weight to the notion of prudent bank management. This was not the case for the special banks. For them, the issue of debentures was permitted, and these funds were to be used in particular areas. The Hypothec Bank was to use its funds for long-term lending on real estate mortgages, and the Industrial Bank of Japan was to use its funds for long-term lending on movable assets or for investment in securities. After a few years, however, the rapid development of industry meant that ordinary banks not only engaged in commercial finance but also, through roll-over of short-term bills, in fact expanded their activities to include long-term lending.

In academic circles of the time there was much criticism of the philosophy of commercial banking, as scholars looked at the rapid progress in industry made in Germany, which had adopted universal banking. But, after several financial crises and the failure of some ordinary banks during the second decade of the new century, the philosophy of commercial banking once again gained strength. And the new Banking Law of 1927 retained this philosophy. It was re-established after the Second World War; that is, the special bank system was reduced substantially in scope. In 1952 a special Long-term Credit

Bank Law was enacted, and there were once again established financial institutions that could float financial debentures and specialize in long-term finance. Trust banks were a special hybrid. These banks were converted from trust companies into banks in 1948 and were permitted to carry out both trust business and banking business together. In 1952 they were permitted to introduce so-called 'loan trusts' as a means of collecting stable sources of funding and thus of facilitating long-term finance.

For financial institutions that rely on gathering deposits as the primary means of collecting funds (and particularly for ordinary banks), there are currently no legal provisions regarding the maturity of funds raised and funds used. However, the Ministry of Finance carries out administrative guidance concerning the terms for fixed deposits with the intention of preventing conflicts between such deposits and financial debentures or loan trusts. It is not entirely clear when such administrative guidance originated, although the origins go back to the pre-war period. Accords among banks dealt with fixed-term deposit rates, but specified rates only for the shortest term, six months. There were no agreements about deposits with longer maturities. In May 1947 guidance was issued concerning three-month, six-month, and one-year deposits. In 1971, an eighteen-month deposit was permitted, and in 1973 a two-year deposit was permitted, while the eighteen-month deposit was abolished. In 1981 so-called 'fixed-date' time deposits were permitted, with a maximum contract length of three years. However, such deposits may be withdrawn upon prior notice, after having been on deposit for one year, and are thus not true three-year time deposits.

Administrative guidance also limits the issue of financial debentures by institutions other than the long-term credit banks. In 1950 the Law Concerning Bond Issue by Banks was implemented, and it permitted ordinary banks to issue financial debentures. However, this law was repealed in 1952 with the passage of the Long-Term Credit Bank Law. The offer of loan trusts is *de jure* permitted to financial institutions other than trust banks, under a 1943 law that is still in effect. (This law was the Law Concerning Joint Operation of Savings Bank Business and Trust Business by Ordinary Banks. In 1981 a revision of banking laws rescinded the sections concerning operation of savings bank business, and hence the name of this law is now the Law Concerning Joint Operation of Trust Business by Ordinary Banks.) These legal provisions notwithstanding, however, administrative guidance *de facto* prohibits ordinary banks from engaging in such business.

Thus, the principle of separation of long- and short-term finance is realized in Japan through two means—the existence of long-term credit institutions, such as long-term credit banks and trust banks, and administrative guidance concerning the maximum maturity at which ordinary banks may raise funds. There are, however, no controls at all on the maturity composition of ordinary bank use of funds, that is, on the asset side of their balance sheets.

c. Separation of banking and trust business

The separation of banking business and trust business is very strict in Japan. This is also the case in the United States, which not only requires banks to separate banking accounts from trust accounts but also has detailed restrictive customs concerning the flow of personnel and information between banking and trust operations within banks, the so-called Chinese Wall, with the purpose of preventing conflict of interest. A single bank is not, however, forbidden from conducting both types of business.

The separation of banking and trust business in Japan first became clear in the Trust Law and Trust Business Law, both of 1922. The origin of these laws was the concern about conflict of interest. The most pressing concern during the Second World War was to acquire long-term funds, and this concern was the origin of the 1943 Law mentioned above. The permission for banks to engage in the trust business was only a temporary measure, so that after the war, once again, the policy of separating banking and trust business was re-established. In this case, however, the primary concern was not conflict of interest, but rather separation of long-term finance from short-term finance. The trust business in Japan, in contrast with that of the Western countries in which individual assets are managed, focuses on joint management through such instruments as money trusts and loan trusts.

The trust business in Japan got off to an extremely rocky start in the early post-war period because the severe inflation of the time sharply reduced incentives for long-term savings. As a result, trust companies were converted into banks in 1948 and were permitted to carry out both types of business under the legal provisions of the law concerning joint operations. This was how the trust banks got started. But thereafter, the Government limited permission to offer loan trust to the trust banks (in 1952), and also promoted separation of banking and trust business through encouragement of mergers between the trust departments of city banks and trust banks proper.

The policy on administrative guidance concerning separation of banking and trust businesses was given in the Sixth Annual Report of the Banking Bureau of the Ministry of Finance in 1958. This publication stated:

'If it is to be permitted that a trust system based largely on money trusts may be established separately from deposit-based business, and if the usefulness of such a system is recognized, then such business must nevertheless be limited to long-term financial functions. Actual conditions in Japan make it inappropriate to have a system such as that in the United States, in which one financial institution may simultaneously manage various types of financial business. In Japan, the areas of business were separated well before the War, and it is thought that the superior system is one in which institutions specialize in managing one type of business on the basis of the abilities and experience appropriate to that business.'

d. Separation of banking and securities business

The separation of banking and securities business has one of its roots in the concept of commercial banking. This is the idea that a bank may harm its own stability by holding equities or long-term securities, which experience large fluctuations of price. Another root of this separation is the problem of conflict of interest. Many problems could accompany the clash of interests between depositors and investors for a bank that also engaged in the securities business. The countries that attach relatively great importance to the separation of banking and securities businesses are the United States, the United Kingdom, Canada, and Japan.

In the pre-war period, there were no legal provisions concerning the separation of banking and securities businesses in Japan. But the mainstream of thought was that banks should stick to commercial banking and not extend their business into other areas such as securities transactions. But it is important to distinguish between the underwriting business and other phases of the securities business. In the pre-war period, banks and the trust companies with excess funds played a rather important role in the underwriting of public and corporate bonds. In fact, financial institutions monopolized the underwriting of corporate bonds, and the original underwriting syndicate for Government bonds, which was established in 1911, was composed entirely of banks. But even for the underwriting business conducted by the banks, the subsidiary functions were carried out by securities companies. In addition, securities companies underwrote equity issues and conducted trading in bonds because the banks feared the risk involved in such transactions and would not become involved in them.

In the post-war period, the legal separation of banking and securities businesses, in principle, was established very clearly in the Securities and Exchange Law (enacted in 1948). The basis for acceptance of Article 65 of that law, which was based on the Glass–Steagall Act of the United States, was the custom from the pre-war period of separating the banking and securities business. Article 65 of the Securities Law prohibits banks from engaging in the securities business, with the exception of cases in which there is an investment motive or a trust contract. The Article does make exceptions for national Government bonds, local government bonds, and Government-guaranteed bonds. But, in actual practice throughout the high growth period, administrative guidance prohibited all but the underwriting of Government bonds.

On the purposes of Article 65, General Headquarters of the Occupation after the Second World War explained at the time that the underwriting of securities was inherently a dangerous business for 'trust institutions' such as banks and trust companies, and that therefore they should not engage in it because of their responsibility to depositors. There were, however, differences between the Glass–Steagall Act and Article 65. The Glass–Steagall Act imposed strict controls, even on the acquisition of securities for investment purposes. Under Glass–Steagall, financial institutions were permitted to buy only negotiable securities were not permitted to buy more than a certain amount of these securities of any given issuer, and were forbidden to hold equities. Article 65, however, places no controls whatsoever on the acquisition of securities and equities for investment purposes. (There are, however, restrictions on the holding of equities by financial institutions under the Anti-Monopoly Law.) Hence, the purpose of the separation of the banking and securities business according to Article 65 was to create a basis for the development of securities companies, and to prevent an excess of indirect finance [40].

2. INTEREST RATE REGULATION

a. Overview

There are two types of interest rate in Japan—free rates (or market rates) and regulated rates. The free rates are those determined through supply and demand relationships in markets; this category includes the interest rates in the short-term money markets and the yields in bond rates. Regulated rates are determined through discussions among interested parties, including the Government, and by law; this category includes deposit rates, the long- and short-term prime rates used by financial intermediaries in the raising and lending of funds, and the subscriber's yields on public bonds. (For details see Chapter 4.) During the high growth period, a basic framework for determining interest rates was maintained. For short-term lending rates, there was an upper limit and also a lower limit (in the form of the prime rate). Actual contract rates on loans, however, were free to fluctuate within these boundaries. Deposit interest rates, however, were precisely controlled, and thus they became the nucleus of interest rate control. Since 1975, however, there has been a gradual and partial elimination of regulations, and the regulated interest rates have become more flexible.

b. Regulation of deposit rates

The first regulations on deposit rates in Japan were established in 1901 by the Osaka Bankers Association. There was an accord among the members of the Association on upper limits for deposit interest rates. The following year, a deposit rate accord was established among the six major banks in Tokyo. However, these accords lacked provisions for enforcement. It appears that large or long-term deposits sometimes earned interest exceeding the levels specified in the accords, and hence the accords collapsed after several years. The first deposit interest rate accord with enforcement provisions occurred in 1918. The movement for conclusion of such an accord began in

Tokyo, Osaka, and Nagoya but quickly spread to the rest of the country. The accord recognized two classes of banks by size, and established maximum interest limits for deposit rates according to these sizes. The enforcement provision included fines for failure to comply and expulsion from the inter-bank bill trading exchange. As a result of these strict enforcement provisions, the accord was effective. The banks' motivation for establishing such a deposit interest rate accord was the fear that banks might become less sound as a result of interest rates competition aimed at acquiring deposits, which then led to the financial crisis just as had happened in the United States and Europe. This was particularly true during the First World War because the demand for funds was growing particularly rapidly owing to the development of heavy industry. Banks began to establish many more branches in an attempt to gather deposits in order to meet this demand. Interest rate competition was particularly intense because industrial entrepreneurs would often establish banks of their own for the purpose of raising industrial funds and would pay high interest rates in order to attract deposits [4].

Deposit rate accord continued through the Second World War, with the only change being the abolition of the two classes of banks in 1943. The agreements also continued into the immediate post-war period; but with the promulgation of the Anti-Monopoly Law in 1947, doubts emerged about the legality of the agreement, and so it was abolished. Instead, controls on interest rates by the public authorities were instituted. In December of that year, the Temporary Interest Rate Adjustment Law (TIRAL) was promulgated and implemented. Of course, the purpose of this law was to prevent interest rate competition that was destructive to the profitability of financial institutions. That is, the law aimed more at ensuring stable business conditions for financial institutions through external controls on competition than at ensuring prudent management of such institutions based on internal controls. But the law had another important goal: contribution to price stability. The explanation that accompanied submission of the Law said that it intended to contribute to price stability by holding down interest costs and by suppressing the so-called 'unfair' increases in lending rates.

Under the TIRAL, the Minister of Finance would determine whether interest rate regulation was necessary in the light of general economic conditions, and then the Policy Board of the Bank of Japan would set upper limits on interest rates for financial institutions or would change or abolish them as necessary. The Law also provided that the Policy Board of the Bank of Japan would seek the advice of an Interest Adjustment Council. Upper limits for deposit rates were established for ten types of deposit. These were three-, six-, and 12-month time deposits, fixed savings, instalment savings, ordinary deposits, notice deposits, special deposits, current deposits, and deposits for tax payment. In 1970, the regulations under the Law were simplified with the purpose of making interest rates more flexible. This simplification reduced the number of categories to four—current deposits, term deposits, deposits for tax payment, and others. However, based on the opinion expressed in the report of the Interest Rate Adjustment Advisory Board on this simplification, the Bank of Japan was to decide on detailed guide-line rates for deposits within the limits of notification provisions in the Law, in order to avoid the confusion that might accompany the simplification. In fact, regulations were placed on the very same types and maturities of deposit that had been regulated in the earlier period.

3. REGULATION OF INTERNATIONAL TRANSACTIONS (EXCHANGE CONTROL)

Separation of domestic and foreign financial markets meant regulation of financial transactions between domestic and foreign agents. These regulations were an attempt to segment domestic financial markets and foreign financial markets, and implied foreign exchange controls.

Japan first enacted Anti-Capital Flight Laws in 1932 as part of the introduction of exchange controls. This was at a time when active fiscal and monetary policies, such as underwriting of Government bonds by the Bank of Japan, were adopted in an attempt to overcome the recession that had been caused by the reversion to the gold standard under the previous government. But as interest rates fell, capital outflow to foreign countries continued, and the yen weakened considerably in the foreign exchange markets. As a result, foreign exchange controls were introduced. However, the Capital Flight Law had many deficiencies, and capital continued to flee. In 1933, a new Foreign Exchange Control Law was enacted, using the exchange control system of Germany as a reference. This was when comprehensive foreign exchange controls began.

Under the new Foreign Exchange Law, not only were capital transactions completely regulated but current account transactions were regulated as well. As the country moved toward war, the regulations were strengthened. After the War, all transactions with foreign countries were regulated by General Headquarters of the Occupation. However, in 1947, private trade was once again partially permitted; and in 1949, the Foreign Exchange and Foreign Trade Control Act was passed. At the time the law was passed, it forbade in principle all cross-border transactions. These prohibitions could be lifted only on Government order. But as time passed, the regulations were gradually eased as part of the international movement toward liberalization [13]. In 1964, Japan accepted the obligations of Article VIII of the Articles of Agreement of the IMF and, hence, in principle, removed all restrictions on current transactions. In 1967, the programme of liberalization of inward direct investment was implemented. However, in 1971, at the time of the Nixon shocks, there were large-scale speculative inflows of funds from abroad, and regulations of domestic investment in securities were implemented along with an export prepayment scheme.

In this way, throughout the high growth period, exchange controls were gradually eased but still remained rather restrictive, at least with respect to financial transactions. These controls, which separated domestic and foreign markets and regulated transactions in funds between foreign and domestic markets, protected the various regulations and customs in the domestic financial markets, such as segmentation of business, interest rate regulation, and the collateral requirements that will be described below, from disturbances from abroad. Thus, the regulation of foreign transactions played an important role in helping the regulations on domestic transactions to function effectively.

4. COLLATERAL REQUIREMENTS

In addition to the three types of control mentioned above, another practice in Japanese financial markets helped to ensure the safety of transactions: collateral requirements. Most of the important types of financial transaction in Japan, including corporate debenture issue, bank lending, and interbank transactions, require the provision of collateral. This practice is unique to Japan; in the other industrialized countries, the provision of collateral is decided on case-by-case base between the parties to the transaction, and, in fact, there are many cases in which no collateral is required.

The principle of collateralized transactions was established gradually in the first quarter of this century. In lending transactions, the provision of collateral spread on the basis of agreements between banks and borrowers. Practices were standardized in 1962 when the Federation of Bankers Associations published standardized bank loan contracts. This publication established the right of the bank to demand possession of the collateral in cases where there were reasonable grounds for the bank to seek to protect the integrity of an asset.

The use of collateral for corporate bonds goes back to the Law on Collateralization of Securities and Trusts of 1905. Until the financial panic of 1927, collateralized bonds were relatively rare in the domestic economy, but defaults grew in the period between the end of the First World War and the late 1920s, due to the financial crises, the chronic recession that accompanied return to the gold standard, and the continuing stagnation of the economy. Owners of uncollateralized bonds suffered very large losses. Sobered by these experiences, the banks, which accounted for the overwhelming share of bond subscriptions, promoted a 'clean up the bond market' movement. As a result, an agreement was reached in 1933 among the important banks, insurance, and trust companies, who made up the Fifth-of-the-Month Club (of underwriters), that corporate bond issues would have to be collateralized and would have to include provisions for sinking funds.

In call-market transactions, collateral was not required during the early years around the turn of the century. However, the failure of the 74th Bank, a large bank in Yokohama, in 1920 encouraged a gradual shift toward collateralized transactions. Collateralization for call-market transactions became the rule after the financial crisis of 1927. The origins of this crisis lay in the failure of special banks, such as the Bank of Taiwan, whose loan portfolios had deteriorated in the recessions that followed the First World War. This localized panic became a nationwide panic for two reasons. First, the special banks with the bad loan portfolios had gone to the call market to raise funds for consolidation. Second, those who lent to the special banks had a rather lackadaisical confidence in the management of the special banks, and expected rescue measures to be taken by the Bank of Japan or others in the event of default. As a result, collateral had not been required [4] [24]. After these events, the banks that participated in the call market formed the Call-Market Association in 1927. Among the new rules for call-market transactions were a requirement for collateral in the form of Government Bonds and prohibition on long-term call-market lending. Thereafter, collateralized transactions became standard practice.

II. Changes in the financial environment and responses of the financial system

1. CHANGE OF ENVIRONMENT AND PROGRESS OF INNOVATION

Financial innovations were not unknown during the high growth period, but they became quite numerous after 1975. In the 1950s and 1960s, there were such innovations as direct credit of payrolls into bank accounts and automatic payment of public utility charges from bank accounts. These innovations contributed to reducing the costs to firms of paying wages or of collecting fees. In 1972, the so-called *sogo* account was established. A *sogo* account is an ordinary deposit with an overdraft facility that is collateralized by a time deposit. By using such an account, the depositor may increase his liquidity at the low cost of only 0.25 per cent above the interest rate earned on the time deposit, and may do so without withdrawal of the funds in the time deposit account. The introduction of *sogo* accounts was the result of the spread of automatic payment of public utility charges. This was because individuals found themselves using their deposits to settle more bills, and incurring high costs from the withdrawal penalties paid on reducing balances of time deposits and putting the proceeds into ordinary deposits. The banks supplied such innovations because deposit acquisition was the critical factor in bank profitability under the controlled interest rate system. The banks sought first to encourage economies in the use of cash through encouragement of deposits, and next to encourage the larger portion of deposits to be time deposits.

But the tempo of financial innovation was slow until the end of the 1960s. Moreover, the types of financial innovation centred on those which eased the technological limitations of financial transactions or which attempted to lower the cost burden to customers. But the regulations and customs which ruled during the high growth period—that is, interest rate controls, separation of areas of business of financial institutions, exchange rate controls, and collateral requirements—were appropriate to the economic and financial structure of the time; and thus these controls were not particularly costly to corporations or to households.

For example, interest rate controls maintained an upward-sloping yield curve, and thus stabilized the profits based on maturity transformation (that is, financial intermediation in which financial institutions borrowed very short-term from depositors but lent long-term to final borrowers). Market segmentation regulations and foreign exchange controls limited the entry of external parties into the various financial markets within the country and thus guaranteed all the profits to the financial institutions which did participate. This system worked to the particular advantage of financial institutions which engaged in maturity transformation, and was one of the major factors that supported the financial structure with the predominance of indirect finance. In this world of indirect finance, even small firms with scant information could enjoy the same benefits or opportunities for transactions as were enjoyed by large firms, while small lenders had the opportunity to use funds profitably. Collateral requirements contributed to channelling of funds toward fixed investments, because they favoured borrowers with material collateral; thus the regulations and customs of the high growth period were an effective means of achieving growth based on high levels of investment even in an environment of relatively low accumulation of financial assets. The costs of such regulations and customs were not particularly high, and hence there was very little incentive for financial innovations that sought to circumvent controls.

But this situation changed in 1973, after the shift to floating exchange rates and the first oil shock had such large effects on the Japanese economy. Detailed repetition will be avoided, but it is sufficient to recall the emergence of large-scale flotations of Government bonds and the development of open financial markets for both long- and short-term assets. As financial assets were accumulated, both corporations and households became more sensitive to the profitability of the assets that they held. Under the floating exchange rate system, there were stronger incentives for swap transactions for the purpose of risk-hedging, as well as for yen-denominated international transactions. These changes expressed themselves in altered behaviour of corporations, households, and the Government with respect to financial transactions. In order to improve the efficiency of financial transactions, there was a greater need to have methods of transactions that did not limit interest rates or participation. As needs changed, the opportunity cost of interest regulations and exchange controls rose; and higher opportunity costs raised the latent demand for financial innovations that sought to circumvent the controls [13]. These movements on the demand side meant new profit opportunities for banks, securities companies, and other suppliers of financial services. It would be possible for these suppliers to raise their profits through acting as intermediaries in financial markets without controls, and by developing new types of financial instruments with high rates of return. Moreover, technological change accelerated these trends; the remarkable progress of computers and communications technology lowered the costs of acquiring market information and of transmitting and processing market transactions. These technological developments reduced the costs of supplying financial innovations and contributed to a remarkable broadening of profit opportunities.

After 1975, therefore there were higher costs associated with the constraints imposed by the controls of the high growth period. As a result, new types of financial innovation, which attempted to circumvent these controls, became more numerous. There were three such types. The first type made it possible to circumvent deposit interest rate controls by use of medium-term Government coupon bonds, which carried market interest rates based on public subscription of bonds, and of long-term Government bonds issued under more flexible conditions. The second was a partial liberalization of deposit interest rates through, for example, the establishment of certificates of deposit or money market certificates. The third type was circumvention of interest rate controls through the use of free-rate markets abroad or transactions which simulated foreign bond transactions, such as yen-based foreign currency deposits [55].

2. FINANCIAL INNOVATIONS AND SYSTEMIC CHANGE

Financial innovations by the private sector that sought to circumvent controls encouraged the authorities to respond and to react by easing or abolishing regulatory requirements, that is, with liberalization and internationalization. And each innovation in turn led to the next. This interdependence meant that the framework of the financial system of the high growth period had to change its overall form. Let us consider the main developments in this process of liberalization after 1975.

a. Relaxation of deposit rate regulation

First, let us consider the relaxation of deposit interest rate regulation. This relaxation began because of the large-scale flotation of Government bonds, in part because the *gensaki* market expanded substantially. Though this market had existed since the late 1940s, it leapt in size around 1975 due to the large quantities of Government bonds that began to circulate. Because corporations now held surplus funds, they sought to invest those funds efficiently through circumvention of deposit interest rate controls. One method of doing this was to shift funds from three- to six-month time deposits into the *gensaki* market. An innovation for smaller transactions was the medium-term Government bond funds or *chukoku* funds. *Chukoku* funds are liquid assets but also pay yields higher than those on short-term time deposits, and so they were an effective means by which households and small- and medium-sized corporations were able to circumvent interest rate controls. These innovations reduced the ability of banks to gather deposits and caused a rapid decline in the share of banks in total financial intermediation. The share decline for the banks had other reasons as well, such as the shift of funds into postal savings in the form of so-called 'fixed-amount' postal savings, which had very special and advantageous characteristics. The banks, of course, sought to maintain a stable business atmosphere for themselves and reacted, even though only partially, with financial innovations of their own. In 1979, the banks introduced certificates of deposit; these were nego-tiable deposits of up to six months' maturity with free interest rates. In 1980, the upper limit of ¥3m. per person on deposits in foreign currency accounts was abolished. (These accounts had always earned free interest rates.) Such foreign currency deposits could be made *de facto* equivalent to free-rate, yen-denominated deposits by the use of a forward exchange contract to hedge the exchange risk. In 1985, money market certificates were introduced. These had interest rates which were linked to those of certificates of deposit but were made available in units of as little as ¥50m. and thus had the merit of being an asset for smaller investors. These financial innovations of course reduced the meaning of interest rate controls.

Further liberalizations continued in 1985 and after. In October of that year, there was a complete liberalization of interest rates on deposits of three months to two years with a minimum deposit of ¥1bn. In April of 1986, the minimum deposit was lowered to ¥500m. In addition, the maturities of CDs and money market certificates were extended to instruments of up to one year in maturity. Changes scheduled for 1987 include further reductions in the minimum size of deposits with free interest rates and of money market certificates, along with an extension of the maximum maturity of money market certificates to two years.

Though interest rate controls on large deposits have been relaxed in stages, the next issue will be the extent to which the interest rates on small deposits are to be liberalized. For deposits whose interest rates are linked to the interest rates of large-scale transactions in the markets, for example money market certificates, there will be no problems of fairness or market efficiency, so long as the postal savings system follows the same rules as apply to commercial banking. As a result, a considerable liberalization of interest rates on small deposits is possible.

A complete liberalization of small deposit interest rates may, however, be difficult because of the existence of the postal savings system. That is, the postal savings system is one link in the public sector financial network, and there is no guarantee that the interest rates on postal deposits will be determined on the basis of market principles. Precisely because the share of public financial institutions in the financial markets is so large in Japan, the postal savings system would be likely to become the price leader in interest rate determination if interest rates on small deposits, including postal savings deposits, were fully liberalized. The interest rates at private sector financial institutions would certainly be affected, and there is the fear that these interest rates might not reflect the balance of market forces. Barring a major change in the postal savings system, an early and complete liberalization of interest rates on small deposits would appear to be difficult.

b. Reduced segmentation between institutions

The new financial products and services supplied during the process of financial innovation have strengthened competition between banks and securities companies; and as a result there has been a partial relaxation of the segmentation of businesses between the two types of institution.

For example, banks may now supply financial products that are linked to Government bonds, and may also supply Government bond transactions services to their customers. This implies a limitation on the regulations that prohibited banks from engaging in the securities business. The debate about legal interpretations of bank rights to engage in the securities business resulted in very clear clauses in the new Banking Law of 1981, concerning the types of securities operation in which banks may participate. (The Securities and Exchange Law was revised in the same year.) Banks were permitted to engage in placements connected with the underwriting of public bonds, in so-called 'over-the-counter' sales (*madohan*), and in purchase and sale of outstanding bonds (so-called 'dealing'). Over-the-counter sales of long-term Government coupon bonds began in April 1983, and over-the-counter sales of medium-term coupon bonds and discount bonds began in October of the same year. Dealing began in June 1984. Banks have also introduced other innovations, such as the Government bond time-deposit account, which divides the funds that a depositer places with a bank between a time-deposit account and Government bonds, and thus pays a higher yield. Yet another product was developed in order to enhance liquidity by combining the Government bond deposit account with a *sogo* account.

But the securities companies were not idle. In 1984, they developed, in a business tie-up with *shinkin* banks, a combination product, which linked *chukoku* funds with ordinary deposits. This made it possible to transfer funds freely into and out of ordinary deposit accounts, although there was a minimum balance requirement for the ordinary deposit. This meant that *chukoku* funds became *de facto* an asset that could be used to settle payments, even though the settlements had to travel through an ordinary deposit account. In addition, permission was granted for securities companies to lend funds to customers without restriction on the use of the funds when the loans were collateralized by public bond holdings. When such loans were first permitted in 1984, they were done on a case-by-case basis, but since 1985 the only constraint is an upper limit on such loans.

Thus, banks have made a partial entry into the securities business, and securities companies have made a partial entry into the banking business. That is, regulations separating banking and securities business have been eased.

The controls concerning the separation of long- and short-term business and the separation of banking and trust businesses continue to be debated. The ordinary banks are exerting pressure for relaxation or abolition of such controls on the grounds that the maturity structures of their assets and liabilities are becoming unbalanced, and that entry into growing areas such as pension trust management would be desirable. In opposition to this, the long-term credit banks and the trust banks point to the merits of specialization and division of labour and seek the continuation of the controls.

In deciding whether to relax controls on areas of business or to leave them as they are, it is necessary to consider carefully the benefits and the costs of deregulation. (See below for an evaluation of liberalization in general.) If controls are retained, however, two issues must be faced. First is the increased pressure for deregulation that will result from the use of foreign market financing capabilities. Second is the possibility that the controls will be circumvented.

c. Relaxation and abolition of exchange controls

Pressure for the relaxation or abolition of exchange controls gained strength with the increased incentives for international capital transactions that accompanied the shift to floating exchange rates in 1973. Controls were eased in stages after 1977, and the revised Foreign Exchange and Foreign Trade Control Law of 1980 liberalized all capital transactions in principle. In 1984, the Report of the Joint US–Japan *Ad Hoc* Group on the yen–dollar relationship was published, and broad measures for financial internationalization were adopted, which included easing of controls on Euro-yen transactions that had hitherto been subject to regulation. The easing of controls was to be carried out with consideration of the equilibrium between various regulations in the domestic market and the Euro-Yen markets. As one example, Euro-Yen lending by Japanese banks was liberalized in the case of short-term lending, but liberalization of long-term lending to domestic residents was postponed because of the principle of separating short- and long-term financial business. Moreover, Euro-yen CDs were limited to a maximum maturity of six months. Concerning the principle of separation of banking and securities business, a Ministry of Finance publication of 1984 ('The Current Status and Future Prospects for the Liberalization of Financial Markets and the Internationalization of the Yen') stated that 'the international business of Japanese banks and securities companies will be treated flexibly in accordance with the development of liberalization and internationalization, keeping in mind the principle of separation between the banking and securities businesses'. In the process of relaxing regulations, it could well be that the competitiveness of Japanese banks in the Euro-markets may be constrained. In this sense, the current state of affairs is a period of transition toward a state of much greater relaxation of controls or their complete abolition. Yet another example concerns the trust business. In 1985, foreign banks were permitted to enter the trust business. It is quite possible that pressure to relax controls in this area will come from domestic ordinary banks, given the potential profitability of pension trust management.

Another example was the abolition in 1984 of regulations on conversion of foreign trusts into yen. This abolition allowed domestic banks a method of raising long-term yen funds through acquiring long-term foreign currency deposits. Such transactions would in fact allow the circumvention of regulations separating long- and short-term business.

d. Relaxation of collateral requirements

The unique custom of collateral requirements has also been affected by internationalization. In the long-term bond market, there was a relaxation of the conditions for the flotation of uncollateralized securities in 1984. This was done to bring domestic practices into conformity with the eased guidelines for the issue of Euro-yen securities by residents. In the short-term money markets, uncollateralized call money brokering by the money market dealers (see Chapter 5 for a description of money market dealers) began in 1985. In addition, interest rates on interbank time deposits were completely liberalized under the same conditions that applied to liberalization of interest rates on large-scale time deposits. Together with this, there was a major expansion in the opportunities for uncollateralized interbank trading. The possibilities for expansion of uncollateralized trading depend on the costs which must be incurred in order to ensure safety of the transactions. It is a reality, however, that the internationalization of finance has brought a reconsideration of the systems and traditions in the Japanese market, such as the collateral requirements [26].

3. FINANCIAL INNOVATIONS AND THE BANKING SECTOR

The liberalization and internationalization of the financial system will have important influences on bank management. The most important questions are whether the environment for the banking business will remain stable and whether, or to what extent, the financial changes and innovations will affect return and risk in the banking industry [25]. First, we consider return in banking. Rates of return in banking will surely be reduced by the liberalization of deposit interest rates, because this liberalization will raise the cost of acquiring funds. Moreover, the liberalization of other interest rates will promote competition and, under normal circumstances, will lead to a decline in lending rates. As a result, the spead between the lending and the deposit rates will shrink. This is only natural, because one of the most important goals of liberalization has been to provide more advantageous transactions opportunities to both borrowers and depositors.

But the reduction of the spread deposit rates and loan rates will not necessarily lead to a fall in the profitability of the banking sector as a whole. First, it will be possible to economize on so-called implicit interest payments, that is, on the costs of non-price competition which occurred under the regime of interest rate controls. (Such competition included, for example, discount on fees to customers, a home visiting service for deposit collection, and special gifts for new deposits.) It is very difficult to estimate the implicit interest costs because data are insufficient. However, after the liberalization of deposit interest rates, a portion of these services will be discontinued, and where necessary appropriate fees for services will be levied. Second, liberalization will contribute to more efficient management in the banking sector by reducing the scope for so-called x-efficiencies, such as inefficient branches or personnel. Third, it appears that the spreads among interest rates will stabilize with the emergence of so-called 'spread banking'. The spreads will, of course, be determined flexibly in the markets according to demand and supply conditions. But at least it will be possible to avoid situations such as negative spreads which occurred during earlier periods because of the inflexibility of controlled interest rates. Eliminating such occurrences will help to stabilize profitability. Fourth, liberalization and internationalization will expand the areas of activity in which financial institutions may engage. The ability to participate in new markets will broaden the scope of profit opportunities for banks and lead to increases in return. On the other hand, when others enter what have hitherto been banking markets, there could be a decline in return. The net effect of these possibilities is unclear.

But when the business of banks becomes more diversified, there will be the potential for economies of scope, and hence an increase in rates of return [23]. For example, when a single branch is able to carry out both deposit and securities transactions businesses, then the unit costs of conducting the two businesses will fall. By use of appropriate and flexible techniques for balance sheet management, there will be increased opportunities to earn returns that could not have been earned under the controlled interest rate system. For example, there will be better possibilities for matching the maturity structure of assets and liabilities, so that certain interest rate risks and liquidity risks may be avoided, even while earning higher yields. This would be one example of economies of scope.

Bank profits will also be aided considerably by advances in computer and telecommunications technologies. There are, of course, some disadvantages to such technology, such as the huge levels of investment necessary for mechanization of financial business and the large risks associated with it, along with the increase in the optimal size of a bank. On the other hand, joint development of communication systems among banks is not impossible, and such co-operation would lower the costs to banks and raise the rates of return. In particular the joint networks of cash machines, such as automatic teller machines, have lowered the cost of such networks to individual banks and have raised the number of points at which deposit business may be done. The savings from these joint activities cannot be ignored. In the areas of firm banking and home banking, mechanization has clear merits when compared to the cost of offering the same sorts of service with labour instead of with capital.

Thus, liberalization will not necessarily have only negative effects on bank returns but rather, because of the positive effects listed above, may even raise bank profitability.

Risk, however, is another matter. There are four types of risk which liberalization of finance may increase: credit risks, liquidity risks, interest rate risks, and foreign exchange risks.

(i) Credit risk is the possibility of a reduction of expected earnings because the repayment conditions on the asset may not be fulfilled; that is, the loan may be late or uncollectable. (Default risk and country risk belong to this category.)

(ii) Liquidity risk is the possibility of a fall in expected earnings that accompanies the need to acquire liquidity in the case of an unusually large call on one's liabilities. For example, in the case of a run on a bank, or inability to roll over funds raised in markets, assets would have to be sold quickly or sources of finance found. In such cases, the cost of raising money would be higher than usual.

(iii) Interest rate risk is the possibility of a fall in expected profits due to unusual fluctuations of interest rates. The traditional risks of the banking business belong here, as do those which accompany fluctuations of the securities market.

(iv) Foreign exchange risk is the possibility of a decline in expected profits due to foreign exchange losses incurred because of fluctuation of foreign exchange rates.

As banks enter the long-term finance and international finance areas, they will face investment opportunities with higher credit risks. With the liberalization of interest rates, an expansion of spread banking is expected. This will pass the interest rate risks to the borrower, but will also raise credit risks from the point of view of the bank.

Liquidity risk and interest rate risk are basically a matter of maturity imbalance between assets and liabilities. Because maturity transformation is the heart of the banking industry, it will be impossible to eliminate these kinds of risks. But for banks that face controls on the maximum maturity of deposits due to the regulation concerning separation of long- and short-term banking business, liquidity risk is currently on the rise. Moreover, as liberalization of deposit rates progresses, fluctuation of borrowing costs will also rise, and interest rate risk will rise with it. The increase in the share of funds raised on domestic markets has raised interest rate risk, and this rising dependence on unstable market funds simultaneously implies an increase in liquidity risk. As CD issue becomes more flexible and as the bankers' acceptance market expands, these trends will be accentuated. Foreign exchange risk will also rise with the expansion of foreign currency-denominated assets and liabilities and with the expansion of foreign exchange dealing [17].

Thus, it appears likely that liberalization will increase the risks in the banking business, but it is also necessary to recognize that liberalization will stabilize the overall atmosphere, for several reasons. First, bank risk may be reduced because of the advantages of the economies of scope that will accompany the easing or abolition of controls on participation in different types of businesses. As participation is extended and diversified, and the ability to manage both assets and liabilities is very well strengthened, there may occur a substantial decline in various types of risk—particularly in interest rate risk and liquidity risk. Moreover, if it is possible to shift funds between conventional types of asset such as loans and assets with different patterns of earnings such as securities, then the variability of profits for the banking sector as a whole may well fall. (For example, when interest rates fall, the yields on loans would be lower but there would also be capital gains on securities.) Second, bank risks may also be reduced by the elimination of the disintermediation that occurred under the regime of deposit rate controls. For the sector as a whole, the basis for acquiring a stable level of funds would be strengthened, and thus liquidity risk would be reduced. Third, bank risk may be reduced by the equalization of interest rate fluctuations across different types of asset that will be effected by the liberalization of interest rates. For example, is the case when interest rates in deposits are all subject to controls while interest rates on short-term money markets fluctuate freely, it is the free rates which function to adjust the gap between demand and supply; sometimes the fluctuation in these interest rates is extremely large. Once deposit rates are also liberalized, then the equilibration function will also spread to transactions in deposits, so that it is quite possible that the variances of interest rate fluctuations will fall. If so, then interest rate risk will have fallen as well. (There is, however, a subtlety here. The authorities' intentions for the post-liberalization period will not have been realized so long as the variations of interest rates that are due to market psychology and that are peculiar to efficient markets fail to fluctuate widely, and thus fail to move other interest rates substantially.) And finally, as seen above, overall return will not necessarily contract due to liberalizations, though bank risk may not fall.

Two forces, therefore, are at work. On one hand, liberalization will raise the various types of risk for banks. But on the other hand, the ability of the banks to cope with these risks will be strengthened. In establishing the balance between the two forces, an important factor will be the creation of a financial futures market; such a market will allow banks to hedge interest rate risks at comparatively low costs.

Thus, while the changes in the financial system will simultaneously work to lower bank return and to raise bank risk, other forces will still work to raise bank returns and to lower bank risks. That is to say, financial liberalization and internationalization will expand the degree to which banks have a free hand in their operations. Just how liberalization and internationalization will change the stability of the banking business will depend on the degree of risk aversion of banks. In short, liberalization and internationalization will not necessarily lead to either a rise or a fall in bank failures.

4. POLICIES FOR FINANCIAL SYSTEM STABILIZATION

a. The potential for destabilization

Whether any particular bank will be able to maintain stability of operations in the face of changes in the financial system will largely depend on that bank's attitude toward risk aversion and on the level of its buffers against loss, such as own capital. But the stability of the financial system as a whole will depend not only on the stability of the individual banks but also on the possibility that the collapse of any one particular bank might lead to the collapse of other banks through the connections among their transactions. This possibility is called system risk. As fund movements acquire huge proportions, then system risk will rise. Thus, the changes in the financial structure may also raise the level of system risk.

For any individual bank, reducing the probability of failure is achieved largely in two ways, by raising the level of capitalization or by improving the risk-return characteristics in the composition of the bank's portfolio. Both of these require the bank to adjust its own management in order to avoid failure. But there is a third way, to distribute the risk of outside agents. This can be done through methods such as risk-hedging through floating-role loans, or through swap transactions, or by improving the buffer facilities that the bank has, such as stand-by credits with other banks. As financial markets develop, this type of risk diversification expands to a considerable extent. However, when banks increase their hedging of risks or increase their levels of buffer against risk, there is also an increase in system risk. And other developments have also increased system risk, such as the development of the electronic funds transfer system and point-of-sale systems. Settlement through electronic fund transfers is instantaneous and can be carried out in large amounts, whereas settlements through banks is slower. If, for example, one bank were unable to honour payments, then the effects of this would spread from bank to bank, and there would be a heightened possibility of system risk.

In summary, the changes in the financial system will not necessarily destabilize the management conditions for individual banks, but coming to conclusions about changes in the stability of the financial system as a whole is more difficult. A historical perspective is in order here. The financial controls of the high growth period were introduced with the purpose of maintaining the stability of the financial system. As these controls have been eased or abolished in the process of financial liberalization, it is necessary to consider what other policies for ensuring stability could replace the regulations that restricted competition.

b. Policies to maintain financial stability

The most important factor for maintaining the stability of the financial system will be ensuring stability of the real economy. Both the world-wide financial panics of the late 1920s and early 1930s and the credit scares around 1974 in the United States, the United Kingdom, and West Germany took place in recessions that had followed the overheating of these economies. This is why the mission of central banks combines stabilization of the value of the currency and maintenance of orderly credit conditions. On the basis of this historical experience, the next step is to consider the problems within the financial system itself, that is, the potential for monetary destabilization.

Three factors may be identified as possible contributors to monetary destabilization of the financial system. Banks may engage in high-risk investments; capitalization rates may fall; and system risk may expand.

High-risk investments and low capitalization could become the reasons for failure of individual banks. In the United States, observers have pointed out two basic reasons why these risks may increase—the rescue of banks that have fallen into bankruptcy, and a deposit insurance system with uniform premiums. The former problem is one of moral hazard, and the latter problem may be explained as follows. As the insurance premiums which a bank pays on its deposits do not depend on the probability of bankruptcy, it is possible for the bank to move toward higher-risk investments without increasing its insurance costs. For a bank without a strong sense of risk aversion, there is a possibility that such behaviour may, in fact, occur. Under a system with uniform insurance premiums, the bank's dependence on insured liabilities rises and its own capitalization ratio falls. In such cases, banks may engage in such behaviour because depositors do not have a strong incentive to distinguish among banks.

In general terms, the deposit insurance problem is also a problem of moral hazard; and precisely because moral hazard is neither wrong nor irrational but rather results from quite rational behaviour, it is very difficult to uproot. The problem of moral hazard has been widely discussed in the United States, and the problems in Japan are similar [10]. The term 'convoy regulation' has been used to describe the Japanese system, and this term by itself contains a nuance of self-criticism with regard to the occurrence of moral hazard. In short, moral hazard is a problem of the failure of the price mechanism.

The problem of undercapitalization has different origins, both in the tax system and in the methods through which the banks raise their capital. In the tax system, liabilities are treated more favourably than own capital. For a bank, dividends are a type of income and hence are subject to taxation, while interest costs on liabilities are treated as a cost for income tax purposes and thus are deductible. Other things being equal, it is advantageous to reduce as far as possible the bank's dependence on own capital. The problem concerning the methods by which banks raise capital is intertwined with the problem of segmentation of long- and short-term types of financial business. Because of the segmentation of these two kinds of business, it was impossible until very recently to raise capital through equity issue at market prices, rather than at par values, and through convertible debentures.

System risk is a problem which occurs because of transactions among financial institutions. It is obvious that the way to reduce system risk is to improve the supervision of credit extension among financial institutions. The possible methods of doing this are to require collateral to underpin transactions and to establish credit limits according to creditworthiness. And preconditions for improving the supervision of credit are improved disclosure and monitoring. In fact, credit supervision of financial institutions is carried out to a considerable extent, but supervision alone does not guarantee that the bankruptcy of one financial institution will not spread to others. The reason that society bears such huge costs in the case of 'domino' bankruptcies of financial institutions is that such bankruptcies severely disrupt the payments mechanism and cause a substantial decline in the efficiency of the economy.

The externalities involved in domino bankruptcies make it quite reasonable for there to be public intervention to halt their spread [49]. The central bank's function as lender of last resort is one means of accomplishing this goal, while the deposit insurance system is an indirect means of doing so. The function of lender of last resort is to supply funds to fill final shortages of funds in the market, that is, shortages of liquidity of banks. If such shortages are filled, then of course there will be no failures of banks due to insufficient liquidity. Deposit insurance systems, on the other hand, have a dual function. As their name suggests, they were originally used to protect depositors of banks that failed; but at the same time, they also worked to restrain the occurrence of runs on banks and thus may be expected to reduce the possibility of domino bank failures [34]. (For a description of Japan's deposit insurance system, see the appendix to this chapter.)

This public saftey net, which comprises both the lender-of-last-resort function and also the deposit insurance system, has a potent effect in ensuring the stability of the financial system. But precisely because of this potency, the effects of the safety net on the attitudes of management of individual banks will be very great. This, of course, is the moral hazard problem seen above. If the interest rates available at the lender of last resort are continuously below the market interest rates, or if insurance premiums are uniform without respect to the probability of a bank failure, then there is the possibility of moral hazard. Moreover, as the public safety net is improved, expanded, widened, and made more flexible, the possibility of moral hazard only grows [51].

Thus the problem of financial system stability comes down to how, or to what extent, to improve or expand the social safety net in order to achieve the greatest benefit at the lowest cost. One method is to draw clear boundaries between the area that is to rely on the public safety net and the area that is to rely on market discipline; the authorities must then adopt policies that will ensure the effective functioning of the public safety net and market discipline, each in its respective area. One possible breakdown might be, for example, to allow the capital markets and the short-term money markets to rely in principle on market discipline, while allowing transactions in other markets to rely on the public safety net. The bulk of the latter comprises transactions in small deposits for which the costs of acquiring information are relatively high. For areas allotted to market discipline, it is essential that adequate information be supplied. An essential condition for better information is an improvement in the disclosure rules and monitoring practices, including rating schemes, which will apply in capital markets and in short-term money markets.

Some success may be expected from separating responsibilities between the public safety net and market discipline. In the areas allotted to the public safety net, however, there will remain the possibility of moral hazard. Hence, the public safety net will continue to bear a huge burden, and it will therefore be necessary to make the market mechanism work within the public safety net itself [34]. For example, it would be possible in theory to allow the central bank to charge an interest rate on lending or to set premiums on deposit insurance in accordance with the creditworthiness of banks. It might also be possible to levy implicit premiums, such as stricter loan conditions or limits on insurable deposits, but explicit premiums are more likely to be effective. Some implicit premiums of this sort exist already: balance sheet controls, such as capitalization ratios and required ratios of liquid asset holdings, are policies through which the regulatory authorities reduce the moral hazards faced by banks and thus substitute for market discipline. Such policies represent a type of mixed framework in which the public safety net is combined with market mechanisms.

APPENDIX: DEPOSIT INSURANCE IN JAPAN

a. Overview

A deposit insurance system is an insurance scheme established jointly by the financial institutions that accept deposits from the general public. Under such a system, the banks accumulate the insurance premiums, and, in case a member financial institution goes bankrupt and cannot repay its depositors, the system makes direct payments to depositors up to a certain limit in place of the bank member that has gone bankrupt.[1] Along with the protection of depositors, the system seeks to maintain orderly credit conditions.

A deposit insurance system was recommended for Japan by the Committee for Financial System Research Committee (CFSR) in a report dated July 1970. This report, which was concerned with the state of the financial system in general, thought it desirable to introduce appropriate levels of competition into the financial markets in order to increase efficiency. As part of the proposed reforms, measures for depositor protection would be necessary and the deposit insurance system was one of these measures.

On the basis of this report, the Deposit Insurance Law was passed in April 1971, and the Deposit Insurance Corporation (DIC) was established in July of the same year to be the special corporation managing the deposit insurance system. The DIC had several interesting characteristics. First, membership was compulsory for almost all private financial institutions. Second, the business of the DIC would be kept within as narrow limits as possible and thus restricted to the receipt of insurance premiums and payments of insurance claims. Third, the private financial institutions would be represented in the management of the DIC. The institutions would contribute one-third of the capital, and management of the institution would reflect the voluntary intentions of the private financial institutions.

There were, however, some institutions that were not members. Agricultural co-operatives and fishery co-operatives established their own Savings Insurance Corporation for Agricultural and Fishery Co-operatives (SICAFC). Labour credit associations were also excluded from the deposit insurance system because their character differed from those of financial institutions for the general public.

The CFSR once again began to deliberate on the issues of financial liberalization in 1982. In its report of June 1985, it suggested the necessity of planning for the expansion and improvement of the deposit insurance system. In response to this initiative, a review of the deposit insurance system was undertaken in May 1986.

---

[1] The first country to establish a deposit insurance system was the USA. At the time of the great depression in the 1930s, one-third of the banks in the United States went bankrupt. This caused tremendous damage to the populace and generated social unrest. This painful experience brought home the need for protection of depositors, and in the revision of the banking law of 1933, the Federal Deposit Insurance Corporation (FDIC) was established. Other countries followed later. Canada established the Canadian Deposit Insurance Corporation in 1967, while Germany established its system in 1976 and the UK established its system in 1982.

There are some other mechanisms for the protection of banks. *Sogo* banks and *shinkin* banks each have aid and support agreements under which institutions that are experiencing difficulties may borrow funds for reconstruction and thus be rehabilitated. But these mechanisms differ in character from deposit insurance systems, in that the direct goal of these mechanisms is not the protection of depositors.

b. Deposit Insurance Corporation (*DIC*)

The DIC is capitalized at ¥450m., with the Government, the Bank of Japan, and the private financial institutions each contributing one-third of the capital. The participating institutions are city banks, regional banks, long-term credit banks, trust banks, the specialized foreign exchange bank (the Bank of Tokyo), *sogo* banks, *shinkin* banks, and credit co-operatives. The types of deposit liability included under the deposit insurance system are regular deposits (including savings deposits, but excluding foreign currency deposits, public deposits, and deposits of financial institutions), instalment savings, and money in trust with principal guaranteed contracts (that is, joint investment designated money trusts and loan trusts). The premiums are calculated on the basis of deposits outstanding at the end of the previous fiscal year for each financial institution. The current rate of premium is 0.008 per cent.

There are two types of incident which may cause payment of insurance claims. A Class I incident is a suspension of deposit payments by the financial institution. Class II incidents include a loss of business licence and decision to declare bankruptcy or to liquidate an institution. In cases of Class II incidents, payment of insurance claims will certainly be made; but in the Class I incidents, the Management Committee of the DIC considers and decides within one month of the incident whether payment of the insurance claim should be made. The amount that may be paid depends on the amount of the deposit, with total deposits per depositor used as the basis of calculation. But because protection of the ordinary individual depositor is the goal of the system, Government regulations limit the payments to any one depositor to a maximum of ¥3m. In addition, deductions are made in cases in which a depositor has liabilities toward the failed bank or if those deposits have been offered as collateral for the liability of a third party to the institution in question.

The DIC is to finance its payments of insurance claims from liability reserves and insurance premium income. With the approval of the Minister of Finance, it may also borrow up to ¥50 milliard from the Bank of Japan, if necessary. The DIC may also take possession of the assets of a failed bank in cases when the DIC has paid insurance claims, and may then liquidate those assets itself in place of liquidation by the depositors to whom it has paid the claims. Finally, the DIC is limited in the uses it may make of the accumulated insurance premiums; they may only be invested in holdings of Government bonds or other securities or in deposits at financial institutions.

c. Savings Insurance Corporation for Agricultural and Fishery Co-operatives (*SICAFC*)

The DIC does not include either agricultural co-operatives or fishery co-operatives as members, due to the special nature of these institutions. It was recognized, however, that there was a need for a system to protect the depositors of these institutions, and their Savings Insurance Corporation was established in September 1973 on the basis of a special law passed in July of the same year. The Savings Insurance Corporation is capitalized at ¥300m., with the Government, the Bank of Japan, and the *Norinchukin* Bank each contributing ¥75m., while the Credit Federation of Agricultural Co-operatives contributes ¥67.5m., and the Credit Federation of Fishery Co-operatives contributes ¥75m. Because the Savings Insurance Corporation was modelled on the DIC, the types of deposit insured, the types of claim, the reasons for payment, and the amounts of payment are all quite similar to those of the DIC. However, the rate of premium is lower, only 0.006 per cent. In addition, if the need for insurance payments in excess of reserves or premium income arises, the Savings Insurance Corporation may, with the approval of the responsible minister under whose jurisdiction the institution in question is regulated, borrow an amount determined by Government regulation (currently ¥10 milliard) from either the *Norinchukin* Bank or from the Bank of Japan. In the fiscal year 1984, there were 4,385 agricultural co-operatives and 1,790 credit co-operatives that were members of the Savings Insurance Corporation.

d. Reform of the deposit insurance system

Proposals for the reform of the deposit insurance system have been made. In its report of June 1985, the CFSR stated: 'In conjunction with the progress of financial liberalization, it is expected that the deposit insurance system will play an important role in maintaining orderly credit conditions', and made some proposals for the reform of the deposit insurance system. While recognizing the somewhat special character of the Savings Insurance Corporation for Agricultural and Fishery Co-operatives, the CFSR said that it would also be desirable to consider similar changes for this system. On the basis of the recommendations of the CFSR, both the Deposit Insurance Law and the corresponding law for agricultural and fishery co-operatives were revised in May 1986.

The two systems are to be revised and expanded along the following lines.

(i) It was deemed appropriate that the limit of deposit protection per depositor should rise from the current level of ¥3m. to ¥10m.

(ii) It was deemed appropriate that the insurance premiums be raised by about 50 per cent (that is, from the current rate of 0.008 per cent to 0.012 per cent).

(iii) It was deemed appropriate that the limit of borrowing from the Bank of Japan be raised considerably from the ¥50 milliard limit at the present to a much higher level (currently ¥500 milliard). It was also deemed appropriate that the required legal changes be made so that, in cases of borrowing from the Bank of Japan, borrowings from other financial institutions could be made so as to repay the borrowings from the Bank of Japan as quickly as possible.

(iv) It was deemed necessary that improvements be made in the diversity of methods available to aid institutions. Based on actual practices in the Japanese financial climate, forward-looking attitudes were to be taken concerning asset and liability succession[2] and introduction of financial aid accompanying merger.[3]

(v) It was deemed necessary for labour credit associations now to become subject to deposit insurance.

[2] Asset and liability succession is a type of transfer business with the following characteristics. In cases when a financial institution takes over the assets and liabilities, including deposit liabilities, of a failed institution, the DIC will supply funds to the succeeding institution in question in the form of purchasing the bad assets of the failed bank.

[3] Financing aid accompany merger is a type of funding provided by the DIC to a financial institution that merges with or buys another financial institution that has encountered business difficulties.

PART II

Details of the Financial System

3

Financial Assets

I. *Types of financial asset*

THERE are many types of financial asset in Japan today and many uses for them. Previous chapters have shown that the way in which individuals choose among the types of financial asset has significant effects on the financial system. In this chapter, we will consider the details of those financial assets. A classification system will be developed that distinguishes among financial assets according to their function, the certainty of their return, how the returns are determined, where and how the assets originate, and how the assets are traded.

The classification of financial assets by function separates assets into two major classes: transactions account assets and investment account assets. The transactions account assets play the role of means of settlement, i.e., means of payment or medium of exchange, and generally have lower return but higher liquidity than investment account assets. Examples of transactions account assets are cash and demand deposits or, from the viewpoint of financial institutions, deposits at the central bank. Investment account assets, on the other hand, comprise all financial assets other than transactions account assets, i.e., time deposits, trusts, bank debentures, Government bonds, industrial bonds, equities, or securities investment trusts.

The classification of financial assets by certainty of return also separates assets into two major classes, safe assets and risky assets. Safe assets are those whose return is stable, i.e., those with a variance of expected return of zero. Risky assets are those with a variance of expected return that is not zero. All transactions account assets are safe assets, and among the investment account assets listed above, the safe assets include time and savings deposits and time postal deposits or fixed-amount postal savings, which have fixed interest rates and guarantee of principal. All other investment account assets have uncertain interest rates or have the possibility of capital losses, and therefore are considered to be risky assets.

The classification of financial assets by how interest rates are determined separates assets into those with free interest rates and those with regulated rates. Free-rate financial assets are those whose interest rates are determined in the market through supply and demand. In Japan, some interest rates, such as the call rate, have been free rates for many many years, while others are free because they fall outside the jurisdiction of the Temporary Interest Rate Adjustment Law (TIRAL). Among the latter are the interest rates on CDs, foreign currency deposits, yen deposits held by foreign governments, central banks, and international organizations, large-scale time deposits, and already issued public or corporate bonds. But most other assets are regulated-rate assets which fall within the jurisdiction of the current system of interest rate regulations. These regulations include not only legal regulations but also administrative guidance and regulations imposed through customary procedures. Many of the regulated interest rate assets are safe assets such as deposits described above, but even some risky assets have regulated rates, such as subscribers' yields on public bonds, bank debentures, and industrial bonds. Most other risky assets have free interest rates.

The classification of financial assets by origin separates assets into those that are direct securities, which may also be called primary securities, and those that are indirect securities. Direct securities are those that are the liabilities of the final user of funds. Indirect securities are those that are liabilities of financial intermediaries, which stand between the depositor and the final user of the funds. Transactions account assets and safe investment account assets are necessarily indirect securities, but risky investment account assets may be either indirect securities (such as bank debentures or certificates of deposit) or direct securities.

The classification of assets by their method of transaction separates assets into those that are negotiable assets and those which are non-negotiable, (bilaterally-traded), i.e., between assets that can be bought and sold in markets and those which are only transacted between two individual parties. Safe assets are always non-negotiable assets, with the exception of cash, while risky assets are always negotiable assets, with the exception of loan certificates (*kari-ire shosho*).

Table 3.1 summarizes this system of classification. The purpose of the table is only to position the various types of asset that currently exist clearly in relation to each other. This is done at some risk because the classification is based on a static description of their characteristics; however, because of the dynamic nature of the changes in the Japanese financial structure today, there will undoubtedly be some assets that will not fit cleanly into the table. For example, the borders are beginning to blur between transactions account assets and investment account assets, because of the continuing development of financial services that join the payments function with the investment function. Examples of such assets include *sogo* accounts at banks, the 'swing services' that provide for automatic transfer of funds from ordinary deposit accounts to time deposit accounts, and transfer services between ordinary and *chukoku* accounts, which are jointly provided by some banks and securities companies. The distinction between safe and risky assets has also been blurred by the emergence of the so-called 'public bond' *sogo* accounts. These accounts

TABLE 3.1 *Classification of Financial Assets*[a]

Function	Transactions account assets	Investment account assets						
Predictability	Safe assets					Ricky assets		
Interest rate determination		Regulated-rate assets					Free-rate assets	
Form of origin		Indirect securities			Primary securities	Indirect securities	Primary securities	
Form of trading	Negotiable	Bilateral		Negotiable		Negotiable	Negotiable	Bilateral
Examples	Cash	Demand deposits; ordinary postal savings	Time and savings deposits; time postal deposits; fixed-amount postal savings	Newly issued bank debentures	Newly issued public bonds; industrial bonds; Government bills	Securities investment trusts; CDs; foreign currency deposits; bank-sold bills	Already-issued public bond; bank-underwritten bills	Loan certificates

Note:

[a] This table is, as mentioned in the text, a rather bold attempt at a clear classification of currently existing financial assets within a system of categorization in outline form. Strictly speaking, some problems remain. For example, assets that would be safe assets if held to maturity involve, nevertheless, some risk in that the return is uncertain if they are liquidated before maturity. In this case, these assets might be categorized in risky assets. Moreover, even safe assets are not perfectly safe, considering the possible loss of real value due to inflation on the possibility of bankruptcy of financial institutions. The categorization is also made by abstracting from maturity-related market segmentation.

allow the depositor to avoid the potential for capital loss in selling a Government bond before maturity by means of attaching a loan provision to these accounts, under which the depositor may borrow against the Government bonds as collateral. Even the distinction between regulated rates and free rates is not as clear as it used to be. For example, the subscribers' yields and other conditions on public and corporate bonds were formerly decided within rather narrow limits and thus were considered to be regulated rates; now, however, the yields and conditions for these Government and public bonds are set with an extremely high degree of consideration for market conditions, and thus have become very flexible.

Financial liberalization is working both to blur the distinctions among assets and to redistribute assets among the categories. For example, the issue limits for CDs have been eased gradually over the years, and in March 1985 money market certificates with interest rates reflecting market rates were introduced. In October of the same year, the interest rates on large bank deposits were also liberalized. It is expected that the liberalization of interest rates on large-lot funds will lead gradually to liberalization of interest rates on smaller lots of funds. Through this process, the funds will be redistributed from regulated-rate assets to free-rate assets and simultaneously the shares of negotiable assets and non-negotiable assets will shift.

Let us now turn to the specifics of each type of financial asset.

II. Monetary assets

1. CONCEPTS OF MONEY

a. Money

Money was classified above as a safe transactions asset. The important function of means of payment is currently fulfilled by money, in the forms of currency in circulation (bank notes or subsidiary coin) along with current deposits, ordinary deposits, and other types of demand deposit. Currency in circulation is called cash currency, while demand deposits are called deposit money, but the boundaries between those financial assets that may be termed money and those that may not is flexible. In Japan in the immediate postwar period, the definition of money focused on cash currency, i.e., bank notes and subsidiary coin, and then in 1949 a redefinition of the money supply was calculated that included both currency in circulation and deposit money. Deposit money, however, was defined at the time to include only current deposits. Only in 1954 was the money supply definition expanded to include all demand deposits. The reason for these changes in the definition of money was the substantial growth—in conjunction with that of the economy—of the use of deposit money as a main medium of transactions. In addition, the accepted monetary theory of the day suggested that all liquid demand deposits should be included in the definition of money.

b. Quasi-money

Under today's definitions, cash currency and deposit money together are defined as 'narrow money', while this quantity plus the quantity of time deposits is termed 'broad money'. Thus, time deposits or substitutes for money—i.e., quasi-money—are included within the definition. That is, time deposits differ from cash currency and deposit money, which are held for transactions matters, in that time deposits are held for investment purposes and are investment account assets; nevertheless, because time deposits can be made liquid if the depositor is willing to forego the interest available if the asset had been held to maturity, it is not appropriate to exclude time deposits from the concept of money. In Japan, as in other countries, there have been large-scale shifts of funds from time deposit accounts to demand deposits in times of tight money, while there have also at times been shifts from demand deposits into time deposits at times when interest rates seem about to fall. Under such circumstances, time deposits must of course be included in money if one is to measure the quantity of money accurately. Time deposits have been included as quasi-money in the Japanese conception of the broad money supply since 1967, the time of creation of the money supply framework that is still used today.

On the other hand, one cannot deny that there is a difference in the so-called 'moneyness' between demand deposits and time deposits. For this reason, there have been attempts to construct so-called 'Divisia monetary indices', which measure the money supply as a weighted average of monetary assets, with weights determined according to the degrees of moneyness of the respective assets.

2. CURRENT DEFINITIONS OF THE MONEY SUPPLY

The money supply is defined today as the quantity of money held domestically by the private non-financial sector, i.e., by corporations that are not financial intermediaries, by individuals, and by local and municipal authorities. But because the money supply statistics are such important indicators for the management of monetary policy, there is a necessity for short reporting lags; and in turn because of this necessity, certain distinctions must be made in constructing the statistics. We must therefore consider in some detail the boundaries of the definition of money and the boundaries of the institutions which supply it. (The scope of money supply statistics in Japan is nearly identical with that in other countries because international comparability of money supply statistics has been pursued, particularly within the framework of the IMF.)

a. The scope of the money supply

The scope of the money supply as defined in the statistics of today includes currency in circulation (i.e., cash currency), deposit money, and time deposits (quasi-money). The sum of cash currency and deposit money is called M1 and that of all three components together is called M2. Deposits denominated in foreign currencies, though they are not a direct means of payment is the domestic economy, may nevertheless be converted into yen and used for the purchase of domestic goods and services regardless of whether they are demand or time deposits, and hence they are included in quasi-money along with the yen deposits of non-residents. In addition, the money market certificates, which were established in March 1985, are similar to the time deposits that were already in existence, except that the interest rates on such certificates fluctuate along with the interest rate on CDs. Hence money market certificate accounts are included in quasi-money, and CDs themselves are also considered to be a type of quasi-money. With CDs, however, there is the possibility of a capital loss when sold, and hence they are of a somewhat different character from M2. Despite this difference, it is common practice to add the outstanding amount of CDs to the various indicators of the money supply when analysing the movements of the money supply. The most commonly used indicator in Japan is M2 plus CDs.

There are two other types of financial asset that are similar in nature to time deposits, specifically the principal in trust accounts (either in money in trust or in loan trusts) and bank debentures. The principal in trust accounts is included in the broader indicator of money called M3 (see below), but the funds invested in bank debentures are not currently included in any monetary indicator, and the same is true of other types of bond such as Government bonds, local authority bonds, and industrial bonds even though they too are assets of high liquidity in the sense that they can be easily exchanged for current deposits. So long as these securities are bought and sold within the private non-financial sector, then the total amount of liquidity in the economy does not change. It is, of course, useful to include such securities in the calculation of liquidity of different sectors or different industries. There is, however, an increase in the quantity of currency or deposits held by the private non-financial sector only when private non-financial agents sell these securities to financial institutions. It is thus sufficient to measure money at this stage of the process. This method of treatment also corresponds to the idea of treating money in the context of credit granted by the financial institutions.

b. Institutions that supply money

The institutions that supply money are the domestic financial institutions, but the scope of coverage of institutions depends on the definition of the money supply being used. That is, for M1 and M2, the institutions concerned are the Bank of Japan, the banking accounts of all banks, *sogo shinkin* banks, the *Norinchukin* Bank, and the *Shokochukin* Bank. The scope for M3 statistics includes all the financial institutions covered for the M2 statistics but also includes the postal saving system, agricultural co-operatives, fishery co-operatives, credit co-operatives, labour credit associations, and the trust accounts of all banks. The reason for the difference in scope between M2 and M3 is primarily the long reporting lags of data for the financial institutions that are included only in the measure of M3. In the past, there was a notion that only credit-granting institutions, centring on commercial banks, should be classified as institutions that could supply money, but today it is more common to agree that savings institutions are also suppliers of money. Foreign banks resident in Japan are excluded from the money supply statistics even though they are also suppliers of money, largely due to data constraints.

c. Current definitions of money supply

Table 3.2 gives an overview of the money supply classifications in Japan. Because of the importance of the money supply as an indicator for monetary policy and because of the importance of a broad judgement of its level, various indicators are constructed. But among these indicators, M2 plus CDs, on an average outstanding basis, is the one considered most important. This indicator is used because it has several important characteristics: first, it has a closer relationship with future prices than do other indicators; second, the Bank of Japan can control it better than the other indicators; and third, the reporting lag is relatively short.

But financial innovation has made defining money more difficult. Since 1975, there have been continuous financial innovations, and the diversification of financial assets has increased the number of assets that have the character of deposits. In the United States, the huge shift of funds into money market accounts required a complete overhaul of the money supply statistics in 1980 [12]. In Japan, the pace of the financial innovation is not quite as rapid as in the United States and things have yet to come to this; nevertheless, the Japanese authorities are continuously reviewing the monetary statistics, their relationships to prices, and their controllability with the object of accurate understanding of domestic liquidity conditions.[1]

---

[1] Because the purpose of the current money supply statistics is to identify the money supply in the domestic economy, deposits outside of the country such as Euro-deposits (i.e., yen-denominated deposits placed in branches of financial institutions outside the country) are not included.

TABLE 3.2 *Money Supply Concepts*[a,b]

Indicator name	Breadth of definition	Financial institutions concerned	Reporting lag	Comments
M1 (end of period or period average)	Cash currency plus deposit money			Most liquid of money supply indicators; deficient as money indicator because it fails to capture temporary shifts into time and savings deposits
M1' (end of period)	M1 + quasi-money of corporations	The Bank of Japan; all banks (banking accounts); Sogo banks; Shinkin banks; Norinchukin bank; Shoko Chukin Bank	2 months +	Monetary indicator most closely related to corporate activity; activity outstanding amounts not available
	M1' + CDs			
M2 (end of period or period average)	M1 + quasi-money		2 months +	Most typical monetary indicator; BOJ currently emphasizes
M2 + CDs (end of period or period average)	M2 + CDs			M2 + CDs; increasing trend due to inclusion of savings deposits of individuals
M3 (end of period)	M2 + deposits in postal savings; agricultural co-operatives; fishery co-operatives; credit co-operatives; labour credit associations + principal in trust accounts of all banks	Institutions concerned with M2; the post offices; agricultural co-operatives; fishery co-operatives; labour credit associations; all banks (trust association accounts)	6 months (preliminary reports in 2 months +)	Monetary indicator most inclusive of various financial assets; increasing trend due to high weight of savings deposits of individuals; reliable data have long lags (preliminary data published only after 5 months)
M3 + CDs (end of period or period average)	M3 + CDs			

Definitions:

Cash currency
 Total bank notes issued plus subsidiary coins less total currency and coin held by financial institutions subject to observation.

Deposit money
 All general deposits, public deposits that are demand deposits and that are liabilities of financial institutions subject to observation, less cheques and bills of those institutions. National Government and financial institution deposits are excluded.

Quasi-money
 All general deposits, public deposits, and instalment savings financial institutions subject to observation less those of the nature of demand deposits. National Government and financial institution deposits are excluded, but non-resident yen deposits and all foreign currency deposits are included.

CDs
 All negotiable certificates of deposit issued by financial institutions subject to observation, excluding those purchased originally by financial institutions.

Agricultural, fishery, and credit co-operatives, and labour credit associations deposits
 All deposits excluding cash accounts (checks plus currency) and savings deposits of financial institutions.

Trust account principal
 All principal of money trusts and loan trusts excluding those established by financial institutions and the cash accounts (cheques plus currency) of trust accounts.

Postal savings deposits
 Final data based on calculation from local post offices that accept deposits; preliminary reports based on daily statements.

Holders of money:

Treatment of Government
 Central Government is not considered to be a holder of money.

Treatment of financial institutions
 In addition to financial institutions subject to observation, other financial institutions (foreign banks, Credit Federation of Agricultural Co-operatives, credit federation of fishery co-operatives, Zenshinren Bank, National Federation of Credit Co-operatives, insurance companies, Government financial institutions) are not considered to be holders of money.

Treatment of non-residents
 Non-residents are considered to be holders of money (M2 and broader definitions; excluding non-resident Government and financial institutions).

III. Description of the types of financial asset

This section outlines the major characteristics of each of the important financial assets (with the exception of cash currency) that are held by the private non-financial sector.

1. DEPOSITS

Deposits are one of the typical financial assets held very broadly by households and corporations. They are both a means of payment and a means of short- and medium-term savings. Deposits are offered by a very broad range of financial institutions, including all banks, *sogo* banks, *shinkin* banks, credit co-operatives, labour credit associations, agricultural co-operatives, fishery co-operatives, and the postal savings system, (see Chapter 5 for more details on institutions). Types of deposit are classified according to whether their term is fixed and whether there is an upper limit on the interest rate that may be paid. That is, the distinction is between demand deposits and time deposits on one hand, and between regulated-rate deposits and free-rate deposits on the other. Regulated-rate deposits and free-rate deposits will be distinguished according to the existence of interest rate regulations, but because such interest rate regulations are gradually being eased or abolished as time goes on, it is not clear that such a method of categorization will be appropriate in the future.

a. Deposits with regulated interest rates

(i) Demand deposits

(1) Current deposits (Toza Yokin).　Current deposits are deposits that the depositor may demand freely as his needs require. They are mostly used by corporations as settlement accounts; deposits and withdrawals may be made in units of ¥1 or more. Usually, a corporation will conclude a current account transactions contract (or a generalized payments management contract), and the corporation will make payments through this current deposit account by means of cheques drawn on the account and payable through the bank or by means of promissory notes or bills of exchange that are payable at the bank. Current deposits have paid no interest since 1944 (in 1944 the zero-interest provision was based on the interest rate agreements among banks at the time; since 1947 it has been based on the TIRAL).

(2) Ordinary deposits (Futsu yokin).　Ordinary deposits are similar to current deposits in that they are demand deposits with free deposits and withdrawal privileges in units of ¥1 or more (for trust banks, the units are ¥10 or more). Ordinary deposits are held mostly by individuals, or by corporations with temporary excesses of funds. They differ from current

deposits in that they are not subject to withdrawal by cheque-writing but rather require presentation of a passbook, which has been given to the depositor by the bank, and a previously registered seal (the Japanese substitute for signature) or secret identification code. In addition, deposits and withdrawals may be made at automatic teller machines or cash dispensers through the use of cash cards. Ordinary deposits are also used for automatic payment services such as transfers of funds, pension and dividend payments, and payments of public utility charges, taxes, insurance premiums, and instalment credit payments. Thus, ordinary deposits are a means of holding short-term savings but are also a type of settlement account. Interest is paid semi-annually to units of ¥100 and becomes part of the principal of the account when paid.

In recent years, ordinary deposit accounts have been used in combination with other financial products, and new financial services involving ordinary deposits have been presented one after another. Three types of such product are so-called *sogo* accounts, swing services, and transfer services between ordinary deposits and medium-term Government bond funds.

A *sogo* account is a combination account that unites an ordinary deposit account with a time deposit account. A *sogo* account has a facility by which there is an automatic lending provision that uses the time deposit as collateral. Such accounts date from August 1972, and are offered by city banks, regional banks, *sogo* banks, *shinkin* banks, credit co-operatives, labour credit associations, and agricultural co-operatives. When funds in the ordinary deposit account are insufficient, a loan to the deposit-holder may be made automatically in an amount of up to ¥1 m. (as of April 1986, with increases foreseeable), so long as this does not exceed 90 per cent of the funds outstanding in the time deposit account. The interest rate on the loan is 0·25 per cent above that on the time deposit. The proceeds of this loan are then automatically transferred from the ordinary account for the payment in question. This type of account is similar to cash management services in the United States, and is a type of financial innovation that makes possible the economization of transactions accounts.

There are two other types of *sogo* account that combine an ordinary deposit either with a bank debenture or with a loan trust. The bank debenture *sogo* account was initiated in October 1981 at the Bank of Tokyo and spread in January 1985 to long-term credit banks. The loan trust *sogo* account combines an ordinary deposit account with a loan trust, and has been offered by trust banks since January 1981. Both of these accounts function in the same way as do regular *sogo* accounts.

A swing service is a type of service that may be added to a *sogo* account. The swing service allows automatic transfer from the ordinary deposit to the time deposit. Such services were initiated by city banks in October 1983. When the balance outstanding on a given day of the month in an ordinary deposit account exceeds a certain fixed level (which must be above ¥ 100,000 and which has been pre-arranged according to contract between the depositor and the bank), then the amount exceeding the pre-arranged level, and usually in units of ¥100,000, is transferred automatically into the time deposit account. In this way, the management of funds becomes more efficient for the depositor. In cases when the ordinary deposit balance becomes insufficient, then an automatic loan will be made against collateral at the time deposit, according to conditions identical to those of the regular *sogo* account.

Another new type of *sogo* account combined an ordinary deposit with a medium-term Government bond fund (described below). This type of account also has an automatic transfer facility. It was first offered in April 1984 as the result of a business link between certain *shinkin* banks and securities companies. In addition, there were some business links with *sogo* banks. When the ordinary deposit exceeds a certain limit, currently ¥300,000, the amounts of ¥100,000 or more in units of ¥10,000 are transferred automatically into the medium-term Government bond fund. There is also a minimum balance for the ordinary deposit account. When the balance in the ordinary deposit account is below that minimum, then the medium-term Government bond fund is reduced by ¥100,000 or more, in units of ¥10,000, and the ordinary deposit account is replenished with the proceeds. Because funds are automatically transferred into the medium-term Government bond fund once the balance in the ordinary deposit account exceeds the certain limit, this type of account is similar to the swing service account and improves the efficiency of fund management for the depositor. This innovation is similar to sweep accounts in the United States.

(3) Notice deposits (Tsuchi yokin).   Notice deposits are deposits that must be left in the account for seven days after placement but may be withdrawn with two days' notice at any time thereafter. These deposits are used mostly by corporations as a means of investing temporary surpluses of funds. The interest paid on such deposits is 0·25 per cent above that paid on ordinary deposits, and the interest is paid *pro rata* for the number of days deposited on the day of withdrawal. For banks, minimum amounts of deposits and units on which interest is paid are in units of ¥50,000 or ¥10,000.

(4) Deposits for tax payments (Nozei junbi yokin).   Deposits for tax payments are deposits made of funds that will be used to pay taxes, and the interest rates paid on these accounts are 0·75 per cent above those paid on ordinary deposits (units on which interest is paid are ¥100 units, so long as the amount outstanding in the account is ¥1,000 or more). In addition, the interest paid on these accounts is tax free. Deposits in these accounts may be made in units of ¥1 or more, or, for trust banks, in units of ¥10 or more. Withdrawal is limited to times at which taxes are paid, however, and in cases when the purpose of withdrawal is other than for tax payments, the interest and the tax thereon are treated as if they were from an ordinary deposit account.

(5) Special deposits (Betsudan yokin).   Special deposits are miscellaneous deposits of other types which are used for such purposes as repositories for temporary funds in transit or held in custody. Examples would include revenue payments to Bank of Japan agencies or to revenue agencies that are credited to the Bank of Japan on the second day after payment, funds deposited by public revenue processing centres, dividend payments on equities that are managed by banks, principal or interest being paid on public and corporate bonds, funds used for stock purchases, and payments in transit between banks. These special deposits are categories that were established in order to account for temporary deposits at banks, so that most have no fixed period of deposit, and most pay no interest.

(ii) Time and savings deposits

(1) Time deposits (Teiki yokin).   Time deposits are deposits for which the term of the deposit is fixed and which in principle cannot be withdrawn during this period. Time deposits account for the largest share of savings deposits in Japan, and depositors include not only individuals but also corporations. The minimum deposit is ¥100 and there are four types of such deposits according to the guide-lines of the Bank of Japan (see Chapter 6), deposits of three and six months and of one or two years (the TIRAL regulates only those deposits with fixed terms, defined to be those of three or more months in maturity). The interest rate paid depends on the maturity of the deposit, with the minimum amount for full payment of interest being ¥ 100. Interest is paid on the date of maturity of the deposit (however, for two-year deposits, a mid-term interest payment is made after one year and the remaining interest is paid on maturity of the deposit; in most cases, there is no compounding of interest on time deposits). Interest on time deposits may be applied to tax exemption of small savings (so-called *maruyu*). Time deposits are also in principle deposited for the period up to the date of maturity, so that, in cases when a withdrawal prior to this date is necessary, a penalty rate proportional to the length of the actual deposit is applied. For funds left in time deposits after the date of maturity, two interest rates may apply. If the deposit is withdrawn, then the ordinary deposit rate applicable on the day of withdrawal is applied to the period between the date of maturity and the date of withdrawal. If, however, the time deposit is renewed, then the time deposit interest rate from the time of the renewal is applied to the period between the maturity and the renewal.

In cases when a depositor wishes to extend a time deposit past the date of maturity, in general the funds must be redeposited. However, it is possible with prior notice to extend a time deposit automatically from the date of maturity at the original conditions of the deposit. Such time deposits are called 'automatic renewal time deposits', and there are two types, those which redeposit only the principal and those which add the interest to the principal for the periods of extension. In addition, instalment time deposits are possible for such purposes as education or house purchase; in such accounts, the deposit places small amounts of funds at regular intervals into the account.

New products involving regular time deposits have been developed, either through altering the method of interest payment or by combining them with other financial products. Examples include maturity-designated time deposits, Government bond time deposit accounts, and public bond *sogo* accounts.

Maturity-designated time deposits are the time deposits for individuals using the *maruyu* system. These deposits may be for periods of one year or more up to three years; after having been left on deposit for one year, the funds may be withdrawn on a given day after prior notice of one month has been given. Such deposits were initiated in June 1981 in response to the fixed-amount postal savings which are described below. The minimum deposit in a maturity-designated time deposit is ¥100, just as for a regular time deposit, but the maximum is ¥3m. The interest rate on such deposits is the same as that for time deposits of the same maturity, but for maturity-designated time deposits the interest rate is compounded annually so that the yield on the account rises with the maturity. Moreover, the interest payments on the account may fall within the *maruyu* system so long as the original principal deposited in the account was below the *maruyu* limit. Thus, even if the total funds in the account together with interest already credited into the account exceed the *maruyu* limit, the interest earnings remain tax-free. The units on which interest is paid and the conditions on early withdrawal are the same as those for time deposits.

Government bond time deposit accounts are a new financial product that was introduced in 1983 at the time of opening of over-the-counter sales of Government bonds by financial institutions. These accounts are aimed at the individuals, offered by ordinary banks, *sogo* banks, and *shinkin* banks, and combine a time deposit with a newly purchased long- or medium-term Government coupon bond; the interest on the Government bond is credited to the time deposit. The original principal at the time of the deposit is usually divided between the Government bond and the time deposit in shares of about 60 per cent and 40 per cent respectively, the purpose of this division being to raise the yield.

When a time deposit is taken in the form of a maturity-designated time deposit for use within the *maruyu* system, then it is possible to have the interest on Government bonds (which is paid twice annually) paid automatically into the maturity-designated time deposit and thus reinvested. In addition to saving the depositor time and trouble, such accounts may also be established together with a *sogo* account using an ordinary deposit. There are ten-year and two- to four-year maturities of such deposits, with the ten-year maturity based on a long-term Government coupon bond (such deposits were started in August 1983) and with the two- to four-year maturities based on medium-term Government coupon bonds (such accounts were started in October 1983).

The minimum deposit for these types of account is ¥500,000 per account, with additions in units of ¥50,000 for Government bond accounts and ¥10,000 for maturity-designated time deposits, and both these types of account may be used in connection with the first or second tranches of the *maruyu* system. In addition, maturity-designated time deposits may be used as the basis for *sogo* accounts, i.e., used as collateral for an automatic provision function or as the back-up for automatic transfer of payments for pensions, dividends, public utility charges, and other credit charges.

Public bond *sogo* accounts are a new type of financial product based on the Government bond time account, and were instituted in June 1985 by city banks and other banks. Such accounts add the facility of using public bonds as collateral to a *sogo* account, which already combines both an ordinary deposit and a time deposit. As a result, the possible overdraft becomes larger. The banks developed this type of account in response to lending facilities granted by securities companies using public bonds as collateral, which had started operation in June 1985.

(2) Instalment savings (Teiki tsumikin).   Instalment savings are a type of savings instrument aimed at individuals. Under the contract, a fixed amount, called the *kakekin*, is deposited on a regular basis, i.e., every month or every day, and accumulated over time until maturity. Compensation benefits, i.e. interest, are paid on on the date of maturity, and principal is returned on that date. For instalment savings, the usual practice is for financial institutions to come to the depositor in order to collect the *kakekin*. Instalment savings are similar to instalment time deposits in that both are used for education, travel, housing, and other targeted savings. Instalment savings accounts are mostly concentrated in financial institutions such as *shinkin* banks, credit co-operatives, and agricultural co-operatives, which have strong local ties. Periods of accumulation are required to be of six months or more, but most such accounts are for one to five years in length (three-year contracts comprise the largest share). Monthly instalments are the most common and are made in units of ¥1,000 with a minimum of ¥1,000 (daily instalments are in units of ¥100). These deposits fall under the provision of the TIRAL and hence are treated as are time deposits. However, according to the interest rate guidelines, the interest rates are paid without regard to the length of the contract, and are lower in most cases than those paid on three-month time deposits. The compensation benefits at the end of the contract period are treated as miscellaneous income under the tax laws, but there is no requirement of declaration if the compensation benefits are below ¥200,000.

The *sogo* banks (see Chapter 5 for a description of these institutions) offer a unique savings account which is similar to instalment savings; this unique account is called the *sogo kakekin*. Under such accounts, a fixed amount of funds is deposited at regular intervals for a set length of time and accumulated until the expiration of the contract. The form of such accounts in terms of units of the *kakekin*, contract length, and tax treatment are similar to those of instalment savings. The differences with instalment savings accounts are that (1) withdrawal is possible before the expiration of the contract (i.e., within the limits of the agreed amount) and the *kakekin* paid thereafter are augmented by an amount equivalent to the loan rate for the funds withdrawn; (2) upon application, it is possible to increase the amount of the *kakekin*; and (3) the yield is higher than that on instalment savings.

b. Deposits with free interest rates

(i) Certificates of deposits (CDs)

Certificates of deposit may be issued by financial institutions that are authorized to collect deposits. The first CDs were issued in May 1979, and differ from regular deposits in that they are short-term deposits with free interest rates that may be sold to third parties. There are no specific restrictions on who may purchase the certificates, but the units of issue are so large that most are purchased by corporations, public-sector co-operatives, and local government bodies. When first issued, the minimum maturity was ¥500m., but this was gradually lowered to ¥300m. in January 1984 and then to ¥100m. in April 1985, and the unit of purchase is ¥10m. The maturities are for one month up to one year (the upper limit was six months until March 1986), and the CDs usually mature on a specific date. The issuing bank is not permitted to buy back the CDs before maturity or to cancel the asset during its period of life, but CDs may be liquidated by holders through sale in the market (see Chapter 4). The interest rate on CDs is a free rate and does not fall within the jurisdiction of the TIRAL, and thus is decided through bilateral negotiation between the issuing financial institution and the purchaser. However, the arbitrage relations with the *gensaki* and bill markets are very strong, so that CD rates are strongly influenced by these other markets. Because CDs are considered to be deposits and not securities, the securities transaction tax is not levied on transactions of CDs, as it is on *gensaki* transactions with repurchase agreement. But *maruyu* limits may not be applied to CD holdings.

In addition to CD issue in the domestic market, a short-term Euro-yen CD issue outside Japan by both foreign and domestic banks was permitted from December 1984 (bringing the proceeds of such issues into Japan is not permitted on the grounds that to do so might allow circumvention of regulation on conditions of CD issue in the domestic market). There are no issue limits or minimum denomination restrictions on foreign CD issues, as there are on domestic ones.

(ii) Foreign currency deposits *(Gaika yokin)*

Foreign currency deposits are free-rate deposits denominated in foreign currencies that are offered by authorized foreign exchange banks. The varieties of deposits offered are similar to those of domestic yen deposits, i.e., current, ordinary, notice, special, and time deposits. The maturity of deposits is left to negotiation between the bank and the depositor, but the largest portion of such deposits are short-term deposits of less than one year. The minimum unit of deposit for demand deposits is one unit of the foreign currency (e.g. $1) or, for time deposits, 100 units of the foreign currency (e.g. $100). There is no upper limit on the quantities of such deposits.

The interest rates on such deposits do not fall within the jurisdiction of the TIRAL. For large deposits, usually of $100,000 or more, the interest rates are determined through individual negotiation on a bilateral basis and take into consideration the maturity and quantity deposited, along with the Euromarket interest rates. Conditions for foreign currency deposits of small amounts are posted on a weekly basis. Because these deposits are denominated in foreign currencies, the depositor bears the foreign exchange risk; however, in most cases this risk is hedged through the use of a forward exchange contract written for the day of maturity of the deposit. This practice locks in the interest rate on the deposit on a yen basis. Foreign currency deposits are not applicable to the *maruyu* system, and hence there are almost no cases of individual small amount deposits in such accounts.

(iii) Non-resident yen deposits

Non-resident yen deposits are deposits received by authorized foreign exchange banks from non-residents. The interest rates on deposits by foreign governments, foreign central banks, and international organizations were removed from the jurisdiction of the TIRAL in March 1980. This measure was taken in the light of developments in the foreign exchange markets at the time, in order to encourage foreign governments, foreign central banks, and international organizations to hold yen deposits and thus to help stabilize the yen market. At the time, there were two types of non-resident deposits, the so-called 'free yen accounts', and other yen deposits. These two types of deposit differed in their liquidity and transferability. But with the revised Foreign Exchange and Foreign Trade Control Law of December 1980, all yen became freely convertible and transferable (in times other than emergencies), so the purpose of the distinction disappeared; all such deposits were renamed non-resident yen deposits.

(iv) Money market certificates (MMCs)

Money market certificates are large denomination time deposits (minimum deposit ¥50m.). Any financial institution authorized to take deposits may offer money market certificates with maturities of between one month and one year (until March 1986 maturities were limited to between one and six months). Such certificates were introduced in March 1985 by *sogo* banks, *shinkin* banks, and credit co-operatives; ordinary banks began to offer them in April that year.

MMCs are in fact a type of time deposit (included as time deposits in the classification on bank balance sheets), but the method of determining of the interest rate on them differs from that for regular time deposits. MMC interest rates are established freely by each bank according to the maturities, but the maximum rate is computed as the average CD issue rate published each week by the Bank of Japan minus 0·75 per cent, in the framework of the TIRAL through notification by the Ministry of Finance. Thus, the MMC only appears to be an asset with a controlled rate formerly established under the TIRAL, but in fact is a free-rate asset, because the MMC interest rate is based on that of certificates of deposit, which are the most typical free rate in the money market. The spread of 0·75 per cent below the CD rate reflects the differences of cost due to the large-unit issue of CDs and the smaller units of MMCs. The introduction of MMCs was an important step toward liberalization of deposit interest rates, and detailed interest rates for MMCs are not established under the Bank of Japan guide-lines.

But the MMC differs from the CD in that the MMC is not negotiable, i.e., in principle an MMC cannot be redeemed until a certain time has passed, currently one month, from the original deposit. In cases of premature redemption, no interest is paid. When redemption is made after the obligatory holding period but before maturity, the interest rate for ordinary deposits is applied. The total quantity of MMCs that a bank may accept is set in relation to the broadly defined capital of the bank. Currently the ratio is 200 per cent, although it was 150 per cent until March 1986. For foreign banks resident in Japan, the ratio is 100 per cent of the total of yen-denominated loans and securities or ¥20 milliard, whichever is higher. The maturities for MMCs are currently scheduled to rise from the range of one month to one year at present to one month to two years, in line with the maturity of time deposits. In addition, the minimum deposit units are scheduled to be reduced.

(v) Large-scale time deposits

Large-scale time deposits are, as the name implies, simply time deposits of relatively large size. There are four types of such deposit, just as with usual time deposits, i.e., those of three months, six months, one year, and two years. The interest rates on such deposits, which are in units of ¥1 milliard or more, were fully liberalized in October 1985. This liberalization measure was taken along the lines of the action programme announced in July of the same year, and the minimum deposit was set at ¥1 milliard in consideration of the conditions of competition and substitutability between large-scale deposits and the short-term money market. In April 1986, the minimum deposit was lowered to ¥500m. with a further lowering to ¥300m. scheduled for autumn of 1986, and yet a further lowering for the spring of 1987.

Large-scale time deposits are similar to ordinary time deposits in most respects. In cases of redemption before maturity, an appropriate penalty must be charged. In principle, the rates in such cases are determined by each bank, but when the funds are withdrawn before they have been held three months on deposit, an interest rate below that of ordinary deposits is considered appropriate. For large-scale time deposits of maturity of two years, an interest payment is paid after the passage of one year. There is, however, one difference between large-scale and ordinary time deposits: if funds are left on deposit after the date of maturity, no interest is paid, because the large-scale depositors should be carefully supervising the management of their assets.

2. POSTAL SAVINGS DEPOSITS (*Yubin chokin*)

Postal savings deposit accounts are those offered by the post office for the small savings of individuals. There is a limit of a total of ¥3m. per depositor, and the interest on these accounts is non-taxable under the income tax law. There are several types of postal savings deposit, including ordinary postal deposits, fixed-amount postal savings, time deposits and instalment postal deposits (residential instalment deposits and educational instalment deposits). Among these, fixed-amount postal savings are a unique financial product offered by the postal system, and comprise 90 per cent of total postal deposits outstanding (as of the end of March 1985). Fixed-amount postal savings may be withdrawn without prior notice at any time after having been on deposit for six months, but may also continue on deposit for up to ten years if there is no need of withdrawal. The interest rate that applied on the date of deposit applies for the entire period of deposit (though there are different maturities for such accounts with different interest rates), and interest is compounded twice annually. For most deposits with regulated interest rates, the interest rates are usually set so that is is advantageous to have longer-term deposits. In contrast to the interest rate paid on private financial institutions' two-year time deposits, which must change with changing financial conditions, the interest rates on these ten-year deposits, along with having the merit of twice per year compounding, are set in a unique way that would be impossible on a commercial basis in the private sector. For example, if the deposit were made during a period of tight money, the interest rate would be guaranteed for ten years (this is why the so-called postal deposit shift often occurs at the end of periods of monetary tightness). The minimum deposit is ¥1,000 and deposits may be made above that in units of ¥1,000.

A type of *sogo* account was instituted by the postal savings system in June 1981. Under this type of account, called a *sogo* passbook service, a fixed-amount postal savings deposit and an ordinary postal savings deposit are listed together in one passbook. The fixed amount postal deposit may be used as collateral for borrowing of up to 90 per cent of the amount in the fixed-amount deposit. The maximum borrowing, however, was ¥1m. as of April 1986.

The accounts of the postal savings system other than fixed-amount postal savings correspond to the deposits offered by private financial institutions. Ordinary postal deposits, time postal deposits, and instalment postal deposits correspond to ordinary deposits, time deposits, and instalment deposits offered by private sector financial institutions.

3. TRUSTS *(Shintaku)*

The trust accounts offered by trust banks may be separated into two general classes according to the type of asset to which the funds invested are applied when the original deposit is made. These two types of trusts are called money trusts and non-money trusts (for details see Chapter 5). Among money trusts, the securities investment trust is of a special nature and will be dealt with below. The other types of money trust, however, are treated here: ordinary money trusts, loan trusts, special-purpose trusts, and pension trusts.

a. Ordinary money trusts *(Kinsen shintaku)*

An ordinary money trust is one that accepts funds in the form of money and invests them in loans, discount bills, securities, and other deposits. The return on the funds in trust is then paid to the beneficiary in the form of money at a rate according to the amount and the maturity of the trust at the time that the trust is dissolved. The largest portion of money trusts is held in the form of so-called 'joint investment designated money trusts', under which the two or more trust accounts of customers may be joined according to the trust contracts written with the trust bank. Such trusts are primarily used by individuals for investment motives, along with the loan trusts that are described below. Joint investment designated money trusts may be in amounts of ¥5,000 or more per account and may be of one of three types, one year or more, two years or more, or three years or more (referring to the designation date of the contract). The trust bank guarantees the principal in the trust through the contract. Distribution of the dividends is accounted for twice per year according to an expected dividend rate, and depends on the performance of management and investments of the funds. The most common form of money trust pays the dividends into the principal of the account and is thus a form of compound interest. The expected dividend rate is not under the jurisdiction of the TIRAL. Notification of the rates is, however, given to the Ministry of Finance and to the Bank of Japan, so that in fact money trusts are a regulated-rate asset. The dividends from money trusts may be included within the tax exemptions of the *maruyu* system.

Two kinds of new account involving money trusts are of interest. The first is the Government bond trust account, initiated in September 1983 and nicknamed the 'double trust'. Such money trusts may reinvest automatically in newly issued long- and medium-term Government bonds and thus achieve high rates of return. Such assets were developed with private individuals in mind as investors. The minimum investment is ¥300,000 or more per account in units of ¥50,000, and in principle all the funds are invested in Government bonds. The second new type of money trust became available in December 1985 and was the result of newly permitted participation of foreign banks in the trust business based on the Japan–US yen-dollar agreement. These trusts are nicknamed 'hit trusts', presumably because they were expected to be a big hit. Hit trusts are quite similar to existing money trusts in the maturities available, the uses of funds, fees for the trustees, and tax treatment. They do, however, differ in certain important respects. Their maturities must be of one year or more; the maturity is not fixed exactly; and the account may be dissolved voluntarily by the depositor after one year. The minimum deposit is ¥100,000 and additions may be made in units of ¥10,000. The expected rate of return is determined from the portfolio of investment and is based on a weighted average of interest rates in that portfolio after deduction of trustee remuneration. And finally, there are no balloon principal payments that guarantee the principal in the account.

b. Loan trusts *(Kashitsuke shintaku)*

Loan trusts are a type of ordinary money trust such as described above, but loan trusts are permitted on the basis of a special law, the Loan Trust Law of June 1952. Under a loan trust, a trust bank issues beneficiary securities and invests the funds so accumulated primarily in long-term loans. The returns are then distributed in proportion to the investment of principal with rights to benefit allocated according to holdings of beneficiary certificates. A special point about loan trusts is that the trust banks are very active in selling them. Just as with money trusts, loan trusts are based on the principle of distribution of actual profits but the principal is guaranteed and the *maruyu* system applies to them. There are two types of maturity for loan trusts, two and five years, and applications are made in units of ¥10,000. Early withdrawal of funds is not permitted; however, after one year from the closing date for funds for a loan trust, the trust bank may repurchase the certificates, thus adding an element of liquidity. Dividends are paid twice yearly according to the expected dividend rate (in case of the earnings/distribution type of loan trust).

A new type of loan trust was instituted in June 1981, the so-called 'big' account. These accounts are exclusively for the use of individuals investing in tax-free deposits (the upper limit on subscription is ¥3m.), and do not pay interest semi-annually but rather compound it semi-annually and pay in a lump sum at the end of the period, thus achieving a higher yield. But maturities, units of investment, liquidity provisions, etc., are identical to those of the usual types of loan trust.

c. Special-purpose trusts *(Tokutei kinsen shintaku)*

Special-purpose trusts differ from ordinary money trusts and loan trusts in that the client, i.e., the depositor, has specific control over the investment of the funds; for example, in the case of a loan, the client directs who will borrow how much, for what period, at what interest rate, and with what collateral. Thus, the return on a special-purpose trust depends on the actual performance of the investment that is made after deduction of the trustee fee, which is the income of the trust bank. The trust bank bears no responsibility for guaranteeing either the principal or rate of return above a certain amount, and thus the entire risk is shouldered by the client.

Special-purpose trusts have grown rapidly since the end of the 1970s, for two reasons. First, as the securities markets expanded, both industrial enterprises and smaller financial institutions that did not have the know-how for equities or foreign bond investments increasingly sought the help of investment advisers, in order to invest their funds in a planned manner. Second, in December 1980, special-purpose trusts were permitted a special tax concession concerning book value calculations for tax purposes (this was based on a revision of the basic regulations concerning corporate taxes). In general practice, when new quantities of a given security that is already held in a portfolio are bought for the securities account of a corporation, then the end-of-period valuation of such stocks or bonds must be an average of the original price and the new market price. For example, if 1,000 shares of a certain stock are owned at book value of ¥500 each and then 1,000 more shares are purchased at a market price of ¥1,000, then the book value of these stocks at the end of the period must rise to ¥750. But special-purpose money trusts may be managed separately from the securities held in the securities portion of the corporation's balance sheet and may be valued separately. Thus, special-purpose money trusts allow avoidance of paying tax on unintended implicit profits or on increases in book value. In addition, so-called accumulation accounting,[2] was permitted as of August 1982 along with cross-sales at theoretical prices, which is a similar practice. Both of these methods permit the earning of a higher rate of return in times when bond markets are weak.

d. Pension trusts *(Nenkin shintaku)*

Pension trusts are pension funds whose management and investment has been undertaken by trust banks or life insurance companies. There are two types: Tax Qualified Pension Plan and Employees' Pension Plan (also called Adjusted Pension Plan).

Tax Qualified Pension Plan was initiated in April 1962. Under the system,

---

[2] Accumulation accounting is a method of crediting dividends that are part of capital gains on a security on a period-by-period basis before the maturity of the asset.

a corporation, which is the client, and a trust bank or life insurance company, which is the trustee, sign a trust contract. The contract stipulates that the funds provided by the corporation or the employees of the corporation are entrusted to the trust bank or life insurance company and that, in addition to managing the funds in trust, the bank or insurance company will make pension payments to the employees, who are the beneficiaries of the pension system of the corporation in question. This system involves the grant of special privileges with respect to the tax laws and is deemed beneficial as an element of social policy; to have this privilege, it is necessary for the National Tax Administration Agency to make a prior investigation of the qualifications of the scheme in question and to grant permission for the establishment of such a pension trust. In return for the tax privileges, it is necessary that assets of very safe and certain return be purchased with the resources of the trust, and therefore rather strict regulations are placed on the funds.

There are eleven types of asset in which the funds may be invested including ordinary money trusts, loan trusts, equipment and real estate trusts, and pension investment trusts. It is also required that more than 50 per cent of the trust assets be invested in instruments with guarantee of principal or with a high degree of certainty of protection of principal. Moreover, since such trusts are long-term assets, it is necessary to protect the buying power of the funds invested, and therefore certain portions of funds may be invested in assets without a guarantee of principal or in assets with uncertain principal up to a given limit. Thus, some consideration has been given to flexible management. The limits are, for example, less than 30 per cent invested in equities or securities investment trust beneficiary certificates and less than 20 per cent in real estate or real estate equipment trust beneficiary certificates.

Adjusted Pension Plan dates from October 1966. This pension is organized as part of the national welfare pension system. The Adjusted Pension Plan manages the welfare pension fund established by corporations along with one portion of the funds accumulated under the Government-managed welfare pension insurance scheme, that is, the portion applying to the return-related part of old-age pensions. Adjusted pension schemes both gather contributions and make the pension payments according to contracts of the trust banks and life insurance companies with the national welfare pension fund. The management of the entrusted assets is in principle treated exactly as that for Tax Qualified Pension Plan.

4. SECURITIES INVESTMENT TRUST *(Shoken toshi shintaku)*

A securities investment trust is one type of money trust but the funds are invested in certain types of security. There are four parties to a securities investment trust: the investor (beneficiary), a securities company, a securities investment trust management company (the client), and a trust bank. In the first step of the process, an investor purchases a beneficiary certificate from a securities company (in units of ¥10,000), and the securities company then pays the proceeds of the sale of the beneficiary certificate to a securities investment trust management company. In the next stage, the trust management company concludes a trust contract with the trust bank and entrusts the funds raised from the sale of the beneficiary certificates to the trust bank. The trust bank then purchases various types of asset according to the directions of the trust management company. The permitted objects of investment include not only public bonds, corporate bonds, equities, and other securities, but also call loans, bills purchased, and money trusts or other money market instruments used for the investment of excess funds. The earnings from these investments, both interest and capital gains earnings, are distributed after deduction of expenses.

Securities investment trusts provide several advantages. First, they make it possible for small amounts of funds to be invested in securities. Secondly, they allow diversification of the risk of securities investment even though there is no guarantee of principal as is the case with money trust or loan trusts. And thirdly, they allow the seeking of high returns through the principle of distribution of actual profits. There are two types of securities investment trust, according to how the funds are invested. One is the stock investment trust, which began operation in 1951 with the passage of the Securities Investment Trust Law. The second is the public and corporate bond investment trust, which was created in January 1961.

a. Stock investment trust *(Kabushiki toshi shintaku)*

Stock investment trusts are trusts that concentrate the investment of their funds in equities, although bonds, deposits, money trusts, and call loans may also be the objects of their investment. There are two types of stock investment trust, unit-type investment trusts in which the funds are treated as a unit for purposes of investment, liquidation, and distribution of earnings, and open-ended investment trusts under which extra funds may be added voluntarily even after the trust fund has been established.

(i) Unit-type investment trusts

Even within unit-type stock investment trusts, there is a further distinction between 'family funds' and 'spot funds'.

A family fund is a group of unit-type trusts that are managed and invested together. First, a parent fund is established in order to carry out the joint investment in equities and public and corporate bonds; then subsidiary funds, which are established during the normal course of month-by-month business, buy the beneficiary certificates of the parent fund. In this fashion, the parent fund is able to acquire new funds of its own whenever subsidiary funds are established (in addition, since the trust has no fixed maturity, such funds are in character very much like the open-ended investment trusts described below). Family funds allow a more efficient management and investment of funds, and thus nearly all the unit-type trusts in recent years have taken this form.

Spot funds do not seek new funding every month, as is the case with family funds but rather do so occasionally as the tenor of the stock market dictates. There are several types of spot funds. One is the capital fund that has no upper limit on the share of securities in the total fund, so that it is possible to seek capital gains aggressively; another is the balance fund that balances equities and public bonds; a third is the public bond fund that *de facto* holds more than half of its assets in Government or public bonds; and a fourth is the convertible debenture fund that concentrates on investment in convertible debentures.

(ii) Open-ended investment trusts

Open-ended investment trusts are established with a pre-announced upper limit on the total size of the fund, and beneficiary securities are sold continuously until this limit is reached. In principle, the beneficiary certificates are sold in groups of ten units, with each unit costing ¥1,000, at the original offering price. But after the original units are offered, the price depends on the market value of the trust (the standard price). There are no fixed maturities for these trusts, and, in the absence of unforeseeable factors, these funds may continue indefinitely. The sale of beneficiary certificates is totally free, and certificates that have been bought by securities companies may be resold. Settlements usually occur either once or twice per year.

There are several types of open-ended trusts. An ordinary stock investment open-ended trust faces no upper limit on equity holdings and is managed according to market conditions. There are also formula funds that buy and sell equities in response to market price movements according to fixed rules; foreign securities funds that actively invest in foreign securities; balance funds that establish an upper limit on the equity composition and thus balance overall holdings between equities and bonds; large capital stock funds that concentrate on large capital stocks; and instalment funds that specialize in accumulating investment funds over time.

b. Public and corporate bond investment trusts *(Koshasai toshi shintaku)*

Public and corporate bond investment trusts restrict themselves to investing almost wholly in public and corporate bonds and do not buy equities. Excess funds are invested in call loans or discount bills. As with stock investment trusts, there are two types, unit-type trusts and open-ended trusts, according to whether funds may be added after the original fund was established. Typical of open-ended funds are medium-term Government bond funds (*chokoku* funds), interest earnings funds (*rikin* funds), and large-unit public and corporate bond investment trusts. Typical of unit-type trusts are the non-distributed-dividend Government bond funds. All of these have been developed by securities companies in recent years in their competition with banks to develop new financial products.

Chukoku funds are open-ended public and corporate bond investment trusts that invest 50 per cent or more of principal in medium-term Government bonds of two- to four-year maturities (remaining funds may be invested in call or bill markets). Operation of these funds began in January 1980. Withdrawals are permitted freely after one month of the original investment, so that the liquidity of the *chokoku* funds is very high. The minimum investment is ¥100,000, and additions may be made in units of ¥10,000; thus *chukoku* funds are short-term, small-denomination assets and are very much of the character of deposits, but they pay relatively high rates of return compared to notice deposit or three- or six-month time deposits. Investors are mostly individuals or small corporations. Yields are calculated daily and the distribution of actual profit is then automatically reinvested on a monthly basis so that the compounding is continuous, thus raising the rate of return. In addition, the interest earnings are available for use within the *maruyu* system. Though *chukoku* funds are a free-rate financial asset for investors, the expected rates of return are set with reference to bank deposits (these expected rates of return on *chukoku* funds are generally slightly lower than the interest rate on one-year fixed-term deposits).

Interest earnings funds (*rikin* funds) are aimed at investors whose public bond (national Government bonds, local government bonds, Government-guaranteed bonds) holdings are held in custody. *Rikin* funds accept the interest earnings on such bonds automatically in units of ¥1 or more and invest these funds in other public and corporate bonds of maturity of three years or less or in call lending. They began operation in November 1982. As with *chukoku* funds, there are no limits on maturity above one month and withdrawals are fully free after funds have been left on deposit for one month. The return to investors is based on the actual performance of the fund, and distributions are made and reinvested on a monthly basis. *Rikin* funds may also be included within the *maruyu* system.

Large-unit public and corporate bond investment trusts are aimed at large-capital investors and are open-ended public and corporate bond investment trusts, also called free financial funds (FFF), that invest 60 per cent or more of principal in bonds. They were first established in August 1985 by securities companies as an innovation to respond to money market certificates (MMCs) which had been initiated by banks in March of the same year. FFFs are essentially *chukoku* funds aimed at large-capital investors. The minimum investment is ¥50m. and additions may be made in units of ¥1m. Interest rates are similar to those earned on MMCs but they differ from *chukokus* funds in that the proceeds are not subject to the *maruyu* system.

Compound *sogo* accounts, also called 'high packs', are investment trusts aimed at individual investors, and combine Government bonds of both long- and medium-term maturity with public and corporate bond investment trusts.

These accounts were first established in September 1983. The principal is invested originally in Government bonds only, but the interest earnings on the government bonds, which are paid semi-annually, are then reinvested in *chukoku* funds, *rikin* funds, or public and corporate bond investment trusts. The reinvested earnings may be withdrawn at any time, and the investor may borrow against the account using the government bonds as collateral, up to an amount of 80 per cent of the face value of the bonds or ¥1m. The minimum investment is ¥50,000 and units above that are of ¥50,000 each. Maturities are of four types of two, three, four, and ten years. Holdings may be included in *maruyu* and special *maruyu* limits.

Non-distributed dividend Government bond funds, also called 'jumbos', are unit-type investment trusts that invest their funds in outstanding long-term Government bonds and are solely for use within the *maruyu* system (i.e., the maximum investment is ¥3m.). The earnings are not distributed during the life of the trust, and hence high interest rates are possible because the earnings are reinvested and then paid together with the principal at the time of maturity. The establishment of 'jumbo' funds is subject to approval by the Ministry of Finance on a case-by-case basis, and so far only two have been created, in July–August and in November of 1982. The maturity is for five years and earnings are credited monthly.

5. PUBLIC AND CORPORATE BONDS *(Koshasai)*

Public and corporate bonds are certificates of indebtedness issued by Government, local Government, or corporations. This type of bond includes national Government bonds, local Government bonds, Government-guaranteed bonds, bank debentures, industrial bonds, and convertible debentures. These types of bond have several features in common. First, fixed rates of interest are paid during the period until maturity (i.e., they are fixed-interest securities). Secondly, they are classified as risky assets according to the system described above, and thus issuers must be of high credit worthiness. In addition, certain measures are taken for the protection of investors, including mortgage debentures in trust and articles for limitations concerning financial conditions. Thirdly, they have longer maturities than other types of saving; they have higher yields; and for instruments of less than five years of original maturity, they may be included within the *maruyu* or the special *maruyu* system.

Traditionally, bonds have been sold to the public through securities companies, but in recent years banks have also acquired the right to sell certain types of bond. Based on the revised banking law of April 1982, banks may now sell public bonds, i.e., national Government bonds, local Government bonds, and Government-guaranteed bonds, to the public. Actual sales were first permitted in April 1983, but at that time were limited to new issues of long-term Government coupon bonds, Government-guaranteed bonds, and local government bonds. In October of that year, however, medium-term Government coupon bonds and Government discount bonds were added.

From June 1984, banks were permitted to buy and sell outstanding public bonds; this was the start of so-called 'dealing'. In addition, newly issued financial debentures may be sold directly to the public by the issuing bank.

Bonds that have already been issued, i.e., outstanding bonds, may be purchased either at the price listed by the stock exchange or on the basis of the over-the-counter price published by the Securities Dealers Association of Japan. In addition to the price of purchase, the investor also pays, first, a purchasing commission (to the Stock Exchange if the purchase is through the Exchange), and second, an amount equal to the interest for the period from the day after the previous interest payment to the date of purchase, i.e., the accrued interest.

In principle, bonds are redeemed on the date of maturity at face value. A common practice, however, allows certain premature redemptions for one portion of the issue. The bonds repurchased in premature redemptions are determined either according to lottery or by purchase from the open market. The periods for premature redemption for the various types of bond are as follows: for fifteen-year industrial bonds, eight years after the original issue; for twelve-year industrial bonds, five years; for ten-year local government bonds, Government-guaranteed bonds or industrial bonds, three years; and for seven- or six-year industrial bonds, two years.

In cases when an investor wishes to sell a bond before the date of maturity, he must bring the security (or the depository receipt in the case of the security held in custody) to the securities company or the bank from which it has been purchased, and then the proceeds of the sale are transferred in principle on the fourth day after the sale. The proceeds of a sale are determined either on the basis of the market rate published at the Stock Exchange or on the basis of the over-the-counter market price published by the Securities Dealers' Association of Japan. When a bond is sold, the sales commission is deducted from the proceeds, but the seller does receive the accrued interest from the day after the last interest payment until the date of sale. In addition, there is a securities transactions tax of 0·045 per cent (although in the case of national Government bonds, the tax is 0·03 per cent).

There is also a 20 per cent withholding tax on the interest income of bonds, but in the case of corporations interest income is deducted from total income when corporations file tax returns.

a. National Government bonds *(Kokusai)*

National Government bonds are issued by the Government. They are issued within the limits established by the National Diet for every fiscal year and are used to cover payments from the general account of the government and to raise funds in order to cover maturing debt. One type of national Government bond is called an Article 4 bond, because it is issued under the jurisdiction of Article 4 of the Finance Law; such bonds are usually called construction bonds, because the proceeds are used for public works projects such as roads, harbours, and housing construction. The other type of national Government bond is called the special bond (*tokurei kokusai*), because it is controlled by Special Bond Flotation Laws passed every fiscal year; such bonds are usually called deficit bonds, because the proceeds are used to cover the deficits in the general account. Bonds issued to cover maturing debt are called roll-over bonds (*karikae-sai*) and are issued under the Law Concerning Special Account of Government Bonds Consolidation Fund, Articles 5 and 5-2, paragraph 2. Until 1976, only long-term coupon bonds were issued by the Government, but with the advent of large-scale national bond flotations, there began a period of large-scale redemptions, so that diversification of the types of national Government bond occurred in order to ensure smooth absorption of the new issues. Currently, the types of national Government bond issued are long-term coupon bonds, discount bonds, medium-term coupon bonds, and short-term bonds. In addition, apart from the bonds issued in order to raise financial resources, the Government also issues Government bills, which are issued to smooth Government cash flows.

Certain non-marketable types of inscribed national Government compensation bond also exist, though these are of minor importance. Examples include Farm Bonds, War-bereaved Family Treasury Bonds, Repatriation Treasury Bonds, and Non-interest Special Benefit Treasury Bonds.

In June 1983, the holder of Government bonds, local government bonds, or Government-guaranteed bonds was permitted to take loans from a securities company if the securities company acted as custodian for the bonds and if the bonds were used as collateral for the loan. The maximum loan was ¥5 m. or 90 per cent of the market value of the national Government bonds at the time of collateralization, or 80 per cent for other bonds. The loans were in principle to be short-term, i.e., less than six months. In June 1985, the securities companies were permitted to make an agreement on loan facilities up to a given amount (¥2m.) also with Government bonds as collateral. In addition, both banks and securities finance companies were allowed, under certain conditions, to make loans to the holders of Government bonds using those bonds as collateral.

(i) Long-term coupon Government bonds *(Choki ritsuki kokusai)*

Long-term coupon bonds form the major share of national Government bond flotations in Japan, and in principal are of ten years' maturity with fixed interest rates. Such bonds are issued every month, and issues are separated into two portions, the market portion and the portion purchased by the Trust Fund Bureau. The market portion is underwritten by the syndicate for underwriting Government securities (hereafter 'the syndicate').[3]

---

[3] The Government, through its agent the Bank of Japan, which is actually the party to the contract, and the bond underwriting syndicate sign a contract for the subscription of Government bonds. According to this contract, the syndicate conducts the public sales of the bonds (with

(Long-term fixed coupon bonds include not only ten-year bonds but also issues from time to time of six-year, fifteen-year, and twenty-year bonds; these issues, however, are private placements at fixed rates.)[4] There are six types of Government bond by face value, those of ¥50,000, ¥100,000, ¥1m., ¥100m., and ¥1 milliard. However, under the Government bond accumulated investment system (also known as Government bond savings), an investment may start at ¥5,000 and be increased in units of ¥1,000. The conditions of issue are determined at the Government Bond Facilitation Committee (*Sewanin Kai*) which is composed of the Ministry of Finance, the Bank of Japan, and eleven firms representing the syndicate. Interest is paid twice yearly and is included in the consolidated taxable income for corporations. For individuals, there is special tax treatment of bonds. For bonds purchased within five years of issue, not only does the normal *maruyu* system apply, but there is also a special tranche of ¥3m. face value of securities on which interest is not taxed. This is the so-called 'small amount public bond interest exemption system', also known as the *tokubetsu-maruyu* system.

(ii) Medium-term coupon Government bonds *(chuki ritsuki kokusai)*

Medium-term coupon Government bonds were first issued in June 1978 as a means of diversifying the types of Government bond offered and thus of smoothing their absorption in the market. These bonds are of two to four years' maturity, and were the first to be issued through public auction.[5] Medium-term Government bonds are mostly issued through these public subscriptions, but a certain portion is issued through fixed-rate private placements or through the Trust Fund Bureau. There are six varieties of face value: ¥50,000, ¥100,000, ¥1m., ¥10m., ¥100m., and ¥1 milliard. Issue of three-year bonds commenced in June 1978, of two-year bonds in June 1979, and of four-year bonds in June 1980. Redemption is on the 20th of the month

the exception of life insurance and fire and casualty insurance companies) and the syndicate also agrees to purchase any bonds that are not purchased by the public in case the sales fail to reach the desired limit of fund-raising. The syndicate is comprised of city banks, long-term credit banks, regional banks, trust banks, *sogo* banks, *shinkin* banks, the *Norinchukin* Bank, the *Shokochukin* Bank, life insurance companies, insurance companies, securities companies, and certain foreign banks and foreign securities companies.

[4] As of Dec. 1985, there have been ten such private placements at fixed rates with particular subscribers. Recently, variable-rate Government bonds have been placed privately on several occasions. These were placement of twenty-year bonds with a five-year period forbidding sale of bonds in the market, which took place in Sept., Oct., and Nov. 1983, and were sold to life insurance companies. The other issue was of fifteen-year bonds, which were not negotiable during their lives; these issues took place in Sept., Oct., and Nov. 1985, and were placed with trust banks, life insurance companies, the *Norinchukin* Bank, and the *Zenshinren* Bank.

[5] Participants in the auction are designated by the Ministry of Finance, and currently include city banks, long-term credit banks, trust banks, regional banks, *sogo* banks, *shinkin* banks (who participate through the *Zenshinren* Bank, their representative trade federation), the *Norinchukin* Bank, the *Shokochukin* Bank, securities companies, life insurance companies, non-life insurance companies, and certain foreign banks. Individuals purchase newly issued medium-term coupon Government bonds through these institutions (except for life and non-life insurance companies).

in which the bond matures. Interest payments are made twice yearly, every six months.

(iii) Discount Government bonds *(Waribiki kokusai)*

Discount Government bonds are medium-term bonds of five years' maturity and were first issued in January 1972 in an attempt to improve the absorption of Government bonds by individual investors. Currently they are issued in principle six times per year in the odd-numbered months. They are issued through 'the syndicate', and the underwriting shares of the member financial institutions are the same as in the flotation of long-term coupon bonds. There are seven types of face value: those of ¥50,000, ¥100,000, ¥500,000, ¥1m., ¥3m., ¥10m., and ¥100m. The maturity is five years and redemption is five years to the day after the issue. The interest rate is usually fixed at a level such that (1) the pre-tax interest rate does not exceed the face value interest rate on five-year coupon bank debentures, and (2) the after-tax yield is not lower than discount bank debentures. The capital gain on discount Government bonds is treated as miscellaneous income, and thus individuals cannot apply it to the tax-free interest limits. There is a separate withholding tax of 16 per cent on the capital gain at the time of issue. For corporations, the capital gain is classified as general income, and the corporations face the same withholding tax as do individuals; deduction of this tax payment is permitted at the time corporations pay their income taxes.

(iv) Short-term Government bonds *(Tanki kokusai)*

Short-term Government bonds are discount bonds of maturity of six months or less. They were first issued in February 1986 in order to smooth the redemption and refunding of large amounts of Government bonds coming due from 1985 onwards. They are floated through public auction, and are intended to be a short-term money market product aimed at institutional investors. They come in two types by face value, ¥100m. and ¥1 milliard, and the minimum unit of issue is ¥100m. The capital gain on short-term Government bonds is also subject to withholding tax just as is that on discount Government bonds, but the capital gain is also treated in a way that does not disturb smooth circulation of the bonds.[6] Short-term Government bonds are a type of roll-over bond and hence differ in character from Government bills, which are used to smooth Government cash flow; hence the Bank of Japan is prohibited from underwriting short-term Government bonds.

---

[6] In principle all discount bonds, including Government discount bonds, only allow for a deduction of tax paid on the bonds for the holding period of the final holder. However, an exception is made for short-term Government bonds and for Government bills such that a tax deduction is allowed throughout the entire life of the bond, on the presumption that trade will take place among corporations.

(v) Government bills *(Seifu tanki shoken)*

Government bills are intended to cover temporary shortages of funds of the Treasury. They are issued every Monday, Wednesday, and Friday within limits established by the National Diet and are redeemed either within the fiscal year or within one calendar year from the date of issue. They are usually of about sixty days' maturity and are discount bills. Under the law, eight types of Government bill are permitted, but only three are in fact issued, Treasury bills, foreign exchange fund bills, and food bills. None of the other five types has ever been issued. Since 1956, the method of issue has been a type of fixed-rate public subscription under which the amounts not purchased by the public are automatically subscribed by the Bank of Japan.[7] In fact, however, the rate of interest paid on these bonds is fixed at a level below that of the Bank of Japan's discount rate and short-term money market rates such as the call rate, so that virtually all the amounts issued are subscribed by the Bank of Japan. Face values for the issues are of two types: ¥100m. and ¥500m. (previously there had been Government bills of ¥1m., ¥5m., ¥10m., and ¥50m., but these were abolished with the establishment of short-term Government bonds). The terms of issues are fixed by the Minister of Finance. The interest rate on these Government bills moves in parallel with that of the Bank of Japan's discount rate, but the two rates do not always move by the same margin. The bills are usually redeemed at maturity. But in cases when surpluses of funds exist, the bills held by the Bank of Japan are redeemed before maturity. The tax treatment of the capital gains on Treasury bills is identical to that on short-term Government bonds. In addition, the securities transfer tax is not levied on Treasury bills or other short-term Government bonds of less than one year's maturity.

b. Local government bonds *(Chihosai)*

Local government bonds are defined as long-term liabilities of local government entities such as prefectures or municipalities under either the Local Autonomous Law or the Local Finance Law. Issue is according one of two methods—a public offering or a private placement, the latter being an issue based on underwriting by financial institutions in the local area. The forms of issue are also of two kinds, either a securities issue or an issue of a certificate of indebtedness. Among these, only those issued in the form of securities, i.e., all publicly placed but only a part of privately placed bonds, are negotiable. For publicly placed bonds, the unit of purchase is ¥10,000 of face value, and maturity is ten years. Interest payments are made twice yearly and

---

[7] Those eligible for these fixed-rate subscriptions are limited to all banks, *sogo* banks, *shinkin* banks, the *Zenshinren* Bank, the *Norinchukin* Bank, the *Shokchukin* Bank, insurance companies, and securities companies or money market dealers doing business with the Bank of Japan. Corporations may purchase the bonds indirectly through direct purchasers such as the securities companies.

the yield to subscribers has been fixed at the same level as that for Government-guaranteed bonds since September 1981.

c. Government-guaranteed bonds *(Seifu hosho sai)*

Government-guaranteed bonds are those issued by Government-related institutions, such as public corporations or public utilities, for the purpose of raising part of the cost of their operations, and which have a Government guarantee on principal and interest payments. (There are, however, some securities by Government-related institutions that do not have Government guarantee, for example special railroad bonds.) Government-guaranteed bonds are issued by public offering and are subscribed and underwritten by underwriting syndicates composed of banks and securities companies. The units of purchase are ¥100,000 of face value and the maturity is ten years. Interest payments are made twice a year, and the yield to subscribers is set only slightly above that on long-term coupon Government bonds since the creditworthiness of Government-guaranteed bonds is assumed to be the same as that of Government bonds.

d. Bank debentures *(Kinyu sai)*

Bank debentures are issued by long-term credit banks, the Bank of Tokyo, the *Norinchukin* Bank, and the *Shoko Chukin* Bank, and come in two varieties, coupon debentures and discount debentures.

(i) Coupon bank debentures *(Ritsuki kinyu sai)*

Coupon bank debentures are of five years' maturity and have face values beginning at ¥10,000 (however, the Bank of Tokyo may issue Bank of Tokyo bonds with a three-year maturity, a practice which began in July 1962). Individuals and institutional investors are the main purchasers. The share absorbed by financial institutions, and particularly city banks, was higher before 1965, but since then this share has declined.

The terms of issue for coupon debentures are determined by taking into consideration the issue conditions on long-term Government coupon bonds, and interest payments are made twice per year. An innovative type of coupon bank debenture, called a 'wide', was initiated in October 1981 by long-term credit banks, the *Norinchukin* Bank, and the *Shoko Chukin* Bank. A 'wide' is paid no interest during the life of the bond, but rather the interest is compounded semi-annually, and a complete payment is made only on maturity after five years. 'Wides' can be purchased only by the investors who can use the *maruyu* system and up to the amount of ¥3m.

(ii) Discount bank debentures *(Waribiki kinyo sai)*

Discount bank debentures may be purchased with face values beginning at ¥10,000, and are of maturity of one year; most are purchased by individual investors. For discount bank debentures, the discount charge—equivalent to the interest earnings—is prepaid to the investor at the time of the investment. In contrast to coupon bank debentures, discount bank debentures may not be used in the *maruyu* system, but the capital gain equal to the profit from redemption is subject to a 16 per cent withholding tax, which is the entire tax liability for discount bank debentures.

A financial innovation involving discount debentures is the Government bond/discount debenture account. Such accounts combine a discount bank debenture with newly issued Government coupon bonds of either long- or medium-term maturity. The interest on the Government bonds, which is paid twice per year, is then automatically reinvested in discount bank debentures.[8] These new accounts were first offered in October 1983 by long-term credit banks, the Bank of Tokyo, and the *Norinchukin* Bank. The minimum deposit for these accounts is ¥300,000 with additions in tranches of ¥50,000, and all the principal for such accounts is invested in Government bonds. It is possible to count the Government bond holdings within the special *maruyu* limit, but because discount bank debentures are excluded from the *maruyu* and special *maruyu* system altogether, these accounts are in fact a product aimed at large-scale investors.

e. Industrial bonds *(Shasai)*

Industrial bonds are the corporate bonds issued by private companies other than financial institutions. Within industrial bonds, there is a distinction made between the electric power bonds issued by the nine electric power corporations and general industrial bonds issued by other corporations. All the electric power bonds are floated through public subscription, but general industrial bonds are issued through either public subscriptions or private placements to fifty or fewer investors. For general industrial bonds, the factories or the equipment of the firm or its other assets are generally the collateral for the principal and interest payments on the bond (this practice is called the collateral principal). However, for firms of particularly high creditworthiness, non-collateralized bond issue is permitted, and the terms of issue are gradually being eased. For electric power bonds, there is no specified collateral, but the investors in the bonds have preferential status over other investors with respect to repayment of principal and interest, as determined in the Electric Power Business Law.

---

[8] However, because the unit of purchase of discount bank debentures is ¥10,000, interest earnings of the Government bonds less than this amount are temporarily invested in ordinary deposits.

The unit of purchase for industrial bonds is the face value of ¥100,000, and there are five types of maturity, for fifteen, twelve, ten, seven, and six years (fifteen-year industrial bonds were first issued in August 1985). Interest payments are made twice yearly and the conditions of issue are determined by an issuing committee comprising the securities companies as managing underwriter and the trustee banks. The rates of interest depend on the ranking of the corporation (AA, A, BB, or B) which in turn are based on the size of the company, as measured by net assets. In April 1985, two new rating corporations were established (one existed already), and the conditions of issue are now starting to be based on the credit ratings of these institutions.

f. Convertible debentures *(Tenkan shasai)*

Convertible debentures are corporate bonds which allow conversion of a bond into equities of the issuing corporation. These convertible debentures combine the advantage of equities (appreciation in price) with those of bonds (certain return). A holder of these bonds may at his own volition eitner hold them as bonds or convert them into equities. The conversion may be made at any time during a conversion demand period, which starts after the passage of a certain length of time. It is not possible, however, to convert the stocks back into bonds. Virtually all convertible debentures are listed on the Tokyo Stock Exchange, and convertible debentures may also be sold before the conversion. In principle, collateral is required for convertible debentures, but there have been cases of non-collateralized issues; the relaxation of the collateral requirement is moving faster than in the case of ordinary bonds.

The conversion from bonds to equities is carried out at a given price, the so-called 'conversion price'. For face-value convertible debentures, this conversion price is equal to the face value of the stock, but for market-price convertible debentures the conversion price is determined on the basis of the market price of the stock at the time of the issue. The rate of interest is determined in the main by the securities companies managing underwriters of the issue, on the basis of a standard rate which takes into consideration market conditions and with certain adjustments. These adjustments mean that the interest rate is determined separately for each individual issue (as of April 1986, the standard rate was 3·3 per cent).

An innovation in the field of convertible bonds is a similar asset called warrant bonds, i.e., bonds that give the holder the right to buy new equity of the firm. The holder has the right to demand new issue of stock from the issuing company up to a certain proportion of his holdings, and also has the right to buy new stock at the price determined at the issue of the warrant bond. Warrant bonds were first permitted under a revision of the commercial code in 1981 and were first issued in December of that year.

g. External bonds *(Gaikoku sai)*

External bonds are of two types, those issued in Japan by non-residents and those issued outside Japan. Of the former type, both foreign currency-denominated and yen-denominated issues exist, but the larger share is in yen-denominated bonds, mostly floated through public subscription (these are sometimes called '*samurai* bonds' in English). Most of the yen-denominated external bonds are floated by international organizations, foreign governments, and Government agencies (the first was issued by the Asian Development Bank in June of 1970), though private-sector yen-denominated external bonds are also issued, usually without collateral. The guide-lines for private issue have been gradually eased since 1984. The terms of issue are fixed according to the actual conditions in the bond markets at the time of issue, and tend to be more flexible than the terms of issue on domestic bonds. Periods of redemption range from five to fifteen years, and thus the yen-denominated external bonds became more diversified than domestic bonds. Yen-denominated external bonds are also issued without collateral and thus have had a major impact on the domestic bond market.

The tax treatment of yen-denominated external bonds is identical to that of domestic bonds with respect to application of the *maruyu* system (there is exceptional treatment of some external bonds such as those issued by the World Bank; for these, withholding of income tax at the source is excused, and instead the interest income is included in general income). The securities transaction tax, which is levied at the time of sale, is 0·03 per cent for the bonds of foreign governments, and 0·045 per cent for other external bonds.

For the bonds issued outside Japan there are also two types: foreign currency-denominated bonds and yen-denominated bonds. The foreign currency-denominated bonds have been issued since 1955 in the United States, West Germany, Switzerland, and Euromarkets. The yen-denominated bonds are called Euro-yen bonds, and until recently only foreign governments and international institutions (among non-residents) were permitted to issue them (an issue by the European Investment Bank in April 1977 was the first Euro-yen bond issue). But since December 1984, the door for foreign private corporations to make Euro-yen bond issues has been opened. For Euro-yen bond issues by residents, the prohibition was lifted in April 1984, and issues began in April 1985 after the abolition of the 20 per cent withholding tax on interest paid to non-residents.

h. Mortgage securities *(Teito shoken)*

Mortgage securities are of a somewhat different nature from regular bonds, but the growth of mortgage securities has been conspicuous in recent years. Some time therefore should be given to considering them.

A mortgage security is a security issued by a mortgage registry office on application by the mortgage creditor and based on a contract between the mortgage debtor and creditor. By endorsement of the mortgage security, both the right of receipt of the mortgage and the right of credit claim collateralized by the mortgage may be traded. Mortgage securities have their legal basis in the Mortgage Security Law, and not in the Securities and Exchange Law and thus are not considered securities under the definition of the latter. The interest rate on mortgage securities is free to be determined, and has certain tax advantages.[9] With the growing preference for high-interest earnings in recent years, mortgage securities have become a suitable object for investment, and the quantity of issues has increased in recent years (at the end of 1985, there were about 100,000 such securities outstanding valued at slightly less than ¥400 milliard—i.e., the share of mortgage securities in total financial assets remains quite small).

Mortgage securities are handled at special mortgage securities companies, of which there existed about 100 at the end of March 1986. These mortgage securities companies carry out very long-term financing usually ten to fifteen years with real estate as collateral. The mortgage securities companies then issue securities based on their mortgage rights and refinance their operations by selling these securities to investors. And the mortgage securities companies also act as intermediary between the mortgage creditor and the mortgage debtor for the details of the transactions such as receipt of interest and principal and custody of the mortgage securities. In addition, mortgage securities companies are regulated under the terms of the Money-lending Industry Control Law.

The issue of mortgage-based securities has been permitted in Japan since 1931 but was hardly ever used because of major differences in the valuation of collateral between the original issuers of the mortgage securities, such as banks and finance companies, and the purchasers of these securities, such as the Hypothec Bank of Japan and other special banks. In the late 1960s there were calls for improvement of the system of mortgage securities as part of the policy of revising the real estate finance system in order to improve residential finance. In 1972 the Japan Mortgage Association was established, and in 1973 the establishment of mortgage securities companies began as the institutions to implement the changes. Nevertheless, mortgage securities were hardly used in residential finance.

However, things have changed with the recent developments in the financial structure. Mortgage securities companies have begun to look for funds demand based on mortgage securities chiefly in the area of finance of small-

---

[9] The interest income on mortgage securities is treated as miscellaneous income under the tax laws and is subject to a final tax declaration. However, for persons whose wage earnings are below ¥15m. and do not have more than ¥200,000 income of interest earnings, dividend income profit from immovables, business returns, profit from forests, assignment charges, temporary income, and miscellaneous income, no declaration of interest income on mortgage securities is necessary.

and medium-sized enterprises. Since about 1982, the mortgage securities companies have offered loans based on issue of mortgage securities, and have dealt in such securities in large quantities with the general public because the demand for mortgage securities which carry free interest rates has increased. Around the same time, both banks and securities companies broadened their efforts to establish mortgage securities companies and thus enlivened the industry.

There remain, however, several problems concerning the development of the mortgage securities market in the future. These include how to find high-quality and stable borrowers, how to strengthen the creditworthiness of mortgage securities companies, how to improve the secondary market, and how to improve the legal system concerning such transactions.

6. STOCKS (Kabushiki)

Stocks are a means of indicating the rank or share rights of the stockholders of a corporation, and have been transformed into stock certificates that are considered to be securities and that are in principle freely negotiable. The rights of stockholders include the right to participate in management (rights of deliberation) and thus interlocking holdings among corporations are an important means of maintaining the rights of control among corporations. Stocks are also widely used by individual investors primarily as a means of making capital gains. The proportion of stocks held by individuals has been declining continuously since the 1960s, and stood at 26 per cent at the end of the fiscal year 1984.

Capital increase consists of the issue of new stocks to be purchased and the free issue of new stocks. For issues of new stocks to be purchased, there is a further distinction among three types, those for which the rights to purchase the new stock are allocated among current stockholders, those for which the rights to purchase new stock are allocated among specified parties, and those for which the funds are gathered from the general public. In earlier years, the common practice in Japan was issue at par value to current stockholders, but in recent years issue at market prices to the general public has become the most common.

Transactions in stocks listed on the Stock Exchange are in principle executed through securities companies. Since October 1982, the unit of transactions for listed stocks has been determined by the company in question as a specifically defined unit share; however, the usual units of transaction were 1,000 shares for the shares of par value of ¥50 or 100 shares for those with par values of ¥500. Payment for stocks is made together with the brokerage commission on the fourth day counting from the day on which the order was placed (e.g. the brokerage commission is 1·25 per cent for transactions valued at more than ¥200,000 but less than ¥1 million). When a stock is sold, a securities transactions tax of 0·55 per cent of the sales price is levied (no tax is levied on purchases). No tax is levied on the capital gains for individuals so long as the number of transactions within a year does not exceed fifty and the total number of shares of transactions does not exceed 200,000 shares. For corporations, the capital gains are taxed as general income.

7. INSURANCE

The types of insurance sold in Japan include not only life insurance and non-life insurance sold by private insurance companies, but also various types of mutual aid insurance, from agricultural co-operatives and the postal life insurance sold through the post office. Here we will consider only two representative types of insurance (see Chapter 5 for the details of the institutions in the insurance industry, such as insurance companies, the types of mutual aid insurance and postal life insurance system).

Non-life insurance includes various types of contract including fire insurance, marine insurance, and automobile insurance, but in recent years automobile insurance has accounted for 60–70 per cent of the total. In previous years, the maturity of insurance contracts was one year or less, and the premiums were not subject to return after the expiration of the contract. However, in recent years insurance contracts with savings provisions for return of premium payments have been growing, beginning with the long-term general insurance of 1968 and the instalment family traffic injury insurance of 1974. Rates of premium are established by the casualty insurance premium calculation committee or the automobile insurance premium calculation committee, and are charged by the individual companies subject to approval by the Ministry of Finance. This method is adopted because of the difficulty of predicting accident rates, unlike in the case of life insurance. For tax purposes, corporations may deduct the payments of premiums as losses, and individuals may also deduct a portion of the premiums on fire insurance paid during a year from their income (the maximum deduction is ¥15,000 for a long-term insurance contract of ten years or more).

Life insurance is of three varieties. The first is insurance against death (term insurance), which pays insurance money in the case of death of the insuree during the period of the contract; the second is pure endowment insurance (e.g. child support insurance, saving insurance, annuity insurance), which pays insurance money so long as the insuree survives for a specified period of time; and the third type is the insurance which combines the two (e.g. endowment insurance or term insurance with survival benefit). Each of these three types includes several sub-types. In addition, many new types of insurance contract which have special conditions concerning casualty, injury, and sickness are being developed. In recent years, savings-type insurance contracts (lump-sum endowment insurance) have become popular because of increased individual awareness of interest rates. In addition, group insurance has also become conspicuous as corporations seek better welfare protection for their employees. The insurance premiums are based on the expected mortality rates and the expected rates of return for investing premium income; the determination and change of premium rates falls within the jurisdiction of the Ministry of Finance. A tax deduction of up to ¥50,000 is possible according to the amounts of premiums paid during a year for life insurance. Benefits of matured insurance contracts are counted as income if the recipient is the signer of the contract and are considered to be gift income for other recipients. Death benefits are considered to fall under the inheritance tax while benefits paid for a sickness and injury are not subject to tax. Some life insurance contracts also have loan provisions for the signer of the contract so that loans are possible on a temporary basis depending on the type of insurance contract and the period since the origination of the contract, usually in amounts of up to 80 or 90 per cent of the amount that would be returned if the contract were terminated.

8. PENSIONS

A pension is a system under which a certain amount of money is paid every year to people with certain qualifications. There are two general types, public pensions and private pensions, classified according to who manages the assets. Public pensions are managed by the Government, and in principle all citizens are members of the pension scheme. Private pensions come in two sub-types, corporate pensions that are established by corporations for their employees, and individual pensions that are established by direct contract between an individual and a financial institution.

a. Public pensions

The public pension system has undergone a major overhaul in the last several years. Originally the system was composed of seven types of pension, the national pensions, the welfare pensions, seamen's pensions, and several mutual aid co-operative pensions such as public employee mutual aid co-operative pensions. But problems arose when so many different types of pension existed simultaneously because of the differences in payment levels among the systems and occasional multiple coverage. In addition, the ageing of the population in the future will cause a substantial burden on the Treasury as well as a substantial burden on the insurance premiums paid by those enrolled in the system. In response to these problems, two new pension laws were passed in 1985. The Revised National Pension Act of April 1985 and the Revised Mutual Aid Co-operatives Act of December 1985. The new public annuity system was implemented in April 1986.

Under the new system, the national pension of previous years became the so-called 'basic pension' for all Japanese citizens. The welfare pension of earlier years was added on top of this basic pension as an 'income proportional pension', according to the length of employment and average remuneration during the period of enrolment. The pension portion of seamen's insurance was amalgamated with the new welfare pensions. The mutual aid co-operative pensions of earlier years are now paid in three parts, the basic pension, the income proportional pension, and a 20 per cent addition which is called the 'occupational area pension'.

A major purpose of these changes was to reduce the burden that both the Treasury and the contributors would have to bear. For example, for the welfare pension system, large increases in pension payments were inevitable based on rising average earnings. Under the new system, there will be a gradual decrease in the rate of pension payments relative to average earnings. In addition, the revision includes basic pensions for enrollees' spouses who have never been enrollees themselves. Thus the new system ensures pension rights for spouses.

The recent pension revisions have also standardized the treatment of injury pensions paid in case of any injury to the enrollee and survivors' pensions for survivors of the enrollee. For those who were enrolled only in the national pension system, there is now a 'basic injury pension' and a 'basic survivor's pension'. For those who were enrolled in the welfare pension system there are in addition 'injury welfare pensions' and 'survivor's welfare pensions' added to the basic pensions in proportion to the earnings and length of enrolment of the enrollee.

Further adjustments are to be made on both the contribution and the benefit sides of the public annuity system. A Cabinet decision has been made to unify the various pension systems by 1995.

b. Corporate annuity

Corporate annuity is a means by which a corporation may accumulate funds in an outside trust institution, such as a life insurance company or a trust bank, in order to pay the pensions for employees after their retirement. There are two such types of pension, so-called 'qualified pensions' and so-called 'adjustment pensions'. 'Qualified pensions' are those that meet the qualifications for preferential tax treatment and that corporations establish on their own (such qualified pensions were introduced in 1962). 'Adjustment pensions' are a part of the system under which a corporation establishes its own so-called 'welfare pension fund' and acts as agent in payment of the regular welfare pension while also adding an extra payment of its own. This system was initiated in 1966. Under both of these systems it is possible for an employee to request a lump-sum payment on retirement. Both systems also receive preferential tax treatment and have been growing steadily in scale (total assets at the end of fiscal 1984 were ¥10·5bn. for 'adjustment pensions' and ¥6·2bn. for 'qualified pensions').[10] The growth of corporate pensions is expected to continue because of the population structure and ageing of

[10] Under the tax preferences, corporations may consider their contributions to the pension funds as costs while employee contributions are considered to be life insurance premiums for the qualified pensions and to be social insurance premiums for the adjustment pensions. Hence both are eligible for deduction in the computation of taxable income.

Japanese society. As a result, interest in managing the funds of corporations, an activity which was previously limited to life insurance companies and trust banks, has grown substantially. Both domestic and foreign financial institutions are showing an increasing desire to enter the trust business, and these desires have been the basis for demands that the separation of banking and trust businesses should be reconsidered.

Originally, foreign banks, which had a long history of participation in trust business, intended to enter the corporate pension business through Japan–US links with domestic securities companies. But with the yen–dollar committee agreement of May 1984, it was agreed that permission would be granted for nine foreign banks to enter the trust business in association with domestic trust banks from June 1985 (the actual entry occurred in October of that year). Both domestic city banks and securities companies are also planning to participate in this growth business of corporate pensions by using investment advisory companies as their method of entry (see Chapter 5 for description of investment advisory companies). There have also been calls recently from the owners of corporate pension rights for improvement of the efficiency of management through expansion of the number of institutions that can manage the pension assets. In response to this, the Securities Exchange Advisory Committee proposed the enactment of an Investment Advisory Industry Law, which included permission for 'investment entrustment accounts' in November 1985. This Law was in fact adopted in May 1986, and it is believed that the management of corporate pension funds will become more active and competitive in the future. Trust banks, however, are continuing to emphasize strongly the importance of separating the banking and the trust businesses, and it is thought that debate on this issue will continue.

c. Individual pensions

Individual pensions are based on direct contracts between a financial institution and an individual according to his own needs, and pay the pension payments directly to that individual. There are two general types of individual pension, the savings-based pension and the insurance-based pension. Savings-based pensions use existing savings accounts as a basis and then repay these amounts to the individual as pension payments. Insurance-based individual pensions use pure endowment insurance contracts as their basis and pay the insurance contract amount to the insuree during his lifetime as pension payments.

With the ageing of society, demand for individual pensions has risen. The types of individual pension offered are as follows. Among the savings-based individual pensions, banks offer a fixed-term, deposit-based pension; trust banks offer an individual pension trust; and securities companies offer so-called 'pension plans' (*nenkin*). Among the insurance-based individual pensions, life insurance companies offer an individual pension insurance; agricultural co-operatives offer a co-operative pension; and the post office offers a postal pension.

4

Financial Markets and Interest Rates

I. Financial markets

1. TYPES OF FINANCIAL MARKET

A DISTINCTION is usually made between short-term and long-term financial markets. Short-term markets, usually called money markets, are those in which assets of maturity of less than one year are traded, and long-term markets are those in which assets of maturity greater than one year are traded. Most long-term financial markets are securities markets, but the reverse of this is not true; that is, every securities market is not always a long-term market. This distinction between short- and long-term markets is reflected in the yield curve, which distinguishes between short- and long-term interest rates.

At the centre of the money market is the interbank market, in which lending and borrowing among financial institutions occurs. There are, in addition, open markets in which the non-financial sector may participate. There is also a foreign exchange market in which currencies of foreign countries are traded, and this foreign currency market is further divided into an interbank market in which financial institutions trade among themselves, and a customer market in which there is trading between financial institutions and their customers. The foreign exchange market differs slightly from other financial markets, in the sense that actual purchasing power is not transferred in the market; but it resembles the money markets, in the sense that short-term assets are also traded.

The securities market, by contrast, is the place where final borrowers from the non-financial sector directly issue securities (except for the case in which financial institutions float debentures) and is also the place where such securities are traded. There are some markets in which the distinction between short and long term appears to be blurred, such as financial innovations like the *gensaki* market, which is a money market that deals in securities originally issued in the long-term market. But, in fact, the *gensaki* market is really part of the money market, and so it is quite possible to separate the transactions of financial markets into short- and long-term types.

This section will describe the various types of financial market, including the money market, such as call, bill, the dollar-call, securities repurchase (*gensaki*), certificates of deposit (CD), bankers' acceptance (BA); and Euro-yen markets, along with the foreign exchange market. In addition, explanations will be given of the structure of the securities market. The following section will discuss determination of interest rates in the various markets.

2. MONEY MARKETS

a. Overview

As described above, the money markets are separated into two types—the interbank markets, whose participants are only financial institutions, and the open market, in which there are no restrictions on participation. In Japan, the interbank market includes the call market, the bills market, and the dollar-call market, while the open market includes the securities repurchase (*gensaki*) market, the certificate of deposit(CD) market, the bankers' acceptance (BA) market, and the Euro-yen market. The interbank market is the place in which the Bank of Japan conducts both lending and bill operations and carries out monetary control (see Chapter 6 for a description of Bank of Japan activities). And it is from these markets that interest-rate effects of policy spread to other markets through arbitrage relationships. If, in the future, the Government bills (TB) market becomes the core of the open market, then it will be possible to conduct open market operations in TBs and strengthen the influence of the Bank of Japan over interest rates.

The first short-term funds market in Japan was a discount market, established around the turn of the century along the lines of the London bill-discount market. But the discount market did not, in fact, develop very much, and so for many years the short-term financial market was synonymous with the call-transactions market among financial institutions. This call market included not only very short-term lending but also slightly longer-term, fixed-period transactions such as over-the-month lending. In May 1971, the slightly longer-term lending was shifted to the newly established bills market, and the call market reverted to its pure and original form of very short-term lending.

The major changes in the Japanese money markets came in the late 1970s. At this time, there was explosive growth in the open markets, along with trading in the call and bills markets in the interbank sector (see Table 4.1). By the end of 1985, the scale of the major money markets in Japan had reached ¥52.3bn., this being the total outstanding in the call, bill, *gensaki*, and CD markets, etc. Compared with the situation at the end of 1975, the interbank markets were 4·5 times larger and the open markets were 11·4 times larger. The share of the open markets has risen from about 20 per cent at the end of 1975 to just under 40 per cent at the end of 1985.

The first particularly interesting characteristic of the major changes in money markets over the recent years has been the diversification of financial

TABLE 4.1 Outstanding Amounts of Money Market[a]

	1970		1975		1979		1980		1981		1982		1983		1984		1985	
	¥bn.[b]	%	¥bn.	%	¥bn.	%	¥bn.	%	¥bn.	%	¥bn.	%	¥bn.	%	¥bn.	%	¥bn.	%
Interbank markets	1·8	75·0	7·1	79·8	11·0	57·0	12·2	57·0	13·9	55·2	17·5	58·1	21·4	58·8	23·6	56·3	31·7	60·6
Call market	1·8	75·0	2·3	25·9	3·5	18·1	4·1	19·2	4·7	18·7	4·5	15·0	4·5	12·4	5·0	11·9	5·1	9·7
Bills market	—	—	4·4	49·4	6·3	32·7	5·7	26·6	4·0	15·9	5·4	17·9	6·8	18·7	8·0	19·1	14·7	28·1
Dollar call market[c]	—	—	0·4 (1·3)	4·5	1·2 (4·9)	6·2	2·4 (11·7)	11·2	5·2 (23·8)	20·6	7·6 (32·1)	25·2	10·1 (43·4)	27·7	10·6 (42·0)	25·3	11·9 (59·2)	22·8
Open markets	0·6	25·0	1·8	20·2	8·3	43·0	9·2	43·0	11·3	44·8	12·6	41·9	15·0	41·2	18·3	43·9	20·6	39·4
Gensaki (in securities)	0·6	25·0	1·8	20·2	4·0	20·7	4·5	21·0	4·5	17·8	4·3	14·3	4·3	11·8	3·6	8·6	4·6	8·8
CDs	—	—	—	—	1·8	9·3	2·4	11·2	3·3	13·1	4·3	14·3	5·7	15·7	8·5	20·3	9·4	18·0
Euro-yen[d]	n.a.	—	n.a.	—	2·5	13·0	2·3	10·8	3·5	13·9	4·0	13·3	5·0	13·7	5·5	13·1	5·9	11·3
BAs	—	—	—	—	—	—	—	—	—	—	—	—	—	—	—	—		0·03
Government bills[e]	0	0	0	0	0	0	0	0	0 (0·3)	0	0 (0·8)	0	0 (0·4)	0	0 (1·0)	0	0 (1·4)	0
Foreign CDs and CPs	—	—	—	—	—	—	—	—	—	—	—	—	—	—	0·7	1·7	0·7	1·3
TOTAL	2·4	100·0	8·9	100·0	19·3	100·0	21·4	100·0	25·2	100·0	30·1	100·0	36·4	100·0	41·9	100·0	52·3	100·0
Foreign currency deposits[c]	—	—	0·1 (0·3)	—	0·4 (1·5)	—	0·8 (4·0)	—	1·2 (5·3)	—	2·1 (8·8)	—	6·0 (17·1)	—	4·0 (24·6)	—	7·1 (35·3)	—
Non-resident yen deposits[f]	—	—	0·1	—	0·4	—	1·1	—	1·2	—	1·3	—	1·3	—	1·9	—	2·3	—

[a] Calendar year-end.

[b] ¥bn. = ¥1 million millions. Cf. ¥1 milliard = ¥1,000m.

[c] For the dollar call market and foreign currency deposits, figures in parentheses are outstanding amounts in dollar denomination (in billions of dollars) converted at year-end exchange rate.

[d] Euro-yen data according to the Euro-deposit statistics of the BIS. The figure for 1985 is that for September.

[e] Figures for Government bills are outstanding amounts of those that were sold to the market by the BOJ. Figures in brackets represent the average outstanding for the year.

[f] Portion subject to free interest rates.

Sources: BOJ, Economic Statistics Annual, and others.

assets traded in the open market. In June 1985, a bankers' acceptance (BA) market was added to the already existing securities repurchase (*gensaki*) market and certificate of deposit (CD) market. Government bills (TBs), however, are not traded in large quantities because the method of issue is not public auction but rather a fixed-rate offering at interest rates that are held below the central bank discount rate and below market interest rates. Therefore, almost no such bills are sold in the market, and nearly all are purchased by the Bank of Japan. The Bank of Japan has sold some of these TBs at market prices in an attempt to foster the growth of a secondary bills market, but a TB market in the true sense of the word has yet to form. Nevertheless, due to the character of the financial assets that would be traded in a Government bill market (that is, their creditworthiness, liquidity, and amount of issue), such a market would be the most appropriate place for the Bank of Japan to carry out monetary policy. For this reason, it is expected that there will be concerted efforts to foster and to develop this market [16].

The second characteristic of the changes in the money markets is that there is now more flexibility than there was in the high economic growth period concerning who lends and who borrows in the interbank markets. Chapter 1 mentioned that the maldistribution of funds in the money markets during the high economic growth period is now gradually being diminished, and that participation in the interbank markets is being diversified. In particular, the city banks are looking very closely at the timing of when to lend funds in the call market and when to invest funds in the bill markets. In contrast to earlier times, these banks are thus becoming active lenders and borrowers in the market. Thus the interbank market is no longer a place where only the funds adjustment for retail banking occurs, but has also become a place where investment and fund raising for wholesale banking occurs.

Thirdly—and this goes almost without saying but is nevertheless important to note—interest rate formation in the money markets is entirely determined by market forces, even though the regulated interest rate structure continues to play an important overall role. In fact, interest rates in the money markets have been determined freely in response to supply and demand in principle since 1955. But this liberalization was carried a step further in 1979 with the abolition of the quotation system, under which a uniform rate for all transactions was established between lenders and borrowers. Under current rules, all transactions are completely liberalized and the interest rates move frequently within the day according to demand and supply of funds.

b. Call and bills market

(i) Participants in the markets

The call money market and bills market comprise the lender and borrower financial institutions (in the bill market, the Bank of Japan is also a participant) and certain specialized intermediaries known as money market dealers (*tanshi gaisha*). The money market dealers borrow funds from financial institutions with temporary surpluses (that is, those seeking to lend in the call market or to purchase bills), and lend to institutions with temporary shortages of funds (that is, those seeking to borrow call money or to sell bills). For call or bill transactions that are collateralized, the money market dealers act as dealers trading on their own account; but in fact their function is closer to that of brokers, who only bring together demand and supply in the markets (For non-collateralized call transactions, the money market dealers act only as brokers. This is described below). While transactions in the bills market differ from those in the call market in maturity and interest rate, they function in fact as an extension of the call market.

City banks have by far the largest share as borrowers of funds in the call and bills markets, taking 50–60 per cent of total funds in the call market and accounting for 90 per cent of the bills sold in the bills market. The shares of city banks have been on a slight downward trend since 1975; but the shares of foreign banks and securities companies have risen because they have gradually borrowed funds in the call and bills market with a good sense of timing in comparing the costs of fund-raising in these markets with the costs in other markets. In addition, the share of the securities finance companies cannot be overlooked. Although these interbank markets were originally a place where the surplus and shortage in reserve deposits of each bank were adjusted among banks, the changes just mentioned have brought these markets some significance as a place for raising the funds to finance inventories of securities or to finance other lending.

The lenders in the call market are generally financial institutions other than city banks; the largest shares of lending come from trust banks, the *Zenshinren* Bank, *shinkin* banks, the *Norinchukin* Bank, and the Credit Federation of Agricultural Co-operatives. Regional banks had a large share in previous years, but their liquidity has deteriorated along with the growth of underwriting of Government bonds. Now the regional banks are active both as borrowers and as lenders in the call money market. In the bills market, the largest buyer is the Bank of Japan, through its bill-buying operations. But other than this, the largest buyers are the *Zenshinren* Bank, *shinkin* banks, agricultural financial institutions, and trust banks.

(ii) How trading is carried out

(1) Call-money transactions. The typical call transaction is a so-called 'market call' transaction in which money market dealers mediate between the borrowers and the lenders. There is, however, another type of transaction called the direct call, in which the financial institutions trade directly with each other without going through the money market dealers. (However, the proportion of direct-call transactions is low.) Transactions similar to call dealings are interbank loans and interbank deposits. Three types of call fund currently exist, classified by the time limit on settlement of funds. These are half-day loans, unconditional call loans, and fixed-date loans.

Half-day loans are the shortest type of call money and are settled within the day of the loan. There are two types—morning loans and afternoon loans. Morning loans are for cases when a bank needs funds early in the morning for purposes, for example, of transfer of funds to local banks or cash needs. These loans are settled by the time of the clearing of the bill market, which is at 1300 hours in Tokyo on weekdays, but at 1130 hours on Saturdays. Afternoon loans are for funds that are necessary for transfer to local areas or other purposes after the daily clearing. These funds are settled by the end of the business day, that is, by 1500 hours on weekdays or by 1200 hours on Saturdays. In principle, dealing in half-day money is unsecured, and payment is made with cheques drawn on the Bank of Japan that are labelled with the time of settlement. (Because these lendings are settled within the day of the loan, they are not reflected as outstanding balances in the statistics on the call market.)

Unconditional call money is, in principle, settled on the day after the date of the transaction at the time of clearing of the market. However, if neither party to the transaction indicates a desire for repayment of the loan, it is automatically extended. (Because of this extendability, unconditional call money differed from next-day call-money loans—which were abolished in April 1979.) In addition, there is a type of morning repayment call loan which is settled at 0900 hours on the morning after the transaction. Currently, unconditional call transactions account for between 70 and 80 per cent of the total call market.

Fixed-date loans are those which are outstanding for a fixed period that is greater than two days, including the day of the transaction. Traditionally, there were two-day, three-day, four-day, five-day, six-day, and seven-day loans, but from August 1985 two extra types were added, two- and three-week loans. (For example, a two-day fixed-date call loan is settled at the time of clearing on the second day of the transaction.) Fixed-date call loans are always settled in a lump sum on the value date, and early repayments are not permitted. Fixed-date transactions account for 20 to 30 per cent of the market.

(2) Bill transactions.   A bill sale occurs when the holder of a bill that has not matured endorses the bill over to the buyer, and the buyer then pays the seller an amount which deducts the interest payment and other costs of the transaction from the face value of the bill. There are two types of bill that are eligible for transactions in the bill market. The first type consists of bills of various sorts, including high-grade commercial and industrial bills, trade bills, high-grade promissory notes, and yen-dominated fixed-term export and import bills. The second type consists of bills of exchange (so-called 'cover' bills (*hyoshi tegata*). To make a cover bill, a financial institution bundles a group of other eligible bills and uses them as collateral for a bill that it underwrites itself and whose payee is a money market dealer. Most trans-actions are in the form of cover bills because the underlying securities are not necessarily either in perfect order or in round sums.

The types of bill transaction in the market are classified according to the value date as follows: (*a*) one-month bills—those that are due on the corresponding day of the month succeeding the month of the transaction or within fifteen days of the day after that corresponding day (that is, thirty to forty-five days); (*b*) two-month bills—those that are due on the corresponding day of the month two months after the month of the transaction or within fifteen days around that day (that is, forty-five to seventy-five days); (*c*) three-month bills—those that are due in the third month after the month of transaction on the corresponding day of the month or within fifteen days around that day (seventy-five to one hundred days); (*d*) four-month bills—those which are due in the fourth month after the transaction on the cor-responding day of the month; (*e*) five-month bills—those which are due five months after the original transaction on the corresponding day of the month; (*f*) six-month bills—those that are due six months after the month of the transaction on the corresponding day of the month; (*g*) resale bills—these are bills which may be resold after the corresponding day in the month succeeding their original issue (if no corresponding day exists, then after the end of the succeeding month) before the day of maturity. The financial institution that has purchased a resale bill may then once again resell it without restriction.

The five- and six-month bills are new types of transaction which began in June 1985. These bills were established in response to the growing need for longer-term transactions, and to have maturities of bills corresponding to financial assets in open markets, such as CD, BA, and Euro-yen markets, and thus to facilitate interest rate arbitrage among the markets.

(3) Collateral requirements.   For bills transactions, the bills themselves serve the function of collateral; but for call transactions, it is necessary to provide collateral that can be made liquid with ease and with certainty. The requirement for collateral in call transactions was introduced because the financial panic of 1927 was, in part, caused by the uncollateralized call funds

that had been borrowed by the Bank of Taiwan. In the pre-war period, financial institutions had large holdings of Government bonds and thus, in principle, Government bonds were used as the collateral for call transactions. In the post-war period, however, there were in fact almost no new issues of long-term Government bonds through the 1950s, and hence there was a tremendous decrease in the amount of call transactions collateralized by Government bonds. After 1965, however, with the new issues of long-term Government bonds, bond-collateralized call transactions were once again used alongside those collateralized by bank debentures or high-grade bills. Currently, Government bonds are the chief collateral in call transactions.

Because call transactions involve such large amounts of funds, the amounts of collateral are also very large and require frequent transfer. In order to reduce the trouble of transfer of the collateral and to reduce risk as well, several systems have been devised, including the substitute-certificates system and the depository-certificate system. The certificates issued under the systems are honoured only among the members of the individual systems, and so it is necessary to become a member of each of the systems in order actually to use them for handling collateral.

The first of the systems is the 'registered Government bond substitute-certificate system for call loan transactions collateral'. This system was established in December 1944 in order to reduce the risk that accompanied the transfer of collateral during war-time. The Bank of Japan issued substitute-certificates based on registered Government bonds and allowed their use as collateral for call loan transactions.

The second system is the 'debentures depository-certificate system for call loan transactions collateral', which was established in November 1969. Under it, bank debentures are entrusted to the Bank of Japan, and the Bank of Japan issues depository certificates based on these bank debentures. The depository certificates are then used as collateral for transactions. The system was introduced because bank debentures had not been in use for collateral, even though Government bonds and Government-guaranteed bonds had for many years been used as the basis of substitute certificates.

The third system is the 'equities depository certificate system for call-loan transaction collateral', which was established in May 1951. Under it, securities finance companies entrust equities that they hold to the Stock Exchange, and the Stock Exchange issues depository certificates based on them. These depository certificates are then used as the collateral.

The fourth system is the 'registered corporate bond substitute certificate system for call-loan transactions collateral', which was established in June 1955. Under it, transactions may be collateralized by certificates that are created and issued by the Industrial Bank of Japan, which is the trustee bank for the original bonds. Currently, only two types of issues are used in this system—Government-guaranteed railway bonds and bonds floated by the Nippon telephone and telegraph Corporation.

Collateralized call-market dealing has been carried out by money market dealers for many years, but non-collateralized call-market broking by money market dealers began in July 1985. At first, there were only overnight and seven-day call broking, but in September of that year, two- and three-week calls were added. In addition, if market needs dictate, consideration will be given to introduction of the remaining types of uncollateralized transaction, such as two- to six-day calls. Uncollateralized call loans are settled every day, and so there is no instrument resembling unconditional call loan, which is extendable. But in place of such extendable loans, there exist overnight uncollateralized loans. The reason for the introduction of non-collateralized call loans was the substantial growth of Euro-yen and foreign currency deposits and other such non-collateralized funds under the development of financial liberalization and internationalization. In addition, within the domestic market, the foreign banks resident in Japan were encountering larger needs for non-collateralized transactions. The interest rates on non-collateralized call loans are slightly higher than those on collateralized ones.

The reason for the emergence of the collateral principle in call transactions was the maintenance of financial orderliness. And for this very reason, the introduction of non-collateralized call loans brings up the question of how to ensure the safety of transactions after their introduction. Now in Japan, money market dealers are limited to the role of broker as a means of ensuring stability of the call market, as is the case in European countries and the United States where call loans are normally non-collateralized (with the exception of England, where they are collateralized). In addition, it appears that a rule will develop for the lending banks to establish credit limits *vis-à-vis* borrowing banks in the future.

(4) Seasonality of the call and bill markets.   The call and bill markets reflect the surpluses or shortages of funds in the financial markets in an extreme way. The sources of such deficits or surpluses are changes in demand for base money (that is, currency, i.e. banknotes, plus Bank of Japan deposits), the balance of Government transactions, and the balance of the foreign exchange account. As a result, there is substantial irregularity in the seasonal volumes of trading in the call and bill markets. Most specifically, the demand for currency is high in March and April, due to preparations for the farming season, to the start of the new academic semester, and to the high demand from the leisure season; currency demand is also high in June, due to payments of bonuses, and also at the year-end, due both to high commercial activity and to bonus payments. Early in the year, the bank notes issued at year-end return to the Bank of Japan. Fluctuations of the fiscal balance are also very great, due to the seasonality of economic activity and systemic factors relating to the fiscal structure. From April to June, there is a small deficit; from July to September, a small surplus; from October to December, a very large deficit; and from January to March, a very large surplus. Increases in the demand

for banknotes and fiscal surpluses cause a tightening in the call and bill markets, while inflows of banknotes into the Bank and fiscal deficits cause an easing in the call and bill markets. There is even seasonality within months, due to tax payment dates early in the month, or payment dates for wages (which tend to concentrate in the middle and latter parts of the month), and various types of settlement that concentrate at the month-end. These factors lead to a tendency toward tightness in the money markets.

It is also obvious that the demand and supply for funds in call and bill markets fluctuates with the business cycle. In times when the cycle is overheating, the high demand for currency, due to expansion of the economy, and the fiscal surplus lead to tight call and bill markets; when the cycle is headed downwards, decrease of the demand for currency and the fiscal deficit both lead to easing of the call and bill markets.

The Bank of Japan operates directly in the bill markets, both buying and selling, and adjusts the level of its lending in order to smooth out the seasonality or the irregular movements in the call and bill market. In addition, these markets feel the direct impact of monetary policies. For example, when the Bank of Japan wishes to reduce the growth of money or total credit, the Bank will purchase smaller amounts of bills relative to the shortage of funds in the market or take a more strict attitude toward lending. As a result, the rate of accumulation of reserves that are counted against reserve requirements is slowed, while the demand for base money increases. These factors put pressure on the demand–supply balance in the call and bill markets so that the interest rates rise and financial institutions then reduce their extension of credit. (For further details, see Chapter 6.)

c. The short-term foreign currency money market (the dollar call market)

(i) Establishment of the dollar call market

The short-term foreign currency money market, that is, the so-called 'Tokyo dollar-call market', is the market in which financial institutions borrow and lend foreign currency funds among themselves over relatively short periods. While the dollar-call market is not directly related to the foreign exchange market (which is explained below), it nevertheless facilitates the foreign currency funding operations of foreign exchange banks and has been an important factor in the growth of the foreign exchange market. The Tokyo dollar-call market was originally used as a place to adjust for very short-term shortages or excesses of foreign funds. In recent years, however, it has also functioned as a place either to borrow or to lend foreign currency funds at hand. During 1985, turnover in the dollar-call market passed the billion dollar level, indicating the huge (almost twenty-five-fold) growth during the last ten years. Even now, overnight and other such very short-term funds are the main part of the market, but the proportion of relatively long-term funding (of one month or more) has risen to between 10 per cent and 20 per cent. As this market grows, the tendency for the interest rates to be relatively high compared to Euro-rates is weakening.

The history of the dollar-call market is relatively short. It began operation in April 1972 on the basis of the Foreign Exchange and Foreign Trade Control Act. The purpose was to allow interbank short-term lending and borrowing in foreign currency funds in order to smooth out the short-term surpluses and deficits of foreign currency. Originally, there was a limit of six months for the maturity of transactions, but with the revision of the foreign exchange law in December 1980, the maturity of transactions was deregulated and currently faces no limit.

(ii) Characteristics and recent developments

The participants in the Tokyo dollar-call market are authorized foreign exchange banks (as of end-March 1986, there were 170 domestic banks and 77 resident foreign banks) and brokers. At present, non-resident participation is not permitted. The transactions in the dollar-call market take the form of lending and borrowing transactions and thus differ from the deposit transactions of the Euro-markets, but they are identical on the point of being non-collateralized. Although the dollar-call market also has the word 'dollar' in its name, there are no restrictions on the currencies which may be transacted; in fact, however, almost all transactions are denominated in US dollars. Transactions go through brokers, who are the same brokers as in the Tokyo foreign exchange market explained below. The minimum transaction value is $100,000 or the equivalent, and payments of funds are generally made to the foreign currency deposit accounts of the transacting banks. Delivery is on the business day following the transaction.

d. The *gensaki* market (repurchase market)

(i) Participants in the market

A *gensaki* transaction is one in which there is a prior promise either to repurchase or to resell the same security as originally transacted after a fixed time and at a fixed price. Although *gensaki* transactions are securities buying and selling in form, they are short-term lending and borrowing in substance, and are similar to call and bill transactions with the securities functioning as collateral. Thus, *gensaki*s are in fact financial transactions in which securities act as the catalyst. There are, however, many other motivations for their use. For example, when the *gensaki* rate is below the direct interest rate on the securities in question, a firm may temporarily sell some bonds it holds in the *gensaki* market and then write them down after the repurchase is completed. In addition, *gensaki*s which go over the end of an accounting period may be used to avoid end-of-period revaluations of securities.

The *gensaki* market is a free, open financial market in which any corporation may participate (a Ministry of Finance directive prohibits the participation of individuals because of the difficulty of determining creditworthiness and because of circumstances concerning development of the market as a place for corporate fund-raising and investment). The actual participants include securities companies, financial institutions, corporate entities, public financial institutions (such as the public mutual aid co-operatives), and non-residents, such as foreign investors. Among the buyers of *gensaki*s (that is, lenders in the market), corporate entities have the largest share at 30–40 per cent. But lending has been on the decline in the *gensaki* market since the introduction of the market for certificates of deposit (CD) in May 1979. The creation of CDs market meant that the short-term open money market was no longer limited to the *gensaki* market, and, as a result, the share of corporate entities in the *gensaki* market has been declining since 1980. (An important reason for the decline of the *gensaki* market is taxation; *gensaki* transactions are legally considered to be securities transactions and thus are subject to the securities transactions tax.) On the other hand, May 1979 was also the time when foreign participation through securities companies in the *gensaki* market was liberalized, and, with the revision of the foreign exchange law of December 1980, capital transactions became fully liberalized in principle. As a result, the share of foreign investors in the *gensaki* market has risen, and currently stands at just under 10 per cent. Foreign transactions in the *gensaki* market concentrate on interest rate arbitrage transactions which link foreign interest rates, *gensaki* rates, and foreign exchange swap costs.

The largest sellers of *gensaki* (borrowers in the market) are securities companies. The share of securities companies is 70–80 per cent, largely because securities companies use *gensaki* transactions as a method of financing inventories of securities, although impact loans and the financing systems for the circulation of public and corporate bonds are also used. City banks, which are the largest borrowers in the call and bill markets, are also major borrowers in the *gensaki* market. In earlier years, the Bank of Japan regulated the total amount of *gensaki*s that could be sold by banks, but with the growth and maturation of the *gensaki* market and the large-scale flotations of Government bonds, these regulations were gradually eased, starting in October 1978, and fully abolished in April 1980.

(ii) Transactions in the market

There are three types of *gensaki* transactions—own-account *gensaki*s, consignment *gensaki*s, and direct *gensaki*s.

Own-account *gensaki*s are those in which a securities company sells a bond in its possession with a repurchase agreement; such transactions are carried out for the purpose of raising funds. Securities companies always have very large inventories of securities held on their own account because of the necessity of smoothly performing their function as dealers. *Gensaki* transactions are an important method of financing these inventories. Regulations on the total outstanding amounts of own-account *gensaki*s were imposed in January 1978 in order to ensure the safe development of the *gensaki* markets and the soundness of securities companies' management.

Consignment *gensaki*s are repurchase agreements under which the bondholders other than securities companies carry out a *gensaki* transaction through securities companies. That is, the seller will sell a security with a repurchase agreement to the securities company, and then the securities company will sell the very same security with the very same date of maturity on its own account to another buyer in the market, such as a corporate entity or a financial institution with excess funds. Such transactions do not cause a change in the balance of securities inventories in the securities company. Limits on the upper levels of amounts outstanding in consignment *gensaki*s have been enforced since May 1974 and were raised seven times between then and June 1980.

A direct *gensaki* is a transaction between a bank or other financial institution with surplus funds and a buyer such as a corporation. This type of transaction does not go through a securities company as intermediary.

With respect to composition of outstanding amounts in the *gensaki* market, own-account *gensaki*s have about 70 per cent of the total and consignment *gensaki*s about 30 per cent. (Data for direct *gensaki*s are not available).

Similar in nature to the *gensaki* is another type of transaction called a *chakuchi*, which has become common since the autumn of 1975. A *chakuchi* is a type of forward contract that stipulates that, on a certain date between one and six months in the future, a certain security will be delivered and a certain amount of cash paid in return. Both the security and the price are specified in the contract. These contracts were first developed between securities companies and small financial institutions specializing in agriculture. (The contracts were signed during the summer at about the time when the extent of the harvests became known and fell due when the payments for rice would be coming in. The securities companies linked these transactions to own-account *gensaki*s.) As monetary policy eased between 1976 and 1978, *chakuchi* transactions expanded on the basis of bullish sentiments about the bond market. But the *chakuchi* market contracted sharply with the fall in the bond market and tight money policy from the middle of 1979, and this, along with regulation of individual agricultural co-operatives by the Ministry of Agriculture, Forestry and Fishery, has meant that the *chakuchi* market does not have its former vigour.

e. The certificate of deposit (CD) market

(i) Composition of the market

(1) The primary market. Issue of CDs began in May 1979. CD issue is permitted to financial institutions that are permitted to accept deposits. City banks have the largest share of the issues outstanding at 50–60 per cent, followed by regional banks, *sogo* banks, *shinkin* banks, and foreign banks. The primary market is the centre of activity in the CD market, and there are no restrictions whatsoever on which investors, that is, depositors, may purchase CDs. Corporations, individuals, residents, and non-residents may all be purchasers. Though there are no statistics on quantities purchased, it is believed that the largest purchasers are corporate entities, followed by public mutual aid co-operatives and local government entities.

(2) The secondary market. The CD is not only a free-rate asset, but also a negotiable one. There are no controls on who may participate in the secondary CD market, but an official designation is required. Firms that have been designated to participate or to act as intermediaries include money market dealers, financial intermediaries (though they may not act as such in trans-actions of their own CDs), and firms related to financial intermediaries, such as factoring firms, leasing firms, and credit-guarantee corporations. Securities companies were permitted to operate in the secondary CD market in June 1985. When the secondary market first began, the money market dealers were the major traders, but since then the financial intermediaries and their associated companies have become more important.

(3) The character of the markets. The issue of CDs is normally carried out as a direct bilateral negotiation between the issuing institution and the individual investors, either by telephone or at a place of business. But there are also cases where financial institutions act as intermediaries between the issuing institutions and investors.

When the CD market was first established, there were constraints in many areas, such as upper limits of issue, minimum denominations, maturity, and forms of negotiability, but these constraints have been gradually eased over time. Concerning issue limits, the original regulation held issue to 50 per cent of own capital of the issuing institutions, but since then this limit has been raised to 200 per cent as of April 1986 (for foreign banks, the limit is 100 per cent of yen-denominated assets). The minimum denomination was lowered from the original level of ¥500m. to ¥300m. in January 1984 and to ¥100m. in April 1985. Maturity restrictions originally limited issues to maturities between three and six months, but in April 1985, the minimum maturity was lowered to one month; in April 1986, the maximum maturity was extended to one year. These changes were a response to the needs of deposit banks, which were suffering from a decline in market share, and also to the need for more efficient fund management by corporate entities. As a result of the regulatory easing, the CD market has developed steadily, and currently is one of the largest money markets.

There are two types of transaction in the secondary market—unconditional and conditional (the latter are called CD *gensaki*). Unconditional purchases and sales occur when a CD is bought outright for the period up to maturity (or sold outright) through a dealer. Conditional purchases and sales use the same technique with *gensaki* (repurchase agreement) transactions, so that the CD is purchased or sold with the promise to be repurchased or resold after a specified period (usually less than one month). The dealers are market-makers in such transactions, seeking buy and sell orders and then matching sellers and buyers. Currently, there are few unconditional sales; the largest part of CD market is conditional.

Secondary market transactions have developed gradually since the autumn of 1980, with the money market dealers in the centre of the business. In the early period, there was about ¥100 milliard of monthly turnover (buying and selling volume), but there was a huge increase after fiscal year 1981. Both financial institutions and their associated companies followed the money market dealers in actively seeking such business, so that, by the end of 1985, the monthly trading volume had reached ¥10bn., (nearly equal to the money market dealers' trading volume ¥8bn.). There has been another large increase in the transactions since the securities companies were permitted to participate in the market (by ¥4bn., buying and selling volume). Reasons for this remarkable increase in the secondary CD market include the searching for new profit opportunities on the part of the money market dealers in the light of the slow-down of growth of the interbank markets and the desire to diversify business on the part of financial institutions in light of the lower interest rate spreads that have accompanied intensification of competition. In addition, the growth of the secondary market has been aided by the *de facto* shortening of the maturities of transactions through the use of CD *gensaki*s, which allowed circumvention of the earlier constraint on maturity of issue of originally three to six months, and now the current constraint of issue of maturity between one month and one year.

Though both the primary and secondary CD market have achieved stable development over the last several years, there is a need to reduce certain remaining restrictions in order to develop the markets further. In addition to expanding the issue limits and reducing the minimum denominations, another problem is somehow to change the form of negotiability from the current form of a registered security to a form with a higher level of liquidity.

f. Bankers' acceptance (BA) market

(i) Establishment of the yen-BA market

The yen-BA market is the newest of the money markets and was established in June 1985. A yen-BA is a yen-denominated fixed-term bill of exchange that has been underwritten by a bank but was originally issued by an exporter or importer for the purpose of settling a trade transaction. Yen-BAs circulate in the market through resale to dealers and investors. (Previously, financial institutions were able to sell yen-BAs in the bill market when necessary, but, because of complicated administrative procedures, most were in fact discounted and held until maturity.)

In the United States, the BA market has been one of the major money markets, along with the CD, commercial paper (CP), and federal funds markets. In Japan, because the proportion of yen-denominated financing of trade was extremely low, and because the interbank market centred primarily on call and bill markets, a yen-BA market hardly existed. But as part of the financial internationalization and liberalization, the Japan–US Yen-Dollar Committee agreed in May 1984 that a BA market would be established in Japan in order to contribute to the diversification of financial markets and to the internationalization of the yen. The yen-BA market was then established after discussion in the Committee for Financial System Research.

(ii) Outline of the BA market

The BA market is an open, free-rate, short-term money market in which financial institutions, corporate entities, non-residents, and others may freely participate. For the present, however, those who are permitted to bring bills to the market for the first time are limited to the authorized foreign exchange banks that have underwritten the bills. This measure was adopted in connection with an ongoing debate concerning the establishment of a commercial paper (CP) Market.[1] That is, the so-called *jikihane*-type bills (see below for description) in the BA market might be used as a type of commercial paper, so that limiting the original seller of BA in the market to foreign exchange banks would reduce the possibility that use of *jikihane* bills would spread and become the *de facto* introduction of a commercial paper market. In addition,

---

[1] There is disagreement within Japan between the banking industry and the industrial sector concerning the introduction of a CP market. The industrial sector believes that the introduction of such a market would provide a substitute for bank loans as a means of raising funds and would allow more flexible funding of operations at lower cost. The banking industry believes that, because commercial paper is non-collateralized, the introduction of such a market would violate the principle of collateral in markets and would be undesirable from the point of view of maintaining financial orderliness and protecting investors, in that it would have an ill effect on the bill market which has hitherto avoided the use of non-collateralized means of finance. In addition, banks point out that introduction of a CP market would further weaken the close relationship between particular banks and firms (the so-called 'main bank system'), and for this reason as well the banks have a negative attitude.

in the secondary market for yen-BAs, there was originally a restriction that participants would be only financial intermediaries, money market dealers, and the associated firms of financial institutions. But from April 1986, permission for participation by securities companies was also granted.

There are five types of bill which may be issued or traded in the yen-BA market. First are yen-denominated fixed-term bills of exchange, which are issued on the basis of letters of credit used for settlement of trade finance by either domestic or foreign exporters. Second are so-called 'accommodation' bills, which are issued as convenient sources of finance by either domestic or foreign exporters in cases when the original bill has been sent abroad for collection or some other purpose. Third are the so-called *jikihane* bills, which are issued by either domestic or foreign importers for the purpose of raising yen funds necessary for sight payments for imports. Fourth are refinance bills, which are issued by foreign banks that have financed yen-denominated trade and are used for the purpose of raising yen funds. Fifth are so-called 'cover' bills (*hyoshi tegata*), which are issued by an authorized foreign exchange bank with itself as the payee and which use bills of the types mentioned above as collateral. The conditions on eligibility of these bills are that (i) they must be accepted within thirty days of the loading of the ship (for non-Japanese exporters, the limit is forty-five days), (ii) the date of maturity must be within six months of loading with the addition of mailing time, and (iii) the bills must be of over ¥100m. in denomination (the same as the minimum unit on certificates of deposit). These bills are all eligible for discounting by the Bank of Japan.

g. The Euro-yen market

(i) Expansion of the Euro-yen market

Euro-yen are yen-denominated financial assets that are traded outside Japan.[2] The Euro-yen market is the market in which such assets are traded. There are Euro-yen markets in London, Singapore, Hong Kong, New York, and other places, but the London market is the most important, having a share of about 60 per cent.

According to data compiled by the Bank for International Settlements (BIS), Euro-yen outstanding were equivalent to $2.7 milliard at the end of 1977. But the outstanding level of Euro-yen grew to $21.7 milliard equivalent by the end of 1984, due to the rapid growth of interest arbitrage transactions, and to the increases in yen-denominated Japanese exports, yen-syndicated loans, and yen-denominated external bonds.

The reasons for the rapid growth of the Euro-yen markets in recent years include the relaxation of regulations and guidance over Euro-yen

[2] An alternative definition is that Euro-yen are yen-denominated deposits that are deposited in financial institutions located outside Japan.

transactions. But more important have been several basic underlying advantages of such Euro-market business. For example, Euro-yen transactions are free from domestic controls and transaction rules such as legal reserve requirements for deposits, interest rate regulations, and collateral requirements. And Euro-yen transactions are also advantageous in their tax treatment, for example, in the absence of withholding tax on interest income. In addition, the concentration and accumulation of know-how and information concerning international financial transactions allows diversification of risks and lower costs, and also allows a specialized efficiency and competitiveness in international transactions. Because of these advantages, the Euro-yen market is not simply a place for interest rate arbitrage or earning profits on spreads, but rather a substitution for certain domestic financial transactions, that is, a so-called 'parallel market'. Indeed, one may view it as one of the open markets of the financial system. Due to these factors, authorized foreign exchange banks in Japan have raised their dependence on the Euro-markets for yen financing in recent years. And remittances of funds from foreign branches to the main office branches of domestic banks through inter-office accounts have increased tremendously, particularly after the abrogation of swap limitations on the conversion of foreign currency into yen in June 1984.

(ii) An overview of Euro-yen transactions

Euro-yen arise from various sources. When a non-resident is the principal party in a transaction, these sources may include current trade transactions (for example, when a foreign exporter receives yen proceeds from an export sale and holds them abroad), overseas remittance of yen proceeds from a yen-denominated foreign loan or a yen-denominated bond flotation, or conversion of another currency into yen in the Euro-market. When a resident is the main source of the transaction, the Euro-yen will arise from overseas remittance of yen by a domestic financial institution through the inter-office account or from that by a domestic non-financial institution.

The transactions that create the Euro-yen through such routes as described above are termed 'primary transactions'; and the transactions that follow thereafter, the secondary transactions, are split into two types according to the form of the transaction: these types are currency transactions and bond transactions. Currency transactions include Euro-yen deposits, Euro-yen CDs, and Euro-yen lendings, while bond transactions include the issue or circulation of Euro-yen bonds. As of now, the types of Euro-yen transaction are shown in Table 4.2, a portion of which are still subject to regulation; but a gradual deregulation is continuing in part because of the Japan–US Yen–Dollar Agreement of May 1984.

Japanese banks have the largest share in a Euro-yen transactions, an overall share of about 70 per cent, including about 40 per cent of funds borrowed and 80 per cent of funds lent. The remainder arise from foreign banks, foreign monetary authorities, and other non-financial institutions. The important

TABLE 4.2 *Treatment of Euro-yen Transactions under the Foreign Exchange and Foreign Trade Control Law and Other regulations, March*

Type of transaction	Counterpart in transaction	Regulatory treatment
Foreign exchange aspects Euro-yen deposits	Non-resident Resident	Free Interbank transactions are free in principle. (Administrative guidance makes impossible the introduction of medium- or long-term Euro-yen borrowings by domestic branches.) Also, foreign deposits by non-bank residents are prohibited in principle (i.e. require approval).
Euro-yen CDs	—	Free issue if less than 6 months in maturity (for institutions designated as not requiring notification). Sales to residents are prohibited.
Euro-yen lendings (offshore)	Non-resident	Free. (But free only for institutions designated as not requiring notification. Voluntary restraint advised concerning medium- and long-term lendings to foreign branches of domestic corporations.)
Euro-yen impact loans (foreign→domestic)	Resident	Short-term ones are free; medium- and long-term ones are subject to advice of voluntary restraint.
Yen inter-office remittance	From domestic office to foreign office From foreign office to domestic office	Free. Short-term ones are free; medium- and long-term ones are subject to advice of voluntary restraint.
Issue of bonds Euro-yen bonds Issue by residents	—	Can be issued by corporations qualified to issue bonds domestically without collateral or with only general collateral. (Prior notification required; 180 days after issue required before sale in Japan permitted.)

Issue by non-residents	—	Clearance of issue standards needed to issue.
		  For public bonds, A or better rating as non-issuer.
		  For private bonds,
		  (*a*) AA or better rating as new issuer; or
		  (*b*) A or better rating plus clearance of financial standards for yen-dominated external bonds; or
		  (*c*) for unqualified firms, clearance of financial conditions on issue of yen-denominated external bonds that were in effect before April 1985.

characteristics of Euro-yen transactions are that they are non-collateralized and may be of any maturity (about 60 per cent of transactions are of less than one month's duration, and almost all are of less than three months' duration). Transactions may be either direct or through brokers, but the largest proportion do go through brokers (for Japanese banks, direct transactions account for only about 20–40 per cent). Delivery of yen funds is carried out on the business day following the date of contract. Interest rates on the transactions are determined individually for each transaction on the basis of a spread formula.

(iii) The Tokyo offshore market

The Tokyo offshore market, which is expected to be established by the end of 1986, has many points of similarity with the Euro-yen markets. The offshore market is one in which banks mediate between non-residents in transactions; that is, the banks are limited to transactions between non-residents but not limited with respect to currency of denomination. The regulation of the market will be approximately as free as that of the Euro-yen market concerning interest rate regulations, reserve requirements on deposits, and exemption from withholding tax. Thus, the difference between the Tokyo offshore market and the Euro-yen market will be that the offshore market is prohibited to residents (though for reasons of settlement of funds, certain transactions will be permitted to the parent bank). That is, the offshore market will be isolated from the domestic markets.

There will, of course, be difficulties of a technical nature in separating the Tokyo offshore market and domestic financial markets effectively from the viewpoint of monetary policy and tax treatment. But there are advantages to establishing a Tokyo offshore market. The Tokyo market will function as a centre for the world's transactions in yen and thus aid the expansion of Euro-yen transactions and the progress of internationalization of the yen. Also, for domestic financial institutions, the offshore market will be lower in cost than placing branches abroad, and will allow an opportunity for increased profits through the expansion of Euro-yen activity.

On the basis of these considerations, the Committee on Foreign Exchange and other Transactions agreed in October 1985 to establish a Tokyo offshore market.

3. THE FOREIGN EXCHANGE MARKET

The Foreign Exchange and Foreign Trade Control Law (FEFTCL) prohibits virtually all direct transactions between individuals and enterprises: in principle, almost all foreign exchange transactions have to be carried out by authorized foreign exchange banks.[3] Under the broad definition, the foreign exchange market is the place in which transactions in foreign exchange occur.

---

[3] Authorized foreign exchange banks are of two types. The first type, organized under the Foreign Exchange Bank Law, requires a licence from the Minister of Finance and is a specialized

However, under the narrow definition, which is the more common usage, the term means an interbank market, that is, the place in which transactions among foreign exchange banks occur. In what follows, we shall refer mostly to the narrower definition.

a. The current state of the foreign exchange market

(i) Composition of the market

The foreign exchange markets in Japan are in Tokyo and Osaka, but the overwhelming share of transactions, 99·8 per cent, take place in Tokyo. As in New York and London, almost all transactions take place over the telephone and there exists no course for foreign exchange as in some countries on the European continent. Participants in the market are the foreign exchange banks, foreign exchange brokers, and the Bank of Japan, which operates to smooth the market.

(ii) Growth and internationalization of the market

Since opening in July 1952, the foreign exchange market in Japan has expanded continuously against a background of continuing liberalization of trade and capital transactions with foreign countries and the growth of the economy. There were, of course, many changes and disruptions over this period, such as the Nixon shocks of August 1971 in which the convertibility of US dollars into gold was suspended, and the shift from fixed rates to floating rates (which first occurred in August 1971, was interrupted by a temporary return to fixed rates under the Smithsonian system in December of that year, but was then re-established with the final move to floating rates in February 1973). In 1985, there was a total transaction volume in the Tokyo foreign exchange market of $1·4 trillion (the total of spot, forward, and swap transactions), which was 125 times the amount traded in 1970 just before the Nixon shocks.

   Throughout these years, there was a steady internationalization of both the system and the transactions practices in foreign exchange markets. These changes were very important in promoting active exchange of funds between Japan and foreign countries. Among the major changes were the complete revision of the FEFTCL which took effect in December 1980. The basis of the new law was that transactions would be permitted in principle unless specifically prohibited, as opposed to the previous law which prohibited

foreign exchange bank. Currently there is only one such bank, the Bank of Tokyo. The second type requires only the approval of the Minister of Finance on the basis of FEFTCL. As of March 1986, there were a total of 247 authorized foreign exchange banks classified as follows: specialized foreign exchange bank, 12 city banks, 3 long-term credit banks, 10 trust banks (including foreign-owned trust banks), 61 regional banks, 49 *sogo* banks, 31 *shinkin* banks including the *Zenshinren* Bank, the *Norinhukin* Bank, the *Shokochukin* Bank, the Export–Import Bank of Japan, and 77 foreign banks.

transactions unless specifically permitted. Another major change was the abolition of the actual demand principle, under which an underlying actual transaction was necessary in order for individuals or corporations to conduct a forward exchange transaction with an authorized foreign exchange bank. This change occurred in April 1984. Other major changes included abolition of regulations on conversion of foreign funds into yen in June 1984 and the introduction of international broking by foreign exchange brokers and direct dealing between domestic banks.

These developments have made the Tokyo foreign exchange market one of the most important exchange markets, along with New York and London, in the Worldwide network of foreign exchange trading.

(iii) Methods of trading

(1) Trading hours. Most foreign exchange markets in foreign countries have no fixed hours of trading. But in Japan there are fixed hours—from 0900 to 1200 hours (the morning market) and from 1330 to 1530 hours (the afternoon market). The markets are closed on Saturdays and Sundays, as are most other foreign markets, as well as on national holidays.

(2) Types of market transaction. There are two types of transaction on the foreign exchange market, depending on the delivery of the funds, that is, when the sale is effected: these are spot transactions and forward transactions. Spot transactions in most cases are those in which the date of delivery of the funds is the second business day after conclusion of the contract, though there are also spot transactions in which the date of delivery is the day of the transaction or the following business day. Forward transactions, on the other hand, are transactions in which the delivery of the funds is at a point in the future defined from the second business day after conclusion of the contract. It is most common for contracts to be defined in terms of round months; that is, delivery is one month hence, two months hence, etc., from the second business day after conclusion of the contract. For interbank trading, however, simple forward transactions are uncommon; they usually take place as part of swap transactions, which are described next.

In analysing the form in which foreign exchange transactions occur, it is possible to distinguish between outright transactions and swap transactions. Outright transactions are those in which the foreign currency is either sold outright or bought outright, while swap transactions are those in which the foreign currency is simultaneously bought and sold but with different dates of delivery. For example, one might sell US dollars and buy yen spot and simultaneously buy US dollars and sell yen forward. There are various types of swap transactions, including so-called 'overnight' transactions in which the two transactions are concluded on the current business day and the succeeding business day, tomorrow–next transactions in which the two transactions are concluded on the succeeding business day and the next business day, other transactions in which special dates for a spot and a forward transaction are specified, and yet other transactions in which two dates for forward transactions are specified.

(iv) Composition of trading

Yen-dollar transactions form the largest proportion, about 80 per cent, of trading in the Japanese foreign exchange market because of the large share of foreign transactions that are carried out in US dollars. Nevertheless, reflecting the growth of internationalization and the diversification of Japan's foreign transactions, an increasing share is being conducted in German marks and Swiss francs. During 1985, yen-dollar transactions were 81·8 per cent and those in other currencies were 18·2 per cent of the total. By type of contract, the growth of swap transactions has been the largest. This reflects the growing level of interest arbitrage transactions and the fact that foreign exchange banks are covering the largest portion of forward transactions with customers through swap transactions. Of the yen–dollar transactions carried out during 1985, 32·2 per cent were spot transactions and 67·8 per cent were forward and swap transactions.

b. Market operations by foreign exchange banks

As banks carry out foreign exchange transactions with individual or corporate clients, there will result either net excess sales or net excess purchases of foreign exchange, either on a spot or a forward basis. The resulting balances are called 'oversold' or 'overbought' positions. If a disequilibrium in the net foreign exchange position of a bank is allowed to continue, then the bank bears a risk of fluctuation in the foreign exchange rate. For example, if a bank has an overbought position in foreign exchange when foreign exchange is expected to weaken or if the bank has an oversold position when foreign exchange is expected to strengthen, then there is a possibility of loss. It is common for a bank with an overbought position to sell foreign exchange in either the spot or the forward markets, or for a bank with an oversold position to buy in either the spot or the forward markets. Such operations are called 'covering an exchange position'. As a result, the disequilibrium in the net position of the bank is eliminated, and this situation is called having a 'square position'. In this fashion, sales of foreign exchange by individuals and corporations become, through the foreign exchange banks, sales to the market; or, conversely, purchases of individuals and corporations become purchases from the market.

But foreign exchange banks need not stop at merely linking the foreign exchange transactions of customers with the market; they may also, on the basis of their own expectations of exchange rates, intentionally take a disequilibrium net position by not linking transactions of their customers with the market, as they attempt to earn foreign exchange profits. They may even create a disequilibrium net position through their own sales and purchases in the market. Such adjustments of the net position of a foreign exchange bank are called foreign exchange position operations. In order to prevent banks from engaging in excessively speculative operations, Japanese law provides for regulations on the overall foreign exchange positions of banks. These regulations require that the overall positions in spot and forward exchange be kept within certain limits by the end of market transactions on every business day.

But regardless of disequilibrium in the net positions, every foreign exchange bank at times faces either surpluses or excesses of either foreign currency or yen funds. In order to deal with such situations, the banks adjust for their surpluses or deficits of either foreign currency funds or yen funds in the foreign exchange markets or in the Tokyo dollar-call markets or in both domestic and foreign yen short-term money markets. This is done as part of their foreign exchange position operations with a sharp eye to the possibilities for interest arbitrage.

c. Foreign exchange operation by the Bank of Japan

The Bank of Japan from time to time carries out a foreign exchange operation, also called market intervention. This is done by buying and selling foreign currency at suitable times in order to influence price formation in the market. This intervention is carried out under the 'Foreign Exchange Fund Special Account', with the Bank of Japan operating as the agent for the Ministry of Finance, in order to stabilize the foreign exchange market and support orderly conditions. This operation was introduced in April 1963 as part of the expansion of margins of exchange rate fluctuation under the Bretton Woods system to plus or minus 0·75 per cent from the IMF parity (before then the band had been plus or minus 0·5 per cent). Having experienced several large fluctuations of international currency conditions over the last decades, the Bank of Japan currently follows the actual developments in the markets and undertakes market intervention when necessary in suitable amounts and at suitable times.

4. SECURITIES MARKETS

a. Recent characteristics

In the financial structure of the high growth period that favoured indirect finance, the securities market had a tendency to be underdeveloped. But after 1975, the securities market grew extremely rapidly under the influence of the large-scale flotations of Government bonds and internationalization. This process is symbolized by three major developments.

First, the securities market both broadened and deepened. This occurred because of the expanded flow of funds through the securities market and particularly through the Government bond market (Table 4.3). One measure of this development was the ratio of total securities outstanding to nominal GNP, which rose from 45 per cent at the end of 1970 to 99 per cent at the end of 1984. There was also a diversification of the financial assets in the market, such as medium-term Government bonds, along with an expansion in the types of investor from banks alone to institutional investors, individuals, and non-residents.

Secondly, flows of funds across international boundaries became more active. This is particularly true for the period since the revision of FEFTCL in December 1980. A large part of the movement of long-term funds is carried out on an uncovered basis, including the foreign securities investments and foreign bond flotations of residents and the domestic securities investments and yen-denominated securities flotations of non-residents. There were many factors accounting for the direction and scale of these movements, but among these factors the most important were long-term interest rate differentials and exchange rate expectations.

Thirdly, there has been a blurring of distinction between the banks and securities companies with respect to Government bond business, and competition has become more active. Banks were permitted to sell both newly issued long-term Government bonds and medium-term Government bonds over the counter from 1983, and were permitted to buy and sell outstanding Government bonds over the counter (so-called 'dealing') from June 1984. Securities companies, on the other hand, were permitted to make loans using deposited Government bonds as collateral from June 1983, though only within certain limits and only on the basis of individual contracts. A further blurring occurred in June 1985, when banks were permitted to offer public bond *sogo* (integrated) accounts, which were combined Government bonds, and securities companies were permitted to make loans on the basis of agreement on loan facilities up to a given amount using Government bonds as collateral. So far as government bonds are concerned, one may say that the boundary between banks and securities companies has ceased to exist.

b. The primary market

(i) Institutions

The primary market for securities comprises essentially the issuers and subscribers, but an important role is also played by intermediary institutions that stand between the issuer and subscriber in order to carry out the issue procedures and to use their good offices to facilitate the issue. Another important aspect of the primary market is disclosure, which is required when the total face value of a bond issue or sale of equities exceeds ¥100m. The

TABLE 4.3 *Securities Outstanding*[a,b]

	1965		1970		1975		1980		1984	
	¥100m.	%	¥100m.	%	¥100m.	%	¥100m.	%	¥100m.	%
Government bills	11,500	6·9	23,700	7·1	46,600	5·9	139,600	7·5	142,700	4·9
Government bonds (medium- and long-term)	3,100	1·9	31,900	9·6	139,100	17·7	673,400	36·3	1,223,800	42·1
Local government bonds	5,100	3·1	14,800	4·4	63,100	8·0	167,700	9·0	206,800	7·1
Public corporation bonds	20,300	12·2	59,700	17·9	127,900	16·3	253,400	13·7	390,600	13·4
Bank debentures	28,900	17·3	61,800	18·6	154,900	19·7	258,400	13·9	391,000	13·4
Industrial debentures	17,500	10·5	30,400	9·1	66,500	8·5	101,700	5·5	130,100	4·5
Equities	68,200	41·0	97,700	29·4	153,900	19·6	201,500	10·9	249,700	8·6
Securities investment trust beneficiary certificates	11,700	7·1	13,100	3·9	33,500	4·3	58,400	3·2	174,700	6·0
TOTAL (A)	166,300	100·0	333,100	100·0	785,500	100·0	1,854,100	100·0	2,909,500	100·0
GNP (B)	326,600		731,300		1,478,700		2,358,300		2,928,000	
A/B (%)	50·9		45·5		53·1		78·6		99·4	

[a] Calendar year-end.
[b] Securities denominated in foreign currency not included.

Sources: BOJ, *Flow of Funds Accounts Application Tables*; *Economic Statistics Monthly*.

types of intermediary institution are as follows:

(1) Underwriters.   An underwriter is a firm that, at the time of an issue of securities, agrees to purchase either the entire amount or a portion of the issue from the issuer with the purpose of selling it, or agrees to purchase whatever may be left of an issue in case the issue is undersubscribed.

Article 65 of the Securities and Exchange Law prohibits such business to banks and trust banks, with the exception of the issue of national Government bonds, local government bonds, and Government-guaranteed bonds. As a result, most of these securities are underwritten by securities companies.

(2) Sub-underwriters.   Sub-underwriters are companies that contract with the primary underwriters and agree to sub-underwrite either an entire issue or a portion of an issue and to accept responsibility for subscribing this sub-underwriting amount. This business is currently carried out mostly by small and medium-sized securities companies, and in fact is simply the handling the subscription procedures for securities.

(3) Trustee corporations.   There are two types of trustee corporation—trustees for subscription and trustees for collateral. The trustee for subscription is entrusted by the issuer to take care of the necessary clerical work concerning the subscription of an issue of a corporate debenture. The trustee for collateral administers the collateral that is attached to a collateralized bond on behalf of the bond-holder. Ordinary long-term credit banks, and trust banks are permitted to be trustees for subscription, while becoming a trustee for collateral requires a licence from the appropriate authorities In fact, client banks of the issuers play the role both of trustee for subscription and of trustee for collateral.

(ii) The primary market for issue of bonds

The types of bond issued in Japan today are Government bonds, local government bonds, Government-guaranteed bonds (the above as a group are called public bonds), bank debentures, corporate debentures, convertible debentures, warrants (bonds that come with a right to purchase new stock issue), and yen-denominated foreign bonds.

These types of bond were described in Chapter 2, so let us here add only a note about the primary market for the issue of such securities.

First, there is a distinction between types of issue, that is, between private placement and public issue. Private placement is a method by which an issuer sells the securities to specific investors through direct negotiation. Public issue is the method through which there are no specified limits on who may purchase the balance. In reality, however, public issue in Japan includes many cases in which the issue is not necessarily made to the general public. Among the methods of public issue are public auction, fixed-rate auction, indirect public issue, and offer for sale (*uridashi*). For example, medium-term Government coupon bonds are sold through public auction, Government-guaranteed bonds through fixed-rate public subscription, and bank debentures through offer for sale; but the largest share of bonds, that is, long-term Government coupon bonds, are sold through indirect public subscription. In the latter case, a syndicate for the subscription is formed and in the case of an undersubscription of the issue, the remainder is subscribed by the syndicate.

Secondly, certain regulations remain in the primary market concerning the issue terms (i.e., yields to subscribers) of bonds (see section II below). While the issue terms now change frequently and are becoming more flexible, there remains a narrow band of interest rates within which the rate for a particular issue is determined on the basis of differences among issues in the creditworthiness, liquidity, and maturity. In the case of Government bonds, from time to time no issues will occur in a given month because the revision of issue terms has not gone smoothly. Moreover, there are more uncollateralized bonds being issued. There is undeniably a growing impression that the principle of collateralization of issue of bonds is a regulatory measure, especially considering the environment of increasing financial internationalization. Another inflexibility is that the quantities of issue depend on the *Kisaikai*, which is an underwriters association composed of the trustee banks and the underwriting securities companies.

Third, the issues of bonds in the primary market are largely made within the framework of indirect finance. This is particularly true for long-term Government coupon bonds and local government bonds, more than half of which are subscribed directly by financial institutions and by banks in particular (see Table 4.4). For bank debentures, however, the bulk of the subscription switched from financial institutions to individuals in the late 1960s, and even for public bonds the share of subscription by financial institutions has been falling; efforts have been made to increase the weight of individual subscription, particularly because the large-scale Government bond flotations exceed the subscription power of the financial institutions. This expansion of subscription by individuals has been possible because of the strengthened preference on the part of individuals for high-interest earnings and the diversification of asset choice away from skewness toward savings-type deposits. In this sense, the primacy of indirect finance is weakening.

(iii) The primary market for equity issues

One way to classify equity issues is according to whether they require pay-in of new capital; that is, issues are separated into compensated capital increases and non-compensated capital increases. There are also types of capital increase which stand between these two polar types, that is, half compensated and half non-compensated capital increases. Another way to classify issues is by who the new stockholders are. There are three types of issue by this classification: allocation to current stockholders, allocation to related parties,

TABLE 4.4 *Bond Absorption during 1984ᵃ, Public Placements*

	Long-term government coupon bonds		Local government bonds		Government guaranteed bonds		Industrial bonds		Bank debentures	
	¥100m.	%	¥100m.	%	¥100m.	%	¥100m.	%	¥100m.	%
City banks and long-term credit banks	7,948	13·2	3,336	40·5	6,499	24·9	973	13·5	413	2·6
Regional banks	3,475	5·8	347	4·2	4,136	15·9	288	4·0	538	3·3
Trust banks	1,017	1·7	249	3·0	861	3·3	166	2·3	47	0·3
Sogo banks	1,385	2·3	125	1·5	1,346	5·2	55	0·8	341	2·1
Shinkin banks and the Shokochukin Bank	3,415	5·6	403	4·9	1,952	7·5	191	2·6	298	1·9
Agricultural co-operative and the Norinchukin Bank	7,402	12·3	336	4·1	2,191	8·4	144	2·0	9	0·1
Insurance companies	2,769	4·6	72	0·9	1,089	4·2	50	0·7	386	2·4
Investment trusts	0	0	—	—	—	—	—	—	—	—
Households	10,153	16·8	361	4·4	5	0	4,139	57·5	14,077	87·3
Other	22,713	37·7	3,001	36·5	7,982	30·6	1,194	16·6	14,077	87·3
TOTAL	60,278	100·0	8,230	100·0	26,060	100·0	7,200	100·0	16,111	100·0
Amount outstanding at end of financial year 1984 (¥m.)	107·1		5·7		14·5		9·3		39·5	

ᵃ Excludes absorptions by the Trust Fund Bureau, the Special Account for Post Office Life Insurance, etc.

Source: Koshasai Hikiuke Kyokai (Bond Underwriters Association), *Kochasai geppo* (Bond Monthly).

and public subscription. In the first two types, the issue of new equities is limited to certain persons who are either current stockholders or have some relationship to the issuer. In the last type, public subscription, new equity is sold to general investors; there are, however, two sub-types of public issue. These are direct and indirect subscription, the former being when the firm sells the issue by itself, and the latter when the subscription is carried out through underwriting by a securities company.

The traditional method of compensated capital increases in Japan was par-value issue with allocation to current stockholders. Public subscription at market prices began in 1969, and although it receded temporarily after the oil crisis in autumn of 1973, it began to rise once again after 1975. Currently between 70 per cent and 80 per cent of corporate equity flotations in the market are market-value issues, and such issues have become the norm for capital increase. These issues are useful in strengthening the business base of a company, because the difference between the market price and the par value may be retained within the corporation as capital reserves—this is why corporations prefer market-price issues. There is, however, a tendency for market-value public subscriptions to occur when stock prices are high; because the procedures for capital increase are time-consuming, it is possible for the market price to fall below the subscriber's price at the point of payment and thus disappoint the expectations of investors. For this reason, the Securities Exchange Council (*shoken torihiki shingikai*) is considering a policy that will improve the use and strengthen the benefits of the market-price public issue system. (For example, the Council is considering the shortening of the calendar for market-price capital increases.) One problem with the primary equities market is the prohibition in principle of firms with equities registered over the counter to carry out public subscription capital increases. This makes it difficult for small and medium-sized firms which do have good prospects but which are not listed on the Stock Exchange to raise funds. To address this problem, measures were adopted in November 1983 in order to ease the standards for over-the-counter registration, and to permit public subscription capital increases.

c. The secondary market

(i) Types of transaction

Secondary securities transactions are separated into two types–transactions on the Stock Exchange and over-the-counter transactions that occur primarily outside the Exchange and in offices of securities companies. In the pre-war period, Stock Exchange transactions had a very strong speculative character and, therefore, most of the spot trading in both equities and bonds was carried out over the counter. In the post-war period, however, transactions on the Stock Exchange came to occur through spot trading on a cash basis. And in order to facilitate transactions through fair price formation, over-the-counter transactions in listed stocks were prohibited in principle. For these reasons, the secondary market in equities came to centre on the Stock Exchange. On the other hand, for bonds, with the exception of Government bonds, yen-dominated foreign bonds, convertible debentures, and warrant bonds, there was no need to concentrate the market; hence the share of the trading on the Stock Exchange was small, and most transactions were over the counter. For large-scale trading in Government bonds (amounts greater than ¥10m.), the large-scale transactions system was introduced in April 1979, after it was decided to use the Stock Exchange for these transactions. This change was introduced to improve the method of price formation and notification. In October 1985 the bond futures market was also added to the Tokyo Stock Exchange.

(1) Transactions on the Stock Exchange.   The Stock Exchange is a corporation formed by its members for the purpose of creating the market that is necessary for transactions in securities. Membership in the Exchange is limited to securities companies, and the highest decision-making body of the Exchange is the General Meeting of members. A board of directors is the administrative body, and the managing director represents the Stock Exchange and has general responsibility for its business. There are in fact eight such Exchanges in Japan—Tokyo, Osaka, Nagoya, Kyoto, Hiroshima, Fukuoka, Niigata, and Sapporo. In comparing these markets, the indicator which most clearly shows the scale of the secondary market at each is trading volume of equities, measured either in the numbers or in the value of shares traded. By both measures, the Tokyo market has more than 80 per cent of the total trading volume of all exchanges, and is thus considered the central market. The Osaka market is the centre for the western part of Japan, and these two markets together account for more than 90 per cent of all transactions.

(2) Over-the-counter transactions.   Transactions in non-listed stocks or those in odd lots (units other than 1,000 shares) are implemented outside the Stock Exchange. These transactions are carried out bilaterally with individual customers at the offices of securities companies, and are called 'over-the-counter' transactions. Along with the post-war boom in equities, there was a sudden increase in the amount of transactions in non-listed stocks, and as a result the need to organize this trading was felt keenly. The response to this need was the establishment in October 1961 of a second section of the stock market jointly listed by the Tokyo, Osaka, and Nagoya Stock Exchanges. As a result, the level of over-the-counter stock transactions is very small compared with that of transactions on the Exchange.

For bonds, on the other hand, over-the-counter trading is generally permitted, even in listed bonds, and about 95 per cent of the trading volume in bonds is over the counter. To aid in determining prices for over-the-counter trading, two indices are used—a daily index including about twenty securities with high trading volume and good indicator characteristics, and a weekly index published every Thursday, which includes about 230 representative bonds chosen according to type of maturity and interest rates.

(ii) The secondary bond market

At the time of the first major post-war issue of Government bonds in 1966, the Tokyo and Osaka Stock Exchanges reopened exchange trading in bonds in order to promote the development of a bond market. Thereafter the market grew very rapidly, particularly after 1975. The biggest impact on the market came from the large-scale flotations of Government bonds and the easing of the resale regulations on Government bonds held by banks. Both of these measures encouraged development of the secondary market in Government bonds.

But in looking at the performance of the secondary bond market, one need not limit oneself to the large growth in the scale of transactions; one may also look at the diversification of participation in the market to financial institutions, institutional investors, corporate entities, individuals, and foreign investors. With the relaxation of the resale controls on Government bonds, the secondary market yields on the Government bonds came to reflect actual market conditions and to represent the long-term bond yields. These changes were a major improvement, had feedback effects on the issue market, and were also one of the major causes of interest rate liberalization [13].

(iii) The bond futures market

Bond futures trading is simply one type of financial futures transaction in which securities are delivered or paid for as of a certain date in the future or by a certain date in the future at a price determined by contract on the date of the transaction. No such market existed in Japan until October 1985, when a bond futures market was established on the Tokyo Stock Exchange. One major reason for the establishment of this market was the growing need to avoid price fluctuation risks. These risks had increased because the accumulation of outstanding bonds was causing large movements in prices of the bonds in the spot market and thus affecting the earnings of bond-holders. Another major reason was the existence of such futures markets in major foreign countries, which could lead to reductions in investment in domestic bond markets.

There are 138 institutions that participate in the bond futures market, including the eighty-three member securities companies of the Tokyo Stock Exchange, twenty-one non-member securities companies (including eight foreign securities companies resident in Japan), and thirty-four financial institutions that are licensed in public bonds dealing. Clients who wish to trade in this market must go through the market participants, and only the securities companies are permitted to be brokers.

The trading in the bond futures market is trading of so-called 'long-term standard' Government bonds, which are actually fictitious bonds with a coupon rate of 6 per cent and a remaining maturity of ten years. The unit of trading is ¥100m. Dates of settlement are 20 March, June, September, and December, and contracts may be signed for five such delivery dates, including the nearest and the next four thereafter, meaning that the longest period which can be traded is one year and three months.

Customers are not required to make payment for a futures contract on the date of the contract, but must place a consignment margin payment of 3 per cent of the transaction value with the securities companies (with a lower limit of ¥6m.). Profit and loss are calculated every day, and in the case when a loss rises to 1 per cent or more of the face value of the transaction, then a extra margin requirement must be paid in. There are limits on the price fluctuation in a given day such that the loss may not exceed 1 per cent per day.

There are two types of settlement for these transactions—cover settlement, under which uncovered positions are settled through reverse transactions (that is, sale of overbought positions or repurchase of oversold positions), and delivery settlement, for cases in which reverse sales are not carried out before the final trading day in question (the ninth business day after each delivery date). Under delivery settlement, the seller must deliver an amount of Government bonds equivalent to the contract amount to the purchaser and the purchaser must pay in funds to the seller. (The price for the standard long-term Government bond which is the basis for the settlement is the price as of the final transaction day.) In order to ensure an identical price for the standard bond and actual Government bonds, a prescribed ratio of exchange is used. In addition, the precise bond used for the delivery may be selected at the discretion of the seller from long-term coupon Government bonds of more than seven years' maturity. The securities transactions tax is not levied on standard bond transactions but is levied on delivery settlements.

Since the establishment of the bond futures market, several types of trading have developed, including hedge transactions against price fluctuations, arbitrage trading between future and spot bonds, spread transactions that arbitrage between different maturities of futures, and open-position trading (i.e., speculative transactions in futures). Thus the bond futures market has led to an overall expansion in the bond market itself, including the spot market.

(iv) The secondary equities market

Of those securities markets in Japan in which movements of demand and supply determine prices freely, the secondary market in equities is the most typical. In terms of trading volume it is an extremely lively market, just as is the Stock Market in the United States.

The composition of equity ownership in the post-war period has shown a conspicuous trend: the share of equities owned by individuals has fallen continuously. This share fell from about 61 per cent at the end of March 1951 to about 26 per cent at the end of 1984. The reasons for the fall include decline in the attractiveness of stock investment (for example, the average yield on stocks fell from about 4–5 per cent in the mid-1960s to about 1 per cent in 1976), but, more importantly from the point of view of equity investment aimed at capital gains, there was a corporatization of stockholdership due to strengthening of corporate combinations among firms and an increase in corporate holdings for the purpose of stable stockholder operation. There is strong consciousness that a continuation of these trends might reduce the function of the secondary equities market; measures to encourage individual stock ownership have been considered. One of these measures was the revision in October 1982 of the Commercial Code, in order to facilitate stock split. Whether this measure in fact promotes equity holding by individual investors will be an issue in the future.

d. Regulation of the securities markets

Strengthening the role played by the securities markets in the economy and simultaneously protecting investors are both important goals. And for those purposes, both issue of securities and transactions in securities must be carried out fairly and smoothly. To these ends, the Securities and Exchange Law was implemented in 1948, and since then this law and its related regulations have been the general framework of regulation of the securities market in Japan. In addition, there have been administrative guidance by the Ministry of Finance and voluntary restraints by the Stock Exchange and by the Securities Dealers Association of Japan. In recent years the basic thrust on the regulatory side has been to promote the market conditions to enable the securities market to fulfil its function through the price mechanism (that is, the promotion of policies for fair price formation).

The Bank of Japan has little contribution to make to the regulation of securities markets. The Bank of Japan Law stipulates, in the articles concerning operation of the Policy Board, that the Bank will adjust the conditions of lending which financial institutions carry out *vis-à-vis* securities companies. But the law lacks any specific prescriptions in this regard, so that the powers are only nominal.

The Bank of Japan does, however, have some direct relationships to the securities markets through business operations, based on provisions of the System of Collateral Receipt for Call Loan Transactions. Such operations occur in cases when the Bank of Japan makes loans to money market dealers on the collateral of a promissory note issued by securities' finance companies for a call borrowing. (See Chapter 5.) In such cases, the Bank of Japan may decide, in consultation with the stock exchange and securities finance companies, about changes in the assessment rate of standard collateral and the particular equities for which securities finance companies may demand the issue of the collateral receipt. The Bank of Japan may also, if necessary, change the assessment rate of collateral that backs a money market dealer's bill. In addition, the Bank of Japan may issue guidance concerning the borrowing of call money in an effort to secure funding for securities finance companies. And the Bank of Japan may lend directly to securities finance companies, in order to smooth the conditions in the bond market. In 1964 and 1965, at a time of depression in the securities market, the Bank of Japan carried out special lending operations to certain securities companies on the basis of Article 25 of the Bank of Japan Law [14]. These were measures aimed at forestalling a financial collapse. The Bank of Japan may also express its opinions when necessary concerning flotation of bonds through underwriting securities companies or the trustee banks, may treat bonds of high credit-worthiness as qualified collateral for loans on bills, and may also influence the bond market through market operations in Government bonds and Government-guaranteed bonds.

II. Interest rates

1. THE DETERMINATION MECHANISM FOR MAIN INTEREST RATES

The previous section has demonstrated that there was a gradual progression toward liberalization of interest rates in Japan after 1975, and that the mechanism by which interest rates are determined is in the process of major change compared to the mechanism of the high economic growth period. This section will classify the mechanisms by which important interest rates are now determined, in the second half of the 1980s.

In general terms, there are three mechanisms, which result in three types of interest rates—policy rate, regulated rates, and free rates. Policy rate is the official discount rate, which is determined at the discretion of the Bank of Japan on the basis of its policy judgement. Regulated rates are those such as long- and short-term prime rates, deposit and savings interest rates, and subscriber yields for bonds, which are determined by certain rules but with consideration of market forces by those concerned. Free rates are those such as call rate, CD rate, and secondary market bond yields, which are determined by demand and supply of funds in the markets. (See Table 4.5 for an overview of the levels of important interest rates.) Let us consider these types of interest rate in some detail.

a. Policy rate (the official discount rate)

The official discount rate, or simply the discount rate, is the standard interest rate applied to lending by the Bank of Japan. Since April 1973, there have in fact been two discount rates. The first is that on discount of commercial

TABLE 4.5   *Principal Interest Rates, 31 March 1986*

	Annualized interest rate (%)
Official discount rate	
Interest on discount of trade bills or on loans collateralized by Government bonds, etc.	4·0
Interest rate on loans collateralized by other items	4·25
Bank lending	
Short-term loan rates [a]	
Upper limit on loans and discounts	6·75
Upper limit on current overdrafts	7·75
Standard rate (prime rate)	4·5
Long-term prime rate	6·4
Average contracted interest rates on loans and discounts of all banks	6·266
Lending rate of Government financial institutions (base rate)[b]	6·4
Deposits, etc.[c]	
Banks	
Ordinary deposits	0·5
Notice deposits	0·75
3-month time deposits	2·5
6-month time deposits	3·75
1-year time deposits	4·5
2-year time deposits	4·75
The post office[d]	
Ordinary savings	1·92
Fixed-amount savings (of less than 1 year)	3·0
Fixed-amount savings (of more than 3 years)	4·75
Money trusts: expected dividend rate (5 years or more)[e]	5·38
Loan trusts: expected dividend rate (5 years)[f]	5·52
Bond yields	
Government bills, 60 days	3·899
Long-term Government bonds, 10 years	5·778
Government guaranteed bonds, 10 years	5·959
Local government bonds, 10 years	5·959
Bank debentures	
Coupon debentures, 5 years	5·5[g]
Discount debentures, 1 year	4·755[h]
Industrial bonds (AA), 12 years	6·108
Call rate (unconditional)	5·375[i]
Bill rate (2 months)	5·3125[j]

[a] For loan rates, discount rates, and overdraft rates, upper limits based on TIRAL.

[b] The base rate is identical to the long-term prime rate.

[c] Details of deposit rates are based on BOJ guidelines. (The upper limits under the TIRAL are 5·75% for time deposits and 1·75% for other deposits.)

[d] Based on Cabinet Order under the Postal Savings Law.

[e] As of 6 April.

[f] As of 6 April.

[g] Applies to bonds floated in April.

[h] Applies to bonds floated in April.

[i] Rate for the lender.

[j] Rate for the purchaser.

Source: BOJ, *Economic Statistics Monthly.*

bills or on lending that is secured by Government bonds, specially designated bonds, or bills corresponding to commercial bills; the second is that on lending collateralized by other instruments. The discount rate for the latter always exceeds that for the former by 0.25 per cent. In most cases, the term 'discount rate' refers to the former.

The official discount rate is determined and changed solely at the discretion of the Policy Board of the Bank of Japan, as specified in the Bank of Japan Law. Changes in the discount rate have two effects on the level of economic activity—a cost effect through changing the fund-raising costs of private financial institutions and a psychological effect, or announcement effect, on activity in the private non-financial sector, particularly that of corporations. (For details, see Chapter 6.) In addition, since November 1962, there have been credit ceilings on Bank of Japan loans to the city banks, which borrow large amounts from the Bank of Japan. When the Bank of Japan supplies loans to these institutions in excess of the ceiling, then a special penalty rate, 4 per cent above the discount rate, is applied to the loans in excess of the limits.

A separate lending facility, apart from that to which the discount rate applies, was established in March 1981, for the purpose of providing temporary or exceptional loans to help adjust the money market. This separate facility is called the special lending facility (or Lombard facility), and a special interest rate in excess of the discount rate applies to loans under it. The purpose of the facility is to help flexibility in cases when there is a special need for well-timed action in the financial markets. (An example would be cases in which the foreign exchange market is influenced disruptively by the active capital flows that may accompany movements of foreign interest rates.) The interest rate on loans from this facility is not established in any permanent way, but rather is determined or changed by the Bank of Japan Policy Board in cases when such loans are necessary and in response to movements in the market, to foreign interest rates, or to other factors.

b. Regulated interest rates

(i) Lending rates

(1) Short-term lending rates of private financial institutions. Japanese law provides for an overall upper limit on the short-term lending rates that may be charged by private financial institutions. The Temporary Interest Rates Adjustment Law of 1947 (TIRAL) regulates the maximum interest rates for loans of under one year in maturity and over ¥1m. in amount that are granted by all banks, trust banks, insurance companies, and the *Norinchukin* Bank.[4] The Minister of Finance has the right to propose establishment or

---

[4] The maximum interest rate regulations apply to the loans that trust banks make from designated money in trusts but exempt loans made under insurance contracts and loans from the *Norinchukin* Bank to an affiliated organization.

change of the upper limits on interest rates, and, on the basis of these proposals, the Bank of Japan Policy Board will determine the rates in consultation with the Interest Adjustment Council;[5] the Minister of Finance then notifies the financial community.

For *sogo* banks, *shinkin* banks and credit co-operatives, the maximum interest rates are determined on the basis of the laws concerning these particular institutions, such as the *Sogo* Bank Law, the *Shinkin* Bank Law, and the Law for Small Business Co-operatives. These laws empower the Minister of Finance to determine the maximum rates; details of such determination are regulated through the business codes for the respective sectors.

In principle, financial institutions may determine the level of short-term interest rates within the limits of the legal maximum rates, but in fact the actual maximum rates for short-term loans for all banks have been linked to the official discount rate since June 1958. When the official discount rate was cut at that time, the Federation of Bankers Associations of Japan made an arrangement for a voluntary cut by the same amount, and since then, every time the discount rate has been changed the maximum short-term rate for loans has also been moved with it, in a type of self-regulation by the Federation of Bankers Association of Japan. (Of course, the rate determined by the agreement may not exceed the maximum rate based on legal notification, but in fact the notification itself has at times been changed when there was a need to do so in order to maintain compliance with the rules.) In addition, a so-called 'standard rate' (*hyojun kinri*) system, which is similar to the American prime rate system, was introduced in March 1959 just after the discount rate cut in February of that year. This system also is an arrangement of the Federation of Bankers Associations of Japan, and under the arrangement the standard rate is moved by exactly the same amount as the discount rate whenever the latter is changed. The standard rate is applied to loans and discounts of bills of particularly high creditworthiness, and thus is the *de facto* lower limit for lending rates. It is also called the 'short-term prime rate' and was originally divided into four categories, but these were unified in October 1970. The standard rate is currently set 0·25 per cent above the official discount rate.

The arrangements concerning these interest rates ran into some difficulties with the Anti-Trust Laws and were officially abolished at the time of the discount rate cut in April 1975. Since that time, however, the Governor of the Bank of Japan has requested that banks follow changes in the official discount rate; the banks voluntarily move their actual upper limits on short-term lending and their prime rates in line with the discount rate. (In fact,

[5] The Interest Adjustment Council (*Kinri Chosei Shingikai*) is an advisory body to the Policy Board of the Bank of Japan, and is composed of fifteen members. These members are the head of the Ministry of Finance's banking bureau, the head of the co-ordination bureau of the Economic Planning Agency, the Deputy Governor of the Bank of Japan, seven representatives of the financial industry, three representatives of the industrial sector, and two people of learning or experience.

certain banks lead their interest rates and other banks follow them, according to the so-called 'leading bank' system.) And at the time of the discount rate cut in March 1977, across-the-board cuts in deposit rates, including the fixed-term deposit rates, were difficult. Hence the Bank of Japan did not request interest rate cuts of the same amount as the cut in the discount rate, but instead requested that banks make every effort possible to cut lending rate levels in the light of these circumstances. The Bank of Japan has not requested it at the time of the official discount rate changes since then, and in fact it was not until March 1981 that the short-term prime rate moved by a different amount from the official discount rate. In this case, the official discount rate cut was by 1 per cent but the cut in the short-term prime rate was only 0·75 per cent, and as a result, the spread between the short-term prime rate and the official discount rate rose to 0·5 per cent, where it has remained.

The interest rates that are applied to individual loans, i.e., rates on con-tracted loans, are determined within the band between the maximum interest rates and the prime rates. There are no regulations on rates on contracted loans themselves. The factors that determine the level of interest rates in individual cases are primarily the creditworthiness of the borrower and the closeness of its business relationship to the bank. During the high economic growth period, the borrowers to whom the short-term prime rate applied were only a portion of the best firms in the country. After the oil shocks, however, the reliance of corporations on borrowings fell, and the bargaining power of the corporations relative to that of the financial institutions rose, so that the prime rate gradually came to apply to a very large number of corporations and industries. This trend was particularly conspicuous in the easy money policy in the first half of the 1980s. After the prime rate cut of November 1983, fully 70 per cent of the short-term loans outstanding were made at either the prime rate or the quasi-prime rate. (In this connection, only about 30–40 per cent of the loans outstanding in the period of monetary ease in the last half of the 1970s were made at the prime rates.)

These changes in the mechanism of determination were not merely tem-porary phenomena accompanying a period of monetary ease. Rather, they reflect the reduction of corporate fund demand and the diversification of funding sources. The changes thus demonstrate how difficult it was to main-tain a method of prime rate determination that was not based on market interest rates.

(2) Long-term lending rates of private financial institutions.   In theory, each financial institution is free to determine long-term interest rates—those apply-ing to loans of more than one year in maturity. The Minister of Finance Notification based on the TIRAL does not apply to these rates; there are no maximum limit regulations; and there are no formal arrangements for self-regulation. In fact, however, the rates are determined through implicit rules among concerned parties, including official authorities. These rates are those

that long-term credit banks and trust banks charge on long-term loans to high-quality corporations such as electric power companies, the so-called 'long-term prime rate'. On the basis of implicit rules among the concerned parties, each financial institution changes its own long-term prime rate at the same time by the same amount. The level of the long-term prime rates is determined as a fixed spread above the fund-raising costs for five-year money of long-term credit banks and trust banks. The spreads are 0·9 per cent above the interest rate on coupon-bearing bank debentures and 0·88 per cent above the expected dividend rate for loan trusts.

In earlier years, the long-term prime rate was the rate of interest on long-term borrowings to the most preferred customers and was the *de facto* lower limit for longer-term lending. But, as described above in the section concerning the short-term prime rate, the structure of corporate finance has changed; since the middle of the 1980s city banks have been applying an interest rate that is below the long-term prime rate to medium-term loans of one to three years' maturity. Long-term credit banks have also been lending at rates that are mixtures of long- and short-term rates, so that in fact there is an increasing tendency to use interest rates that are below the prime rate. As a result, the long-term prime rate is losing some of its character as the basic rate for long-term lending.

Additional flexibility is achieved by the choice between fixed and floating rate loans. The long-term lending rate charged by an institution may be either fixed or floating, depending on the type of institution. For example, long-term credit banks raise most of their own funds through fixed-interest bank debentures and thus make most of their loans on a fixed-rate basis. For trust banks, however, because the dividends on the main source of funding (i.e. trusts) are calculated on the basis of actual earnings, the floating rate system for long-term lending is more common. For city banks, which raise most of their funds through deposits, the general practice is to have floating rate formulas under which there is a periodic review of interest rates.

(3) Interest rates charged by Government financial institutions. The lending rates charged by Government financial institutions are determined either by the laws under which the institutions are chartered or by the business codes of the institutions. (For most such institutions, approval of rates by the responsible Minister is required.) For the Japan Development Bank, the People's Finance Corporation, and the Small Business Finance Corporation, the basic lending rate is set at the same level as the long-term prime rate of the private sector. But all Government financial institutions, including these, have a special lending rate that is below the long-term prime rate for loans whose funds are used for purposes of Government policy. Movements of the basic rates follow those of lending rates of private financial institutions, and most of the special lending rates also move in parallel. But for some loans that are thought to require public assistance, the lending rates are kept at

relatively low levels; these include equipment loans for agriculture, forestry, fishery, and medical undertakings.

(ii) Deposit rates, savings rates, and trust dividend rates

(1) Interest rates on deposits and savings at private financial institutions
Almost all deposit and savings interest rates of private financial institutions are regulated under TIRAL in the same way as are short-term lending rates. The Minister of Finance proposes the establishment or charge of rates, and the Policy Board of the Bank of Japan determines maximum rates in consultation with the Interest Adjustment Council. Thereafter, the Minister of Finance notifies the financial community, (see Fig. 4.1), but, unlike the case of short-term lending rates, the regulations concerning deposit and savings rates apply not only to banks and *sogo* banks, but also to *shinkin* banks, to credit co-operatives, to agricultural co-operatives, and indeed to all private financial institutions. Deposits with an affiliated organization, however, do not come under the deposit rate controls.)

In the 1960s, the maximum interest rates on deposits and savings deposit

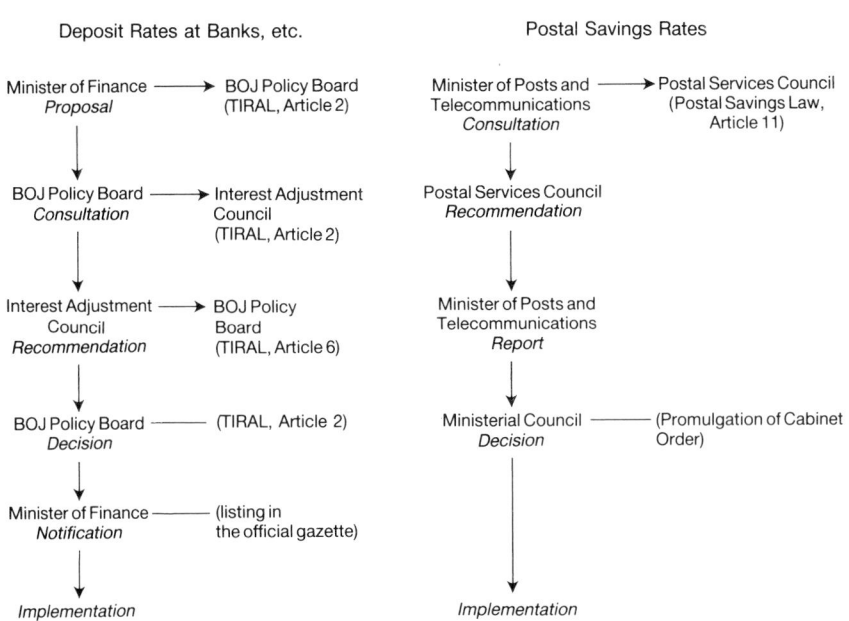

Figure 4.1   *Deposit Rate Determination*

were determined in great detail under TIRAL, according to type of deposit. But in order to promote the more flexible movement of interest rates, simplification and rationalization of the methods of regulation were sought, and in April 1970 a new system was developed. Under this system, the Bank of Japan establishes guide-lines for deposit rates according to maturity, but within the limits of the regulations of TIRAL. The Bank of Japan then publishes these guide-lines and requests that each financial institution observe the guide-lines. The institutions then set their own deposit rate levels voluntarily at the maximum level of the guide-lines. (For *shinkin* banks, agricultural co-operatives, and other small institutions, deposit rates may be set between 0·1 per cent and 0·25 per cent higher than for other institutions.)

Since 1970, the deposit rates in the guide-lines and the maximum rates acording to TIRAL have moved simultaneously. When these deposit rates are moved, their relationship with lending rates is given great weight. There has, however, been a gradual increase in the number of types of deposit and savings deposit to which the regulations of TIRAL do not apply, in part because of the liberalization of interest rates in recent years. These developments are discussed below.

(2) Postal savings rates.   The interest rates on postal savings are determined by the Cabinet on the basis of a report by the Minister of Posts and Telecommunications in consultation with the Postal Services Council (*Yusei Shingikai*), and published through the Cabinet Order. This method of determination is defined in the Postal Savings Law. The Postal Service Council is composed at the most of twenty-five individuals who represent a spectrum of opinions, including those of academics, postal savings depositors, postal life insurance policy-holders (such insurance is issued by the post office), and postal annuities owners.

Interest rates on postal savings and interest rates offered by private financial institutions are therefore determined quite separately. This separation may hinder the flexible operation of monetary policy, as has been pointed out for many years. This possible hindrance was addressed in a report to the Prime Minister by a special committee, the Consultative Committee Concerning the Role of the Public Sector in the Field of Finance (*Yucho Kon*), in August 1981. The Committee's report emphasized the necessity of creating a unified system for determination of deposit rates.

The result of the report was a tripartite agreement in September of the same year between the Minister of Posts and Telecommunications, the Minister of Finance, and the Director of the Cabinet Secretariat. The agreement stated that 'in cases of determination or changes of interest rates on deposits of private financial institutions, the Ministries of Posts and Telecommunications and of Finance would seek a mutual understanding concerning determination or changes of postal savings rates and would respond flexibly with due consideration to conformity'. This tripartite agreement was approved by the

Cabinet. The agreement was reaffirmed in the final report of March 1983 by the Temporary Investigative Committee on Administrative Reform. This latter report stated that 'concerning interest rate policy, it is thought necessary to create a system under which all deposit interest rates are determined in a unified fashion, but the Government will for the moment give due consideration to flexible and elastic interest rate policies based on the tripartitie agreement'.

Despite the agreement and the reports, however, there were difficulties at the time of the cut in the official discount rate in October 1983. The problems related to an improvement in the commercial attractiveness of the fixed amount postal savings deposits. Determining the cut in the deposit and savings interest rates took longer than ever before. In November 1983, after this event, the Interest Adjustment Council expressed its deepest regret about the occurrence of such events to the Policy Board of the Bank of Japan. It made a representation to the Policy Board that the spirit of the tripartite agreement and of the Temporary Committee on Administrative Reform be carried through, and that the responsible authorities take appropriate measures in order to facilitate unified determination of interest rates. The Ministry of Posts and Telecommunications replied to this representation by stating that each institution should set its own interest rates in order to reflect market conditions as the liberalization of interest rates progressed; this was the natural means of setting interest rates, and unification of interest rates with the goal of having postal deposit rates follow the private-sector rates would run counter to true liberalization. The Bank of Japan issued a strong rebuttal to the Ministry of Posts and Telecommunications. According to the Bank of Japan, once interest rates are liberalized, a single interest rate formed through the market mechanism should apply to similar types of deposits according to financial market conditions. Because of the non-profit nature of the postal savings system, it was difficult to say that the interest rates decided by the postal system in fact reflected market conditions. Hence it was a necessity to unify the determination of interest rates in the sense of setting postal rates on the basis of private-sector rates and thus preserving equilibrium between the public and private systems. This was true at the time and would remain true after the liberalization of interest rates. (The Bank of Japan's report was issued in December 1983 and was entitled 'The State of Deposit and Savings Interest Rates'.) The Ministry of Posts and Telecommunications responded once again in August 1984 in a report entitled 'The Liberalization of Deposit and Savings Interest Rates'. This report stated that a liberalization of deposit rates for small deposits was essential and that, in the transition period to such liberalization, creation of deposits with interest rates linked to market rates was under consideration.

(3) Dividend rates on trusts.   The dividend rates on money in trusts and on loan trusts offered by trust banks (these are the anticipated dividend rates) have been excluded from the Notification based on TIRAL since April 1961, though before that time the rates on money in trusts were included under that Notification. In theory, each institution voluntarily determines its own rates but in fact there is an implicit rule among the banks and other concerned parties on unified rates that take into consideration a balance with such other interest rates as those on deposits and the interest rates on bonds.

(4) Interest rates on bonds.[6]   With the exception of certain types of bonds such as medium-term Government coupon bonds, the subscribers' yield (issue terms) on new bonds are determined by the issuer or the underwriter, in consultation with the concerned parties and on the basis of market conditions. The specific mechanism differs by type of bond. For long-term Government coupon bonds, the issue terms are decided by the long-term Government bond facilitation committee (*sewanin kai*), which consists of the Ministry of Finance, the Bank of Japan, and representatives of the underwriting syndicate. This committee consults every month concerning the quantity of bonds to be issued and the issue terms for that month. For medium-term Government coupon bonds, which began issue in 1978, issue terms are set through a public auction system. For corporate bonds, the issue terms are determined with reference to discussions in the Bond Issue Committee (*Kisaikai*), with consideration of the opinions of the public authorities. (The actual terms for a particular issue are determined by one of the major securities companies considering a rating for the bond; the other securities companies will follow these terms.) For Government-guaranteed bonds, public subscription local government bonds, and bank debentures, the issue terms are determined by the issuer setting a balance between these terms and other long-term interest rates.

The above shows that in theory the issue terms for new bonds are determined voluntarily; but in fact they are determined within rather narrow limits that give consideration to balance with other interest rates. *De facto*, therefore, issue terms are mostly regulated rates, even though there is no legal basis for this. It remains true, however, that the ways of determining these interest rates change between the high economic growth period and the period since 1975.

During the high economic growth period, until 1975, it was viewed as most important to have an interest rate structure which reflected differences in the certainty of repayment and liquidity of the various types of long-term bonds. (The factors included the length of the period until repayment and the convertibility of the securities into money.) Long-term Government bonds had the lowest interest rates, followed by Government-guaranteed bonds,

[6] Each type of bond has two relevant yields—the yield to subscribers and the yield in the secondary market. The secondary market yields are free interest rates and will be treated below.

TABLE 4.6 *Major Liberalization Measures in Short-term Markets*

	Interbank markets	Open markets	Other
1976		March: Official recognition of *gensaki* transactions	
1977			April to October: Measures to make national Government bonds more liquid
1978	June: First set of market flexibility measures: Relaxation of the quotation for the call rate Permission for resale of bills one month after purchase (at free rate) October–November: Second set of market flexibility measures: Creation of 7-day call loans at free rate Creation of 1-month bills at free rate Liberalization of rates on over-three-month-ends bills		June: Issue of medium-term Government bonds through bidding; BOJ starts bid-based market operations in Government bonds
b 1979	April: Third set of market flexibility measures: Abolition of quotation system for the call rate (call rate liberalization) Creation of 2- to 6-day call loans October: Fourth set of market flexibility measures: Liberalization of rate on over two-month-ends bills	May: Start of CD transactions Liberalization of non-resident participation in *gensaki* transactions	February: All restrictions on non-resident acquisition of domestic securities lifted June: Permission for short-term impact loans among Japanese foreign exchange banks December: Permission for selection of either 'cost or market' methods or cost method
1980	May: Fifth set of market flexibility measures: Change of pricing system from over-the-month to fixed-date contracts November: Permission for large securities companies to borrow in the call market	April: Permission for city banks to be sellers (i.e. borrowers) in *gensaki* transactions	January: First sales of medium-term bond funds (*chukoku*) March: Liberalization of interest rates on yen deposits of foreign public entities December: Implementation of revised FEFTCL; liberalization of foreign currency deposits of residents and of impact loans to residents
b 1981	December: Permission for medium sized securities companies to borrow in the call market (and expansion of borrowing limits for large securities companies)	April: Permission for city banks to be buyers (lenders) in *gensaki* transactions May: Start of BOJ sale of Government bills in the market	

TABLE 4.6

	Interbank markets	Open markets	Other
b 1982			April: Implementation of the revised Banking Law and of the revised Securities and Exchange Law
b 1983			April: First over-the-counter sales of long-term Government bonds June: Abolition of prohibition on short-term Euro-yen loans to non-residents October: First over-the-counter sales of medium-term Government bonds
b 1984	June: Abolition of regulations on conversion of foreign funds into yen	January: Reduction of minimum CD denomination from ¥500m. to ¥300m. December: Abolition of prohibition on Euro-yen CD issue	April: First transactions in foreign CDs and commercial paper June: Start of dealing in public bonds by financial institutions; liberalization of short-term Euro-yen lending to residents; BOJ starts small-lot, flexible operations in Government bonds
b 1985	June: Creation of 5–6 month bill transactions July: Start of uncollateralized call transactions August: Creation of 2–3 week call transactions	April: Reduction of minimum CD denomination from ¥300m. to ¥100m., and shortening of allowable maturity from 3 months to 1 month June: Creation of the yen BA market; entry of securities companies into the secondary market for CDs	March: First issue of money market certificates April: Abolition of prohibition on medium- and long-term Euro-yen lending to non-residents June: Expansion of public bond dealing by financial institutions (more institutions and types of issues) August: First sales of large-scale public bond investment trusts October: Interest rate liberalization on large-scale (¥1b. or more) deposits
b 1986		January: BOJ starts repurchase agreements in Government bills (so-called TB *gensaki*) February: Issue of short-term Government bonds by bidding April: Lengthening of allowable maturity for CDs from 6 months to 1 year	April: Lengthening of maximum allowable maturity of MMCs from 6 months to 1 year; reduction in minimum size of large-scale deposits from ¥1b. to ¥500m.

local government bonds, and bank debentures, with corporate bonds having the highest interest rates. As a result, the issue terms for new bonds were rather inflexible, and also were determined at levels rather below the secondary market yields, particularly in periods of monetary tightness. It was possible to an extent to separate the issue terms for new bonds from secondary market fields because the scale of the secondary market was so small in comparison with that of the primary market.

The basis for this separation was undermined after 1975. The open secondary market grew tremendously, with Government bonds as the most active issues, because of the large-scale flotations of such bonds and the expansion of excess investible funds in the hands of corporations. Moreover, in 1978, three-year medium-term Government coupon bonds were introduced, which were issued through public auction. In addition, the Bank of Japan switched from a bid system to an auction system for its purchases of Government bonds. It therefore became increasingly difficult to maintain the independence of the terms of issue for new bonds from the demand and supply conditions in the secondary markets, and thus to maintain the interest rate structure of the high growth period. This structure was first violated in fact in March 1979, when the subscribers' yield on ten-year Government bonds was set above that for five-year bank debentures. In March 1983, the subscribers' yields for Government bonds were set above even those of corporate bonds. Thus, even though the issue terms for bonds are regulated in a broad sense, they now reflect the market environment at the time of issue.

For short-term Government bills, the Law Concerning Government Bonds states that the Minister of Finance will determine their terms of issue (that is, their discount rate) 'while considering the financial conditions of the time'. In fact, these issue terms are moved in parallel with the official discount rate, but their level is unrelated to the short-term financial markets and the rates are held below the official discount rate.

c. Free interest rates

(i) Interest rates in the short-term financial markets

There are two types of interest rate in the short-term financial markets, the interbank rates (such as the call and the bill rates) and the open-market rates (such as the CD rate and the *gensaki* rate). Both of these types, however, are free rates, and are determined through the interaction of demand and supply in the markets. Even in the short-term financial markets, the rates have become more flexible since 1975, with the implementation of measures of liberalization (see Table 4.6). They now reflect better the stance of monetary policy of the Bank of Japan and the trends of demand and supply of funds.

Liberalization in the interbank market was carried out in steps through the late 1970s. In June 1978, the agreement of market participants was obtained in order to change the quotation system for call and commercial bill rates to one which better reflected the market conditions. This change was implemented, and free-rate call loans of seven days' maturity were established in October 1978. In April 1979, a wide variety of fixed-date transactions of less than seven days were permitted, and the quotation system for call rates was completely abolished. Similar liberalizations occurred in the bill market. In June 1978, both the resale of bills of over one month's outstanding maturity and the interest rates on them were liberalized; in November 1978, free-rate bills of one month's maturity were created, and the interest rates on over three month-end bills (bills whose maturities cross three month-ends) and over four month-end bills were liberalized; in October 1979 the quotation system for over two month-end bills was abolished, and through this the interest rate liberalization in both the call and the bill markets was completed. Since 1980, the regulations on participation and transactions have been eased, for example through the permission for city banks to lend call funds and permission for securities companies to borrow them.

In open markets, the first step in the liberalization process was the start of issue of certificates of deposit (CDs) with free interest rates in May 1979. Diversification and expansion of the market for free-rate instruments continued thereafter, with liberalization of interest rates on yen-denominated deposits held by foreign public institutions in May 1980, abolition of holding limits on free-rate foreign currency deposits by residents in December 1980, sales of Government bills in the market by the Bank of Japan in May 1981, and liberalization of the minimum size of CD and the maturities of such issues in January 1984, April 1985, and April 1986. In parallel with these developments, the regulations on city bank participation in *gensaki* markets were eased, with the abolition of the sales limits in April 1980 and the granting of permission for purchases in April 1981. In addition, the issue limits for CDs were expanded in steps after April 1980.

The characteristics of the financial markets changed after such liberalization measures [3]. First, functioning of the call and bill markets became extremely smooth after the liberalization of the interest rates, even in times when there were sudden changes in expectations in the markets. Under the quotation system prior to these liberalizations, the quoted rate was established through an agreement between the major lenders (such as the financial institutions for agriculture, forestry, and fishery) and the major borrowers (the city banks). As a result, changes in the quoted rate were prone to a lack of flexibility, and the actual rates seemed not to reflect the day-to-day changes in demand and supply for funds. Particularly in cases when the expected interest rates were subject to rapid change, there were situations in which it was difficult for the market to clear. However, after liberalization, rate changes have occurred every day and have reflected even minor changes in demand and supply conditions and in expectations.

The second major change in the character of short-term markets has been the more elastic yield curve of interbank interest rates. Under the quotation system, the relatively long-term bill rate was always higher than the shorter call rates, but after liberalization the yield curve came to reflect the expected interest rates of market participants. And from time to time there have occurred cases when the bill rate was below the call rate.

Thirdly, there was an increase in interest rate arbitrage both between the interbank markets and the open markets and within the open markets. As a result, the tendency towards coherence among interest rates in various markets increased, and there ceased to be large deviations. As a result (and as will be described below), the policy-induced interest rate effects in the interbank markets flowed very quickly into the open markets. And because of the very large growth of the open markets, interest rate formation in the interbank markets came to be affected by conditions in the open markets.

And finally, very clear interest rate arbitrage relationships developed between foreign financial markets and domestic ones. The nearly perfect international interest rate arbitrage came about because of the liberalization of foreign exchange transactions accompanying the amendment of FEFTCL in 1980, and because of the abolition of regulations on conversion of foreign funds into yen based on the report of the Japan–US Yen–Dollar Committee in 1984. Since these liberalizations, there has been a stronger relationship of parallelism between domestic short-term money market rates and Euro-yen rates.

(ii) Lending rates of private financial institutions

As seen above, the long-term and short-term prime rates for lending by private financial institutions are in fact part of the regulated interest rate structure; but lending rates for general loans by these institutions are freely determined within the upper bounds set by TIRAL. Hence there is a significant amount of arbitrage between the lending rates on one hand and the short-term money market rates and secondary bond market yields on the other [31].

At first glance, the levels of loan rates appear in general to be lower than the other free interest rates in the financial markets. But, in fact, compensating balances raise the effective rates of interest on loans. Lending rates that are adjusted for the effects of compensating balances are called effective loan rates. Business decisions concerning interest rate levels include consideration of many general and longer-term factors, such as the average levels of compensating deposits, foreign exchange fees, collateral, and the long-term customer relationships of the borrowers with the banks. The types of compensating balances are not restricted to those forced through clear provisions in contracts such as *buzumi* and *ryodate* deposits[7]; the motivation for such

---

[7] *Buzumi* and *ryodate* are compensating deposits which must retain a part of the amount lent at the time of lending.

deposits may be seen as the result of voluntary rational behaviour on the part of the borrower from the viewpoint of a long-term customer relationship [52]. Moreover, practices have changed over time. Even the *buzumi* and *ryodate* deposits have been on a downward trend; according to calculations of the Fair Trade Commission, which measured the ratio of non-voluntary deposits to total loans, the proportion of such deposits fell from 16·9 per cent in May 1974 to 7·4 per cent in May 1985. But voluntary compensating deposits have also been falling, because corporations have been able to lower them in view of the higher levels of corporate liquidity and the increased financial power of firms. This was particularly true in the last half of the 1970s during a major round of corporate cost-cutting. Thus, the divergence between nominal loan rates and effective loan rates is not so large at present as it was during the high growth period.

(iii) Deposit and savings rates at private financial institutions

While most of the deposit and savings interest rates at private financial institutions remain regulated rates, some are being liberalized as part of the overall trend of changes. The first such interest rates to be liberalized were those on large-scale deposits.

The types of deposit and savings rate to which the regulations of TIRAL do not apply are determined by the Ministry of Finance. At present, the following types of deposit or savings deposit have been liberalized: interest rates on CDs, interest rates on the non-resident yen account deposits of foreign governments, foreign central banks, and international institutions, and interest rates on foreign currency-denominated deposits. In October 1985, very large-scale time deposits were also liberalized; this applied to deposits of between three months and two years, with a lower limit on such deposits of ¥1 milliard; this lower limit was reduced to ¥500m. from April 1986 (see Chapter 3). The interest rates on all of these free rate assets are determined through bilateral negotiation between the issuing financial institution and the depositor on a case-by-case basis, but there are important interest rate arbitrage relationships between these interest rates and those in short-term money markets. For example, the interest rates on CDs are strongly influenced by the rates on *gensaki*'s and the bill market rates, while interest rates on foreign currency deposits are strongly influenced by Euro-market rates.

The interest rates on money market certificates (MMCs), which were introduced in March 1985, do fall within the regulation of TIRAL, but the upper limit on rates for these deposits differs from that for general deposits. As explained in Chapter 3, the interest rates on MMCs are set at the average CD issue rate minus 0·75 per cent, and hence are not actually regulated rates.

With respect to small-scale deposits, the Government published a clear statement of policy in July 1985 entitled 'Outlines of an Action Programme to Improve Access to Markets'. This document stated that liberalization of small-scale deposits would be promoted in the wake of that of larger-scale deposits, on the basis of consideration at the earliest possible time of the concrete problems of such liberalization, which included protection of depositors and maintaining an overall balance with the postal savings system.

(iv) Interest rates on bonds

Although the issue terms for most bonds are part of the regulated interest rate structure, the issue terms for some bonds have been liberalized. For medium-term Government interest-bearing bonds, a public tender formula was adopted in 1978 when the issue of such bonds began, in order to facilitate their issue. In the original auctions, the buyers would bid on the overall yield for the securities; but since August 1979, the coupon rate on the bonds has been set prior to the auction, and the buyers have bid on the price.

Unlike the issue terms for new bonds, the secondary market yields on outstanding bonds are formed in the long-term open markets, and change in response to conditions of demand and supply. This was largely true earlier, but was extended by the formation of the huge secondary market in Government bonds and the easing of regulations concerning sale of Government bonds held by banks (which was done in order to facilitate the absorption of new issues). The most interesting facet of recent developments in the secondary markets is the strenthened influence on the formation of secondary market bond yields brought by the internationalization and liberalization of securities markets and the extension of trading in securities by banks [15].

Foreign developments also have important influence on the determination of secondary bond yields in Japan. The relaxation of regulations after the revision of FEFTCL in 1980 brought a huge increase in foreign investment by residents, much more flotation of securities in foreign markets by residents, steady increases in the flotation of yen-denominated bonds by foreigners, and much greater investment in Japanese markets by non-residents. In addition, the attitudes of domestic banks toward investment in securities markets became more active because of approval for over-the-counter sale and dealing in public bonds by banks after 1983 and because of the difficulties of lending in the market. The increased liveliness of fund transfers between domestic and foreign securities markets has worked toward strengthening the influence of foreign interest rate movements on the formation of secondary market yields in the domestic securities markets. For example, after the summer of 1984 the stance of monetary policy in the United States eased because of the slow-down in the tempo of expansion in the American economy and in the growth rate of the money supply; as a result, both long- and short-term interest rates in the United States fell. Lower interest rates in the United States in turn lowered secondary bond yields in Japan. These effects were accelerated by the expectations of lower domestic short-term rates accompanying the fall of American rates and the resulting upswing in the bond market. In turn, financial institutions became more active in bond investment and further accelerated the decline of secondary market bond yields [8].

2. PRESSURE AGAINST MAINTENANCE OF THE REGULATED INTEREST RATE STRUCTURE

In view of the discussion above concerning the formation of interest rates and how these processes of formation have changed, it would be fair to say that there has been a liberalization and movement toward more flexibility in the determination of interest rates since 1975. We shall next consider how this liberalization and move toward flexibility has affected the relationships among interest rates.

There are very close relationships between both the levels and the movements of interest rates. For regulated rates, these relationships were known during the high growth period as the 'structure of regulated interest rate'. This structure was viewed as extremely important for the determination of these interest rates by the regulatory authorities and by the parties in the market-place. The structure of regulated interest rates had no basis in law, but did have a basis in three implicit rules. Rule 1 was that long-term assets and liabilities of low liquidity should always have higher interest rates than short-term assets and liabilities of high liquidity. Rule 2 was that it was normal for the yields of bonds of issuers with high creditworthiness to be lower than those of issuers with low creditworthiness. Rule 3 was that a stable margin should be maintained between the cost of raising funds for financial institutions and the interest rates on their provision of funds. These rules had a very close relationship to the predominance of indirect financing and over-borrowing during the high growth period. The system of the regulated interest rate structure, which had the official discount rate as its corner-stone, functioned smoothly, at least until the middle of the 1970s.

But free-rate markets both expanded and diversified in the wake of the changes in money flows after the first oil crisis and the progress toward financial internationalization after the move to floating exchange rates. With the expansion of markets in free-rate assets, relationships were formed among the interest rates on these assets, and sharp contradictions began to occur between the open-market interest rates and those of the regulated interest rate structure. This was particularly true during periods of monetary tightness, and had important effects on the structure of regulated interest rates.

After about 1975, with the expansion of open markets for both short- and long-term assets, there developed in the open markets a clear yield curve, that is, a relationship between the maturity and the yields of assets. This yield curve for free-market assets came to influence the structure of regulated interest rates, including short-term ones [28], [29], [30].

The yield curve implied by the structure of regulated interest rates was always upward-sloping (see Figure 4.2). As a result, in the final phase of monetary tightness, when expectations of falling interest rates were common,

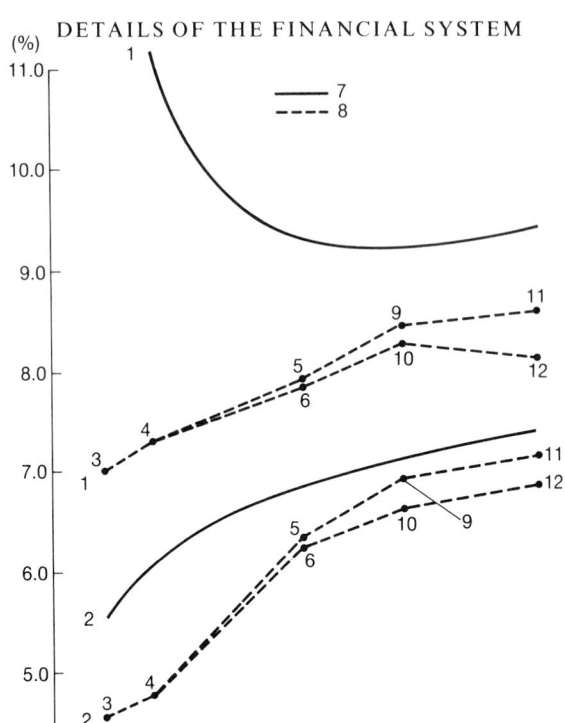

Figure 4.2 *Yield Curves for Outstanding Government Bonds and for Regulated Interest Rates (in percent) – March, 1979 (easy-money period) and March, 1980 (tight-money period) –*

1. March 1980
2. March 1979
3. 1-year time deposit
4. 2-year time deposit
5. 5-year loan trust
6. 5-year bank debenture
7. Yields on outstanding Government bonds (representing free interest rates)
8. Regulated rates
9. 7-year B-rated industrial bond
10. 7-year AA-rated industrial bond
11. 10-year B-rated industrial bond
12. 10-year Government bond
13. years to maturity

the upward-sloping yield curve of regulated interest rates was entirely different from the downward-sloping yield curve of free interest rates. This phenomenon first occurred after the second oil crisis in 1979 during the period of monetary tightness. Looking at the yield curve for long-term Government bonds in the secondary market, one saw not only that it shifted upwards as the tightness of monetary policy spread, but that its shape shifted from upward-sloping to downward-sloping after the middle of the year. In contrast, the yield curve formed by deposit rates, trust rates, and the issue terms on bank debentures and public bonds remained upward-sloping as usual under the structure of regulated interest rates. As a result of the differences, there was a shift of funds from regulated-rate assets into free-rate assets, such as *gensakis*, medium-term Government coupon bonds, and outstanding long-term Government coupon bonds, particularly at the shorter maturities. And even among assets with regulated interest rates, those with longer maturities and higher interest rates (such as fixed-amount postal savings that one could keep at high interest rates for as long as ten years, five-year loan trusts, or bank debentures) were preferred to shorter-term assets such as bank deposits with a maximum maturity of two years [41].

The shift of funds from regulated-rate assets to free-rate assets and from short-term assets to long-term assets within regulated-rate assets meant nothing other than disintermediation, i.e., a decline in the ability of deposit banks to attract funds. As a result, the banks were no longer able to continue relying on the regulated rates which had until then stabilized their business climate. They had no choice but to ease, even if only partially, the regulation of deposit interest rates and to supply to depositors new types of deposit that guaranteed higher yields. Large-denomination CDs with free interest rates were introduced in 1979, and the upper limit of ¥3m. equivalent for foreign currency deposits under free rates was abolished at the time of the revision of FEFTCL in 1980. Also in 1980, the securities companies introduced the medium-term Government bond funds, and when these began to attract smaller deposits from small businesses and individuals, there occurred a gradual relaxation of the regulations on minimum sizes and maturities of CDs in banks. In 1985, MMCs were introduced, which were of a smaller denomination than CDs but had interest rates which moved in parallel. In the same year, there was a liberalization of the interest rates on large-scale time deposits, and there is an expectation that the minimum denominations for large-scale time deposits will be lowered. The pressure put on financial institutions by the regulation of interest rates was one reason for changes in the structure of regulated rates, and was an important influence and contributor to liberalization of interest rates [13].

Nor could the Government live in peace with regulated interest rates. When terms of issue for new Government bonds remained under regulation, there emerged large deviations between the secondary market yields on old Government bonds and the issue terms for new ones, due to the huge expansion of the secondary market in Government bonds. (Under the regulated-rate structure, it was common for the regulated interest rate at a given maturity to be below the free rate at that maturity.) Under these circumstances, the absorption of large-scale issues of Government bonds could not be smooth. For example, the syndicate refused to underwrite Government bond issues on several occasions during 1981, 1982, and 1983, and no bonds were issued during several months in these years. As a result, the issue terms for Government bonds gradually became more flexible, i.e., came to reflect market conditions better, and the long-term interest rate structure—in which Government bonds always had lower subscribers' yields than bank debentures or corporate debentures—began to crumble.

The trend toward more flexibility in the lending rates of banks also became stronger. Effective loan rates were made relatively flexible by changing the volume of compensating balances and the number of borrowers applying the prime rate. On the other hand, it is difficult to deny that there remain constraints on the flexible movement of nominal loan rates due to the existence of the prime rates. With the partial relaxation of regulation of deposit interest rates, however, the fund-raising costs of banks became more flexible, and thus the banks, at least to the extent that they raised short-term funds and lent long-term funds, began to bear a much larger risk of interest rate movements. In order to reduce the risks of interest rate movement, the banks had either to hedge the risks through carrying out swap transactions in the interest rate futures markets or to seek more flexibility in the interest rates that they earned on the asset side of their balance sheets. Loan rates are also more influenced by international factors because of increased competition from foreign funds in the lending market. Two such factors were the increase in foreign currency impact loans after 1979 and the introduction of short-term Euro-yen impact loans to residents after their liberalization in 1984 [7].

Because of these circumstances, there has been a trend for interest rates on current overdrafts and spot loans to be determined less by the prime rate and more by the spread method, in which a margin is applied over and above the interest rates of the short-term markets. For loans to large trading companies, the nominal interest rates on loans may still be based on the prime rates, but in fact the loans are flexible-rate loans based on the bill rate, with the flexibility achieved through changes in compensating deposits.

5

Financial Institutions

I. General framework

1. CLASSIFICATION OF FINANCIAL INSTITUTIONS

J A P A N 's financial institutions may be classified into seven categories according to their main types of business[1] (1) Commercial banks focus on short-term finance as their main area of business; this category includes city banks, regional banks, and foreign banks resident in Japan. (2) Financial institutions for long-term credit concentrate chiefly on the supply of long-term funds for industry; this category includes long-term credit banks, trust banks, and similar institutions. (3) Specialized foreign exchange banks focus on foreign exchange and trade finance as their main area of business; this category includes only one bank, the Bank of Tokyo. (4) Financial institutions for small businesses concentrate on lending to such businesses; this category includes such institutions as *sogo* banks, *shinkin* banks, credit co-operatives, labour credit associations, the *Shokochukin* Bank, and similar institutions. (5) Financial institutions for agriculture, forestry, and fishery concentrate on financing agricultural activities and others; this category includes such institutions as the *Norinchukin* Bank, agricultural co-operatives, and fishery co-operatives. All of the above are private sector financial intermediaries. (6) Securities companies concentrate on operations in the securities markets. (7) Augmenting the functions of private financial intermediaries is a group of Government financial institutions such as the Japan Development Bank and the Export–Import Bank of Japan, and others.

This categorization is not so much functional as historical, based on the establishment of various types of financial institution since the Meiji period under the general framework of the English type of commericial banking system. That is to say, ordinary banks were born first, followed by the special financial institutions for various branches of industry; after this, institutions for small businesses and those for trust businesses came under the jurisdiction of the authorities [4], [9]. Viewed in the light of this history of development financial institutions, the distinctions become more meaningful.

But one need not categorize the financial institutions of today by merely historical criteria; a categorization based on theoretical concepts is possible,

[1] The Bank of Japan, the nation's central bank, is excluded from this system of classification.

and would separate financial institutions in general terms into two types according to whether they act as intermediaries. The first type will be called financial intermediaries and the second other financial institutions.

A financial intermediary is one which transfers funds from the ultimate lender to the ultimate borrower by means of issuing indirect securities such as deposit certificates, bank debentures, trust certificates, or insurance certificates to the ultimate lenders and then purchasing primary securities such as loan certificates or bills from the ultimate borrower. The various types of financial institution that issue indirect securities, beginning with commercial banks, belong to this category. In contrast, other financial institutions are those which sell the primary securities issued by the ultimate borrowers to the ultimate lenders. Securities companies and money market dealers belong to this category.

Financial intermediaries may be further subdivided according to whether the indirect securities they issue may be called deposits. The deposit-issuing institutions are called 'depository institutions' and the others 'non-depository institutions'. It is common to call the depository institutions that handle demand deposits and that create deposit money 'banks'.[2] So defined, banks play an important role in the financial system as the suppliers of deposit money (which is a means of payment), as operators of the institutions for settling payments, and as media for the transmission of policy effects through their relationship to monetary policy.

2. THE FINANCIAL INSTITUTIONS OF JAPAN

According to the functional taxonomy given above, the financial institutions of Japan today may be classified and organized as in Figure 5.1, although the financial liberalizations of recent years and the intensification of competition among financial institutions have brought major changes to virtually all. These changes include diversification, internationalization, and mechanization of their lines of business. Because of these changes it is difficult to grasp the dynamics of the structure of financial institutions, and therefore a little extra explanation is in order.

The private financial institutions that have played the essential role in the historical development of the Japanese financial system have been depository institutions. Among these depository institutions are city banks, regional banks, resident foreign banks along with long-term credit banks, trust banks (the banking accounts thereof), *sogo* banks, *shinkin* banks, credit co-operatives, labour credit associations, the *Shokochukin* Bank, and the financial

---

[2] Under the Banking Law, a Bank is defined as an incorporated financial institution that operates in the banking business once having received a licence from the Minister of Finance. The banking business is defined as the joint operation of taking either deposits or instalment savings and making loans or discounting bills, and carrying out domestic exchange transactions (according to Clause 2 of the Law). This notion of the bank according to the Banking Law as a financial intermediary that simultaneously borrows and lends is nearly identical to the concept of a bank under the functional classification scheme given above.

institutions for agriculture, forestry, and fishery. The Japanese system is slightly different from that of other countries because of the nature of ordinary banks. Even though ordinary banks (city banks and regional banks) are established in principle as commercial banks, their means of raising funds are somewhat longer-term than that of commercial banks, while on the asset side they are very active in making medium- and long-term loans; a small portion even have trust accounts. Thus, ordinary banks serve the function not only of credit creation but also of credit intermediation, and thus they cannot be called commercial banks in the pure sense of the word but rather must be called mixed banks. On the other hand, among the types of business of long-term credit banks, which are not ordinary banks, are not only the use of bank debentures as the main method of raising funds but also the acceptance of demand deposits. Other depository institutions also accept demand deposits. To this extent, the long-term credit banks and others have the same role as creators of credit as do ordinary banks.

Thus it is difficult to make very precise distinction in a functional sense among the depository institutions. But through the lengthy period of high economic growth, a distinction was made based on law and custom between the city banks, which serve the short-term financing needs of large corporations, and the regional banks and other specialized financial institutions, such as *sogo* banks and *shinkin* banks, which played the major role in financing small businesses. In different dimension, there were two other types of institution, the long-term credit banks and trust banks, which catered for the medium- and long-term financial needs, and the financial institutions for agriculture, forestry, and fishery, which served the agricultural sector, etc., under the general organizational structure of the *Norinchukin* Bank.

After 1975, the distinctions became even harder to make. There was an intensification of competition as the environment surrounding financial institutions changed with the reduction in the funds deficit of the corporate sector. That is, each type of financial institution began to invade the turf of others. Diversification of business, including internationalization and business links in other areas, became the basis for activity, as institutions sought stable profits and a stronger business base.

For example, the ordinary banks in Japan, and particularly city banks, have for many years participated as mixed banks in both short- and long-term finance. But in recent years they have put extra effort into the longer-term end of the business, and have also taken a very aggressive stance in expanding into lending to small business and to individuals (for housing loans or consumer loans), both of which fields were formerly only marginal to them. As areas of business become similar among financial institutions, the meaning of the distinction between long- and short-term financial fields has been called into question, and there have even been calls for the complete conversion of *sogo* banks into ordinary banks.

One of the important parts of diversification of business has been the

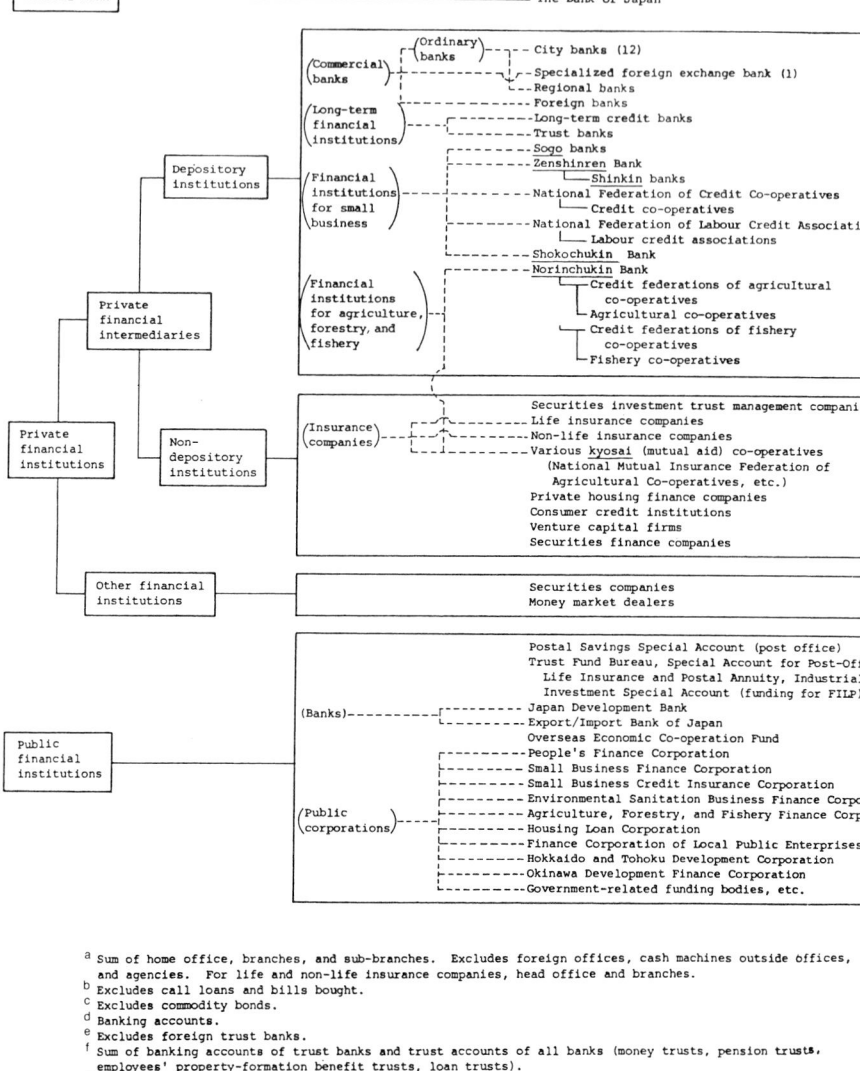

^a Sum of home office, branches, and sub-branches. Excludes foreign offices, cash machines outside offices, and agencies. For life and non-life insurance companies, head office and branches.
^b Excludes call loans and bills bought.
^c Excludes commodity bonds.
^d Banking accounts.
^e Excludes foreign trust banks.
^f Sum of banking accounts of trust banks and trust accounts of all banks (money trusts, pension trusts, employees' property-formation benefit trusts, loan trusts).
^{f'} Sum of banking accounts of trust banks and trust accounts of all banks.
^g Includes instalments.
^{g'} Includes mutual instalment loans.
^h Total net assets.
ⁱ Excludes foreign life insurance companies.

Sources: BOJ, <u>Economic Statistics Monthly</u>, etc.

Number of institutions	Number of business office [a]	Capital (or capitalization)	Deposits and debt issued	Loans outstanding [b]	Securities held [c]
13	3,059	12,091	1,282,185 [d]	1,234,712 [d]	221,017 [d]
64	6,907	6,885	907,333 [d]	708,535 [d]	194,058 [d]
77	114	-	17,116	48,883	5,158
3	64	2,821	345,015	285,248	85,577
7 [e]	363	2,467	666,857 [f]	370,726 [f]	324,909 [f]
69	4,279	1,900	375,486 [g]	305,887 [g]	60,383
1	17	200	57,573	17,546	26,700
456	7,090	2,679	501,844	365,419	83,300
1	12	41	14,819	8,003	7,375
448	2,835	1,429	125,764	95,692	13,256
1	1	150	11,123	559	8,702
47	600	531	49,082	25,244	11,670
1	95	1,913	89,611	80,307	12,802
1	38	450	187,374	97,261	92,391
47	240 (85/3)	2,010	290,134	38,860	101,323
4,286 (85/9)	15,491 (85/9)	9,117	397,221	125,383	20,414
35	124 (85/3)	204	15,474	8,204	459
1,753	2,125 (85/10)	1,458	15,528	10,896	289
11 [i]	11	47	199,722 [h]	-	-
23 [i]	16,652 (85/3)	143	504,885 [j]	242,123	180,775
23 [k]	3,896 (85/3)	3,081	102,422 [j]	24,009	52,781
48 [l]	48	422 (85/3)	101,986 [j]	27,714	57,640
8	148	122	-	50,431	-
n.a.	n.a.	n.a.	-	265,159 [m]	n.a.
3 [n]	3	177	-	387 [o]	-
3	9	63	-	17,311	73
212 [p]	2,281	4,574	-	29,495 [q]	3,840
6 [r]	12	14	189,748	193,039 [s']	186
1	23,654 (85/9)	-	987,467 (85/10)	4,728	-
3	-	-	-	1,304,037	571,359
1	10	2,339	67,122 [t]	76,092	240
1	2	9,673	46,618 [t]	57,467	658
1	1	16,092	18,055 [t]	32,915	-
1	152	260	51,085 [t]	51,124	1
1	59	312	50,661 [t]	53,862	333
1	1	3,948	-	3,165	-
1	1	10	6,669 [t]	6,582	229
1	22	1,682	50,733 [t]	51,466	1,189
1	14	972	244,610 [t]	245,752	47
1	1	124	95,145 [t]	93,540	1,283
1	4	330	8,354 [t]	8,683	155
1	6	275	7,356 [t]	7,764	86
13	-	-	-	81,122 (85/3)	-

[j] Operating assets.
[k] Excludes foreign non-life insurance companies.
[l] Sum of National Mutual Insurance Federation of agricultural co-operatives plus 47 prefectural mutual insurance federations of agricultural co-operatives.
[m] Figure for 1984, estimated by the Japan Consumer Credit Industry Association.
[n] Figure for small business investment companies.
[o] Outstanding investments.
[p] Excluding branches of foreign securities companies in Japan and saitori members who match the sell and buy orders placed by the regular members.
[q] Margin trading loans.
[r] Excludes foreign currency intermediators.
[s] Sum of call-money borrowing and bills sold.
[s'] Sum of call-money lending and bills bought.
[t] Sum of borrowings and securities (including external bonds).

Figure 5.1

expansion of international business. A specialized foreign exchange bank was established very early on to concentrate in the areas of foreign exchange and international finance, but the city banks have played a major role in these areas for many years already. Both the specialized foreign exchange bank and the city banks have taken a very aggressive posture in diversifying their types of international business by adding to the traditional functions of foreign exchange and trade finance. Among these new areas are international business such as syndicated loans and international securities operations. As a result, the share of the profits from international operations in total profits for the city banks has risen very rapidly and in the financial year 1984, for example, stood at about 20 per cent of total profits (specifically, the ratio is the gross operating profits from international operations to total gross operating profits). Internationalization has also been pursued strongly by long-term credit banks and trust banks, and other depository institutions are eager to catch up in the international fields with the city banks and to make such international operations one of the major areas in which they are diversifying.

The most important reasons for the growth of internationalization of the financial institutions' operations have been the major expansion and diversification of the needs of corporations for international and foreign exchange-related services because the international business of Japanese corporations has become more active. One cannot, however, overlook the fact that it has become easier for financial institutions to expand their international business because of changing conditions both at home and abroad, such as the huge growth of the Euromarkets and the liberalization in principle of foreign transactions under the revision of FEFTCL in December 1980.

But depository financial institutions are not the only ones to have expanded actively into new business. The non-depository institutions and the other financial institutions have done so as well. Among the non-depository financial institutions, those that have been active include trust banks (the trust accounts thereof), securities investment trust management companies, insurance companies, private housing finance companies, consumer credit institutions, small business investment companies (similar to venture capital firms), and securities finance companies. The first three of these issue indirect securities, i.e., trust certificates, investment trust beneficiary certificates, and insurance securities, respectively, but also compete more vigorously with depository institutions by creating new financial products in order to attract funds. The remainder of the institutions, such as private housing finance companies, raise funds through borrowing from other financial intermediaries and then concentrate on aggressive lending to consumers or other types of borrowers.

The class of 'other financial institutions' includes securities companies and money market dealers; securities companies in particular have been undermining the pre-eminent position of indirect finance through their role as the primary institutions in the securities market. The money market dealers, on the other hand, have become even more active in the interbank markets and have aggressively increased their new types of business such as the handling of the secondary market in CDs. Moreover, even firms in the retail industries, which are not financial institutions at all, have taken a more eager attitude towards entering financial activities through such instruments as loans to consumers, as one part of their package of services.

Even while the competition between the depository institutions, the non-depository institutions, and securities companies is becoming stronger, an interesting trend of recent years has been the joint development of new financial product through business associations between different types of institutions. For example, the *shinkin* banks and the securities companies have treated a new product that is a combination of an ordinary deposit and a medium-term Government bond fund. Another example is the new product provided together by banks and life insurance companies, which combines a maturity-designated time deposit with payment in a lump sum endowment insurance (for details see Chapter 3). Some constraints, such as units of transaction, still remain on such accounts, but they are important because they suggest the direction of development that will accompany financial liberalization in the future. These developments also make necessary a reconsideration of the state of the regulations that separate the banking business from the securities business.

Quite separate from private financial institutions is the other major characteristic of the Japanese financial system, the entrenched existence of public financial institutions.

The first of these is the postal savings system. Postal savings deposits are gathered through the network of post offices that is scattered throughout the country. Part of these deposits are lent directly, but the largest share is redeposited in the Trust Fund Bureau (*Shikin Unyo Bu*) of the Ministry of Finance. The Trust Fund Bureau takes the postal savings deposits and adds to them the surpluses from special Government accounts such as the Welfare Pensions and the National Pensions and uses the totality of these funds to finance its lending operations to Government financial institutions, public corporations, and local government organizations.

The Government financial institutions carry out the lending programme of the Government. The capital of these institutions comes entirely from funding by the Government, and the institutions are used to implement national policy such as industrial development (through the Japan Development Bank and the Hokkaido and Tohoku Development Corporation), foreign trade and economic co-operation (the Export–Import Bank of Japan and the Overseas Economic Co-operation Fund), construction of houses, (the Housing Loan Corporation), small business (the People's Finance Corporation, the Small Business Finance Corporation), agriculture (the Agriculture, Forestry, and Fishery Finance Co-operation), and others. Financing by these institutions is intended to supplement that of private financial institutions, and is carried out on the basis of the fiscal investment and loan programme (FILP). The post office provides further funding for FILP through another route, the postal life insurance and postal annuities system. These funds are not deposited in the Trust Fund Bureau but rather are the accumulations of the special Government account for postal life insurance and annuities; but, like funds that are deposited in the Trust Fund Bureau, they are used as a source of financing for FILP.

These public financial institutions were established gradually, with the idea that it was necessary to supplement the funding from private financial institutions when this funding was insufficient to achieve the goals of national economic policy. But since 1975, as the demand for funds in the private sector has weakened, there has developed a trend towards increasing competition between private and public financial institutions. On the deposit side, there was a shift of funds into the unique financial products, such as fixed-amount savings deposits, offered by the postal savings system, and on the lending side the Government financial institutions exceeded the boundary of their supplementary role in relation to private finance and began to compete with private financial institutions. As a result, the share of public financial intermediation in total intermediation rose from less than 20 per cent during the high growth period to just under 30 per cent [46]. Because of this rise, there have been calls for a reconsideration of the role of public financial institutions in the light of the significance they have acquired in the financial system and the fact that they are intended merely to supplement the role of private financial institutions. On the other hand, they have been a factor in prompting private financial institutions to develop new and revolutionary types of financial product.

II. Types of financial institutions

1. PRIVATE DEPOSITORY FINANCIAL INTERMEDIARIES

a. City banks and regional banks

(i) Overview

In Europe and the United States, the main pillar of the financial system is the commercial bank; in Japan, the commercial bank is called the ordinary bank or simply a bank, or to put it more accurately, a bank defined by the Banking Law. The commercial banks comprise the city banks and the regional banks. A bank has two functions. The first is to act as financial intermediary by accepting deposits from corporations and individuals and investing these funds either in loans or in securities; the second is to perform the function of supply of deposit money through dealing in demand deposits and thus to perform a function of settlement of payments. Banks also have an important influence over the direction of the economy through their credit creation function, i.e., the supply of deposit money that is many times the size of their cash reserves and that occurs in the course of their credit-granting activities. The banks' performances of these many functions makes them indeed the pillar of the financial system. As seen in the previous section, however, there are various financial intermediaries in Japan other than ordinary banks that deal in demand deposits, though at a very different degree of intensity. In this sense, these other financial intermediaries carry out banking business just as do ordinary banks; but here we will give an overview of the business of city banks and regional banks, i.e., ordinary banks, as the representative type of organization that carries out banking. In addition, in the explanation that follows, we will deal separately with the specialized foreign exchange bank that is usually considered as part of the category of city banks. First, let us provide a simple overview of the organization and special traits of each of the types of ordinary bank.

(1) City banks. City banks are banks that have their headquarters in a large metropolitan area and that have nationwide networks of many banking branches. As of the end of 1985, there were twelve city banks (excluding the Bank of Tokyo, with which we deal below). These were the *Daiichi Kangyo* Bank, the *Fugi* Bank, the *Sumitomo* Bank, the *Mitsubishi* Bank, the *Sanwa* Bank, the *Tokai* Bank, the *Taiyo Kobe* Bank, the *Mitsui* Bank, the *Kyowa* Bank, the *Daiwa* Bank, the *Saitama* Bank, and the *Hokkaido Takushoku* Bank.

These city banks have been at the centre of the private financial sector in Japan ever since the Meiji period. Even today, they hold 20 per cent of the total deposits of all financial institutions and 60 per cent of the deposits of all ordinary banks. They also provide about 20 per cent of the credit needs of private corporations, and thus have an extremely large influence on the national economy.

The lending of city banks goes in large part to large corporations. At the end of 1985, over 30 per cent of the total lendings of city banks were to corporations capitalized at over ¥1bn. On the deposit side, too, about 60 per cent of total deposits are corporate deposits, and 90 per cent of these are large-scale deposits of ¥10m. or more. But in recent years, banks have watched a declining trend in funds demand from large manufacturing corporations, and have put efforts into cultivating trade with small businesses and individuals. As of the end of 1985, the shares of total lending going to small businesses and to individuals were 40 per cent and 10 per cent respectively at the end of 1975. In addition, there has been a conspicuous increase in international operations and securities operations of city banks, and they have taken an aggressive attitude toward mechanization of their operations.

The funding position of city banks has been one of a net deficit throughout the post-war period, as explained in Chapter 1. This deficit has been financed through borrowing from the Bank of Japan and through raising funds through the short-term financial markets, such as call money borrowing or sale of bills.

(2) Regional banks. Regional banks are banks that have their head offices in large or medium-sized cities throughout the country and carry on most of their business in the prefecture in which the head office is located. Like city banks, they are organized as corporations, and at the end of 1985 there were sixty-four such banks. Among regional banks, there are several that are almost equal in size to some of the city banks, but the largest majority of the regional banks are of medium and small size. The main borrowers from regional banks are small- and medium-sized firms in the area in which the bank is located, and more than one half of regional bank lendings are to firms with under ¥100m. in capital. Over half of the regional banks' deposits are from individuals and about 80 per cent are time deposits, almost all of which are of one year or more in maturity. Because regional banks have such a high share of stable deposits from individuals and because their main lending is to local corporations in the area of their business, they have a relatively easy funds position compared to city banks. As a result of this good funds position, they have a high ratio of securities holdings and are among the most important lenders in the call and bill markets. There are very few regional banks that are chronic borrowers from the Bank of Japan on the bill market.

Like city banks, regional banks have also been undergoing a diversification of their operations in recent years, but with respect to international operations they have been late, relative to city banks, in establishing foreign points of business. As a result, their international operations centre on trade financing, and exchange transactions that depend on correspondent relationships.

(3) Specialized foreign exchange banks. Specialized foreign exchange banks are banks that are established under the Foreign Exchange Bank Law of 1954 and that have as their main line of business foreign exchange transactions and foreign trade transactions. Currently there is only one such bank, the Bank of Tokyo. It is organized as a corporation and is a purely private financial institution. There is no qualitative difference between the trade and exchange transactions carried out by a specialized foreign exchange bank and those carried out by an authorized foreign exchange bank. The only differences are that the specialized foreign exchange bank centres its activity on trade and foreign exchange operations, that it gets some preferential treatment from the Government in deposit of the Government's foreign exchange balances and the approval of foreign branches, that its placement of domestic branches is limited to cities that are important for the purpose of carrying out trade and foreign exchange operations, and finally, that it does not make loans which are unrelated to trade or foreign exchange. In view of the

difficulties that this bank had in raising deposits, there was a revision of the law under which it is organized in 1962. This revision allowed the specialized foreign exchange bank to augment its raising of yen funds through the issue of debentures. Between 1962 and 1982, the limit on debenture issues was set at five times the total of capital and reserves, but, after 1982, a further revision of the law allowed total issue of up to ten times capital and reserves. The specialized foreign exchange bank is also permitted securities operations such as those that are permitted to ordinary banks, for example, over-the-counter sale of public bonds.

(4) Bankers' associations. The city banks (including the Bank of Tokyo) and the regional banks have formed, together with the long-term credit banks and trust banks described below, clearing houses and bankers' associations in each of the major cities, including Tokyo. They have also formed the Federation of Bankers' Associations of Japan as their nation-wide representative body. The regional banks also have their own individual organization on a national scale called the Regional Banks' Association of Japan (for descriptions of the clearing houses, see section 3 below).

The Federation of Bankers' Associations of Japan was formed in September 1945, and its members are the Banker's associations in each city. As the representative organization for the banking industry, it has carried out research on economics and finance, has facilitated communication between the Bankers' Associations and other economic groups, has communicated the desires or suggestions of the banks to the appropriate authorities, and has accomplished the undertakings that were necessary in order to achieve progress and improvement in a broad sense for the banking industry. In particular, it has carried out various activities relating to self-regulation by the banking industry, the most typical of which were self-restraint concerning compensating balances and the self-regulation of advertising. In earlier years, the Federation of Bankers' Associations of Japan was also the basis for the arrangements concerning setting the standard interest rate (the short-term prime rate) for the banks' short-term lending. However, these arrangements were abolished at the time of the discount rate cut of April 1975 because the view was strengthening that this arrangement was one of collusion, which might violate the Anti-Monopoly Law.

The Regional Banks Association of Japan carries on the tradition of a similar association that was formed in 1936, and thus has a longer history than the Federation of Bankers' Associations of Japan. In contrast to the latter, which is a confederation of the bankers' associations in each city, the Regional Banks Association of Japan is formed from individual regional banks and is a stronger organization, since the interests of the members clash less often. This association of regional banks carries out many activities, including the joint training of bank employees, the payment and receipt of public funds, joint underwriting of national Government bonds and

Government-guaranteed bonds, and active representation of its suggestions and desires to those concerned with such issues.

(ii) Operations

The New Banking Law that was implemented in 1982 establishes detailed provisions concerning the extent of operations in which banks may engage. According to the Banking Law, there are four types of operation in which banks may engage: first, exclusive operations such as taking deposits or instalment savings and making loans, discounting bills, or engaging in domestic exchange transactions (Clause 10, Section 1); second, auxiliary operations (Clause 10, section 2); third, securities operations (Clause 11); and fourth, other operations pursuant to laws (Clause 12).

For our purposes, however, a division of six types of operation is more convenient. These are: deposit operations, lending operations, domestic exchange operations, securities operations, international operations, and other operations such as auxiliary businesses and peripheral businesses.

(1) Deposit operations. Deposit operations are the most basic receiving operation of banks and for this reason were made the exclusive activity of banks, along with lending operations and domestic exchange operations.

Banks may accept as deposits either cash currency or cheques, bills, or other securities that can immediately be realized as funds through the clearing mechanism. There are no particular restraints on parties from whom banks may accept deposits, and in fact deposit transactions are carried out with individuals, corporations, foundations, organizations without juridical powers, and associations as defined under civil law. The types of deposit that banks accept are divided into two major categories, deposits with a prescribed term, which have a determined length of deposit, and demand deposits, which have no determined length of deposit and which may be withdrawn according to the request of the depositor. Deposits with a prescribed term include term deposits, instalment savings, and CDs, while demand deposits include current deposits, ordinary deposits, notice deposits, deposits for tax payments, and special deposits. Foreign currency deposits and non-resident yen deposits are conceptually identical to the other types of deposit but are separated from domestic yen deposits for purposes of statistical classification.

Except for current deposits and special-purpose deposits, interest is paid on deposit accounts. The interest rates paid on deposits must fall below the limits notified under the provisions of the Temporary Interest Rate Adjustment Law (TIRAL), the details of which are determined by guide-lines from the Bank of Japan that specify interest rates by the type of deposit concerned (of course, the guide-lines do not apply to free-rate deposits). In actual practice, the interest rates paid by the banks are identical to those in the guide-lines. As a result, there are no differences among banks on the interest rates paid on deposits. In fact, the deposit contract provisions used by each bank are created as models for each type of deposit by Federation of Bankers' Associations of Japan, and at least so far as the basic types of deposits mentioned above are concerned, these deposits are entirely uniform products across different banks.

In recent years, however, banks have responded to stronger demands from customers for high interest rates and have gone to great lengths in order to develop new types of deposits through tie-ups with other types of industry or through combining deposit accounts with Government bonds in some fashion. As a result, there has been a substantial diversification of the types of deposit offered in response to various needs, primarily of small depositors. There has also been a gradual approval of new types of financial product with free interest rates, i.e., those which fall outside the application of TIRAL. These are primarily for large investors, and include non-resident yen deposits that are held by foreign governments, central banks, and international institutions, all foreign currency deposits, CDs, and large fixed-term deposits of at least ¥500m. in size (for MMCs, the Minister of Finance notifies banks of the upper limit, but this upper limit moves with the interest rate on CDs). Looking slightly into the future, it seems likely that there will be a gradual expansion of the limits to which free interest deposits apply to include smaller and smaller deposits (for details see Chapter 3).

(2) Lending operations.   Lending operations are the central credit-granting operations of banks. There are two general types of lending, discount of bills and loans, and within loans there is a further subclassification of loans on bills, loans on deeds, and overdrafts. At the end of 1985, the respective shares of the types of lending in the total lending of ordinary banks was as follows: bill discounts, 14 per cent; loans on bills, 44 per cent; loans on deeds, 36 per cent; and overdrafts, 7 per cent.

Discount of bills. The discount of a bill is the purchase of an outstanding bill at its face value less fees and the amount of interest that will accrue up to the date of maturity. Most such loans are discounts of commercial bills.

A commercial bill is a bill issued for the purpose of settling the payment concerned in a commercial transaction, and usually is of about three months' maturity. Because these bills, by their nature, can be settled in short terms and with certainty through sale of the goods of the bill-payer, there are several names associated with a bill; in the event that the bill-payer cannot make settlement, such bills may be collected even from the discount guarantor who has endorsed the bill. The highest-quality commercial bills may be rediscounted with the Bank of Japan or may be used as collateral for a loan from the Central Bank.

In addition to commercial bills, other bills that a bank may discount include bankers' acceptances whose payments have been guaranteed by the bank and documentary drafts (also known as exchange bills, *nigawase tegata*), to which bills of lading or way-bills are attached as collateral. The former are considered to be particularly safe, but nevertheless, few of these types of bill are used except in foreign trade activities.

Loans on bills. Loans on bills are lendings of funds in the form of a discount of a bill by a bank; the bill in question is a promissory note issued with the borrower as the issuer and the bank as the payee (a promissory note is also known as a single name bill because there is only one name listed as the debtor on the bill).

Unlike discount of commercial bills in which the bill discounted is one based on a commercial transaction, the bills in question for loans on bills are issued for the purpose of borrowing from the bank. Loans on bills are used to supply working capital to corporations and are usually of three to four months' maturity. However, a roll-over of such bills is not uncommon, and hence the funds may be used for long-term working capital or for equipment investment.

In contrast to loans on deeds, which are described next, loans on bills have several merits for the financial institution. First, in cases in which the borrower defaults, the collection procedures are simple. Secondly, interest may be paid in advance. And thirdly, loans on bills may be converted to cash through such methods as endorsement on sale or attachment of collateral (the latter would include conversion to cash through sale of the bill on the bill market).

Loans on deeds. Loans on deeds are loans that require a lending certificate as the evidence of indebtedness rather than a bill. These loans are most often used for long-term lending, primarily as a means of lending for plant and equipment investment collateralized by real estate or for lending to local governments or public authorities. In recent years, loans on deeds have been increasing, which reflects the expansion of consumer lending and housing loans. They are also used together with bills in order to ensure the safety of assets.

Overdrafts. Overdrafts are facilities that are concluded with holders of current deposits and that allow the payment of cheques issued above the level of the outstanding balance in the current deposit so long as this extra payment remains within a pre-arranged limit and is repaid within a pre-arranged time. For banks, managing such loans is more difficult than managing discounts of bills or loans, and in addition is not eligible for refinancing by the Bank of Japan. As a result, Japanese banks have not been particularly active in granting overdraft facilities. From the viewpoint of corporations, however, such facilities have several merits. They are extremely convenient for borrowers who have a large turnover of funds through accounts. Moreover, the corporations may move funds at their own discretion for purposes of either borrowing or making repayments. Just at the time when the preference for high-yielding assets was growing in the period of monetary ease in the first half of the 1980s, there was an increasing trend towards the use of overdrafts. (The share of overdrafts in the lending of city and regional banks together rose from 1 per cent at the end of 1975 to 7 per cent at the end of 1985.) In addition, the overdrafts on *sogo* accounts were one form of overdraft, and the banks themselves emphasized the merits of such overdrafts as part of their policy of attracting more individual deposits.

Interest rate and collateral. The rates of interest chargeable on loans are subject to an upper limit in TIRAL, currently 15 per cent irrespective of the type of loan (with the exception of loans of more than one year in maturity, loans of less than ¥1m., and foreign currency-denominated loans). This upper limit of 15 per cent is of only limited significance, because it is rather high, and exists independently of the practice of compensating balances. In the light of these circumstances, each bank voluntarily decides the maximum limits on its loans and its standard loan rates within the limits laid down by TIRAL. For long-term loans, including housing loans that are of more than one year's maturity and that are outside the regulation of TIRAL, each bank also will decide its own interest rates (for details of interest rate determination mechanisms, see Chapter 4).

For loans other than bill discounts, it is common to require collateral, either personal or physical, in order to assure the quality of the loan asset. For physical collateral, the most common assets used are deposits at the bank in question (either time deposits or notice deposits) or real estate such as land, structures, ships, or factories. In cases where the borrower is of low creditworthiness, an individual guarantee from a representative or guarantee from a credit guarantee association or related company may also be required. Loans that are collateralized by stocks, debentures, or commodities are relatively rare. In earlier years, it was common to allocate portions of loan funds received to time deposits or notice deposits and to use these compensating balances as security, but when used to excess these practices raised the effective loan rates and led to a false increase of the deposit base. Arrangements among banks have fostered self-restraint in this area; in addition, interest rates on loans that use deposits as collateral have lower stated interest rates than general loans.

(3) Domestic exchange operations. Domestic exchange operations are the operations in which a bank acts as the intermediary for payment or collection of funds from various parts of the country. The parties to the transactions gain by economizing on the danger and trouble of sending cash.

There are four methods of sending funds through banks: ordinary remittance, telegraphic remittance, ordinary account payments, and telegraphic account payments. An ordinary remittance is one in which a sending bank creates a remittance cheque drawn on a paying bank in a certain area of the country; the paying bank must be a member of the nation-wide bank domestic exchange system. The sending bank then sends the remittance cheque to the remitter, who in turn transfers it to the recipient. The recipient then presents the cheque to the paying bank and receives payment. A telegraphic remittance is used when a remittance cheque will not be sufficiently rapid; such a remittance informs the recipient and the paying bank of the transaction by telegraphic means. Ordinary account and telegraphic account payments are those in which the recipient is the holder of a current or ordinary deposit account; the sending bank notifies the bank that holds the account and pays the funds directly into this account. This is the safest and surest method of transferring funds, and is more broadly used than the previous two types of remittance.

When a creditor wishes to collect funds from a debtor by going through a bank, the most common method is the use of a bill. The bank that receives the bill will then send the bill to its own branch in the place of payment, or to a bank which is a member of the domestic exchange system, and clear the bill through the clearing house or collect it directly.

When such exchange transactions are carried out between the branches of a single bank, the settlement is made through internal procedures of the bank on the books of the various branches; but when the transactions are carried out with other banks, there is a rapid and centralized settlement of the exchange balances through the nationwide Data Telecommunications System of All Banks in Japan (see section 3 below).

(4) Securities operations.   The permissible limits for banks to engage in securities operations such as underwriting and subscribing of new bonds, dealing in already issued bonds, and brokering bonds with customers has been debated for many years, chiefly through interpretation of Article 65 of the Securities and Exchange Law. Under the revised Banking Law of 1982, a legislative interpretation of these issues was attempted (Clauses 10 and 11).

Public bond operations. The Banking Law clearly establishes that banks may undertake securities operations concerning public bonds, that is, Government bonds, local government bonds, public offering, and Government-guaranteed bonds. There are two general categories of such business: underwriting through the syndicate and sales of Government and other public bonds over the counter, and the total underwriting, dealing, and brokering operations in Government and other public bonds.

The Banking Law establishes that syndicate activities and over-the-counter sales of Government bonds by banks are auxiliary operations in the legal sense. The former is the purchase of newly issued Government bonds without the intention of selling them, and is carried out by the banks in their role as members of the National Government Bond Underwriting Syndicate. The second, called over-the-counter sales, is the handling of subscriptions to such bonds, which is part of the syndicate underwriting process. Over-the-counter sales were permitted to the banks recently for the chief purpose of lightening the risk burden that accompanied the large-scale underwriting of Government bonds. But because these operations require direct contact with general investors, they require authorization not only under the Banking Law, but also under Securities and Exchange Law because of the need for investor protection. Over-the-counter sales began with selling of long-term Government coupon bonds, Government-guaranteed bonds, and publicly subscribed local government bonds in April 1983. In October of the same year, medium-term Government coupon bonds and Government discount bonds were added to the list of securities eligible for such business.

It is not at all obvious that the banking business ought to include the underwriting of Government bonds outside of the syndicate and with the intention of selling bonds, subscription of bonds outside of the syndicate, dealing in already issued bonds, or brokering the transactions of already issued bonds. The Banking Law does not recognize such transactions as belonging either to the main business of banking or to auxiliary businesses, but does make special provision for them in Clause 11. This clause provides that such activities shall be permitted only up to the limit at which they do not interfere with the achievement of the main business of banking. Moreover, since banks themselves have not for a long time carried out such types of business in the domestic markets, it is required for a certain period that the banks obtain approval from the Minister of Finance before carrying out such business with investors from the general public.

Of the businesses mentioned above, dealing in Government and other public bonds has been permitted in stages since June 1984. At the end of 1985, the institutions that carried out such dealings were city banks, long-term credit banks, trust banks, regional banks, the *Norinchukin* Bank, and foreign banks, eighty-seven in all.

Other securities operations. In addition to the securities operations in public bonds mentioned above, banks carry out other operations and securities, such as securities investment operations, securities lending operations, trustee operations, and securities agent operations. These activities have been carried out by banks for many years, and under the new Banking Law are listed as specific types of auxiliary operation, with the exception of some types of trustee operation (specifically excluded are activities carried out under the Mortgage Debenture Trust Law).

Securities investment operations are a type of operation in which the bank either acquires securities for the purpose of investment or disposes of such securities to a limited and specified number of clients. The securities concerned are not limited to public bonds. For many years, it was common for securities investment operations by banks to be merely a different form of lending. Banks would hold the corporate bonds or bank debentures or equities of firms with which they had client relationships or hold Government bonds or Government-guaranteed bonds as members of the underwriting syndicate (the latter type of bond was qualified for use as collateral in borrowing from the Bank of Japan). In recent years, however, the banks' attitude toward securities investment operations has changed, and the proportion of securities in total assets has risen as underwriting increased along with the large-scale flotations of Government bonds and as growth of lending to corporations stagnated. At the end of 1975, the share of securities in total assets of banks was 12·1 per cent, but the share had risen to 13·8 per cent by the end of 1985. In addition, banks will make transactions in securities as part of the business of taking orders from their clients; such transactions, along with the transactions in securities for the investment motives mentioned above, will naturally occur in the course of the deposit operations that are the main work of banks. In the Banking Law both of these types of securities transaction are listed as auxiliary operations.

Securities lending operations are operations in which the bank will lend a security that it holds to a customer in return for a fixed lending fee. In most cases, the client will use the securities as collateral for borrowing from a third party. There are two forms of such lending of securities, one in which the actual security is delivered to the client and one in which the right of pledge for a registered bond is registered in the borrower's name.

Trustee operations are operations that banks carry out in trusteeship for the issuers of securities in order to implement the issue, to pay interest, or to redeem bonds smoothly. Such operations include the clerical work in connection with the subscription or with the collateral for an issue. Trustee operations concerning subscription include preparation of the certificates of application and the clerical work concerning receipt of funds paid in. Trust operations concerning collateral include activities covered by the Mortgage Debentures Trust Law, specifically valuation, preservation, and management of the collateral, execution of collateral rights, convening of bond-holders' meetings, and implementation of the particulars of the decisions at such meetings. Because mortgage debentures trust operations require specialized knowledge in order to protect bond-holders, the banks that carry out such operations require a licence from the Minister of Finance.

Securities agent operations are those in which a bank acts as the agent of the issuer of a security in transactions involving the security. The bank uses its network of branches in order to receive payments for the stocks and to make payments of dividends and interest or principal on bonds. In return for providing these services, the bank receives a fee from the issuer.

(5) International operations. Ordinary banks may carry out international operations if qualified as either a specialized foreign exchange bank or an authorized foreign exchange bank (both are called foreign exchange banks hereafter). International operations have grown tremendously over the last several years because of the progress of internationalization of the Japanese economy. Particularly after the liberalization in principle of foreign transactions under the revised FEFTCL of December 1980, the types of international operation diversified tremendously because of a series of measures.

Foreign exchange banks carry out many different types of international operation. In the domestic market, these include the sale, purchase, and remittance of foreign currency or travellers' cheques, foreign currency deposit transactions with individuals, the collection and settlement of payment for imports and exports, trade financing, provision of impact loans, and exchange contracts for corporations. In international markets, they include loans extended overseas to subsidiaries of Japanese corporations, financing of foreign governments, underwriting and sales of Eurobonds, and transactions that use new financial products centred in the Euromarkets.

Banks also carry out exchange operations in the foreign exchange markets both at home and abroad in order to even out the surpluses or deficits of foreign exchange or disequilibria of foreign exchange positions that occur as the banks carry out transactions with their individual or corporate customers. But in addition, banks also promote international payments through concluding correspondent contracts with foreign banks, and are active in borrowing in foreign currencies from such foreign banks. The following sections explain foreign exchange operations, lending operations (both trade financing and general lending, which includes lending of foreign currencies in Japan and lending abroad), international securities operations, and foreign exchange borrowing operations.

Foreign exchange operations. The foreign exchange operations carried out between banks and their clients are usually thought of as including not only the transactions in foreign exchange but also various procedural operations such as the issue and receipt of letters of credit and acting as a proxy in procedures required by the foreign exchange law. Here, however, we will restrict ourselves to considering foreign exchange transactions that are the means of settlement for our foreign transactions. Discussion will centre on the representative types of business such as foreign remittance operations and settlement operations for export and import payments.

Foreign remittances are carried out through the so-called 'ordinary remittance' (*nami gawase*) in which the remittance is made through a foreign exchange bank from a domestic debtor to a foreign creditor. There are three such types of foreign remittance; demand drafts, mail transfers, and telegraphic transfers. In the case of a demand draft, the domestic debtor, i.e., the remittance guarantor, purchases a foreign currency draft from an exchange bank and sends this directly by mail to the creditor in the foreign country. The creditor then presents the draft to the paying bank in order to receive payment. In the cases of mail transfers and telegraphic transfers, the foreign exchange bank receives payment from the remitting party and then carries out the instructions for payment to the creditor through a postal or a telegraphic notification either to its own branches abroad or to its correspondent banks abroad.

In contrast, the settlement of payments for exports and imports usually uses the so-called 'reverse remittance' (*gyaku gawase*), in which the creditor collects the funds from the debtor through the foreign exchange bank. For example, when an exporter is recovering the payment for freight that has been shipped, the exporter will in general issue a foreign currency-denominated bill of exchange drawn on the importer; this bill must be either paid or under-written in order for the exporter to deliver to the importer the bill of lading or other shipping documents such as marine insurance certificates that are necessary for taking possession of the goods in question. Such exchange bills are called bills for collection. When settlements are carried out through bills with fixed maturity dates (so-called 'usance bills'), then the foreign exchange bank is granting finance to the exporter for the period of the bill through the bank's purchase of this bill (this is called export usance).[50] There are many cases in which the purchase of foreign exchange is effected simultaneously with export finance. Actually, the transactions in foreign exchange and trade finance, which is described below, have a very close relationship. But foreign exchange operations are used not only in connection with trade and invisible transactions, but also for capital transactions, such as foreign currency deposits of residents and impact loans. Because such dealings were liberalized with the revision of FEFTCL, there has been a substantial growth in the amount of such business. There has been, therefore, a huge expansion in the turnover of foreign exchange transactions of foreign exchange banks in recent years, reflecting such liberalization.

Trade financing operations. Trade financing is the supply of funds, either in yen or foreign currency, that are necessary to settle export and import transactions and together with foreign exchange transaction *vis-à-vis* clients is one of the basic businesses of foreign exchange banks. But trade financing operations have become less important over the years because of the increase in the scale of capital account transactions outside the scope of trade finance, and also because of the increase of non-traditional methods for trade financing such as impact loans. Currently, the outstanding balance of trade bills purchased is only one fifth of the amount of total loan extended overseas and not even half the amount of impact loans or securities holdings (see Figure 5.2). A more detailed consideration requires a distinction between export finance and import finance.

Export finance is the general term for supply of the funds necessary for the export of goods, and can be divided into short-term and medium-term finance. The former is also divided into finance before and after shipment.

Short-term finance before shipment is credit in the form of overdrafts or loans on bills that provide the yen funds necessary for the production, processing, or collection of goods before they are loaded aboard by the domestic exporter or manufacturer. The bills generated through such trans-actions may be treated as 'bills corresponding in credibility bills' by the Bank of Japan for purposes of rediscounting if these bills fulfil certain conditions such as existence of an assured export contract and a maturity of the shortest possible period up to six months. In cases of rediscount, the Bank of Japan supplies necessary yen funds to the banks with these bills as collateral.

Short-term finance after shipment is credit supplied to an exporter for the period between the time of loading the goods aboard and the completion of

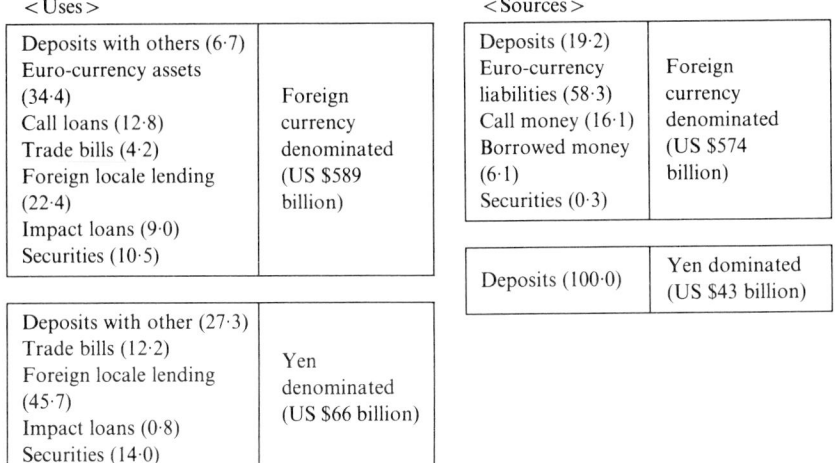

< Uses >

Deposits with others (6·7) Euro-currency assets (34·4) Call loans (12·8) Trade bills (4·2) Foreign locale lending (22·4) Impact loans (9·0) Securities (10·5)	Foreign currency denominated (US $589 billion)
Deposits with other (27·3) Trade bills (12·2) Foreign locale lending (45·7) Impact loans (0·8) Securities (14·0)	Yen denominated (US $66 billion)

< Sources >

Deposits (19·2) Euro-currency liabilities (58·3) Call money (16·1) Borrowed money (6·1) Securities (0·3)	Foreign currency denominated (US $574 billion)
Deposits (100·0)	Yen dominated (US $43 billion)

Note: Inter-office accounts, on a basis excluding the net actual balance.

Source: BOJ.

Figure 5.2   Sources and Uses of Funds for Japanese Foreign Exchange Banks (percent of total sources or uses; end-September, 1985)

payment from the importer by means of purchase by a foreign exchange bank of the export exchange bill issued against the foreign importer. For yen-denominated export financing (financing that matures within six months of loading of the goods), a foreign exchange bank may refinance in the yen-BA market, a portion of the credit it has given to its customer (for yen-denominated import financing, the same is true). The yen-BA market was established in June 1985. The Bank of Japan treats export bills that fulfil specified conditions, such as being yen-denominated and having maturity within five months from the acceptance of the bill by the foreign exchange bank, as bills corresponding in credibility to commercial bills; thus these bills are eligible for use as collateral in the supply of yen financing to private-sector banks by the Bank of Japan. In addition, yen-denominated fixed-period export bills became eligible for Bank of Japan bill market operations in November 1973.

There are also several types of medium- and long-term export financing. In some cases, an exporter will receive financing from a financial institution and provide supplier's credits to the importer in the form of deferred payment. Much of this type of export financing comes in the form of co-operative financing, mostly from the Export–Import Bank of Japan. Another type is buyer's credits, which are direct credits supplied by the financial institution of the exporting country to the importer. Yet another type is lending by a financial institution in the exporting country to a financial institution in the importing country, the amount of which is then rolled over in a bank loan to the importer. This type of financing is provided mostly in cases of very large-scale exports of capital goods with a very high degree of value added, such as manufacturing plants or ships.

Import financing is credit granted to an importer for the purpose of deferring a payment of imports for a fixed period of time. There are two general types of import finance: import usance, in which a foreign exchange bank provided the credit, and shipper's usance, in which the foreign exporter provides the credit. It is also possible to include within import financing so-called 'boomerang' yen financing (*hanekaeri kinyu*) after the settlement of the import bill. Under this type of financing, a foreign exchange bank will discount a bill issued to an importer by those who purchase the imported goods from him.

There are three forms of import usance: the acceptance method, the BC-usance method, and the Japan loan method. The first two are subject to a usance maturity limit of two years under the provisions of FEFTCL, while the latter is not subject to any maturity restriction. The interest rates on such lending are based on the BA rate in the United States plus a bill discount fee plus a margin for the foreign exchange bank. Under the acceptance method, the foreign exporter issues a fixed-term bill based on a letter of credit opened by a Japanese foreign exchange bank. This bill is then discounted either by a foreign bank or by the foreign branch of a Japanese foreign exchange bank. Under the BC-usance method, a foreign branch of a Japanese foreign exchange bank buys a fixed term bill, i.e., a bill for collection, issued by the foreign exporter but not based on a letter of credit, and the funds from the bank's purchase are used to pay for the imports and thus give the importer a certain postponement of the collection of the funds. This type of financing is primarily used between the home offices and branches of Japanese trading companies. Under the Japanese loan method, a foreign exchange bank acts in place of the importer in settling a sight bill issued by the foreign exporter, and thus gives the importer a certain period of extension before collection.

Moreover, the Bank of Japan treats yen-denominated fixed-term import bills as bills corresponding in credibility to commercial bills so long as they fulfil certain conditions, such as being less than four months in maturity. Such bills may then be used as collateral in the supply of yen funding to banks by the Bank of Japan. Yen-denominated fixed-term import bills may also be the object of bill operations by the Bank of Japan. In addition, an import settlement bill system was established in May 1978; under this system, the Bank of Japan carries out yen loans to banks using import settlement-related, quasi-commercial bills, etc. as collateral. This system was established in order to improve the foreign position of foreign exchange banks through encouraging shift towards yen-denominated import financing, but was also intended to lower interest costs for businesses and to encourage imports.

Domestic lending operations (to residents). Under the old FEFTCL, a foreign investor was required in principle to obtain approval in order to acquire a loan asset *vis-à-vis* a domestic resident. There was a distinction between two types of foreign currency lending to residents: tied loans which were limited to a specified purpose for the funds, and impact loans which had no specified purpose. Each loan had to be approved individually. Short-term impact loans, those of less than one year's maturity, were prohibited (until June 1979), and long- and medium-term impact loans, those of more than one year in maturity, were prohibited except when made by foreign banks resident in Japan (Japanese foreign exchange banks were permitted to make such loans after March 1980).

Under the new FEFTCL implemented in December 1980, foreign currency borrowing by residents is divided into two types: foreign currency borrowing from residents, and borrowing, including yen-denominated borrowing, from non-residents. Each of these two types of borrowing is free in principle. Foreign exchange banks are quite active in lending to residents through two particular types of instrument, impact loans and Euro-yen impact loans.

'Impact loan' is the general term for foreign currency lending made by a foreign exchange bank to a resident without restriction on the use of funds. It is distinguished from tied loans on which there are restrictions on the use of the funds. Because of the regulations on impact loans under the old FEFTCL it was often the case that tied loans would be taken because receiving approval was easy. But because of the liberalization of foreign currency borrowing by residents under the new FEFTCL, almost all the foreign currency lending to residents from foreign exchange banks (with the exception of trade finance) is in the form of impact loans.[3]

Impact loans are used for many purposes. Petroleum companies and trading companies use them as a substitute for more traditional forms of trade financing in making payment settlements for imports and exports. Exporters use them as a method of hedging the exchange risks that accompany the holding of foreign currency-denominated claims on foreigners, while securities companies use them as a method for raising the funds necessary to hold foreign securities. Moreover, because an impact loan with a forward foreign exchange risk is in fact the same as yen-denominated borrowing, securities companies have been using impact loans as one method to finance their general holdings of securities. In the last case, securities companies compare impact loan cost with the rate of other methods such as a securities *gensaki* transactions. There has been an increase recently in the amounts of impact loans used for these purposes. The outstanding amount of impact loans (by foreign exchange banks) grew by 4·9 times between the end of 1980, just after the implementation of the new FEFTCL, and the end of 1985, from $10·8 milliard to $53·3 milliard. The share of impact loans in the total loans outstanding of ordinary banks rose from 2 per cent at the end of 1980

---

[3] Foreign exchange borrowing among residents that does not involve a foreign exchange bank continues to require approval.

to 7 per cent at the end of 1985. Moreover, the maturity structure of impact loans has shorted greatly; in earlier years, the largest portion were medium- and long-term loans of more than one year, but recently the majority have been short-term loans of less than one year.

Euro-yen loans are defined as the yen-denominated lending of financial institutions abroad (including the foreign branches of Japanese banks) to residents or non-residents. Euro-yen impact loans are the portion of Euro-yen loans that go to residents. Despite the liberalization in principle of foreign transactions under the new FEFTCL, the Japanese authorities requested self-restraint on the part of financial institutions concerning the extension of Euro-yen impact loans. But short-term impact loans of less than one year in maturity were liberalized in June 1984, in order to aid in the inter-nationalization of the yen.

Foreign lending operations (to non-residents). Lending by Japanese foreign exchange banks, including that by their foreign branches, to non-residents in either foreign exchange or yen is termed 'foreign locale lending'. Such lending started in the second half of the 1960s primarily to the foreign branches or locally incorporated affiliates of Japanese corporations, hence the name 'foreign locale lending', because such lending abroad stands in contrast to domestic lending to these corporations. Foreign locale lending is a major portion of the lending of foreign exchange banks.

The largest portion of foreign locale lending, about 80 per cent of the total outstanding at the end of 1985, remains denominated in foreign currencies, although a larger and larger share has been yen-denominated in recent years. The reason for this high share of foreign currency lending is that such lending became the chief type of business for the foreign branches of Japanese banks, due to its having begun in earnest as the supply of foreign currency funds by the foreign branches of Japanese banks or their affiliates to the locally incorporated affiliates of Japanese enterprises that were of low credit-worthiness in foreign countries; in later years, the increase came from lending to non-Japanese corporations. Another important component of foreign locale lending is medium- and long-term lending to foreign governments and foreign public-sector institutions. Such Euro-lending, also called syndicated loans, is usually carried out as joint funding by the financial institutions of several countries on an international basis, and hence almost all such lending is foreign currency-denominated. This is another reason why foreign currency lending is such a large part of foreign locale lending.

Almost all yen-denominated foreign lending is made to foreign governments or foreign public-sector institutions on a medium- or long-term basis. In most cases, such lending is made by forming a syndicate with a Japanese bank as the leader. Owing part to the decline in demand for funds by domestic corporations, several financial institutions have become very aggressive in making such loans, and the conditions on such loans reflect this com-petitiveness. There has been a diversification in the terms of loans. Historically, most were fixed-rate loans with the interest rates based on the long-term prime rate in Japan, but in recent years floating-rate loans have been more common, and the total outstanding in such loans has risen tremendously. The regulation of such lending has also become easier over the years. Previously, the Japanese authorities requested self-restraint on the part of financial institutions in making yen-denominated loans to non-residents through the foreign branches of Japanese banks (the so-called 'Euro-yen' loans to non-residents); but in order to promote the internationalization of the yen, short-term lending of this nature was completely liberalized in June 1983 (before then, only trade-connected lending had been liberalized), and medium- and long-term lending was liberalized in April of 1985.

But the foreign locale lending, which had been expanding so smoothly, has now come to face certain problems. The greatest of these had been the intensification of country risk difficulties during the early 1980s. Continuing high interest rates in the United States and falling prices for primary commodities have caused a spate of demands for rescheduling from countries with reduced debt-servicing capability in which loans had been concentrated. Because of these problems, reserve for foreign asset loans were established in March of 1983 with a view to ensuring the soundness of bank management.[4]

In recent years, the so-called 'securitization' of loans has been progressing with the emergence of new financial products that are substitutes for loans, such as note issuance facilities and floating-rate notes, chiefly in the Euromarkets. Partly owing to this securitization, foreign locale lending shows slow growth.

International securities operations. Along with expanding lending operations, Japanese foreign exchange banks have diversified their other international activities into securities, trust, leasing, and other areas. Of these activities, they have taken a particularly active attitude in the area of international securities operations.

Among the securities operations carried out in foreign markets, the most important is underwriting of Eurobonds through foreign subsidiaries, called securities affiliates, located in Europe, particularly in London or Switzerland. At first, the securities affiliates handled mostly the foreign currency bond

[4] The general provisions of the reserve for special foreign asset loans are as follows:

(*a*) Eligible countries: the lending of a private financial institution to the government or to government institutions in a particular country may be subject to a reserve for special foreign asset loans if any one of the following facts holds: (1) payment of principal or interest is over one month in arrears; (2) a rescheduling or similar event has occurred at any time during the past five years; (3) one month or more has passed since the request for a rescheduling.

(*b*) Eligible assets in principle are all assets related to the eligible country.

(*c*) Eligible amounts for the reserve: the amount paid into the reserve may be between 1 per cent and 5 per cent of the total eligible assets at the end of the previous period, with the exact amount depending on an expressly recognized expected loss which in turn is related to the country risk of the eligible country.

The gathering and analysis of the domestic and foreign information concerning the country risk problem is carried out by a non-profit foundation, the Japan Centre for International Finance, which was established in Mar. 1983.

issues by Japanese-related corporations. But in recent years, the scope of operations has expanded to include participation in the bond flotations of corporations with no ties to Japan. In addition to operations involving underwriting of securities, the securities affiliates of Japanese banks also perform transactions in foreign securities and act as investment advisers for the foreign securities investments of Japanese corporations.

Banks also perform international securities operations in domestic markets. Examples include the trustee operations on the occasion of issue of yen-denominated bonds by non-residents and the operations concerning the securities investments in Japan by foreign investors (custody of securities, proxy agent operations, and the buying and selling of such securities). In addition, banks have been active in their management of international portfolios. In recent years, the size of such portfolios has exceeded that of the portfolios of trade financing (i.e., trade bills).

Foreign currency fund raising. Much of the Japanese current transactions focusing on exports and imports are denominated in foreign currencies. As a result, most of the international operations of Japanese foreign exchange banks is in foreign currencies and particularly in dollars. It is therefore necessary for the foreign exchange banks to raise foreign currency funds. The chief methods of doing this are borrowing from foreign banks, Euro-funding, and foreign currency call borrowing. Borrowing from foreign banks was, in previous years, the main method of securing funds for financing of trade, and most of such funding came from American banks. The forms of such borrowing included discount of bank acceptance in the BA market (i.e., BA rediscount), refinance borrowing based on import bills, and own-account or single-name borrowing which did not require an import bill as a basis (so-called 'clean' borrowing). Currently, the first two of these methods are the most important. The interest rates on refinance borrowing in general slide with the American BA rate, while the interest rates on clean borrowing are in general determined on the basis of the American prime rate.

For some years, borrowing from foreign banks rose along with the expansion of the scale of Japanese trade, but in recent years its rate has fallen because of the increased ability of Japanese foreign exchange banks to raise funds in Euromarkets. Virtually all the funds required for foreign locale lending are raised through Euro-funding. The form of Euro-funding is for the most part the acquisition of deposits in the Euromarkets (including international banking facilities), but these are deposits in form only and are in fact short-term uncollateralized borrowings of maximum maturity of two years. The share of Japanese foreign exchange banks in deposit acquisition in the Euromarket has been increasing steadily. In addition, in response to the growth of medium- and longer-term lending, there has been expansion of fund-raising through other instruments such as Euro-CDs (of maximum maturity of five years) and Eurobank debentures. Nevertheless, short-term Euro-deposits remain the largest share of Euro-funding, and a problem remains that the maturity structure of funds raised and funds lent may not match adequately.

Despite the fact that gigantic international bank transactions occur in the Euromarkets, the lack of a central bank as the lender of last resort implies a market structure in which isolated credit disturbances may be transmitted very easily. Responding to this situation, private banks have established mutual lines of credit among themselves so that no particular bank will be relied on excessively for the provision of credit. In addition, there have been discussions concerning improvement of the system through appropriate monitoring and management of markets in co-operation with the monetary authorities of the various countries.

Foreign currency call borrowing is actively used by banks in order to raise short-term funds. The most important markets for foreign currency call borrowing are the federal funds market of the United States and the Tokyo Dollar-call market. Recently the Tokyo Dollar-call Market has become the central market for such types of transaction.

(6) Other operations. The operations discussed above are the most important of the international banking activities, but three others also require some explanation. These are auxiliary operations recognized under the Banking Law, operations approved under other laws, and peripheral operations that are carried out through subsidiaries and that are similar to auxiliary operations.

Auxiliary operations. Auxiliary operations are those operations that are normally thought of as naturally accompanying the traditional business of banks as they carry out their social and economic functions. Clause 10, Section 2 of the Banking Law lists ten specific types of such auxiliary operation.

The auxiliary operations concerning securities were described above.

Type 1: Guarantee of liabilities. The Banking Law lists the guarantee of obligations and acceptance of bills as auxiliary operations of banks. Acceptance and guarantee are similar to a loan in being a form of credit-granting operation by the bank, but rather than directly providing funds to the client, the bank allows the client to receive funding from elsewhere but with the use of the bank's good name, or alternatively, allows the firm to enjoy the same benefits as if they had received such funding. In return for providing this credit function, the bank receives a guarantor's fee from the client. In periods of tight money, banks that are in a difficult position with respect to their window guidance quotas or banks with a bad funds position may use acceptance and guarantee and thus secure an identical effect for their clients as if a loan had been made but without any funding burden. Through such actions, the banks may expect long-term client relationships to develop. Banks usually require a collateral for acceptance and guarantee, just as in cases of loans.

Type 2: Acquisition and cession of monetary claims. Securities or deeds for monetary claims here include CDs, commercial paper (CPs), issued abroad, housing mortgage certificates, and beneficiary certificates from mortgage trusts. Factoring operations (under which a bank purchases an outstanding money certificate before its maturity and thus grants funding to the original creditor) were hitherto considered a peripheral operation but are, under the new Banking Law, considered part of the acquisition of money securities.

The handling of CDs and commercial paper issued in foreign countries is recognized as an auxiliary operation under the new Banking Law, in response to the free introduction of such instruments into the domestic market after the revision of FEFTCL. Because foreign CDs and commercial paper have the mixed character of being both securities and short-term money market instruments, the handling of them was also granted to securities companies when such handling was permitted after April 1984. Because of concerns about investor protection and maintenance of orderly domestic credit conditions, operations in these types of money certificate is subject to uniform rules determined by the authorities.

Type 3: Agent operations. Agent operations are those in which a bank acts as the proxy for a portion of the business of some other financial institution. Such operations include agency loan and agency guarantee of liabilities but do not include the simple clerical work of handling money. The specific examples of agent operations are decided by Ministry of Finance ordinance.

Type 4: Receipts and payment of public funds. Banks may be entrusted by the national Government, local governments, or public bodies with the collection of funds or other clerical works concerning money.

Type 5: Safekeeping deposit.

Type 6: Money changing.

Type 7: Other auxiliary operations. In addition to the auxiliary operations described above, banks may carry out other operations such as opening letters of credit, issuing traveller's cheques, credit card business, and over-the-counter sale of gold.

Operations permitted by other laws. Article 12 of the Banking Law prohibits banks from engaging in other businesses outside of the Banking Law except for those which are specifically permitted according to other laws, such as the Mortgage Debentures Trust Law. This prohibition is based on the idea that it is desirable for banks to fulfil their primary function through concentrating on their main business of acting as effective financial intermediaries. Were they to do otherwise, there might occur difficulties in their losing their soundness or even in protecting depositors, or social frictions might arise if banks were to engage in other more general undertakings on the basis of their huge financial power.

Besides the activities permitted under the Banking Law, there are four other activities in which banks may engage. The first is the mortgage debentures trust business, which requires a licence under Article 5 of the Mortgage Debentures Trust Law. Second is trust business that requires approval under

Article 1 of the Law Concerning Concurrent Operation, etc. of Trust Business by Ordinary Banks. Third is bond registration business, which requires designation under Imperial order according to Article 2 of the Law for Registration of Corporate Debentures, etc. Fourth is the lottery business, which requires a trusteeship under Article 6 of the Law for Establishment of Certificates with Prizes.

Peripheral operations. Peripheral operations are those which are less close to the traditional banking business than auxiliary operations. Examples of peripheral operations including leasing, venture capital, consulting, entrustment with calculations, and housing finance carried out with joint capital from banks. These peripheral operations are those that do not belong to any of the other three categories of exclusive bank operations, auxiliary operations, or securities operations. Because the Banking Law forbids banks to undertake the joint management of other types of operation, the banks are not permitted to manage the peripheral operations directly. Instead, banks provide these services and fill the need of their customers through related corporations in which the banks have a capital participation. There are no fixed limits for peripheral operations; rather, the limits are subject to flexible interpretation along with trends in social conditions. In fact, as attitudes have become more flexible toward related company operations, the banks have expanded into such areas as consumer finance and mortgage security operations (from May 1984) and investment advisory operations (from March 1985).

(iii) Assets, liabilities, and income and expenditure

The ordinary banks of Japan engage in all the types of operation described above; but in order to gain some sense of how the importance of these different types of operations has changed in recent years one may look at the assets, liabilities, and income and expenditure of the banks.

(1) Liabilities. The most important liability for banks is deposits, which provide about 70 per cent of total fund sources (see Table 5.1). About 60 per cent of total deposits are time deposits, and of the time deposits, those of over one year account for about 80 per cent. As at the end of 1985, slightly more than 3 per cent of total time deposits were large-scale time deposits, whose interest rates were liberalized in October 1985. The share of CDs in total liabilities was slightly more than 2 per cent at the end of 1985. CDs had been introduced in order to combat the outflow of funds to the *gensaki* market and other open financial markets before the liberalization of interest rates on large-scale time deposits. It is thought that the shares of large-scale time deposits and CDs in the total funding of banks is likely to rise in future years, because the minimum deposit for application of free rates to large-scale deposits is expected to fall while CDs become smaller in minimum amount and more flexible in maturity. The large share of time deposits and

TABLE 5.1 *Principal Accounts of City and Regional Banks, end of 1985*

	City banks		Regional banks		Total	
	¥100m.	%	¥100m.	%	¥100m.	%
Assets						
Cash	95,613	4·9	40,413	3·7	136,026	4·5
Cheques and bills	(87,620)	(4·5)	(23,390)	(2·2)	(111,010)	(3·7)
Deposits with others	55,322	2·9	15,139	1·4	70,461	2·3
Call loans	72,791	3·8	39,306	3·6	112,097	3·7
Bills bought	394	0·0	4,834	0·5	5,228	0·2
Commodity bonds	14,518	0·7	7,521	0·7	22,039	0·7
Securities	221,017	11·4	194,058	18·0	415,075	13·8
Bills discounted	165,941	8·6	103,482	9·6	269,423	8·9
Loans	1,068,770	55·1	605,052	56·1	1,673,822	55·4
(Loans on bills)	(542,658)	(28·0)	(305,195)	(28·3)	(847,853)	(28·1)
Foreign exchange account	51,142	2·6	4,573	0·4	55,715	1·8
Domestic exchange unsettled, Dr.	32,924	1·7	18,391	1·7	51,315	1·7
Customer's liability for acceptances and guarantees	131,794	6·8	26,563	2·5	158,357	5·3
Bank premises and real estate	16,239	0·8	12,772	1·2	29,011	1·0
Other	13,237	0·7	6,822	0·6	20,059	0·7
TOTAL	1,939,702	100·0	1,078,926	100·0	3,018,628	100·0
Liabilities						
Deposits	1,256,195	64·8	907,333	84·1	2,163,528	71·7
Large-scale term deposits[a]	(33,407)	(11·7)	(9,671)	(0·9)	(43,078)	(1·4)
Actual deposits	(1,168,575)	(60·2)	(883,943)	(81·9)	(2,052,518)	(68·0)
CDs	48,905	2·5	17,630	1·6	66,535	2·2
Bank debentures issued	25,990	1·3	—	—	25,990	0·9
Borrowed money	35,435	1·8	3,266	0·3	38,701	1·3
(from BOJ)	(31,210)	(1·6)	(1,267)	(0·1)	(32,477)	(1·1)
Call money	68,345	3·5	21,061	2·0	89,406	3·0
Bills sold	125,900	6·5	5,171	0·5	131,071	4·3
Foreign exchange account	10,330	0·5	491	0·0	10,821	0·4
Domestic exchange unsettled, Cr.	31,746	1·7	19,082	1·8	50,828	1·7
Acceptances and guarantees	131,794	6·8	26,563	2·5	158,357	5·2
Reserves	15,222	0·8	8,428	0·8	23,650	0·8
Capital	12,091	0·6	6,885	0·6	18,976	0·6
Legal reserves	5,161	0·3	5,366	0·5	10,527	0·3
Surpluses	31,311	1·6	22,785	2·1	54,096	1·8
Other	141,277	7·3	34,865	3·2	176,142	5·8

[a] Large-scale deposits are those of ¥1bn. or more, and were accepted after Oct. 1985.

Source: BOJ, *Economic Statistics Annual*.

particularly of time deposits of more than one year's maturity is a special characteristic of the Japanese banking system. This helps to make possible the relatively long-term investment in funds made by Japanese banks.

Following time deposits in importance are ordinary deposits, which have a share of about 15 per cent of total deposits. Both current deposits and notice deposits have shares of about 7 per cent. As seen above, the largest portion of current deposits are used by corporations for settlement of trans- actions. The outstanding balance of such deposits reflects the state of trans- action activity among corporations and displays large fluctuations according to both the state of the business cycle and seasonal factors.

The own capital of banks comprises capital, legal reserves (capital reserves and profit reserves), surplus accounts (voluntary reserve and undistributed profits), and provisions for payment (reserve for loan loss, reserve for retire- ment pension payment, etc.). With the exception of provisions for payment, these funds are sometimes called 'narrowly defined own capital'. The own capital of banks covers the risk of investment of the funds of banks and is also necessary as a final reserve against deposits and other outside liabilities of the banks. Because of these needs, the Banking Law requires that banks accumulate more profits than do ordinary corporations (so-called 'profit reserves'); throughout the post-war period, the Special Taxation Measures Law has permitted that a portion of the provisions for payment may be counted as losses in the calculation of income for the purpose of corporate income tax. In earlier years, the amounts of funds that banks could pay into accounts for provisions of payment were left to the free discretion of the banks, but, since the second half of fiscal 1967, the payments into such accounts are made according to unified accounting standards under the administrative guidance of the Ministry of Finance. In the pre-war period, bank own capital was about 20 per cent of total liabilities (of this, capital was 15 per cent), but in recent years, even including the provisions for payment mentioned above, total own capital is only about 4 per cent of total liabilities (of which capital is 1 per cent). The main reason for the very small size of capital has been the rapid growth of deposits and lending, but capital increases were also constrained by the limits imposed by administrative guidance on dividends payable on bank stock.

Reflecting the declining share of own capital have been rises in outside funding such as borrowing from the Bank of Japan, call-money borrowing, and sales of bills. In particular, for city banks, whose borrowings of outside funds was almost nil in the pre-war period, outside funding has increased tremendously in the post-war period, reflecting the active desire to lend to the corporations with such huge demand for funds during the reconstruction period and the high growth period. Since the end of the high growth period, there have been major increases and decreases in outside funding; at the end of 1985, such outside funds were 11·6 per cent of the sum of outside funds and *de facto* deposits (including bank debentures issued). For regional banks, this ratio was 1·8 per cent, a contrast which reflects the net surplus position of these institutions. But for both city banks and regional banks, there has been an increased reliance on market-related borrowings since 1975. For city banks the ratio of such funding to total assets has gone from 11 per cent at the end of 1975 to 21 per cent at the end of 1985, while for regional banks the ratio has gone from 0 to 10 per cent. These large differences in ratios between city banks and regional banks reflect for the most part the difference in position, judging from the fact that both city banks and regional banks have similarly become more dependent on free interest rate deposits such as CDs and MMCs; for city banks this dependence rose from 3 per cent to 12 per cent, and for local banks from 0 to 8 per cent.

(2) Assets. Lending, both through discounted bills and through direct loans, has been the major asset for banks, in the pre-war and post-war periods alike. Currently the weight of lending in total assets is more than 60 per cent.

Although lending to individuals has risen considerably in recent years due to the increase of consumer lending that has accompanied housing finance and durable good consumption growth (the share of lending to individuals has risen from just under 9 per cent of total assets in 1975 to just under 11 per cent in 1985), the largest portion of bank lending continues to go to corporations. Breaking lending to corporations down by industrial classification, about 30 per cent continues to go to manufacturing industry, although this share has been on a declining trend accompanying the shift of the economy toward lower growth (in 1975, this share was about 40 per cent). The share of going to wholesale trade is the next largest, at 20 per cent. Among the types of loan to non-manufacturing industry, there has been a conspicuous growth of lending to service industries, from just under 6 per cent of total lending in 1975 to 10 per cent at the end of 1985.

There are two types of lending as classified by use, working funds and equipment funds. Equipment funds comprise about 20 per cent of total lending but this share would be larger if one included working funds that are continuously rolled over.

Corporate demand for working funds is of various types. The portion used for the purchase of raw materials or of intermediate goods is largely settled through bills, and most of these bills are brought to banks to be discounted. Also, there are many cases of corporations borrowing pre-production funds and funds for closing of books such as corporate tax funds and dividend payments funds. As a result, lending of working funds by banks rises seasonally at periods of settlement of trade transactions (March, September, and December) and in periods when corporations close their books or make bonus payments (June and December).

Loan portfolios also differ among banks according to the sizes of borrowers. For city banks, about half of funds lent are provided to large corporations, i.e., those with more than ¥100m. capital or more than 300 regular employees. For regional banks, more than half of funds lent are provided to smaller corporations, i.e., those with less than ¥100m. in capital or less than 300 regular employees. These loans are an important source of funding for small corporations.

The second most important form of investment for banks is securities. The share of securities in total assets remained at about 10 per cent from the mid-1950s through to the mid-1970s but rose rapidly after 1975 along with the large-scale flotation of Government bonds (at the end of 1985 their share in total assets was 13 per cent). Classified by type of security held, the share of Government bonds has risen quickly, and stood at 30 per cent of total securities held at the end of 1985. The share of public bonds, which includes not only Government bonds but also local government bonds and the bonds of public corporations and certain public financial institutions, rose to 50 per cent of the total securities held, while the share of private-sector bonds (which had been in the majority during the high growth period) fell to about 15 per cent.

The share of so-called 'front-line' payments reserves, including cash (excluding cheques and bills) and funds on deposits, is currently about 5 per cent of actual deposits. The largest portion of these funds are required reserves that are deposited at the Bank of Japan under the reserve requirements system. Second-line payments reserves, i.e., call loans and bills purchased are also about 5 per cent of actual deposits. For city banks however, the amount of external funds raised, i.e., through call borrowing and bills sold, is substantially greater.

(3) Income and expenditure. The asset and liability composition described above is reflected in the banks' income and expenditure.

Nearly 60 per cent of banks' current income comes from interest on lending (including discount fees for bills and interest payments on loans). The remaining 40 per cent comes from interest on securities, etc. The yield on lendings follows the official discount rate movements, though with some lag, and stood at 7·2 per cent in fiscal 1984. The overall yield on working assets (yield on lendings, call loans, and securities) was about 8 per cent (see Table 5.2).

About 60 per cent of current expenses are interest payments on deposits. The cost of deposits and debentures was 7·7 per cent during fiscal 1984, compared with a total cost of funds (cost of deposit, securities, borrowing, and call money) of 7·8 per cent.

As a result, the overall profit margins, i.e. the difference between the total yield on working assets and the total costs of funds, was extremely narrow at 0·2 per cent. In recent years there has been a conspicuous trend towards narrowing the overall profit margins due to the increase in the interest rate on deposits and securities because of more flexible interest rates applied to these liabilities and to the reduction of yields on lendings that reflect the

TABLE 5.2   *Yield on Assets and Cost of Funds for City and Regional Banks, by Financial Year*

	1965 (first half) %	1970 (first half) %	1975 (first half) %	1980 (first half) %	1984[b] %	1985 (mid-ye. %
Yield on lending, call loans, and securities (A)	7·61	7·67	9·06	8·91	7·98	7·27
Yield on lending	7·72	7·71	9·35	9·02	7·21	6·81
Yield on call loans[a]	7·50	8·91	9·93	12·68	10·62	8·29
Yield on securities	7·05	7·33	7·46	7·30	7·60	7·26
Cost of deposits, debentures, borrowings, and call money (B)	6·75	6·37	8·47	8·67	7·77	7·13
Cost of deposits and debentures	6·72	6·22	8·19	8·32	7·65	7·05
Interest rate on deposits and debentures	4·04	4·16	5·73	6·25	6·19	5·60
Cost ratios	2·67	2·06	2·46	2·07	1·45	1·44
Interests on borrowings	}6·92	}7·46	7·89	10·97	8·35	7·13
Interests on call money[a]			11·37	12·78	8·36	7·19
PROFIT MARGIN (A − B)	0·85	1·29	0·59	0·24	0·21	0·14

[a] For yield on call loans and interests on call money, the calculation includes bills bought and bills s⊙ (and also dollar call market transactions).

[b] Business periods changed to full fiscal year from 1981 financial year.

Source: BOJ, *Economic Statistics Annual.*

longer-term trend toward financial ease.

The contributions to earnings from the international operations of banks have been growing year by year recently, reflecting the expansion of international businesses. For example, for city banks, the ratio of gross operating income from international operations to total gross operating income has risen from 15 per cent in 1975 to 20 per cent in 1984.

b. Foreign banks

(i) Overview

Foreign banks are defined as the branches or agencies established in Japan by banks of foreign countries. There were 114 such branches or agencies at the end of 1985, representing seventy-seven foreign banks. According to the provisions of the Banking Law a licence is necessary from the Minister of Finance for each branch when a foreign bank wishes to establish branches and to conduct banking business in Japan. Thus, foreign banks have the same legal position as Japanese ordinary banks and are considered to be banks according to the Banking Law. Because of their character, the share of foreign currency transactions in their business is high, and hence all the foreign banks are authorized foreign exchange banks. Many foreign banks also have representative offices in Japan, which only require notification to the authorities under the provisions of the Banking Law. The business in which such offices may engage is limited to operations connected with banking business (e.g., a liaison for correspondent banks in Japan), and collection of information, etc. Such representative offices are not permitted to carry out normal banking business, although many are often included in a broad definition of foreign banks in Japan because they represent the preparatory stage for opening a branch. In July 1985, there were 118 foreign bank representative offices in Japan.

In the immediate post-war period, before Japanese banks were able to carry out diversified types of business, the foreign banks in Japan played an extremely important role in the foreign exchange business in the country. But as Japanese banks improved their capabilities in carrying out foreign exchange business, the importance of the foreign banks declined in relative terms. The number of foreign banks and representative offices was stable during the 1950s and 1960s, but because of increasing financial internationalization, this number of offices and branches has grown remarkably since the 1970s. Moreover, there has been a diversification of the nationalities of foreign banks away from the concentration of banks from Europe and the United States. In the last few years, there has been yet another increase in the level of activity of foreign banks seeking to enter Japan, reflecting both the relatively good economic performance in Japan and expectations for the future as well as expectations of further internationalization of the financial and capital markets in Japan.

(ii) Operations

Because foreign banks are defined as banks under the Banking Law, the limits of their operations are not fundamentally different from those of Japanese banks. Moreover, as authorised foreign exchange banks, the foreign banks are an important part of the Tokyo dollar-call market and the Tokyo foreign exchange market, along with the city banks.

The most important types of business for foreign banks are deposits, lending, foreign exchange business, and trade financing, but in recent years lending operations toward domestic corporations (particularly to large firms in steel, shipbuilding, and trading industries) have become the focus of business. The main sources of funds for foreign banks are Euro-money borrowings from the main branch office of the bank in question, because the small branch networks of the foreign banks constrain their ability to attract deposits.

(1) Deposit operations.   Deposits are the most fundamental source of funds for banks, but foreign banks in Japan have not hitherto expected to attract large deposit bases because of their small numbers of branches. In fact, the level of deposits (defined to include CDs) in foreign banks is only about

TABLE 5.3   *Principal Accounts of Foreign Banks in Japan by Year-end*

	1975		1980		1985	
	¥100m.	%	¥100m.	%	¥100m.	%
Assets						
Denominated in yen						
Loans	16,880	33·8	31,898	33·0	30,291	21·2
Securities	9	0·0	1,651	1·7	4,331	3·0
Call loans, etc.[a]	900	1·8	3,525	3·6	16,129	11·3
Inter-office account	1,542	3·1	2,984	3·1	6,001	4·2
Total denominated in yen	*22,062*	*44·2*	*46,750*	*48·4*	*67,252*	*47·2*
Denominated in foreign currency						
Loans	12,830	25·7	14,818	15·3	18,592	13·0
Cash and deposits with others	558	1·1	15,924	16·5	17,305	12·1
Call loans	1,724	3·5	3,729	3·9	14,664	10·3
Inter-office account	2,955	5·9	4,371	4·5	14,260	10·0
TOTAL ASSETS	49,942	100·0	96,585	100·0	142,628	100·0
Liabilities						
Denominated in yen						
Deposits	7,747	15·5	8,643	8·9	5,996	4·2
CDs	—	—	2,572	2·7	7,450	5·2
Borrowed money	125	0·3	5,479	5·7	12,773	9·0
Call money, etc.[a]	4,184	8·4	11,958	12·4	9,843	6·9
Inter-office account	2,471	4·9	6,181	6·4	10,938	7·7
Total denominated in yen	*16,992*	*33·9*	*39,959*	*41·4*	*53,636*	*37·6*
Denominated in foreign currency						
Deposits	2,360	4·7	3,843	4·0	11,119	7·8
Call money	946	1·9	7,735	8·0	13,660	9·6
Inter-office account	20,927	41·9	36,090	37·4	56,651	39·7
Conversion of foreign funds into yen[b]	6,069	12·2	9,987	10·3	18,553	13·0

   [a] Call loans, etc. include bills bought. Call money, etc. include bills sold.
   [b] Conversion of foreign funds into yen are the sum of funds raised by sales of foreign currency to yen in the Tokyo foreign exchange market (in this table, the difference of yen assets and yen liabilities) and yen funds raised from inter-office accounts (in this table, the difference of inter-office assets and liabilities in yen).
Source: BOJ.

¥2·5bn. or 50 per cent of total lending of ¥4·9bn. (see Table 5.3.)
   Most of the ¥1·1bn. of foreign currency deposits in foreign banks are the deposits of Government, Japanese foreign exchange banks, and trading companies, and the share of foreign deposits from other corporations and individuals is very small. Among the yen deposits of ¥1·3bn. the largest

shares are those of non-residents. CDs, and deposits of the debtors of the bank related to lending. The interest rates on the various types of deposit, both foreign currency deposits and yen deposits, are identical to those of Japanese banks.

(2) Lending operations. The lending of foreign banks in foreign currencies was formerly limited to medium- and long-term impact loans (of three to seven years in maturity, with five-year maturities the most common). But since the easing of regulations in 1979, it has been possible to make short-term impact loans. The quantity of these impact loans at the end of 1985 was ¥1·9bn., most of which was denominated in US dollars. The main source of funding for such lending is Eurodollar borrowings from the Euromarket which come through the inter-office account; foreign currency deposits, however, also play some role in funding impact loans. The interest rates on impact loans are usually the Euro-dollar interest rates plus a fixed spread. At times there are surpluses of foreign currency funds from the total amounts borrowed, and these very short-term surpluses are often lent in the Tokyo dollar-call market.

The yen-denominated lending of foreign banks, which was ¥3bn. at the end of 1985, is almost entirely of a short-term nature and comes about through lending on bills within prescribed credit limits established on a client-by-client basis. Though a part of the funds for such lending is raised through yen deposits, this amount is quantitatively limited, and most are raised through conversion of foreign funds into yen in the foreign exchange market or through call borrowings and sales of bills. Conversions of foreign funds into yen were about ¥1·9bn. at the end of 1985, and this amount included narrowly defined conversions of foreign funds into yen, which are the raising of funds in yen through selling foreign exchange on the Tokyo foreign exchange market, and the yen borrowed through inter-office accounts. Call and bill borrowings totalled about ¥1 trillion for foreign banks, most of which are borrowers in the call and bill markets. In most cases, the interest rates on yen lendings by foreign banks are determined on the basis of short-term money market rates such as the commercial bill rate.

(3) Foreign exchange and foreign trade finance operations. The foreign exchange and foreign trade financing operations of foreign banks in Japan are almost identical to those of Japanese foreign exchange banks, but some foreign banks, particularly those from the United States, also act as suppliers of certain foreign exchange funds to Japanese banks through rediscount of export bills that have been bought by Japanese banks and through dollar refinancing of loans made by Japanese banks, for example, through the acceptance or rediscount of refinance bills issued by Japanese banks on the basis of import bill transactions. But the importance of foreign banks in this respect has declined in recent years as a result of the diversification of ways

of raising of foreign currency funds and the expansion of the number of branches of Japanese banks in foreign countries.

(iii) Recent developments

During the high growth period when Japan faced a continuous shortage of capital and shortage of foreign exchange, foreign banks made very large profits through borrowing funds in foreign markets and lending them to Japanese corporations. But the business environment for foreign banks in Japan changed greatly because of the reduction in funds demands by corporations which accompanied the shift to lower economic growth and also because of the decline in the importance of foreign exchange fund raising through bank borrowing due to the internationalization of finance. For foreign banks, the effect of the reduction in corporate fund demand and particularly for yen borrowing has been very important, and has been a major cause of difficulty in the domestic operations sector for foreign banks in recent years. For the six-month business period ending in March 1985, the total current profits of foreign banks in Japan as a group were 30 per cent lower than in the same period of the previous year. As a result, most foreign banks are directing their efforts toward finding demand for funds in the areas that remain relatively strong, such as leasing, factoring, housing finance, and consumer finance. In addition, some of the large US banks have begun to handle underwriting, over-the-counter sales, and Government bonds, and have begun to diversify and expand their operations actively into other areas, such as trust operations.

c. Long-term credit banks

(i) Overview

Long-term credit banks differ from their pre-war predecessors, which were based on special laws and are completely private banks organized under the Long-term Credit Bank Law of 1952. The Industrial Bank of Japan had been organized under a special law in the pre-war period but converted to an ordinary bank in 1950 and then reconverted to a long-term credit bank in December 1952. The Long-term Credit Bank of Japan was established originally in December 1952. The Nippon Credit Bank was organized in April 1957, originally as the Japan Hypoteck Bank.

Long-term credit banks are of course financial institutions that concentrate their operations on making long-term loans. The reason for their establishment was not only to separate long- and short-term financial business, but also to lighten the burden on ordinary banks of providing long-term funds. Long-term credit banks are permitted to issue bank debentures as a means of raising the funds for long-term lending, but are restricted in where they may accept deposits. As a result, their fund-raising differs substantially in character from that of ordinary banks, and they also have many fewer branches.

The long-term credit banks played an extremely important role as institutions specializing in long-term finance throughout the high growth period, but their business environment changed completely with the change in the financial structure at the time of the first oil crisis. In response to this change in the environment, the long-term credit banks put great effort into developing new demands for funds in the domestic market, but also moved very aggressively into international financial operations. On the domestic side, they expanded their financing of the wholesale and service trades, which in recent years have had a strong funds demand, and entered businesses related to demand of individuals for funding through lending to private housing finance companies and consumer credit companies. They have also been active in lending for Government purposes such as petroleum and non-ferrous metal storage as well as in lending to information-processing industries. On the international side, just as city banks, the long-term credit banks have not only lent to the foreign operations of Japanese corporations but have also participated in international syndicated lending to foreign governments, public bodies, and corporations, as well as in the international securities business.

(ii) Operations

(1) Debenture issue.   As noted above, a debenture issue is the main source of financing for long-term credit banks. The limit on debenture issue is thirty times own capital. For regular corporations, the limits on bond issue are normally twice the level of own capital as defined either in the Commercial Law or in the Law Concerning Temporary Measures on Bond Issue Limits, or the net assets of the corporation as seen in the last balance sheet, whichever is lower. But because bank debentures are the main source of funding for long-term credit banks, the limit of their issue have been expanded greatly.

There are two types of debenture issued by long-term credit banks, five-year coupon debentures and one-year discount debentures. In principle these debentures are uninscribed, but if the subscriber or the owner wishes, inscription may be carried out. Moreover, the timing, amounts, and conditions for issue of these debentures must be pre-notified to the Minister of Finance. The total amount outstanding in bank debentures from long-term credit banks stood at ¥28·9bn. at the end of 1985, equivalent to 12·5 per cent of outstanding deposits at all banks.

(2) Deposit operations.   Deposit operations are an indispensable type of business for long-term credit banks if they are to carry out smoothly their asset management and other types of business. However, there are certain restrictions placed on the types of deposit that long-term credit banks may

accept, and as a result, the outstanding amount of such deposits is small. That is, long-term credit banks may accept deposits only from the Government, local government, public bodies, their own borrowers, corporations who entrust bond subscriptions to them, and other clients. One reason for these restrictions was the thought that it would not be appropriate to allow the raising of funds through short-term deposits to long-term credit banks, which were intended to concentrate on longer-term credit business. In addition, it was intended that there should not be express competition for deposits between long-term credit banks and ordinary banks, and that the two types of bank should operate in an independent fashion. The total of deposits and debenture proceeds outstanding at the end of 1985 was about ¥35bn., equivalent to 13 per cent of the total of all such liabilities held by all banks.

(3) Lending operations. The most important funding supply operations of long-term credit banks are lending for plant and equipment and for long-term working capital, discount of bills, guarantee of debts, and acceptance of bills; that is, the long-term credit banks primarily provide credit for plant and equipment and long-term working capital, but, as an auxiliary to these loans, provide funds also for short-term working capital (funds of less than six months in maturity). There is, however, a restriction that the total supply of short-term working capital funds by long-term credit banks must fall within the limits of the deposits. Beside lending for long-term business funds it is permitted for long-term credit banks to lend for other long-term funding, i.e. loans of greater than six months in maturity, such as housing construction loans and consumer loans, on condition that they accept real estate as collateral.

Because of their character, long-term credit banks must take particular care in management of their assets. The Long-term Credit Bank Law establishes special provisions in this regard in Clause 7, and stipulates that long-term credit banks must take special account of the particularities of the assets based on their lending of long-term funds, etc. and must attempt to ensure the safety and collectability of these assets. They must require collateral of certain value, and must give special consideration to methods of operation such as repayment of lending in tranches.

In December 1974, long-term credit banks were included along with city banks in the Ministry of Finance circular that required credit limits to be placed on large-lot loans. A partial revision of the Long-term Credit Bank Law in 1982 made these provisions part of the legal code. For long-term credit banks, total lending to any one borrower must not exceed 30 per cent of own capital.

The lending of long-term credit banks stagnated after the first oil crisis, reflecting the change in the economic environment. This slow-down was particularly conspicuous in lending for industrial equipment. In the early

1980s, there was a noticeable increase in activity relating to short-term working capital loans in order to compensate for the drop in industrial equipment lending.

The composition of lending by industry by long-term credit banks has changed substantially over the last ten years. The share going to manufacturing industries has declined from 47 per cent at the end of 1975 to 23 per cent at the end of 1985, while the share going to so-called 'tertiary' industries such as service industries, wholesale trade, hotels, leisure, etc., private housing finance companies, consumer credit companies, and information-processing industries has increased rapidly and currently takes a large share.

(4) Securities-related operations. The securities-related operations of long-term credit banks are similar to those of ordinary banks and are very diverse, including the securities operations concerning public bonds (such as over-the-counter sales and dealing in public bonds), securities investment operations, securities lending operations, trustee operations, and securities agent operations. Among these various operations, the long-term credit banks join the city banks in playing important roles in the fields of mortgage debenture trust business and trustee business, i.e., the trustee operations concerning subscription of bonds.

(5) Other operations. In addition to the operations mentioned above, long-term credit banks also operate businesses in the same way as city banks and regional banks. Among these are domestic exchange operations and international operations (foreign exchange business, foreign trade financing, foreign locale lending, and international securities operations), along with guarantee of obligation and safe-keeping deposit services.

(iii) Assets, liabilities, income and expenditure

The types of business described above are reflected in the asset and liability composition of the long-term credit banks. Let us consider a few important characteristics of the liability and asset composition through pointing out the trends in the main accounts.

(1) Liabilities. At the end of 1985, bank debentures were the most important source of funding for long-term credit banks, providing about 60 per cent of total liabilities compared to 13 per cent for deposits (see Table 5.4). This is, of course, in stark contrast to the condition of city and regional banks, for whom deposits account for about 70 per cent or more of total liabilities.

(2) Assets. On the assets side, lending was 70–80 per cent of total assets during the high growth period, but has fallen to a little over 60 per cent in recent years. The share of securities investments in total assets was between

TABLE 5.4 *Principal Accounts of Long-term Credit Banks, by year-end*

	1965 ¥100m.	%	1970 ¥100m.	%	1975 ¥100m.	%	1980 ¥100m.	%	1985 ¥100m.	%
Assets										
Cash and deposits with others	790	2·6	2,477	3·8	11,072	6·6	12,536	4·7	23,114	5·2
Call loans[a]	498	1·7	427	0·7	2,466	1·5	2,369	0·9	4,668	1·0
Commodity bonds	—		—		—		—		1,905	0·4
Securities	2,947	9·9	7,133	10·9	23,351	13·9	52,524	19·5	85,577	19·1
Loans and discounts[b]	22,483	75·1	47,293	72·2	110,582	65·8	165,244	61·5	285,248	63·7
Other	3,211	10·7	8,150	12·4	20,630	12·2	36,063	13·4	47,312	10·6
TOTAL	29,929	100·0	65,480	100·0	168,101	100·0	268,736	100·0	447,824	100·0
Liabilities										
Deposits	2,422	8·1	8,092	12·4	27,449	16·3	34,344	12·8	56,463	12·6
CDs	—		—		—		1,964	0·7	5,784	1·3
Bank debentures issued	22,616	75·6	46,401	70·9	110,327	65·6	182,132	67·8	288,552	64·4
Borrowed money[b]	324	1·1	654	1·0	586	0·3	114	0·0	2,971	0·7
Call money[a]	14	0·0	0	0·0	402	0·2	1,503	0·6	27,142	6·1
Capital	430	1·4	740	1·1	1,754	1·1	2,479	0·9	2,821	0·6
Other	4,123	13·8	9,593	14·7	27,583	16·4	46,200	17·2	64,091	14·3

[a] Call loans (or call money) include bills bought (or sold).
[b] Loans (or borrowed money) include those to or from financial institutions.

Source: BOJ, *Economic Statistics Annual.*

3 and 7 per cent during the second half of the 1950s, but has grown gradually since then and currently stands at about 20 per cent. The proportion of liquid assets such as currency and funds on deposit is lower than that at ordinary banks. The reason for this is that long-term credit banks do not need substantial reserve assets, partly because of the higher proportion of substantial securities on the liabilities side.

(3) Income and expenditure. Considering the character of long-term credit bank operations, it is only natural that interest from lending should be the most important source of income and that interest on debentures the most important expenditure.

The overall yield on total funds used is a little higher for long-term credit banks than for city banks and regional banks because of the larger share of funds invested in long-term lending. However, the costs for long-term credit banks are also higher because of the important role played by bank debentures on the fund-raising side. Particularly in recent years, the profit margins for the long-term credit banks has been conspicuously smaller than that for city and regional banks, not only because of the major decrease in yields on working assets due to the reduction in demand for fixed-interest long-term lending but also because of the relatively small decline in the interest rates on bank debentures, which are established as part of the long-term interest rate structure based on the subscriber's yields for long-term Government

TABLE 5.5 *Funding Cost Comparison, 1984*

	Long-term credit banks (%)	Trust banks (%)	City banks (%)	Regional banks (%)
Cost of funds (A)	8·43	9·73	8·15	6·85
Cost of deposits and debentures	8·30	10·34	8·04	6·80
Interest rate on deposits and debentures	7·75	8·03	6·86	4·74
Personnel expenses ratio	0·20	1·31	0·67	1·33
Non-personnel expenses ratio	0·32	0·94	0·44	0·64
Yield on working assets (B)	8·43	8·70	8·35	7·10
Profit margin (B − A)	0·00	—[a]	0·20	0·25

[a] No margin is shown for trust banks because all the indirect costs of the trust sector of their business is included in costs of deposits and debentures.

Source: Federation of Bankers Associations of Japan, *Zenkoku Ginko Zaimu Shohyo Bunseki* (Analysis of Financial Tables of All Banks).

coupon bonds (see Table 5.5). The long-term credit banks, however, have a much lower cost ratio than do ordinary banks. This lower level of cost ratios reflects the special character of long-term credit banks in having a relatively small number of branches and employees compared to the total quantity of funds.

d. Trust banks

(i) Overview

The trust business is a set of transactions in which a trust owner transfers, through a set of legal acts (act of trust), the property rights of his own property to another party (the trustee) and at the same time entrusts the management and disposal of these assets to the trustee for a specified purpose (the purpose of the trust) for the benefit of society, himself, or a third party (the beneficiary). In such cases, the trustee receives a transfer of assets and has the right to manage and dispose of these assets for the specified purpose in his own name and not in the name of the trust owner. Thus, the trust business was originally the business of managing assets, and in the pre-war period trust companies handled some of this type of business. In the post-war period, however, trust companies became primarily institutions of long-term fanance, so that trust banks became institutions that specialized in longer-term transactions and came to hold an important place in this business along with long-term credit banks.

There were many small trust companies in Japan during the early years of the twentieth century, but the modern trust business got its real start in 1926 with the Trust Law and the Trust Business Law. Under the regulation of these laws, the existence of weak and small trust companies became difficult, and in the late 1920s, trust companies organized under the Trust Business Law came to play an important role in long-term finance chiefly through money trusts. Joint operation of banking and trust business under one roof became legal in 1943, as part of an expansion of the means of raising more war-financing funds. The original law was the Law Concerning Joint Operation of Ordinary Banks, Savings Bank Business and Trust Business, which was revised in 1981 to become the Law Concerning Joint Operation of Ordinary Banking and Trust Operations (hereafter called the Joint Operation Law). As a result of this law there were, just after the end of the war, only seven firms left that dealt exclusively in the trust business, and eleven that were jointly operating banking and trust businesses.

In the post-war period, trust companies temporarily faced a difficult situation because of the high inflation and the prohibition on engagement in securities business under Clause 65 of the Securities and Exchange Law of 1947. Under a plan emanating from the occupation authorities, six trust companies converted themselves into banks and carried out their trust operations as joint operations. These institutions were renamed as trust banks, and business actually began in 1948. (The remaining firm was converted into a securities company.)

In 1951, the trust banks began to handle securities investment trusts and in 1952, loan trusts. Thereafter, new forms of business were permitted, such as pension trusts, movable property trusts, and transfer agent operations. In

December 1954, the authorities decided to separate the banking and trust fields and drew a sharp distinction, in their treatment of licensing new branches and regulation of trust business, between banks that jointly operated both businesses but concentrated on banking and those that concentrated on the trust business. The original seven trust banks (Mitsubishi, Sumitomo, Mitsui, Yasuda, Toyo, Chuo, and Nippon) and nine foreign banks that opened for business in October 1985 are the trust banks that concentrate on trust business. One city bank (Daiwa Bank) and two local banks (the Bank of Ryukyu and the Bank of Okinawa) also operate trust businesses but concentrate on banking operations. The major business difference between the two classes of bank is that the former handles loan trusts while the latter does not.

The most important characteristic of Japanese trust banks is their role as important institutions for long-term finance. Particularly since the early 1960s, loan trusts have grown at a tremendous rate, and trust banks have taken a large share in the field of long-term lending. Second most important is that trust banks have a strong character as savings institutions for the general public, a characteristic that has been particularly striking since the end of the war. Important reasons for this have been the fading from view of pre-war investors due to the war, and the subsequent virulent inflation, but also the large share of the general public in the trust banks' clientele, reflecting the rise of levels of income and equalization of income distribution that have accompanied high economic growth. One cannot, however, overlook the fact that measures such as the improvement in the liquidity of beneficiary certificates and reduction in their size, as seen for example in loan trusts, made acceptance of trust business easier during the conditions of the post-war period.[5]

(ii) Operations

Although trust banks jointly manage both trust operations and banking operations, these two types of business are different in character and therefore must be managed separately (according to Clause 28 of the Trust Law). As a result, trust banks have two sets of accounts, the banking accounts and trust accounts.

[5] The important contrasts between trust business in the United States and trust business in Japan are as follows: first, the asset management function is the focus of trust operations in the United States while the financial trust function of earning high interest for funds entrusted and returning those funds to the entruster is at the centre of the trust business in Japan. Secondly, in the field of operations geared toward individuals, individual management of so-called 'asset management' trusts, such as large-scale inheritances, is the main type of business in the United States, whereas joint management of financial trusts, which are primarily loan trusts, and which are composed of small amounts of entrusted assets, are the main source of business in Japan. Thirdly, 90 per cent of the funds in trust in the United States are invested in bonds and equities, whereas the largest portion, that is, about 30 per cent, of funds are invested in loans in Japan. Fourthly, in the United States there is a strict separation in the organization of institutions that jointly manage trust and banking business (the so-called 'Chinese wall') whereas in Japan these institutions are unified even in personnel.

The banking accounts of trust banks are identical to those of city banks and regional banks and therefore we limit consideration here to the trust accounts. Concerning the types of asset that trust banks may accept in their trust operations, Clause 1 of the Joint Operations Law applies the provisions of Clause 4 of the Trust Business Law. Only six types of asset may be accepted. Money, securities, monetary claims, movable property, real estate and fixtures, and surface rights and land lease rights.

(1) Money trusts.   The type of trust asset initially accepted by trust banks is money. There are currently several types of money trusts including ordinary money trusts, pension trusts, loan trusts, securities investment trusts, and entrustments of money other than ordinary money trusts (for details see Chapter 3).

(2) Non-money trusts.

Securities trusts. The types of trust asset initially accepted by trust banks are securities, and there are two kinds of securities trust: management types and loan types (or investment types). The former are called securities administration trusts and the latter securities operation trusts.

Monetary claim in trust. Monetary claim in trusts are those carried out with the object of ensuring and investing monetary claims such as the collection of interest or principal on monetary claims and the administration or preservation of collateral claims. Historically, this type of trust was limited mostly to life insurance claim in trusts, but from June 1973 housing loan claim in trusts were added.

Life insurance claim in trusts are trust contracts in which the insuree is the trust owner and the trust bank, which acts as trustee, is the designated recipient of the insurance claim. When the insurance contract reaches maturity or if a claim occurs, the trust bank receives the insurance money and manages and invests these funds according to the trust contract for the benefit of the beneficiary indicated by the trust owner. Until the insurance funds are received, this type of trust is a monetary claim in trust; after the funds are received it becomes a designated money trust. There are two types of life insurance trust. The first is the so-called 'life insurance trust with revenue source', in which the trust bank not only has the right to receive the insurance funds but also pays the insurance premium to the insurance company in place of the trust owner. The second type is the so-called 'life insurance trust without revenue source', in which the trust bank is entrusted only with the right to receive the insurance monies while the payment of the insurance premium is made by the trust owner.

A housing loan claim in trust is a type of trust in which a private housing finance company, which is the trust owner, entrusts a certain amount of housing loan claims to a trust bank and then sells the beneficiary certificates issued by the trust bank to institutional investors. The purpose of this is to make housing loan claims liquid and thus to make it possible to raise the housing funds in a stable way.

Movable Property in Trusts. Movable property in trusts are those whose purpose is to manage and dispose of commodities or other goods that are the trust asset. In fact, the management and disposal of such goods is normally the business of wholesalers and warehouses owners, and so it is not entirely appropriate that such trusts should be operated in general by a financial institution. However, it is approved for trust banks to be trustees for rolling stock or other transport vehicles, for machinery and for precious metals such as gold bullion (precious metals in trust began in February 1982). Currently the most important types of movable property in trust are shipping trusts and computer trusts.

Shipping trusts operate as follows. First, the shipbuilder, the trust bank, and the ship user conclude a basic agreement concerning the ship trust. When the ship is delivered, the shipbuilder concludes a ship trust contact with the trust bank and the ownership right to the ship is transferred to the trust bank. At that time, the shipbuilder receives beneficiary certificates to prove his rights of receipt and uses these certificates as collateral for financing. At the same time, the trust bank and the user of the ship conclude a ship-leasing agreement conditional on the ship in question being purchased by the user at the expiration of the lease contract. During the term of the lease, the ship user pays leasing fees to the trust bank and then, at the end of the period of the lease, pays the remaining price of the ship to the trust bank and takes possession of the ship.

Real estate in trusts. Real estate in trusts are agreements in which land and structures are entrusted for management or disposal to a trust bank. Formally these agreements are called 'land and fixtures in trust'. Management trusts are concluded for the purpose of collecting rents for land or houses as well as for management and preservation. Disposal trusts are concluded for the purpose of making appropriate improvements to land and selling it, and are also used in cases when the landowner wishes to sell the land in question to the renter.

A land trust is one type of real estate in trust, which has often been viewed in related business as somewhat different from general real estate in trusts. The purpose of a land trust is to use land efficiently in order to reap high profits. The landowner, who is the trust owner, entrusts the land to the trust bank and becomes the beneficiary of the trust. The trust bank, which is the trustee, then builds structures, raises the necessary funding, finds tenants, and manages the structure along the lines of the trust contract. In contrast to general real estate in trusts in which a completed piece of real estate was entrusted, land trusts are special in that the trust bank is entrusted with the implementation of the entire operation of building, raising funds, and finding tenants. There are two types of land trust, one in which a structure is built and leased to tenants and the property managed, and another in which the structure is not leased but instead sold. In both cases, however, there is no guarantee of principal, and the trust bank pays the actual earnings on the operation to the trust owner (the beneficiary) according to the successes of the investment.

Land trusts were instituted in 1984, after increased debate from 1983 onward concerning more efficient use of land through the introduction of more private activity; their introduction also served the purpose of increasing income of trust banks through supply of new products that used their trust function and that depended on asset management operations. Until now, use of land trusts has been limited to privately owned properties, but currently the application of such trusts to public lands is also under consideration.

Mortgage debentures in trust. Mortgage debentures in trust is one in which the corporation issuing the bond is the trust owner and entrusts to the bank or trust bank (trustee) either corporate collateral rights or physical collateral rights on the basis of the status of the corporation as single property including land, ships, railroads, factories, or mines. The trustee then manages the collateral rights on behalf of the creditors of the debenture issue as a whole.

In general, collateral rights are an intangible asset and therefore would not be permitted independently as the object of a trust; only in the case of corporate debenture are they permitted because of the difficulty of dividing collateral rights. Such trusts are based on the Mortgage Debentures Trust Law of 1905 and thus are older than ordinary trusts based on the Trust Law. Engaging in the mortgage debenture trust business requires approval from the Minister of Finance, and currently the seven trust banks as well as the city banks (including the Bank of Tokyo), the three long-term credit banks, and some regional banks engage in such business. The largest portion of corporate debentures currently floated use this system, generally with joint trusteeship by banks and trust banks with which the firm in question has close ties.

(3) Investment of funds held in trust.

Lending. Lending forms the largest share of assets of trust banks held in their trust accounts, excluding the securities investment trusts. In recent years, however, securities have been gaining a larger share.

The lending within the trust accounts of banks is of necessity a lending for plant and equipment funds due to the role of trust banks as providers of long-term finance. At the end of 1985, lending for industrial equipment accounted for about 50 per cent of total lending by the trust accounts of banks, much higher than the 20 per cent for city banks and regional banks.

Secondly, trust banks tend to lend more to large corporations than do city or regional banks. About 64 per cent of trust banks' lending goes to firms with capital exceeding ¥100m., while about 42 per cent of the lending of city and local banks goes to such firms. Because of the character of trusts, the lending within trust accounts is used for large-scale, long-term safe financing.

However, trust banks were also subjected to the overall credit limits to individual borrowers implemented in December 1974, and total lending to any individual borrower may not exceed 30 per cent of own capital (for trust accounts, total lending is defined to include designated joint operating money trust accounts and loan trust accounts).

Classified by type of industry, much of the lending of trust accounts goes to long-term industrial equipment funds supplied to basic industries such as manufacturing, electricity, gas, water, transportation, and telecommunication. Recently, however, lending to real estate industries and individuals has grown very rapidly and the types of borrowing client are being diversified.

Securities investment. Until about 1970, two-thirds of the securities held in the trust accounts of trust banks belonged to investment trusts while only one-third was assigned to other types of trust; since 1975, however, the proportion of securities, and particularly of Government bonds, that are applied to other trusts has risen. By the end of 1985 this proportion stood at about 60 per cent.

(iii) Assets, liabilities, and income position

(1) Assets and liabilities of the trust accounts. Of the liabilities of trust accounts, money trusts account for 97 per cent while the share of non-money trusts in total liabilities has remained at only 3 per cent. Until the second half of the 1960s, ordinary money trusts grew very steadily, but since then they have grown rather less. In recent years, specified money trusts have grown extremely rapidly and have risen to 17 per cent of total liabilities. For example, loan trusts have also grown extremely rapidly because their dividend yield exceeds those on money trusts and the yields on deposits. Between 1965 and 1975 their share was about 50 per cent of total liabilities, but it has fallen to under 40 per cent recently because of the extremely rapid growth of other types of trust. In addition, pension trusts have been growing steadily, a trend noticeable since 1975.

On the asset side of the trust accounts of trust banks, the share of investment trust securities rose temporarily with the increase in securities investment trusts, but after that the share of loans recovered. After 1975, however, the share of loans once again began to decline steadily because of the weak growth of demand for plant and equipment investment funds. In addition, the share of securities other than those applied to securities investment trusts has been rising, and the asset composition of trust banks has undergone considerable diversification.

Because of the character of the trust business, very little is held in cash reserves, either as currency or deposits. In addition, the trust accounts of banks make very few call loans, and even the largest portion of the call loans they make are reserve assets for securities investment trusts. For proper trusts, there are very few call loans indeed (see Table 5.6).

(2) Assets and liabilities in the banking accounts of trust banks.   As described above, even trust banks that concentrate on trust business have banking accounts in addition to their trust accounts (see Table 5.7). In comparing the sizes of the trust accounts and the banking accounts for trust banks that concentrate on trust business the trust accounts are of course much larger. But the sizes of the banking accounts differ widely by bank. For most, the banking accounts are of between 20 and 30 per cent of total assets. The share of the banking accounts of trust banks that concentrate on the trust business in the total banking accounts of all banks was about 4 per cent and 6 per cent, respectively, for deposits and loans and 13 per cent for securities at the end of 1985.

All the trust banks that concentrate on trust business are located in major metropolitan areas, and the banking accounts of these banks concentrate on transactions with large corporations, just as do city banks. As a result, the deposits in the banking accounts of trust banks that concentrate on the trust business are primarily corporate deposits and the share of demand deposits is extremely high. In contrast to their lending by trust accounts (which concentrates on plant and equipment lending), their lending by banking accounts is largely for working capital.

(3) Income and expenditure position.   The most interesting characteristic of the profit and loss calculations for trust banks is the small share of remuneration from trusts received from the operation of trust business relative to the income from banking accounts. Of course, there are large gross income and expenditure flows connected with trust accounts, all of which lie behind the trust remuneration finally received by the bank. However, trust accounts are basically kept for other owners; that is, the investment results are basically a part of the accounts of beneficiaries and of those outside the trust bank. Thus, if one looks at the income statement of the trust bank as a corporation, the remuneration for trust activities is all that shows up in the portion pertaining to the trust accounts (see Table 5.8).

Personnel and non-personnel costs in principle ought to be separated into those incurred for trust accounts and those incurred for banking accounts. Such a separation, however, is difficult, and all such costs are entered under the banking accounts.

It is often said that the interest margin for trust banks is narrower than that for ordinary banks. This is because trust banks operate on the principle of distributing actual dividends of investments so that remuneration for trust services is in the nature of a fee. That is, trust funds are invested on the theory of high volume and low margin. In addition, the charges and commission received are relatively high for trust banks.

TABLE 5.6 *Principal Accounts of the Trust Accounts of All Banks, by Year-end*

	1965 ¥100m.	1965 %	1970 ¥100m.	1970 %	1975 ¥100m.	1975 %	1980 ¥100m.	1980 %	1984 ¥100m.	1984 %
Assets										
Cash and deposits with others	37	0·1	53	0·1	160	0·1	205	0·0	1,518	0·2
Call loans[a]	2,266	6·2	2,995	3·9	4,461	2·1	16,878	3·9	41,410	4·9
Securities	608	1·7	3,115	4·0	19,135	9·1	77,433	17·9	247,659	29·5
Securities held for securities investment trust	9,475	25·9	10,802	14·0	33,315	15·9	58,701	13·6	158,174	18·9
Loans and discounts	21,926	60·0	51,550	66·8	120,149	57·3	175,241	40·5	227,522	27·1
Due from bank accounts	n.a.	n.a.	1,814	2·3	9,427	4·5	35,595	8·2	104,398	12·5
Others	2,236	6·1	6,856	8·9	23,179	11·0	68,453	15·8	57,731	6·9
TOTAL ASSETS	36,548	100·0	77,185	100·0	209,826	100·0	432,506	100·0	838,412	100·0
Liabilities										
Money trust (Ordinary money trust)	4,424	12·1	11,006	14·3	26,071	12·4	58,193	13·5	139,701	16·7
Loan trust	19,533	53·5	43,724	56·6	106,659	50·8	191,094	44·2	322,854	38·5
Pension trust	138	0·4	2,539	3·3	15,775	7·5	50,890	11·8	117,843	14·1
Securities investment trust	11,237	30·8	13,325	17·3	38,396	18·3	74,144	17·1	197,673	23·6
Money deposited other than Money Trust	9	0·0	1,717	2·2	8,712	4·2	33,856	7·8	36,281	4·3
TOTAL LIABILITIES	35,361	96·8	72,311	93·7	195,613	93·2	408,177	94·4	814,352	97·1
Securities in trust	963	2·6	3,545	4·6	8,689	4·1	12,267	2·8	14,056	1·7
Others	224	0·6	1,329	1·7	5,524	2·6	12,062	2·8	10,004	1·2

[a] Call loans include bills bought.

Source: **BOJ**, *Economic Statistics Monthly*.

TABLE 5.7 *Principal Banking Accounts of Specialized Trust Banks[a], by Year-end*

	1965		1970		1975		1980		1984	
	¥100m.	%	¥100m.	%	¥100m.	%	¥100m.	%	¥100m.	%
Assets										
Cash and deposits with others	1,289	11·4	1,874	7·5	5,873	8·2	10,895	8·8	23,601	8·0
Call loans[b]	248	2·2	1,525	6·1	1,981	2·8	1,656	1·3	21,341	7·2
Community bonds	—	—	—	—	—	—	—	—	3,994	1·3
Securities	2,461	21·7	4,826	19·2	14,071	19·7	40,783	33·0	77,250	26·1
Loans and discounts	5,919	52·3	12,401	49·3	32,210	45·1	48,445	39·1	143,204	48·4
Others	1,410	12·4	4,514	18·0	17,309	24·2	21,986	17·8	26,524	9·0
TOTAL ASSETS	11,327	100·0	25,140	100·0	71,444	100·0	123,765	100·0	295,914	100·0
Liabilities										
Deposits	8,112	71·6	17,011	67·7	38,742	54·2	53,375	43·1	86,026	29·1
CDs	—	—	—	—	—	—	2,993	2·4	7,476	2·5
Borrowed money	87	0·8	150	0·6	636	0·9	139	0·1	193	0·1
Due to trust account	n.a.	n.a.	1,814	7·2	8,087	11·3	35,235	28·5	102,641	34·7
Call money	425	3·8	207	0·8	1,179	1·7	4,012	3·2	51,416	17·4
Capital	286	2·5	741	2·9	1,379	1·9	1,819	1·5	2,467	0·8
Others	2,417	21·3	5,217	20·8	21,421	30·0	26,192	21·2	45,695	15·4

[a] Banks engaged mostly in trust business.
[b] Call loans (or money) include bills bought (or sold).

Source: BOJ, *Economic Statistics Annual.*

TABLE 5.8   *Income and Expenditure of Trust Banks, 1984*

	¥100m.	%
Current profits		
Interest on loan	10,614	31·1
Interest on securities	6,059	17·8
Interest on call loan and bills bought	2,560	7·5
Interest on other securities and bonds	8,633	25·3
Remuneration on trust	3,593	10·5
Charges and commissions received	1,759	5·2
Other	917	2·7
TOTAL CURRENT PROFITS	34,135	100·0
Current expenditure		
Interest on deposits	12,955	40·3
Interest on call money and bills sold	4,689	14·6
Interest on other securities and bonds	7,671	23·9
Operating expenditure	4,343	13·5
Other	2,468	7·7
TOTAL CURRENT EXPENDITURE	32,126	100·0

Source: Federation of Bankers Associations of Japan, *Analysis of Balance Sheet for All Banks.*

e. *Sogo* banks

(i) Overview

Sogo banks are based on the *Sogo* Bank Law of 1951, which was part of the post-war restructuring of the financial system. The *sogo* banks were converted from a traditional type of popular financing institution called *mujin* companies, the access to whose resources was determined by lottery.

Sogo banks, which take corporate form, rather than old-fashioned *mujin* companies, specialize in financing small- and medium-sized firms, with the purpose of contributing to smoothing of finance for the general populace and increasing their savings.

There are two major differences between *sogo* banks and ordinary banks: *sogo* banks face restrictions on granting of credit to firms other than small businesses but are also permitted to continue instalment financing operations in just the same way as the *mujin* companies previously. However, in recent years, the instalment savings and lending portion of *sogo* bank business has declined in weight. In fact the *sogo* banks have become similar to ordinary banks; that is, while city banks were lending to large corporations during the high growth period, *sogo* banks were at the same time playing an important role in developing and incubating small and medium-sized firms. But the *sogo* banks achieved very high growth as well during the process, and gradually their instalment lending and instalment savings business withered, while there was an increase in their transactions with firms other than small businesses and while their areas of business expanded and their loans became larger and larger in size. As time passed, they became more and more like ordinary banks. The scale of operations in *sogo* banks came to differ according to the differences in regional development across the country, but it is undeniable that the behavior of *sogo* banks diverged from that which was originally considered for them.

The Committee for Financial System Research considered this problem in a report in October 1967 entitled *The State of Finance for Small Firms.* As a result of this report, two new laws concerning financing of small enterprises were passed. These laws were based on the notion of improving the efficiency and smoothness of financing for small firms: they were the Law Concerning a Revision of a Portion of the *Sogo* Bank Law and the *Shinkin* Bank Law and the Law Concerning Merger and Conversion of Financial Institutions. These two laws were implemented in June 1968.

These legal revisions of 1968 clarified several important points. First, they defined small firms as those with less than 300 employees and less than ¥200m. in capital. Secondly, they raised the minimum capital for *sogo* banks and were intended to improve the financial soundness of the institutions. Thirdly, they abolished the geographical limits within which these instititions could do business. And finally, the merger and conversion law opened the road for conversion of *sogo* banks into ordinary banks so long as certain conditions were fulfilled, such as not causing difficulties for medium- or small-sized firms and contributing to improved financial efficiency.

A next round of legal revision in 1973 both raised the maximum capital in the definition of a small or medium-sized firms from ¥200m. to ¥400m. and permitted *sogo* banks to handle foreign exchange operations because of the increased activity of small firms in foreign trade. The most recent set of legal revisions, in 1981, once again raised the maximum capital in the definition of a small firm from ¥400m. to ¥800m. and also expanded the limits of businesses for *sogo* banks to a level identical with those of ordinary banks. As *sogo* banks expanded over the years, they came to occupy a position of importance as objects of monetary policy, for example through the application to them of the reserve requirements system in April 1963 and through their eligibility for securities purchase operations from the Bank of Japan in March 1966.

The process of development of *sogo* banks was one of convergence in character toward ordinary banks, and it remains the fact that this development diluted their original character. With financial liberalization, with the long-term trend toward monetary easing, and with the intensification of the competition among financial institutions, the *sogo* banks have had to respond to many pressures such as the entry of city banks into financing of medium-sized and small enterprises and the close geographical proximity of *shinkin* banks. It is fair to say that *sogo* banks are currently searching for a particular niche in the financial system.

At the end of 1985, there were sixty-nine *sogo* banks with 4,279 branches and a deposit base, including instalment savings, of ¥37·5bn. and lending, of both regular loans and instalment loans, of ¥30·6bn.

Small firms continue to get a significant proportion of their funds from *sogo* banks. At the end of 1985, *sogo* banks provided 15 per cent of the borrowings of small firms, while the share of financial institutions specializing in loans to small and medium-sized firms, which includes lending by *shinkin* banks and credit associations, was 37 per cent. All banks provided about 51 per cent, and Government financial institutions about 9 per cent, with a small amount being made up from other sources.

(ii) Operations

The business activities of *sogo* banks were made identical to those of ordinary banks through the legal revision of 1981, with the exception that *sogo* banks may still carry out mutual instalment operations. Just like ordinary banks, they may take deposits or instalment savings, make loans, discount bills, and carry out foreign exchange transactions, all activities that are part of the normal banking business, but they may also engage in auxiliary businesses such as over-the-counter sales and dealing in Government bonds and public bonds and in securities-related operations such as securities investments, guarantee of liabilities, proxy and agent operations, and sales of gold bullion. For activities covered under other laws (such as collateralized security trust business) that had not been permitted to *sogo* banks previously, it is now possible for *sogo* banks to operate such businesses jointly upon receipt of approval under the law in question. From the point of view of contributing to smooth financing for small and medium-sized firms, however, *sogo* banks are still in principle limited to lending to such firms (although it is possible for loans in an amount up to 20 per cent of total loans to go to large corporations). The total credit limits to individual borrowers apply to *sogo* banks just as to ordinary banks, and the limit on lending to any one person is 20 per cent of total own capital or ¥1·5 milliard, whichever is smaller. The interest rates on deposits paid at *sogo* banks are subject to the limits under TIRAL. Lending rates are subject to upper limits in the report on business affairs (which describes managerial schemes the details of which are subject to Ministry of Finance approval), and stood at 15 per cent p.a. at the end of 1985, with the exception of loans of less than ¥1m. or of maturity greater than one year.

The instalment (*kakekin*) operations permitted to *sogo* banks are a special type of transaction (not to be confused with instalment savings, *teiki tsumi-kin*). An instalment is a contract concluded with the client for a certain period of time, and under this contract the bank accepts instalment payments at fixed periods on the promise of returning a fixed amount of money at the end of the period or at times during the period of accumulation. The instalment business at *sogo* banks differs from instalment savings in two ways. First, repayments (*de facto* borrow-back) may be made during the period of the contract; and secondly, after such repayments, an extra amount may be added to the instalment corresponding to the interest on the repayment. The somewhat difficult nature of the instalment business meant that it has answered the needs of the times less and less as the years have progressed. Moreover, since April 1963, the payments and receipts in the instalment business from the same individual were treated as offsetting from an accounting point of view, and in recent years the share of the instalment business in total *sogo* bank business has become very small.

(iii) Recent developments

Total deposits plus instalments of the *sogo* banks were ¥37·5bn. at the end of 1985. They had grown by less than 40 per cent over the previous five years, which represents a slow-down since the shift to lower economic growth. Time deposits such as fixed-term deposits and instalment savings have a share of 58 per cent of total liabilities. Instalments had had a share of about 50 per cent of liabilities at the end of 1955, but this share fell to only 3 per cent by the end of 1985.

Total outstanding loans and payments made by *sogo* banks were ¥30·6 trillion at the end of 1985, which had grown by more than 40 per cent over the previous five years, but now represent a relatively low growth on account of the entry of city banks into the borrowing clientele of the *sogo* banks. Of this total amount, the instalment payments are small enough to ignore (see Table 5.9).

f. *Shinkin* banks

(i) Overview

The origins of *shinkin* banks go back to the credit co-operatives of the Meiji period, but their immediate precursors were the credit co-operatives based on the Law for Small Business Co-operatives, etc. of 1949. In June 1951, the *Shinkin* Bank Law was promulgated, and those credit co-operatives that had previously been regular credit co-operatives in fairly urbanized areas and that were relatively large in scale and similar to general financial institutions became *shinkin* banks. The operations of *shinkin* banks centre on taking deposits and making loans and thus are not particularly different from that of ordinary banks. *Shinkin* banks, however, are organized on a membership basis, so that in principle credit operations are limited to members. In addition, they are limited to certain geographical areas because of their character as regional financial institutions, and differ in this respect as well from banks. They are, however, similar to general financial institutions and dissimilar to credit co-operatives in another respect, that of the ability to take deposits from non-members. Credit co-operatives are limited to taking non-

TABLE 5.9 Principal Accounts of Sogo Banks, by Year-end

	1965		1970		1975		1980		1985	
	¥100m.	%	¥100m.	%	¥100m.	%	¥100m.	%	¥100m.	%
Assets										
Cash and deposits with others	4,463	12·2	8,066	10·6	19,364	9·9	27,839	8·4	27,324	6·2
Call loans[a]	1,134	3·1	2,607	3·4	7,269	3·7	10,838	3·3	12,659	2·9
Securities	2,554	7·0	5,440	7·1	16,780	8·6	37,663	11·4	60,383	13·7
Mutual instalment loans (kyufukin)	1,247	3·4	352	0·5	162	0·1	104	0·0	93	0·0
Loans and discounts	24,736	67·8	51,223	67·2	124,604	63·8	213,169	64·6	305,793	69·5
Others	2,346	6·4	8,584	11·3	27,100	13·4	40,463	12·3	33,766	7·7
TOTAL	36,480	100·0	76,272	100·0	195,279	100·0	330,076	100·0	440,018	100·0
Liabilities										
Instalments (kakekin)	2,653	7·2	1,244	1·6	633	0·3	1,985	0·6	14,898	3·4
Deposits	29,547	81·0	62,421	81·8	158,774	81·3	271,668	82·3	360,587	81·9
CDs	—	—	—	—	—	—	1,104	0·3	6,755	1·5
Borrowed money	21	0·0	289	0·4	391	0·2	1,659	0·5	1,627	0·4
Call money[a]	—	—	—	—	—	—	448	0·1	3,492	0·8
Capital	391	1·1	604	0·8	1,142	0·6	1,678	0·5	1,900	0·4
Others	3,868	10·6	11,714	15·4	34,339	17·6	51,534	15·6	50,759	11·5

[a] Call loans include loans to other financial institutions and bills bought; call money includes bills sold.

Source: BOJ, Economic Statistics Annual.

member deposits up to a maximum 20 per cent of total deposits, whereas *shinkin* banks do not face such a limit.

The development of *shinkin* banks in the post-war period was quite conspicuous, and in 1967 they surpassed *sogo* banks in total amount of funds held. *Shinkin* banks, therefore, also held an important position in the field of financing small and medium-sized firms; but, like *sogo* banks, the *shinkin* banks underwent a remarkable change in the content of their business in the process of development. First, the membership system became largely a matter of form. That is, in order to borrow, all one needed to do was to become a member in formal terms, and after this borrowing was easy. On the deposit side, the proportion of deposits coming from non-members grew substantially, and the *shinkin* banks became more and more like ordinary banks. Moreover, the dilution of consciousness of membership reduced the general meetings and general responsibilities of members to a purely nominal form, and thus the management of the *shinkin* banks through the consensus of members was not able to be implemented effectively. Secondly, considerable differences emerged in scale of operations among different *shinkin* banks across the country, reflecting differences in regional development. Thirdly, the various regulations imposed on *shinkin* banks, such as qualifications for membership and limits on lending to any individual, did not necessarily match the development of social and economic conditions. As a result, the laws concerning *shinkin* banks were revised, along with those for *sogo* banks, in 1968, 1973, and 1981.

The important characteristics of the *shinkin* banking system as it is today are as follows. First, qualifications for membership are that members must be operators of businesses with either an address or a place of business within the geographical area served by the bank and must have either fewer than 300 employees or less than ¥400m. in capital; or members must be workers from within the geographical area. Secondly, voting rights are one vote per member regardless of the amount of funding provided by the member and the decision-making body is the general members' meeting. Thirdly, there are minimum limits to the funding provided by a single member and to the total capital of the *shinkin* bank. Fourthly, there are restrictions on types of business in which the bank may engage, as described below, which reflect the character of the *shinkin* bank as an institution for its members. Fifthly, maximum lending to any single individual may be as much as 20 per cent of own capital or ¥800m., whichever is smaller.

On the basis of revisions in the system and the merger and conversion laws, an amalgamation of *shinkin* banks has occurred. The number of *shinkin* banks has been reduced from 520 in May 1968 to 456 at the end of 1985, a reduction of 64. It is expected that the amalgamation of *shinkin* banks will continue, as they seek a stable basis for business through economies of scale in an environment of intensified competition among financial institutions as liberalization progresses.

Shinkin banks were made subject to the deposit reserve requirement system in April 1963 along with the *sogo* banks. According to the system, as of the end of 1985, reserve requirements become binding on *shinkin* banks with total deposits of more than ¥160bn., just as for *sogo* banks.

(ii) Operations

The revision of the law for *shinkin* banks in 1981 made a distinction, similar to that in the Banking Law, between the main businesses and auxiliary operations of *shinkin* banks and established detailed provisions concerning each. The main business of *shinkin* banks is established to be (1) the accepting of deposits and instalment savings from members and non-members (2) lending to members, and (3) foreign exchange business. In addition, *shinkin* banks are permitted to lend to non-members, but such lending must not interfere with lending to members. Lending to non-members is restricted to lending on the collateral of deposits, lending to local public bodies and local government organizations, lending to financial institutions, lending to so-called 'graduates' (those whose growth of capital or growth of the number of employees has caused them to lose their qualifications for membership but who retain rights to borrow for a fixed period after such loss), and so-called 'lending to non-members in small amounts'. Moreover, such lending to non-members (excluding lending to financial institutions and local public bodies) must not exceed 20 per cent of total lending (excluding lending to financial institutions). The 1981 legal revision also opened the way for *shinkin* banks to participate in foreign exchange business, and as of the end of 1985 thirty *shinkin* banks had received permission to operate under FEFTCL and were actually carrying out such operations. In addition, some auxiliary operations for *shinkin* banks have been designated, including securities investment operations, sales of over-the-counter Government bonds and other public bonds (at the end of 1985, 434 *shinkin* banks were handling such business), custody deposits, sales of gold bullion, and agent business for the People's Finance Corporation.

The interest rates on deposits for *shinkin* banks are under the jurisdiction of TIRAL. The *shinkin* banks are permitted to pay 0·1 per cent more than are ordinary banks for fixed-term deposits, and are permitted to pay 0·25 per cent more for deposits for tax payments and other deposits. For lending rates maximum levels are set under the reports on business affairs (which describes managerial schemes the details of which are subject to approval by the Ministry of Finance). Since April 1980, this limit has been 15 per cent p.a., the same restrictions as for *sogo* banks.

(iii) Recent developments

Deposits at *shinkin* banks have grown by somewhat less than 50 per cent over the last five years to stand at ¥50·2bn. at the end of 1985. Time deposits are the largest portion of these total deposits, with a share of about 80 per cent. Lending by *shinkin* banks grew by somewhat less than 40 per cent over the last five years to stand at ¥36·5 trillion at the end of 1985. These levels of deposits and lending exceed those of *sogo* banks by 34 per cent for deposits and 19 per cent for lendings; the share of *shinkin* banks in total lending to small enterprises has risen steadily over the last few years.

Shinkin banks invest their surplus funds in call lending (¥1·4bn. at the end of 1985) and in deposits placed with other institutions (¥7·7bn.). Almost all the deposits with others (about 75 per cent) are placed at the *Zenshinren* Bank, and the largest proportion of these, about 90 per cent of those at the *Zenshinren* Bank, are placed in time deposits in order to increase the efficiency of their investment (see Table 5.10).

TABLE 5.10   *Principal Accounts of* Shinkin *Banks and the* Zenshinren *Bank, by Year-end*

	1965 ¥100m.	1970 ¥100m.	1975 ¥100m.	1980 ¥100m.	1985 ¥100m.
Shinkin banks					
Assets					
Cash and deposits with others	6,398	11,391	29,978	44,971	87,490
Call loans[a]	1,604	4,927	4,380	6,591	13,699
Securities	2,631	6,375	20,605	56,709	83,300
Loans and discounts	23,132	62,307	155,624	263,472	365,419
Liabilities					
Savings and deposits	31,138	77,395	195,568	344,745	501,844
CDs	—	—	—	241	2,139
Borrowed money	264	940	771	2,334	3,595
Capital	696	1,222	1,788	2,296	2,679
The *Zenshinren* bank					
Assets					
Cash and deposits with others	124	317	315	308	5,619
Call loans[a]	1,820	2,917	4,867	9,963	16,239
Securities	456	1,389	6,175	8,111	26,700
Loans and discounts	1,264	4,172	9,341	15,346	17,546
Liabilities					
Deposits	3,128	5,514	16,351	27,215	57,573
Borrowed money	436	3,059	2,895	5,076	5,712
Short-term borrowings from *Shinkin* banks	(413)	(3,034)	(2,802)	(5,012)	(5,588)
Capital	12	50	100	100	200

[a] Call loans include loans to other financial institutions (and for *Shinkin* banks, loans to the *Zenshinren* bank), and bills bought.

Source: BOJ, *Economic Statistics Monthly,* and *Economic Statistics Annual.*

(iv) The Zenshinren Bank

The Zenshinren Bank is established under the *Shinkin* Bank Law as the central institution for *shinkin* banks; the individual *shinkin* banks are members. The precursor of this institution was the National Federation of Credit Co-operatives which was established as the central organization for credit co-operatives in 1950. But with the start of the *shinkin* banks under the *Shinkin* Bank Law of 1951, the Zenshinren Bank was established in November of that year.

The operations in which the *Zenshinren* Bank may engage are listed in Clause 54 of the *Shinkin* Bank Law. These operations are: (1) the acceptance of deposits from members, lending to members, and foreign exchange operations with members; (2) acceptance of deposits from the national Government, local government, and public bodies, and non-profit organizations; (3) the acceptance of deposits from, and provision of lending to, non-members as approved by the Ministry of Finance; and (4) auxiliary operations similar to those carried out by *shinkin* banks, i.e., operations related to securities (securities investment activity, over-the-counter sales of Government and public bonds), and agent operations for the People's Finance Corporation.

The revision of the *Shinkin* Bank Law in 1981 gave special approval for the *Zenshinren* to engage in foreign exchange operations for the convenience of member banks who were not permitted such operations under FEFTCL. In addition, the *Zenshinren* Bank was permitted to borrow short-term surplus funds from members under a special type of account. The limits on lending to any single individual are 25 per cent of total own capital (invested capital plus reserves) for lending to a member, and 20 per cent of this amount to a non-member.

At the end of 1985, the total funds held by the *Zenshinren* Bank were ¥6·3bn.; of this, ¥5·8bn. were deposits (including time deposits of ¥5.7bn.) while borrowing from member banks totalled ¥559 milliard. Lending by the *Zenshinren* Bank was ¥1·8bn., securities holdings ¥2·7bn., and call loans ¥1·6bn. Of these loans, a little less than 60 per cent were entrusted to member institutions and just under 20 per cent were direct lending to member institutions. The remainder went to public bodies, public corporations, and certain corporations or others whose stocks are listed on the Stock Exchange as marginal. The *Zenshinren* Bank is also eligible for the securities operations by the Bank of Japan that began in February 1966.

The *Zenshinren* Bank carried out functions for its member banks as follows.

(1) Smoothing of regional and seasonal funds. Because *shinkin* banks were originally orientated toward specific regions, the demand for funds at each individual *shinkin* bank is subject to large influences from the special characteristics of that region and from seasonal factors. Such regional and seasonal fund demands must be accommodated; the *Zenshinren* Bank does this by accepting deposits from the individual *shinkin* banks and then lending these

funds onwards to other *shinkin* banks with a strong funds demand, either as direct lending or as agency loan.

(2) Efficient investment of funds.   By concentrating the surplus funds of the *shinkin* banks, the *Zenshinren* Bank can improve the efficiency of their investment and obtain a better yield on investment than could the individual banks if they invested these funds on their own. The *Zenshinren* Bank pays specified interest rates on deposits to its member institutions but also adds special incentive payments. This system of borrowing from the member banks is one way of concentrating the funds within the *shinkin* bank system; but because the interest rate on such funds is determined on a sliding scale based on the call rate, there is a conspicuous withdrawal of funds by the member banks when the call rate falls, and transfer to time deposits that are more advantageous. When call rates rise, funds flow in the opposite direction.

(3) Concentrated settlement of exchange.   In order to improve the efficiency of the settlement of domestic exchange among the *shinkin* banks, the *Zenshinren* Bank has become the central institution for a data telecommunications system among the nationwide network of *shinkin* banks. With the establishment of the Data Telecommunication System of All Banks in February 1979, exchange from *shinkin* banks may be sent speedily to any part of the country, but the *Zenshinren* Bank acts as a representative for the *shinkin* banks in transactions through the Bank of Japan for settlement of exchange with other institutions.

(4) Payment intermediation.   The *Zenshinren* Bank has established branches in seventeen major cities of the country, and each of these branches has an account for each of the 456 *shinkin* banks. These accounts form the basis for an intermediate payments operation for over 200 types of payment including payments of public utilities, pensions, lending from Government financial institutions, and credit sales funds.

(5) Mutual aid systems.   Because the *shinkin* banks are mostly so small in scale and limited in their geographical area of business, there is the possibility of major disturbances occurring from natural disasters and unforeseen emergencies. In response to this, the *Zenshinren* Bank established the Promotional Fund System in May 1960 and the Deposit Payments Fund Lending System in October 1971. Through these systems, low-interest loans may be provided to *shinkin* banks that are in special situations of difficulty in their business. In addition, there is a *Shinkin* Bank Mutual Aid Fund System, established in October 1971 in order to improve co-operation among the institutions of the *shinkin* banking industry.

g. Credit co-operatives

(i) Overview

Credit co-operatives are co-operative financial institutions based on the mutual support of owners and workers in small businesses. They are organized under the Law for Small Business Co-operatives, etc. of 1949. As described above in the section on *shinkin* banks, the credit co-operatives that were similar in nature to general financial institutions were converted into *shinkin* banks; as a result, the credit co-operatives of today are more like co-operative societies than like *shinkin* banks. The independence of credit co-operatives is respected, and supervision is made as simple as possible. In principle, their business is conducted only with members of the co-operative, and thus their purpose as co-operative financial institutions is more clearly carried out. Because credit co-operatives also manage financial business, however, it is necessary for them to be managed soundly in order to protect their depositors. To this end, the Law Concerning Financial Undertakings by Co-operative Societies was established in 1949. This law placed limits on how the surplus funds of such co-operatives might be used, and provided administrative guidance concerning a regulation of payment reserves against deposits, limits on size of credits granted, and requirements for retained earnings.

The administrative authority for supervision of credit co-operatives is currently vested in the prefectural governors, who received this jurisdiction in June 1951 from the Ministry of Finance by the enactment of the *Shinkin* Bank Law.

The major expansion of credit co-operatives in the 1950s and 1960s caused a gap between theory and practice of credit co-operative operation, just as in the cases of *sogo* banks and *shinkin* banks. In 1968, several revisions of the system were undertaken, in which the areas of business of credit co-operatives were expanded to include lending collateralized by deposits to local governments and public bodies and lending to financial institutions. In addition, the capital base of credit co-operatives was improved by raising the minimum amount of capital for such institutions; the limit on lending to any single individual was also revised. A second set of reforms in 1973 permitted up to 20 per cent of deposits to be taken from non-members and also strengthened the requirements for membership.

When the conversion of credit co-operatives to *shinkin* banks occurred in the early 1950s, only seventy-two credit co-operatives were left. However, unlike the case of *shinkin* banks, the establishment of a credit co-operative is automatically approved unless particular conditions as defined by law exist; many credit co-operatives were established after the original conversions. By May 1968, there were 544 credit co-operatives. In that year, the Finance Ministry took measures to reduce the founding of credit co-operatives, and thereafter the merger and conversion of such institutions continued. By the end of 1985 there were 448 credit co-operatives remaining.

(ii) Operations

Credit co-operatives may accept deposits and instalment savings only from certain types of depositor: (1) members of the co-operative; (2) the national Government, local governments, local public bodies, and non-profit organizations (only deposits may be accepted from these institutions); (3) spouses and relatives of co-operative members who are living in the household of the member; and (4) non-members (with the exception of those under items (2) and (3)) though only up to a maximum 20 per cent of total deposits. The interest rates payable on these deposits are subject to TIRAL, but for deposits of a fixed term, the upper limits on the allowable interest rates are set at 0.1 per cent p.a. above those for banks, or 0.25 per cent for deposits for tax payment.

On the lending side, credit co-operatives may lend or discount the bills in principle only to members, but some amounts may be lent to non-members. Up to 20 per cent of total loans (excluding loans and discounting bills to financial institutions) may be lent to non-member depositors on the collateral of their deposits or instalment savings, or to local government and public bodies. The limits on lending to any single member are 20 per cent of own capital or ¥400m., whichever is lower. The upper limit on the interest rate on lending is determined in the report on business affairs for the institution in accordance with its accounting conditions.

In addition to the business activities mentioned above, credit co-operatives may engage in domestic exchange, payments connected with securities transactions (such as receipt of funds for purchase or a payment of interest, principal, or dividends), safety deposit business, and agent business for designated public bodies. Domestic exchange transactions were legally mandated under the 1981 legal changes, and in August 1984 the credit co-operatives joined the Data Telecommunications System of All Banks.

(iii) Recent developments

Deposits and instalment savings account for more than 80 per cent of the liabilities of credit co-operatives and stood at ¥12·6bn. at the end of 1985, an increase of just under 50 per cent in the previous five years. This large increase in funds available was due to the rapid growth of the small and medium-sized firms that are members of the co-operatives.

Lending stood at ¥9·6bn. at the end of 1985, an increase of just under 40 per cent in the preceding five years. Lending accounts for 70 per cent of total assets, while securities holdings comprise about 10 per cent (see Table 5.11).

TABLE 5.11 *Principal Accounts of Credit Co-operatives and the National Federation of Credit Co-operatives, by Year-end*

	1965 ¥100m.	1970 ¥100m.	1975 ¥100m.	1980 ¥100m.	1985 ¥100m.
Credit co-operatives					
Assets					
Cash and deposits with others	1,832	3,233	8,599	14,551	25,655
Call loans[a]	n.a.	420	1,147	2,033	4,430
Securities	242	603	3,972	8,600	13,256
Loans and discounts	6,276	17,245	40,256	69,051	95,692
Liabilities					
Savings and deposits	7,721	19,778	49,672	86,471	125,764
Borrowed money	203	460	1,031	2,454	5,435
Capital	290	540	954	1,311	1,429
National Federation of Credit Co-operatives					
Assets					
Cash and deposits with others	225	104	115	76	1,518
Call loans[a]	n.a.	50	844	857	2,010
Securities	155	378	636	2,245	7,375
Loans and discounts	276	1,060	2,571	4,979	8,003
Liabilities					
Deposits	590	913	3,140	6,760	14,819
Borrowed money	46	637	879	1,318	3,568
Short-term borrowings from credit co-operatives	—	583	858	1,308	3,568
Capital	8	22	25	41	41

[a] After 1975, call loans include loans to other financial institutions (and, for co-operatives, loans to the National Federation), and bills bought.

Sources: BOJ, *Economic Statistics Monthly* and *Economic Statistics Annual.*

(iv) The National Federation of Credit Co-operatives

When the largest proportion of credit co-operatives converted into *shinkin* banks in 1951, the original National Federation of Credit Co-operatives converted to the *Zenshinren* Bank. But in 1954, the National Federation of Credit Co-operatives was re-established with the remaining credit co-operatives as members on the basis of the Law for Small Business Co-operatives, etc. The newly formed Federation accepted members from all parts of the country.

The operations of the Federation on the deposit side are similar to those of the *Zenshinren* Bank. The Federation may accept deposits from members, the national Government, local government, and non-profit corporations, and may also accept funds in the form of borrowings, called 'co-operative short-term funds', that are the short-term excess liquidity of credit co-operatives. (The latter type of borrowing has been permitted since April 1969.) At the end of 1985, the total funding of the Federation (deposits and borrowings) was ¥1·8bn., about one-third that of the *Zenshinren* Bank.

The most important lending activities of the Federation are lending and bill discounting to participating co-operatives and their members. In addition, some loans are made to the national Government, local government, public bodies, and non-profit corporations with deposits as collateral. In addition, the Federation makes some loans through member credit co-operatives with the latter acting as agents. At the end of 1985, total loans outstanding were ¥800 milliard, of which about 70 per cent were such lending through members as agents.

h. Labour credit associations

(i) Overview

Labour credit associations are financial institutions in the form of co-operative societies that carry out the financial business that is necessary in order to promote the improvement of living standards for workers and to promote the joint welfare activities of organizations such as labour unions, consumer co-operatives, and other labour bodies.

Membership of labour credit associations is limited to labour organizations with the purpose of improving the economic status of workers (such as labour unions, consumer co-operatives, federations of these two types of body, organizations of public workers or private schoolteachers organized under certain laws, and others). In addition, these organizations must be resident within the geographical area of operation of the labour credit association in question. Certain labour credit associations may also admit individual workers as members if their articles of association so provide.

At the end of 1985, there were forty-seven labour credit associations in Japan, one per prefecture except for Osaka prefecture (which had two) and for Tottori and Shimane prefectures (which had one between them). The labour credit associations had 600 offices and about 290,000 members, of which about 56,000 were organizations.

(ii) Operations

The main businesses of labour credit associations are the acceptance of deposits and instalment savings and the provision of loans. Deposits and instalment savings may be accepted from member organizations from the national Government, local government, public bodies, non-profit corporations, members of organizations that are members, and individual members or relatives of members who live in the member's household. Under the legal revisions of 1981, acceptance of deposits from the general public up to a limit of 20 per cent of total deposits was permitted.

On the lending side, the largest share of loans goes to member organizations, to members of organizations that are members, and to the Japan

Workers' Housing Association. In addition, they are permitted to lend up to 20 per cent of total loans (excluding loans to financial institutions) to non-members on collateral deposits, and to non-member non-profit corporations such as local public bodies and local housing supply corporations. There are no particular requirements on the investment of surplus funds, but the largest proportion go as deposits to the National Federation of Labour Credit Associations or as short-term lending to that Federation or toward the purchase of public and corporate bonds.

(iii) Recent developments

The total deposits and instalment savings of labour credit associations have risen steadily along with the increase in membership, and had risen by over 60 per cent between the end of 1980 and the end of 1985. At the end of 1985, these deposits and instalment savings stood at ¥4·9bn., of which a little less than 90 per cent were time deposits. The trend of lending by labour credit associations has declined somewhat in recent years, reflecting the lower growth of residential lending which is the main type of lending by such associations. At the end of 1985, lending stood at ¥2·5bn.

(iv) The National Federation of Labour Credit Associations

The National Federation of Labour Credit Associations was established in April 1955 as the central organization for labour credit associations around the country.

The Federation may accept deposits and make loans in just the same way as the labour credit associations themselves. Because of the Federation's role as an institution meant to strengthen the mutual support base of labour credit associations and to improve the efficiency of their use of funds, however, the focus of the Federation's operations is the administration of the Domestic Exchange Concentration Payments System (the Nation-wide Labour Credit Association Data Telecommunication System) of the Mutual Rescue Fund, and of special lending systems and others.

The Domestic Exchange Concentrated Settlement System (established in August 1981 and previously known as the Current Account Concentrated Settlement System) was established in order to improve the efficiency of settlements of domestic exchange of the labour credit associations with which the Federation did business. In this Concentrated Settlement System, the various payments among the labour credit associations are settled through current deposit accounts at the Federation, and in addition the Federation acts as representative for its members in dealings with other types of institution in settlement of exchange through the Bank of Japan. The Mutual Rescue Fund System (established in February 1957) is an organization under which the National Federation accepts time deposits from the various labour credit associations and through the use of these funds seeks to improve the protection of depositors in the labour credit associations at times of unforeseen disasters or other incidents. In addition, the National Federation may make special low-interest loans in cases in which a member labour credit association encounter difficulties or is subjected to unusual disasters.

At the end of 1985, the total deposits of the National Federation of Labour Credit Associations were ¥1·1bn. The largest portion of these funds were invested in securities (¥870 milliard) followed by call lendings, deposits and lending.

i. The *Shokochukin* Bank

The *Shokochukin* Bank is a special corporation organized under the *Shokochukin* Bank Law of 1936. Its purpose is to facilitate the financing of co-operative societies of small businesses and also of organizations of small business operators. Originally it was chartered for a fifty-year period, but in a legal revision of 1985 it was converted into a permanent organization. The deposit and lending business of this bank is limited to the organizations that contribute to its capital and to their members; thus it has the character of being largely a financial institution for co-operatives of small and medium-sized businesses. Another of its characteristics is the relatively strong participation of the Government compared to other private financial institutions. The Government contributed one portion of the capital (although dividend payments to the Government are subordinate liabilities), and takes measures to aid the organization such as underwriting a portion of the debentures that the organization issues. In addition, the Ministers of International Trade and Industry and of Finance have the right to appoint the directors of the *Shokochukin* Bank, have individual rights of approval over certain aspects of its operations, and oversee its operations through appointment of the superintendent of the Bank.

Lending by the *Shokochukin* Bank was originally limited to small businesses or their co-operative societies (or, more precisely, organizations qualified to provide capital and their members), in line with the original intention at its founding. In response to the development of financial liberalization, however, the legal revision of 1985 permitted lending to foreign corporations established by member organizations or to the members or member organizations, to foreign financial institutions, to holders of *Shokochukin* bank debentures or Government bonds (when these are used as collateral), and to depositors (when deposits are used as collateral). In addition, the legal revisions abolished the provision that loans be of less than twenty years in maturity, or five years maturity if lump-sum repayment were used. The limits on maximum lending to any borrower are established through a decision by the General Council, which is the decision-making body comprising representatives chosen jointly by the member organizations. In fiscal 1985, these limits were ¥2·5 milliard to any member organization and ¥250m. to any member of a member organization. The interest rates on loans are determined by the managing director within limits set by the responsible ministers. As of the end of 1985, these loan rates were very close to the long-term prime rates of private financial institutions: for example, a standard loan rate of 7·2 per cent for loans of maturity of one to three years extended to member organizations. Total loans outstanding were ¥8·0bn. at the end of 1985, about 50 per cent over the level of the People's Finance Corporation or the Small Business Finance Corporation, and about one-quarter of the level of all *sogo* banks put together. In recent years, the share of total lending to manufacturing industry has been declining and is now below 40 per cent; instead, larger shares have gone to wholesale and retail trade, to service industry, and to transportation and telecommunication industries.

The largest source of funding for the *Shokochukin* Bank is flotation of debentures, on which there is a limit of twenty times capital plus capital reserves. This is permitted because the level of deposits that may be expected from member organizations and members of member organizations is not particularly large. At the end of 1985, total debentures outstanding were ¥ 7bn., about three-quarters of total funding. Deposits account for only about 20 per cent of total funding; the reason for this low proportion is the limitation on who may place deposits to organizations qualified to contribute capital, members of such organizations, public bodies, non-profit corporations, and financial institutions approved by the competent ministers—that is, because deposits from the general public may not be accepted. As was the case with lending operations, however, the legal revisions of 1985 expanded the limits of acceptable depositors to include foreign corporations and individuals, holders of debentures in the bank, or of Government bonds, electricity and gas companies, those who borrow from agents for *Shokochukin* Bank loans, and non-member borrowers added through lending operations. (For certain depositors, however, the opening of time deposit accounts is not permitted.) The interest rates paid on deposits are not subject to TIRAL but rather to the individual determination of the managing director. However, the deposit rates are set at levels which follow the guide-lines of the Bank of Japan.

The revision of the *Shokochukin* Bank Law in 1985 not only expanded the limits of lending and deposit business, but also permitted expansion of securities operations such as over-the-counter sales and dealing in Government bonds, and the investment of surplus funds into money trust and monetary claims in trust. In October 1985, the *Shokochukin* Bank joined the Government bond underwriting syndicate and began over-the-counter sales of Government bonds. Through these measures, the Bank responded to the diversifying needs of small and medium-sized businesses through the development of new types of financial product, and strengthened its base for operations in an environment of financial liberalization.

j. The *Norinchukin* Bank

(i) Overview

The *Norinchukin* Bank is the central financial institution for co-operatives serving the agricultural, forestry, and fishery industries. The financing for these industries is carried out through organizations of co-operatives based on a spirit of mutual support and with Government protection and aid. This system of finance and Government aid and protection are provided because it is difficult for these industries to participate in the normal financing activities of financial institutions owing to their special character (such as their weak collateral endowments, low profitability, and the long-term or seasonal demand for funds). Government aid takes the form of augmentation through so-called 'system finance'.[6]

The co-operative financial institutions for agriculture, forestry, and fisheries are part of a three-tier network of institutions. At the top stands the *Norinchukin* Bank; the middle stage consists of a prefectural level of federations of individual co-operatives; the lowest level is the co-operatives themselves, which are the terminal organizations in individual cities and villages. These lowest-level co-operative societies are in turn split into three branches: those for agriculture, those for fishery, and those for forestry. This section will consider the *Norinchukin* Bank and the individual co-operatives; the federations for agriculture and those for fisheries will be considered in the two following sections.

The *Norinchukin* Bank was established as a special corporation of limited liability based on the *Norinchukin* Bank Law in 1923, and converted to a private corporation in 1986. As the financial institution at the top of the three branches of co-operatives, the *Norinchukin* plays the central role in financing these co-operatives. At the end of 1985, the Bank's capital was ¥45 milliard, all of which was subscribed by private agriculture, fishery, and forestry organizations as specified under the *Norinchukin* Bank Law.

(ii) Operations

The operations of the *Norinchukin* Bank fall into two major categories, intrinsic operations and operations that are entrusted to it under other laws and regulations.

Intrinsic operations include acceptance of deposits, provision of loans,

---

[6] System finance is a series of policies based on financial measures that are in turn based on laws and regulations intended to achieve policy goals. Such measures include direct financing from public funds by the national Government and local government or public bodies, interest subsidies on borrowing from market institutions or the special institutions for agricultural, fishery, or forestries, and guarantee of the liabilities in these industries. Typical of the so-called 'assistance' are the Agriculture, Forestry, and Fisheries Finance Co-operation Fund System, which is based on fiscal funding, and the Agricultural Modernization|Fund|System (which pays interest subsidies on borrowings from private financial institutions mainly from the co-operative financial institutions for agriculture, fisheries, and forestry).

business connected with domestic exchange, and the issue of debentures. Through these operations the Bank adjusts the regional distribution of funds within the branches of the overall system. In the process of doing this, the Bank becomes a very large tender in short-term money markets such as the call and bill markets.

The *Norinchukin* Bank is permitted to accept deposits from organizations that may contribute capital according to the *Norinchukin* Bank Law, from non-member borrowers (the deposits from these borrowers are limited to those other than time deposits), from the subscribers of debentures of the *Norinchukin* Bank, from public bodies and other non-profit corporations, and from financial institutions that have received permission from the responsible minister. Almost 90 per cent of deposits come from organizations that con-tribute capital, and most of these are the deposits of organizations in the agricultural branch of the system. Because the deposits from within the system are mostly excess funds of the member organizations, most are accepted as high-yielding time deposits. (As a result, about 90 per cent of the total deposits were time deposits of some sort as of the end of 1985.) The credit federations of agricultural co-operatives are paid deposit interest rates higher than the usual levels, and extra incentive payments are added. Since September 1969, the *Norinchukin* Bank has been subject to the system of reserve requirements on deposits.

The *Norinchukin* Bank may also issue debentures in order to raise funds. There are two such types of debenture, a five-year coupon bond and a one-year discount bond. The debentures are in principle non-registered (bearer debentures), and the overall limit on their issue is thirty times the sum of capital and reserves that belong to the capital subscriber accounts.

Lending of the *Norinchukin* Bank is in principle limited to organizations that contribute capital; lending to non-members is, however, permitted so long as this lending does not interfere with the lending operations to the member organizations. There are seven types of outside organization to which the Bank may lend: (1) those organizations that are qualified to be members but are not members; (2) producers in the agriculture, forestry, and fishery industries; (3) corporations providing infrastructure (i.e., corporations managing undertakings that benefit agriculture and forestry); (4) cor-porations in undertakings connected with agriculture, forestry, or fisheries; (5) corporations for the improvement of agriculture, forests, or fishing facilities whose primary members are local public bodies; (6) corporations to which lending may be regarded as appropriate from the viewpoint of developing the economy (local government or public bodies, special-purpose corpor-ations, and non-profit corporations whose members, capital subscribers, or basic asset providers are national Government, local government, or public bodies); and (7) financial institutions. For lending to categories (3), (4), and (5), the approval of the responsible ministers is required concerning the maximum lending during a period and the outstanding balance at period-end. In addition, for lending to those in category (6), individual approval is required for each case from the responsible minister. The largest share of lending to non-members by the *Norinchukin* Bank is that going to category (4), so-called 'related industry' lending. In addition, the Bank invests its surplus funds in securities, call loans, and bills bought. Recently, the investments in securities have seen a rapid increase in the share going to Government bonds while the growth of lending has been relatively weak since 1975. Holdings of securities have risen to about the same scale as investment in lending, and the *Norinchukin* Bank has become the largest single institutional investor in the private sector. In addition, lending in the form of call loans and bills bought has reached a very high level, and the *Norinchukin* Bank is an important lender of funds in the interbank markets.

Other intrinsic operations of the Bank include the formation of an exchange communications network on a nation-wide basis for member institutions, i.e., an on-line system. The Bank also carries out remittance transfer and payment collection services connected with domestic exchange settlement. In February 1979, the Bank joined the Data Telecommunication System of All Banks and thus strengthened its function as the centre of the exchange network for member institutions. Reflecting the internationalization of its clients' business, the Bank was permitted to begin to handle foreign exchange operations, based on a legal revision of the *Norinchukin* Bank Law in 1973, and actual operations began in 1974. In March 1981, a foreign exchange on-line system began to be used, and in June the Bank received general approval concerning foreign exchange correspondent business and thus established the basis for further development of its international operations. In October 1982, the Bank opened its first foreign office in New York, and this office took on branch status in October 1984.

The *Norinchukin* Bank Law was partially revised in 1981, along with the revision of the Banking Law in June of that year. Due to this revision, the *Norinchukin* Bank was allowed, as were the ordinary banks, to carry out securities operations such as over-the-counter sales and dealing in Government bonds and other public securities. In addition, the new law made the business of lending securities a usual activity, although this had only been an auxiliary activity previously.

In addition to its intrinsic operations, the *Norinchukin* Bank may act as agent in several types of business if the approval of the responsible minister is obtained. Such types of business include those with the national Government, local governments and public bodies, non-profit corporations, banks, and other financial institutions. Currently, such operations entrusted to the Bank include payment of funds for Government purchases of staple foods and acting as agent in lending the funds of the Agriculture, Forestry, and Fisheries Finance Corporation.

(iii) Recent developments

Deposits placed with the *Norinchukin* Bank have been growing recently, reflecting the weaker growth of lending by member institutions. At the end of 1985, such deposits stood at ¥15bn., an increase of just under 80 per cent during the previous five years. Because of this increase in deposits, the share of funding coming from debentures has declined (as of the end of 1985, debentures outstanding were ¥3·7bn., of which the Trust Fund Bureau had underwritten ¥210 milliard).

Lending stood at ¥9·7bn. at the end of 1985, an increase of 60 per cent over the preceding five years and thus less than the increase in deposits. Lending to the organizations that contribute capital has declined conspicuously, from 38 per cent at the end of 1975 to 15 per cent at the end of 1985. During this period, the proportion of assets held in securities has risen remarkably, and reached ¥9·2bn. by the end of 1985, equivalent to 95 per cent of loans outstanding (at the end of 1975, 31 per cent). Lending in the call and bill markets reached ¥2·1bn. as of the end of 1985, equivalent to 10 per cent of the total of the call and bill market loans outstanding (just under ¥20bn. at the end of 1985).

k. Agricultural co-operatives and credit federations of agricultural co-operatives

(i) Agricultural co-operatives

(1) Overview. Agricultural co-operatives are the basis for the agricultural branch of the co-operative system, and are formed under the Agricultural Co-operatives Law of 1947. The system of agricultural financial institutions comprises not only the *Norinchukin* Bank at the top but also the Prefectural credit federations of agricultural co-operatives.

Agricultural co-operatives are special corporations having a co-operative form and their management is entrusted to the farmers who are the members. The activities of these co-operatives include credit, purchasing, sales, public utility, mutual aid, and processing, but of these credit operations are extremely important.

The number of agricultural co-operatives has been decreasing gradually as a result of the measures for consolidation and merger based on the Law Concerning Aid for the Mergers Among Agricultural Co-operatives of 1961. Nevertheless, these institutions are spread throughout the country, and as of September of 1985 there were 4,286 general agricultural co-operatives that managed credit operations. These co-operatives had a total membership of 8 million persons, comprising nearly all the farmers of the nation. In recent years, however, with the increase in those pursuing farming and other activities simultaneously, there has been a tendency for the agricultural co-operatives themselves to engage in a larger share of their activities outside agriculture. This is also due to the changing composition of membership that has accompanied the movement of workers out of agriculture and the increase in non-farm income of members. These trends have become an important issue in considering the state of this branch of the co-operative system.

(2) Credit operations.   The credit operations in which agricultural co-operatives may engage are the acceptance of savings deposits or instalment savings of members and the provision of loans of funds necessary for the undertakings or livelihood of the members or for improvement of the industrial basis of conditions of livelihood of agricultural areas. In order to ensure the sound operation of these credit activities, Regulations Concerning Financial Standards for Agricultural Co-operatives require that the co-operatives hold certain standard levels of reserves for payment of deposits and also that they maintain certain standards of loans and investment of surplus funds.

The agricultural co-operatives play a very important role as savings institutions for agricultural communities. There are two types of savings deposit handled at co-operatives, savings deposits of a current nature (so-called 'current savings deposits' and 'ordinary savings deposits') and savings deposits of the nature of time deposits (including fixed-term savings deposits and instalment savings). The share of those deposits similar to time deposits is the largest, at over 70 per cent of total savings deposits at the end of 1985. For deposits of non-members, the agricultural co-operatives are limited to accepting deposits within 20 per cent of the total amount (average outstanding balance) of member deposits during any one business year on a co-operative-by-co-operative basis. The interest rates on deposits at the agricultural co-operatives are subject to TIRAL and are set at 0·1 per cent above those paid by banks.

Lending is the second most important activity of the co-operatives. Long-term lending accounts for more than 70 per cent of the total lending outstanding from agricultural co-operatives and includes so-called 'system finance' funds for agricultural modernization and for disaster relief that are provided with back-up from the Government in the form of interest subsidies, etc. For lending as well, a limit of 20 per cent of total lending to members is placed on lending to non-members.

The incidental operations of the agricultural co-operatives include handling of public funds, handling of Government procurement payments for rice and barley, and on-lending of funds from the Agriculture, Forestry, and Fisheries Finance Corporation that are entrusted to the credit federation of agricultural co-operatives.

(3) Recent developments.   Total savings in agricultural co-operatives were ¥39·7bn. at the end of 1985, an amount slightly exceeding the deposits of *sogo* banks as a whole. However, their rate of growth has been moderate in recent years because of the stagnation of the agricultural economy and the reduced rate of use of agricultural co-operatives by farmers. Lending has also

grown very slowly, and stood at ¥11·6bn. at the end of 1985, far below the level of deposits. That is, surplus funds corresponded to 60 to 70 per cent of total deposits. A portion of these excess funds were invested in securities, but the larger portion was transferred to the credit federation of agricultural co-operatives as deposits placed.

In recent years, the agricultural co-operatives have also attempted to improve the functioning of the financial services they provide and to ensure the stability of their deposit base. They have done so through improving current transfer and payments services and creating a nation-wide savings deposit service network. In August 1974, they joined the Data Tele-communications System of All Banks and began to expand their domestic exchange operations. In addition, they began to operate a credit card system in April 1983.

(ii) Credit federations of agricultural co-operatives

There is one credit federation of agricultural co-operatives in each prefecture of the country—forty-seven in all. Each is a special corporation formed form the individual agricultural co-operatives and from federations of under-takings other than credit undertakings, and each is based on the Agricultural Co-operatives Law. As with individual agricultural co-operatives, the credit federations of agricultural co-operatives are not permitted to operate under-takings jointly other than credit undertakings.

The main activities of the credit federations of agricultural co-operatives are to accept deposits and make loans to members, but in addition they also play a role in strengthening the credit operations of agricultural co-operatives through discounting the bills of members or guaranteeing the liabilities of members, and also in smoothing the regional surpluses and deficits of funds among the co-operatives. Deposit and lending operations may be carried out with non-members, but the total amounts are subject to limitations that are the same as those for agricultural co-operatives. In addition, there are limits on lending to any individual borrower that are established through the annual meetings every fiscal year. These limits are usually 35 per cent of paid-in capital for lending to members and 20 per cent of capital for lending to non-members. The credit federations of agricultural co-operatives are positioned in the middle of the exchange settlement system of agricultural co-operatives, and act as pipelines between the *Norinchukin* Bank and the agricultural co-operatives themselves. As a result, the operations of the federations are relatively highly computerized.

Deposits in the federations have grown relatively rapidly with the increase in funds deposited from the agricultural co-operatives themselves. At the end of 1985, total deposits exceeded ¥29bn. In contrast, the lending by the federations (with the exception of lending to financial institutions) has been stagnating in recent years, accompanying the shift to lower economic growth. As of the end of 1985, total loans outstanding were only ¥3·9bn. Taken together, these trends mean that the ratio of loans to deposits declined from 44 per cent at the end of 1975 to only 13 per cent at the end of 1985, implying a rapid increase in surplus funds. Hence, holdings of securities exceeded outstanding loans by a huge margin by the end of 1985, and stood at ¥10·1bn. (compared to being only about half the level of loans outstanding at the end of 1975). Deposits placed by the federations in the *Norinchukin* Bank were ¥15·4bn. at the end of 1985, more than half of total deposits, (53 per cent, compared to 39 per cent at the end of 1975).

l. Fishery co-operatives and credit federations of fishery co-operatives

Fishery co-operatives. The Fishery Co-operatives Law of 1948 established three types of co-operative for the fishing industry. Fishery co-operatives, fishery production co-operatives, and marine products-processing co-operatives. Of these three types, the fishery co-operatives and marine products-processing co-operatives are permitted to carry on credit operations, but the credit operations of these co-operatives are not particularly large when compared to those of agricultural co-operatives. Instead, the fishery co-operatives concentrate on sales operations, ice production, refrigeration, and other economic undertakings. There were 1,757 individual co-operatives carrying out credit operations at the end of 1985, of which fisheries co-operatives were 1,725, or about 98 per cent of the total.

The main credit operations of the individual co-operatives are the acceptance of deposits and the making of loans to members. At the end of 1985, the total outstanding amount of deposits was ¥1·5bn. and that of loans ¥1·1bn., on a much smaller scale than that of the agricultural co-operatives. However, the ratio of lending to deposits remains at the high level of 71 per cent and in some regions there are actually more loans than deposits. As a result, borrowings by fishery co-operatives are relatively high, and stood at ¥1bn. at the end of 1985 or about 70 per cent of deposits.

Credit federation of fishery co-operatives. The individual fishery co-operatives that carry out credit operations have organized credit federations of fishery co-operatives as higher-tier institutions. At the end of 1985 there were thirty-five such federations. These federations are not permitted to carry out operations other than credit operations. Their main types of business are accepting deposits from members and making loans to members. At the end of 1985, the total deposits outstanding were ¥1·5bn. and loans outstanding were ¥820 milliard. As for deposit and lending business with non-members, the federations are permitted to accept deposits and make loans within the same limits as applied to the total amounts of these types of business with members in the case of fishery co-operatives.

2. PRIVATE NON-DEPOSITORY FINANCIAL INTERMEDIARIES

a. Securities investment trust management companies

(i) Overview

Securities investment trust management companies are intermediaries in the securities investment trust business. The investment trust management company is the trust owner directing the management of the entrusted assets. This management company gathers funds from the general investing public (who are the beneficiaries) by selling beneficiary certificates and then entrusts these gathered funds to a trust bank or to a bank carries out trust business (the trustee). The trust bank or other trustee then invests the funds in securities according to the directions of the trust owner and then distributes profits or redemption funds to the beneficiaries. Securities investment trusts are organized for investors from the general public who do not have the necessary funds by themselves or are lacking in sufficient investment knowledge to make the securities investments on their own; such trusts thus assist the efficient investment in securities by such customers.

The system of securities investment trusts was first established under the Securities Investment Trust Law of 1951. Originally the management operations for investment trusts were carried out jointly with other business by securities companies; but in order to maintain the independence of management of the entrusted assets, the management operations were separated from securities companies after 1960 and assigned to securities investment trust management companies that are independent of the securities companies. There are currently eleven such securities investment trust management companies. They must be licensed by the Minister of Finance, and must fulfil the conditions of having more than ¥50m. in capital, of having corporate form, of possessing sufficient qualifications to carry out the management business, and other conditions (before the revision of the Securities Investment Trust Law in 1953, there was a registration system rather than a licensing system).

(ii) Operations

The operations of management companies are carried out on the basis of securities investment trust agreements that have been approved by the Minister of Finance in advance (Article 12 of the Securities Investment Trust Law). There are five areas of operations for these companies: (1) the conclusion and cancellation of trust contracts, (2) the issue and subscription of beneficiary certificates, (3) the direction of investment of the entrusted assets, (4) the payment of distributions of profits, proceeds of contract cancellations, and proceeds of redemptions, and (5) the preparation of prospectuses and investment performance reports concerning the entrusted assets. In the trust agreements it is permitted for designated securities companies (of which there were sixteen at the end of 1985) to act as agents in the sales of beneficiary certificates, payments of distributions of profits, proceeds of contract cancellations, and proceeds of redemptions.

Normally, the beneficiary may liquidate his beneficiary certificates without waiting for redemption. There are two methods of doing this, the redemption request method (under which a request is made of the designated securities company that acts as agent for the management company to redeem the beneficiary certificate) and the partial cancellation request method (under which a request is made of the management company for partial cancellation of the trust contract). In cases of redemption requests, the designated securities companies may ask the management company for a partial redemption of the trust contract concerning the beneficiary certificates that have been redeemed from the beneficiary. When the management company receives a request for contract cancellation, the management company notifies the trustee of the cancellation and extinguishes the beneficiary rights corresponding to the beneficiary certificates concerned.

In its directions of investment of funds, the management company is forbidden by the Securities Investment Trust Law to engage in activities that might harm the interests of the beneficiaries for the purpose of profits of the management company itself, its directors, or its major stockholders. In addition, the assets in which entrusted funds may be invested are restricted to securities designated under the Securities and Exchange Law and may not be placed in such assets as vouchers or franchise securities. Moreover, it is not permitted to underwrite securities by means of trust assets, nor is it permitted to make money loans other than call loans as trust assets. And finally, in order to diversify risk and to ease the influence on the securities market of investment trusts that hold large amounts of funds, there are restrictions concerning securities holdings by any particular management company or any individual fund in a company.

There is an industry association for management companies called the Investment Trusts Association, and it contributes to the protection of investors and the development of the securities investment trust business. These contributions are made through the regulation of the industry and conclusion of agreements concerning self-restraint in the areas of subscription and sales of beneficiary certificates and instructions on the investment of trust assets.

(iii) Recent developments

There are two types of securities investment trust, classified according to how the funds are invested: stock investment trusts, which began at the time of implementation of the Securities Investment Trust Law in 1951, and bond investment trusts, which were newly created in 1961. The total principal of both types of investment trusts surged by 3·3 times in the five years to 1985, compared to growth in bank deposits at ordinary banks of about 50 per cent. At the end of 1985, the principal in these investment trusts reached ¥19·3bn., equivalent to 9 per cent of the total deposits in all ordinary banks. This rapid growth has occurred not only because of the stable growth of the stock and bond markets, but also because of the development of new financial products such as medium-term Government bond funds, new Government bond funds, jumbos (undistributed Government bond funds), and international bond funds, all of which were due to the development of the bond markets since 1975. Against this background, the bond investment trusts have increased their share in recent years, while the stock investment trusts which once formed the largest portion of the securities investment trusts during late 1950s and early 1960s have lost share (see Table 5.12).

Reflecting the increase in bond investment trusts, the outstanding bonds in investment trusts rose to ¥14·1bn. at the end of 1985 or about 70 per cent of the total (the share of public bonds held by securities investment trusts as a proportion of total public bonds outstanding has risen from 2·3 per cent in 1980 to 5·4 per cent in 1985). In contrast, the value of stocks in investment trusts (at market prices) was only ¥3·5bn. at the end of 1985, or 17 per cent of total assets, a decline from the level of 25 per cent in 1980. The securities investment trusts also keep call loans and bills as liquid payments reserves, and are important lenders in both the call and the bill markets.

b. Life insurance companies

(i) Overview

At the end of 1985, there were twenty-three life insurance companies in Japan that had received their operating licences on the basis of the Insurance Business Law. (In addition, there were fifteen life insurance companies operating that had their main offices in foreign countries and were based on the Law Concerning Foreign Insurance Undertakings.) Of these twenty-three companies, sixteen were of the mutual company type while the other seven were of the joint stock form; but in terms of how they functioned as undertakings and in terms of the structure of their earnings, there were hardly any differences among them. The establishment of a life insurance company requires the approval of the Minister of Finance on the basis of the Insurance Business Law. Companies of the joint stock type and those of the mutual company type both require ¥30m. or more in capital or capital funds, respectively, and in addition, mutual companies are established on condition that they have 100 or more members.

Insurance companies are undertakings that operate by accepting payments of insurance premiums on a specific basis from large numbers of people who have concluded insurance contracts in order to seek protection from unforeseen accidents, and then paying the contracted insurance payments in cases of occurrence of the accidents in question. Although insurance companies supply such financial assets to households, at the same time they

TABLE 5.12   *Principal and Distribution of Net Assets of Securities Investment Trusts, by Year-end*

	1965		1970		1975		1980		1985	
	¥100m.	%	¥100m.	%	¥100m.	%	¥100m.	%	¥100m.	%
Principal outstanding										
Stock investment trusts	9,663	81·5	7,316	55·6	19,771	59·0	38,820	66·5	100,314	52·0
Bond investment trusts	2,195	18·5	5,836	44·4	13,731	41·0	19,581	33·5	92,457	48·0
Medium-term Government bond funds	—	—	—	—	—	—	(2,310)	(4·0)	(40,122)	(20·8)
TOTAL PRINCIPAL OUTSTANDING	11,858	100·0	13,153	100·0	33,503	100·0	58,403	100·0	192,772	100·0
Distribution of net assets										
Call loans[a]	1,543	13·7	2,365	18·1	4,100	12·2	13,426	22·2	22,313	11·2
Stocks and shares[b]	6,718	59·5	4,102	31·4	10,409	31·0	15,000	24·8	34,695	17·4
Bonds and debentures[b]	2,733	24·2	6,401	49·1	18,842	56·0	31,435	51·9	140,589	70·4
TOTAL NET ASSETS	11,289	100·0	13,044	100·0	33,625	100·0	60,519	100·0	199,722	100·0

[a] Call loans include bills bought.
[b] For 1965 and 1970, stocks as well as listed bonds are represented at book value and after 1975 at market value, except for non-listed issues which are represented at book value.

Source: BOJ, *Economic Statistics Annual.*

accumulate large sums of insurance premiums to provide against the occurrence of accidents, and use these funds to play an important role as suppliers of industrial funds and as institutional investors in securities markets. Life insurance companies in particular have the character of being long-term financial institutions because mortality rates can be predicted with a great degree of accuracy and because, in normal cases, the contracts are of a long-term nature and the funds so received are relatively stable over a long period of time.

Until recently, the life insurance industry, because of its nature, concluded uniform agreements concerning insurance premiums and profit distributions. However, because of the financial liberalization of recent years, these agreements are to be gradually eased, and a course is to be set toward free competition that will bring out the individual character of each company.

(ii) Operations

There are three general types of insurance: mortality life insurance, in which an insurance payment is made at the time of death of the insuree (term insurance), survival insurance, in which a payment is made on condition that the insuree survives during a set period (savings insurance, individual pension insurance, etc.), and mixed insurance, which combines features of both (endowment insurance, etc.). Each of the life insurance companies deals in these types of insurance, and in recent years many new types of insurance have developed, such as those which attach casualty insurance and sickness insurance to the main contract.

A fixed proportion of the insurance premiums gathered by insurance companies are accumulated for contract-holders (insurance contract reserves), and these funds constitute 90 per cent of funds invested by the insurance companies. The most important of these reserves are (1) required reserves, accumulated against insurance payments of the future, (2) payments reserves, accumulated against payments of insurance funds for incidents that have already occurred, and (3) profit distribution reserves, used to distribute profits. Of these reserves, the required reserves are the most important and the methods of their accumulation are subject to approval by the Minister of Finance.

The assets of life insurance companies are composed of small amounts of funds from many contract-holders and must be paid out in the future to these contract-holders. In order to protect the enrollees, safe and certain investment of the funds must be expected and therefore strict regulation of investment methods is carried out under laws and regulations.[7]

[7] The important points of the regulations are as follows:

(1) The securities which may be held as investments are limited to Government bonds of the Japanese or other governments, local government bonds, Government-guaranteed bonds, corporate debentures, equities, mortgage securities, and the beneficiary certificates of loan trusts and investment trusts. However, holdings of equities and securities investment trust beneficiary

The interest rates on lending are left to the voluntary determination of each company so far as long-term rates are concerned, but tend to be about the same as those of long-term credit banks. For short-term interest rates on lending, maximum limits were previously determined according to agreements within the Life Insurance Association of Japan, but since April 1975 they have been subject to voluntary determination by each company, just as in the case of city banks.

There are three sources of earnings for life insurance companies, the interest rate differential, the mortality rate differential, and the cost differential. The interest rate differential is that between the actual yield on assets invested and the expected yield on investments. The mortality rate differential is that which is caused by the difference between actual mortality rates and expected mortality rates. The cost differential is that between actual costs incurred and insurance premiums. For mutual companies, more than 90 per cent of surplus funds are accumulated as reserves for distribution to contract-holders and are then used to pay dividends to these contract holders. For the joint stock companies, similar amounts to those paid as dividends to contract-holders in mutual companies are calculated from profits and are entered on the books as dividends to contract-holders.

(iii) Recent developments

The volume of business of life insurance companies has shown a steady growth over the last years, with growth in the value of contracts and premium income expanding as a reflection of the growth of the economy and of individual income. As a result, the total assets of life insurance companies stood at ¥51bn. at the end of 1985, roughly doubling in the preceding five years (see Table 5.13). Looking at the total financial assets of life insurance companies through the deposited assets from contract-holders of the life insurance companies (twenty-three companies)—i.e., through the reserve accounts for insurance contracts—there was a stock of about ¥41bn. of such funds at the end of March 1985, or about 8 per cent of the gross financial assets outstanding of the household sector.

In recent years, the amounts of contracts outstanding in endowment

certificates must be together less than 30 per cent of total assets, holdings of foreign securities less than 25 per cent (until March 1986, within 10 per cent), and holdings of the bonds and equities of any single corporation must be less than 10 per cent.

(2) The lending of life insurance companies is limited to lending secured real estate or securities mentioned above (with the total falling within 5 per cent of total assets for loans collateralized by name-designated assets and within 30 per cent for loans collateralized by securities), loans to public bodies (limited to 20 per cent of total assets), loans to contract-holders as determined within insurance agreements, and call loans. Total lending to any one borrower must be less than 3 per cent of total assets.

(3) Limits are also placed on how much in deposits may be placed in institutions. Total deposits in any one bank or total money trusts or insurance securities trusts in any trust bank may not exceed 10 per cent of total assets.

(4) Acquisition of real estate may not exceed 20 per cent of total assets.

TABLE 5.13 Investments of Life Insurance Companies, by Year-end

	1965		1970		1975		1980		1985	
	¥100m.	%	¥100m.	%	¥100m.	%	¥100m.	%	¥100m.	%
Total assets	22,431	100·0	58,548	100·0	128,960	100·0	262,578	100·0	513,682	100·0
Cash and deposits with others[a]	253	1·1	592	1·0	1,620	1·3	4,452	1·7	48,537	9·4
Loans	13,890	61·9	39,290	67·1	87,572	67·9	156,851	59·7	242,123	47·1
Call loans	256	1·1	351	0·6	636	0·5	2,149	0·8	2,468	0·5
Securities	5,391	24·0	12,745	21·8	27,941	21·7	79,760	30·4	180,775	35·2
Stocks and shares	4,732	21·1	11,453	19·6	23,396	18·1	45,201	17·2	75,344	14·7
Corporate debentures	182	0·8	853	1·5	2,019	1·6	14,228	5·4	24,603	4·8
Government bonds	38	0·2	334	0·6	2,117	1·6	6,049	2·3	25,524	5·0

[a] Cash and deposits include money in trust.

Sources: Ministry of Finance, Banking Bureau, Insurance Division, Hoken Nenkan (Insurance Yearbook); and BOJ, Economic Statistics Annual.

insurance and other existing types of insurance product have not been growing particularly quickly, because of the dissemination of life insurance and the strengthening of competition with both the postal life insurance system and the various types of mutual insurance societies. As a result, most companies are putting increased effort into acquiring new types of business in the corporate pension insurance area, in which strong growth of demand is forecast for the future.

On the assets side, lending continues to take the largest share of assets, and stood at ¥24·2bn. at the end of 1985. There has been, however, a conspicuous weakening of growth of lending, reflecting the reduction in corporate funds demand. As a result, the share of lending in total assets has fallen from 68 per cent at the end of fiscal 1975 to 47 per cent at the end of (calendar) 1985. The loans continue to focus on those for plant and equipment for various industries, in particular electric power, steel, and chemicals. The share of securities in total assets has been rising in recent years and stood at 35 per cent at the end of 1985, up from 22 per cent at the end of fiscal 1975, to stand at ¥18·1bn. (this figure excludes securities investments through specified money trusts). In securities markets, the life insurance companies have a considerable influence as institutional investors. About 40 per cent of the securities held are equity investment, but the insurance companies have also been members of the Government bond underwriting syndicate since it was established with the first issue of Government bonds in 1966. Since 1975, the share of Government bonds in the total portfolio has risen.

Since the early 1980s, the share of life insurance company investments going abroad in the form of yen-denominated syndicated loans or of foreign securities has risen, reflecting the fall of corporate funds demand in Japan and the high interest rates abroad. For example, the share of foreign securities in total assets rose from 2 per cent at the end of fiscal 1980 to 9 per cent at the end of calendar 1985. With the approval of individual guarantee business by credit guarantee corporations that are subsidiaries of life insurance companies in June 1983, the life insurance companies themselves have become active in making loans to individuals. Thus, the life insurance companies are diversifying their asset portfolios, in comparison with the condition of the high growth period in which their lending was concentrated on plant and equipment lending to corporations.

c. Non-life insurance companies

(i) Overview

At the end of 1985, there were twenty-three domestic non-life insurance companies in Japan that had received operating licences under the Insurance Business Law. All of these had corporate form (in addition, there were thirty-nine foreign non-life insurance companies operating under the Law

Concerning Foreign Insurance Undertakings). Although there are not many differences in the types of product that these companies sell, the number of companies indicates that there is quite severe competition in the industry. On the other hand, one cannot overlook the quite substantial relationships of mutual interdependence within the industry and the attempts to avoid direct effects on the stability of profits because of claims; such interdependence is seen in the form of use of techniques of risk aversion, such as reinsurance, joint insurance, and group insurance.

In addition to their primary activities as providers of insurance and insurance services, the non-life insurance companies, like the life insurance companies, play an important role as suppliers of industrial funds and as institutional investors. The maturity of their investments, however, is shorter than that of the life insurance companies, and their shares in the loan and securities markets are smaller.

The non-life insurance companies are subject to exactly the same conditions as life insurance companies concerning the establishment of business, and subject to Government supervision under the Insurance Business Law and other related laws and regulations.

(ii) Operations

There are many types of non-life insurance including fire insurance, marine insurance, transportation insurance, automobile insurance, accident compensation insurance, and injury insurance. Originally, fire insurance was the largest share of the non-life insurance industry, but recently the share of automobile insurance has become the largest and at the end of fiscal 1984 accounted for 40 per cent of the total contracts outstanding.

A portion of the insurance premiums in the non-life insurance industry is accumulated as reserves for contract-holders, but the largest proportion is accounted for by required reserves, just as with the life insurance industry. The special characteristic of the non-life insurance companies is that they accumulate extreme danger reserves in view of the possibility of unexpected disasters. Some types of non-life insurance have premium arrangements under which a portion of the premiums are returned when the contract expires if no insurable incident has occurred; such types of premium arrangement occur, for example, in certain types of fire insurance. In most cases, however, the premiums are outright payments, in contrast with the case of life insurance companies.

The investment of assets by non-life insurance companies is subject to the same types of restriction under law as that of life insurance companies, other than the fact that firms that engage in marine insurance are permitted to lend on mortgage of ships. Since insurable incidents under non-life insurance contracts may occur at any time, however, high liquidity of assets must be given consideration. As a result, non-life insurance companies have a character more like short-term financial institutions when compared to the life insurance companies. The interest rates on short-term loans were for many years subject to an agreement of the Marine and Fire Insurance Association of Japan, but currently each firm sets its own interest rates.

(iii) Recent developments

The total contracted amount for non-life insurance companies has grown steadily over recent years. As a result, the total assets of twenty-three non-life insurance companies stood at ¥11·8bn. at the end of 1985, equivalent to about one-quarter of that of life insurance companies and up by more than 60 per cent in the preceding five years. Reflecting the need for maintaining liquidity, 16 per cent of total assets are placed in bank deposits and call loans (see Table 5.14). Lending and securities investments account for 65 per cent of total assets, but the share of securities investments is larger and that of loans is smaller than in the case of life insurance companies.

d. Housing finance companies

(i) Overview

In the field of housing finance, banks and other private financial institutions play the central role, accounting for over 70 per cent of the total of credit extended. The Housing Loan Corporation, which is a Government financial institution, plays an augmenting role (see Table 5.15). Within the financing provided by private financial institutions, there is, along with the direct financing by banks and similar institutions, a portion provided by housing finance companies that were jointly established one by one by the banks after 1971. Currently there are eight such housing finance companies.

There were several reasons that the banks established housing finance companies to specialize in residential lending. Housing loans tend to be small in amount and complicated with respect to administration, and also require specialized knowledge and experience concerning the evaluation of collateral such as land and structures. In addition, it was thought that accepting medium-term funds and lending longer-term funds would contribute to stable supply of housing funds. Thus, it seemed more rational and efficient to leave such lending to specialized institutions rather than to have the banks themselves handle it.

Housing finance companies rely almost exclusively for funding on the financial institutions that have created them. As a result, their lending rates are somewhat higher than those of banks, but their share in total housing credit has expanded very rapidly along with the growth of the number of such companies and the spread of their networks of offices. In the recent past, however, their lending has grown slowly, reflecting the weakness in housing investment because of weak growth of income and rocketing housing prices.

TABLE 5.14 *Investment of Non-life Insurance Companies, by Year-end*

	1965		1970		1975		1980		1985	
	¥100m.	%	¥100m.	%	¥100m.	%	¥100m.	%	¥100m.	%
Total assets	4,768	100·0	14,329	100·0	38,761	100·0	72,017	100·0	117,923	100·0
Cash and deposits with others	944	19·8	2,249	15·7	6,221	16·0	13,063	18·1	17,278	14·7
Loans	602	12·6	3,776	26·4	12,444	32·1	16,398	22·8	24,009	20·4
Call loans	190	4·0	663	4·6	441	1·1	832	1·2	1,993	1·7
Securities	1,957	41·0	4,492	31·3	11,449	29·5	26,959	37·4	52,781	44·8
Stocks and shares	1,582	33·2	3,657	25·5	8,940	23·1	15,689	21·8	21,267	18·0

Sources: Ministry of Finance, Banking Bureau, Insurance Division, *Hoken Nenkan* (Insurance Yearbook); and BOJ, *Economic Statistics Annual*.

TABLE 5.15   *Shares of Residential Credit Outstanding (Instalment Repayments), by Month-end*

	March 1975 %	March 1980 %	December 1985 %	¥100m.
Private housing finance companies	3·9	7·7	8·3	50,431
City banks	16·9	14·6	13·6	82,463
Regional banks	14·3	12·8	10·3	62,205
Trust banks (bank accounts)	0·9	0.6	0.4	2,291
Long-term credit banks	1·2	1·2	1·0	5,810
Trust accounts of all banks	6·8	5·7	4·1	24,625
Sogo banks	7·6	6·5	5·6	34,053
Shinkin banks[a]	11·7	10·3	8·1	48,983
Credit co-operatives[a]	1·6	1·7	1·3	7,942
Labour credit associations	4·0	2·7	2·3	13,939
Financial institutions for agriculture, forestry, and fisheries	7·9	4·5	3·4	20,390
Life insurance companies	3·5	5·0	6·2	37,627
Non-life insurance companies	0·3	0·3	0·4	2,438
Housing loan finance corporation	19·5	26·3	35·0	212,156
TOTAL	100·0	100·0	100·0	605,353

[a] Includes funds supplied by the National Federation of Credit Co-operatives.

Source: BOJ, *Economic Statistics Annual.*

The legal character of housing finance companies is that of money-lenders based on the Law Concerning the Regulation of Receiving of Capital Subscription and Interest Rates on Deposits of 1954. The establishment of a housing finance company requires notification to the Minister of Finance. All eight of the housing finance firms currently operating are under the supervision of the Minister of Finance and have been designated as directly under the Minister's jurisdiction, according to a Ministry of Finance notification based on the Cabinet Order Concerning Transfer of Authority over Notification by Money-Lenders and Examination of Money Lenders.

(ii) Operations

The main business of housing finance companies is the lending of funds for residences on the security of real estate, and the amount of credit granted stood at ¥5bn. at the end of 1985, or about 8 per cent of the total housing credit. In addition, the housing finance companies act as agents in the life and non-life insurance businesses related to housing loans and as agent for the Housing Loan Corporation.

The two major characteristics of loans secured by real estate, the main activity of housing finance firms, are the principle of material collateral (no guarantors or guarantee funds are required) and the long-term maturity of the loans (maximum thirty-five years).

On the fund-raising side, the housing finance corporations of course differ from banks in that deposits may not be accepted, and thus they rely on parent institutions and financial institutions for long-term borrowings (of about five years). In addition, there are three ways of making the loan assets liquid. These are housing loan asset trusts (established in June 1973, and under which the housing loan certificates are entrusted to trust banks and sold to the pension funds of the trust banks), housing mortgage deeds[8] (established in October 1974), and mortgage securities (sold primarily to individual customers). Currently none of these methods has a high share in the funding of housing financing companies. As in the case of residential loans by banks, the housing finance companies usually establish a mortgage over the physical objects of their loans, attach long-term fire insurance to the structures (with premium burden borne by the borrower), and establish right of pledge over the claim rights for the insurance funds in question. In addition, group credit life insurance and housing loan guarantee insurance are used as supplementary means of ensuring the quality of assets.

e. Consumer credit institutions

(i) Overview

Consumer credit (excluding housing loans) is separated into two general types: (1) sales credits, under which credit is provided for the purpose of payment for goods or services purchased by a consumer, and (2) consumer finance, in which the consumer is granted the credit directly. It is difficult to gauge precisely the scale of the market for consumer credit, but an estimate by the Japan Consumer Credit Industry Association (see Table 5.16) of new credit granted to consumers during 1984 was ¥31·6bn., or about 18 per cent of final private consumption expenditures (at the end of 1984, the amount outstanding was ¥26·5bn.). Of the total new credit granted during 1984, 53 per cent was sales credit and 47 per cent consumer finance. Over the last nine years, sales credit has grown by 2·9 times and consumer finance by 3·6 times. Many types of firm have seen rapid growth of their credit lending. *Shinpan* companies (sometimes known as credit sales companies) have expanded rapidly in both sales credit and consumer finance, while credit card companies tied to banks and companies specializing in consumer finance have also seen rapid growth in the consumer finance area. On the other hand, neither lending by private financial institutions nor sales credits by credit card companies tied to distributors and producers for particular goods has grown rapidly.

---

[8] Housing mortgage deeds are a method of raising funds from institutional investors by selling to them name-designated assets that have been issued as housing mortgage deeds on the basis of housing loan assets held by the housing finance companies that have the same lending conditions (interest rate maturity and method of redemption). Not only housing finance companies, but also city banks, regional banks, *sogo* banks and others issue such housing mortgage deeds.

TABLE 5.16   *The Consumer Credit Market: Flow of New Credits*

	1975	1980	1984[a]	Amount outstanding, 1984 year-end
	¥100m.	¥100m.	¥100m.	¥100m.
Sales credit	58,069	108,247	169,037	126,049
Instalment credit	50,870	96,468	144,350	122,974
Shinpan companies	5,208	28,036	57,440	46,348
Distributors	30,267	43,702	45,209	27,886
Manufacturers' credit card firms	9,658	15,789	17,773	21,247
Financial institutions (joint loans)	5,737	8,941	23,928	27,493
Non-instalment credit	7,199	11,779	24,687	3,075
Banks' credit card companies	3,253	6,117	12,972	1,289
Distributors	3,946	5,662	11,715	1,786
Consumer loan	40,309	93,088	147,061	139,110
Instalment credit	10,740	34,279	68,398	75,988
Consumer loan companies	4,660	21,441	28,271	21,896
Financial institutions	5,264	9,159	25,029	42,398
Shinpan companies	523	2,142	9,924	7,631
Banks' cerdit card companies	293	1,246	1,214	1,712
Distributsors	0	291	3,960	2,351
Non-instalment credit	29,569	58,809	78,663	63,122
Financial institutions (including the post office)	26,637	51,990	67,958	61,426
Pawnbrokers	2,040	2,240	2,015	670
Banks credit card companies	892	4,579	8,690	1,026
TOTAL	98,378	201,335	316,098	265,159

[a] Survey base for 1984 differs in part from that for 1975 and 1980.

Source: BOJ, Japan Consumer Credit Industry Association, *Nihon no Shohisha Shinyo Tokei* (Statistics on Consumer Credit in Japan).

These trends demonstrate that the needs of consumers have shifted away from funds for purchase of durable consumer goods such as electric appliances and automobiles and toward education, leisure, and entertainment, and that demand has been increasing for so-called 'free' loans and cash loans based on uncollateralized credits whose uses are not specified in the borrowing contract.

The competition in the consumer credit industry has intensified recently. Large leasing firms, distribution firms, and firms that specialize in consumer finance have moved conspicuously into the sales credit areas while existing financial institutions, *Shinpan* companies, and credit card companies have actively moved into consumer finance.

With this growth in the consumer financing industries, social problems have emerged concerning the excessive interest rates and improper collection procedures used by some firms specializing in consumer finance. In reaction to these problems, two laws concerning the money-lending industry were passed in May 1983. These were the Law Concerning Regulation of the Money-lending Industry and the Law of Partial Revision of Laws Concerning the Regulation of Receiving of Capital Subscription, Deposits, Interest Rates, and Funds on Deposits (the two money-lending industry control laws). It is thought necessary to improve and expand further consumer protection through reform of laws in this fashion and also through reform of the system of obtaining consumer credit information as well as preventing the occurrence of bad debts on the balance sheets of banks. In addition, in the future it will be necessary to promote the further sound expansion of the consumer credit industry in an environment of such reforms.

(ii) *Shinpan* companies

Let us consider the *shinpan* companies, which from very early on have played a central role in the consumer credit industry.

The term *shinpan* refers to firms that are registered with the Ministry of International Trade and Industry as firms that intermediate in instalment purchases on the basis of the Instalment Sale Law of July 1961. In March 1985 there were 126 such firms. There were two types: the so-called 'credit card' firms, which handle the business of intermediating in general instalment purchases, and the instalment claims purchasing companies, which intermediate in instalment purchases of specific goods. In the former case, the credit card holders will purchase goods and services on an instalment basis at stores that are members of the *shinpan* company's network, and the *shinpan* company will pay for the goods immediately. The latter buy the instalment purchase claims generated through the sales of member stores to the general public. In addition, some of the *shinpan* companies, particularly the larger ones, have in recent years become active in consumer financing businesses and credit guarantee businesses.

Shinpan companies hold a share of about 21 per cent in the total consumer credit in Japan, and extended ¥6·7bn. of credit (of which sales credits accounted for ¥5·7bn. and consumer finance, ¥1bn.) during 1984. Credit extended by *shinpan* companies has increased twelvefold during the last nine years.

Originally, *shinpan* companies were established in order to undertake the business of intermediating in general instalment purchases. But currently the share of their business in intermediating instalment purchases of specific products is overwhelmingly the larger (in 1984, this constituted 61 per cent of their credit extension). This is because the instalment sales for individual products are more flexible than credit card sales. For instalment purchases of individual products, there are no upper limits on the amount of credit that may be granted and hence no upper limits on the size of the sale, whereas for credit card sales there are difficulties such as the requirement that card holders be members of the *shinpan*'s credit card system and that credit limits on instalment payments on the card not be exceeded. In addition, instalment payments for individual items may be increased in total amount simply by expanding the network of stores that are members of a *shinpan* company's network. However, all the companies recently put greater effort into expanding their credit card systems because of the high diffusion of durable consumer goods and the expectation that the age of the cashless society will begin soon in earnest. In addition, the *shinpan* companies are beginning to enter new fields such as leasing and housing loans.

As the area of business of *shinpan* companies expands, they have increased their dependence on borrowings from banks and other institutions. In addition, the major *shinpan* companies in particular have diversified their sources of funding by becoming listed on the stock exchange and by issue of convertible debentures in foreign markets.

f. Venture capital

(i) Overview

Venture businesses, i.e., businesses, that break into the market on the basis of managerial know-how and technology, have never been few in any era. Nor, however, has it ever been easy for such firms to raise funds in securities markets or from financial institutions in order for them to expand their production or operations. These difficulties in raising capital have been due to the uncertainty of the growth prospects for venture businesses, the high risk of bankruptcy, the inadequacy of physical collateral, the weakness of profit positions, and the difficulty of obtaining debt guarantees from credit guarantee associations.

Venture capital concerns are those that undertake general consultancy on the management of such venture businesses, supply their funds through acquisition or holding of stock, and thus seek to acquire capital gains on the sales of such stocks at the time that the firm concerned has grown enough to go public. There are several types of venture capital concern in Japan today—the small business investment companies that are partially funded through the Small Business Finance Corporation, private venture capital companies, and private investment societies.

(ii) Small business investment companies

Small business investment companies are established on the basis of the Small Business Investment Company Law of 1963. The first were established in that year in Tokyo, Osaka, and Nagoya through joint investment from the Government (the Small Business Finance Corporation) local public bodies, and the private sector. The investment companies separate their operations into investment operations and consultation operations. Their investment operations are carried out for firms of under ¥100m. in capital and include the subscription of newly issued stock by the corporations that belong to certain industries as specified by Government order (currently twenty-eight types of industry). In addition, subscription of convertible debentures is also permitted. Once a company has increased its capital beyond ¥300m., subscription by the investment companies is in principle not permitted (in calculating the capital of a corporation, convertible debentures are measured as if they had been converted into stock at the time they were subscribed). In addition, the stock subscribed by the investment company (or convertible debentures) must account for between 15 per cent and 50 per cent of the total stock issued by the company. However, a problem arose in 1965 when the Stock Exchanges raised the minimum capital requirement for becoming listed on the Exchanges. In Tokyo and Osaka, the minimum capital was raised to ¥300m. (and in April 1975 to ¥500m.) and in Nagoya to ¥200m. (¥300m. in April 1975). The original purpose of the investment companies of 'incubating' small firms toward listing on Stock Exchanges in the future became impossible. As a result, the regulations concerning operation of investment companies were revised in December 1966. Under these new rules, an investment company may receive approval from the Minister of International Trade and Industry to continue to subscribe new stock of a client until the capital of the client is of a sufficient scale to allow public listing of the stock on securities exchanges.

The investment companies hold the stocks that have been subscribed, and once the stage has been reached at which listing of the stock of the corporation is possible, the stocks held by the investment company are disposed of. The disposal is carried out at market prices when a market price for the stock in question exists.

The consultancy activities of investment companies include the guidance of management and technology for the client firms.

Total investments made by the three investment companies stood at ¥38·8bn. at the end of 1985, with loans extended to 947 specific clients.

(iii) Private venture capital companies and investment undertaking societies

Almost all private venture capital companies have been established and funded by banks, securities companies, and insurance companies. At the end of 1985, there were eighty such concerns. The largest proportion has been established since 1975, and the number in existence before that time was very small. Moreover, it would be difficult to claim that the various venture capital firms have been particularly aggressive in their activities. Reasons for this lack of activism include the low prospects of profitability due to the long periods of time between the original investment and listing of the company on the Stock Exchange, which in turn occurs because of the high standards for listing on the Stock Exchange.

Since 1982, however, the establishment of venture capital companies by banks and securities companies has become quite active because of the boom in high technology of recent years. A large number of venture capital firms has been formed, for several reasons. First, the growth of medium- and small-sized firms that have frontier technologies has been quite conspicuous, while that of corporations in general has been relatively stagnant. Secondly, risk diversification has become easier because of the introduction of such methods as investment undertaking societies (partnerships).[9] Thirdly, reforms of the over-the-counter stock rules are under consideration; the reforms would open the stock markets further to venture businesses. (Specifically, easing the registration standards for over-the-counter business is under consideration.) If this comes about, then recovery of funds invested in venture capital businesses will become easier.

g. Securities finance companies

(i) Overview

Securities finance companies are companies that specialize in the financing of securities in order to supply the funds necessary for smooth issue and circulation of stocks and bonds. The history of these companies begins in the post-war period. Just after the reopening of the Stock Exchanges in 1949, large blocks of stock were dumped on the market because of the dissolution of industrial conglomerates (*Zaibatsu*). As a result, there was a major depression in the stock market. In response to this depression and in an effort to ensure the sound development of the markets, a system of margin trading was introduced, and the securities finance companies were established in 1950 with the purpose of supplying the equities and funds necessary for this trading to the securities companies. Nine such securities finance companies were established. At the time of their establishment, these firms were subject to the Laws Concerning the Money-lending Industry, but in 1955 they became licensed companies under the newly revised Securities and Exchange Law. At that time, several mergers occurred in order to strengthen the function of the securities investment firms, and three firms emerged: the Japan Securities Finance Company, the Osaka Securities Finance Company, and the Chubu Securities Finance Company.

(ii) Operations

The basic type of operation of the securities finance company is lending to securities companies in the form of so-called 'loans for margin transactions'; these loans are used to supply the funds necessary for margin trading in

[9] Investment undertaking societies are co-operatives in the civil law sense of the term and so recognized under civil law. These societies raise funds from domestic and foreign debentures, and the venture capital companies as officers of co-operatives then find venture businesses and make the investments and loans. When capital gains occur, these are received as a type of reward for success. The co-operative structure makes it easier to avoid risks and is an effective policy for ensuring the business foundation for the venture concerned.

equities between the securities company and its customers. But lending collateralized by bonds was begun in 1960 in order to promote development of the bond market; loans for this purpose are called bond dealer financing. In recent years, the quantity of bond dealer financing has exceeded that of the loans for margin transactions because of the large growth of the primary and secondary markets in Government bonds. In addition, the securities finance companies make working capital loans to the securities companies and also lend to general investors on collateral of securities. Apart from lending, the securities finance companies also engage in custody business concerning securities, and handle payments of interest and principal on Government bonds.

(1) Loans for margin transactions

The form of loans for margin transactions. Secondary market transactions in equities were carried out through two methods during the pre-war period, the actual exchange of securities for cash in spot transactions, and the adjustment of net balances through payment either by sales of equities or by buy-backs. With the reopening of the Stock Exchanges in the post-war period, the latter type of adjustment transaction was prohibited, and only spot transactions were permitted (with settlement on the fourth day after the contract). Under this system, however, customers without immediately available funds could not sell or buy, so that smooth formation of prices in the secondary market was difficult to achieve. As a result, with the purpose of facilitating price formation, a margin trading system was introduced in 1951 through the introduction of an appropriate level of speculative demand. Under this margin trading system, the securities companies would lend funds or equities to clients to the extent necessary for purchases within the limits of the spot transactions system.

The credit system allows two types of transactions: a securities company may lend either funds (for a client who wishes to buy on credit) or equities themselves (for a client who wishes to sell on credit) to a client who wishes to carry out a transaction on credit. The securities company may provide the funds or equities from its own holdings or its own funds (these are called 'own-account lending' and 'own-account equity lending') or the securities company may raise the funds by borrowing from a securities finance company. The transaction works as follows. The securities finance company receives an application from a securities company (who must be a member of the Stock Exchanges) and the securities finance company delivers the funds for settlement or the equities to the clearing section of the Stock Exchanges on behalf of the securities company on the day of settlement. Then the securities finance company receives from the Stock Exchange, as collateral, the securities purchased or the payments that should have been received by the security company that took out the loan (in addition, the securities finance company receives a fixed proportion of the loan as collateral on the loan from the borrower). The particular equities that are eligible for such lending transactions (known as marginal stocks) are determined through an agreement between the securities finance companies and the Stock Exchanges.

The conditions on such loans are that they must be of less than six months in maturity and that their interest rates must be within the limits prescribed by the Minister of Finance (as of March 1986, these limits were 13 per cent for lending of funds and 11 per cent for lending of equities). However, the actual interest rates at which transactions are made depend on the financial conditions at the time so long as they are within these limits (in March 1986, lending of funds was at 6·5 per cent and lending of equities at 2·75 per cent).

The securities finance companies provide the largest portion of the funds or securities for loans for margin transactions from their own funds or their own securities holdings (in both cases these come from their holdings of collateral of either funds or equities); but when own funds or equity holdings are insufficient, the securities finance companies may borrow from the call market in order to obtain funds, or may borrow securities from the securities companies or from institutional investors.

Regulation on margin trading. In order to prevent an excess of speculative margin trading, the securities finance companies adjust the total amount of margin trading through changing the terms of their lending. The changes in terms include general measures such as raising the interest rate on loans and raising collateral rates, but also raising collateral requirements for securities companies that borrow above predetermined credit limit amounts and, if necessary, raising interest rates on loans to these companies. In cases in which margin transactions concerning one particular equity issue has risen substantially, the securities finance companies and the Stock Exchanges may jointly decide to take measures such as raising the collateral requirements in transactions for that particular equity or reducing the number of applications for loans.

(2) Bond dealer financing.   Bond dealer financing (loans for the secondary bond market) began in 1960, as a means of short-term financing of the inventories of securities companies that became necessary as the subscription and sales of bonds grew. Such loans use the bonds themselves as collateral. This type of lending grew gradually after it was introduced, but adjustments were necessary in response to the growth of the secondary market that accompanied the large-scale issue of Government bonds after 1975. In December 1977, various systems of bond dealer financing were improved and expanded so that the basis for such loans was consolidated.

Most bond dealer financing at present consists of loans collateralized by bonds; the proceeds of the loans are used as temporary working funds between the time of subscription to a new bond issue and the sale to another party, or between the time of purchase and resale of bonds in the secondary market. There are other such types of loan, however, including so-called 'small bond financing', in which the securities companies receive loans for the time between the purchase of small-sized bonds from customers and the time when enough of such small bonds have been accumulated to sell in a unit. There are also Government bond delivery financing loans which provide funds necessary for large-scale transactions in the Stock Exchanges. Neither of these latter two types of loan, however, is important in the activities of the securities finance companies.

There have been several improvements in the system of bond circulation finance loans. The credit limits have been expanded several times, and preparations have been made for the use of registered bonds for collateral under the system of proxy certificates for registered bonds, which will be used as collateral in bond circulation finance lending.[10]

The interest rates on bond circulation finance loans are determined in accordance with financial market conditions. As of March 1986, they were 5·5 per cent for loans collateralized by Government bonds and 5·75 per cent for those collateralized by public bonds other than Government bonds.

(3) Fund-raising. The securities finance companies rely in part on their own funds for engaging in the lending operations but also borrow from banks and from the Bank of Japan. Of these sources, however, borrowings from the call market and banks constitute the largest share. In raising funds from the call market, the securities finance companies use different types of collateral for different types of lending. For bond dealer financing, the borrowings from the call market are collateralized by bonds, by bond proxy certificates, and by the bills issued by securities companies. For loans for margin transactions, the call money borrowings are collateralized by collateral receipt for call loan transactions.[11] But borrowing from banks is the larger source of borrowings for the securities finance companies, and such borrowings are generally loans on bills that are collateralized by bonds or equities received in the course of bond dealer financing. A portion of the funds necessary for bond dealer financing are also borrowed from the Bank of Japan. These are loans on bills collateralized by bonds.

---

[10] The system of proxy certificates involves the securities companies, the securities finance companies, and the money market dealers. Under the system, a participating securities company delivers a designated registered bond to the Bank of Japan in return for which the security company receives a proxy certificate for the registered bond. On this proxy certificate, the exact type of the designated registered bond is listed. The proxy bond may then be used as collateral for a bond financing from a participating securities finance company. Through this system it became easier to use as collateral the registered bonds that have such a substantial weight in the securities companies' inventory.

[11] The collateral receipt for call loan transactions are issued by the Stock Exchanges in return for the deposit of securities at the Exchanges by the securities finance companies. The equities are originally deposited by the securities finance companies at the Stock Exchanges as collateral for the loans for margin transactions.

(4) Recent developments. For many years, the loans for margin trans-actions were the main business of the securities finance companies. Until the mid-1970s, the securities companies were in a state of continuous need of funds and hence had a high dependence on borrowings to raise the funds necessary for margin trading. In the second half of the 1970s, however, the capital base of the securities companies expanded and allowed them to rely more on their own funds; in addition, there were expansions of other means of raising funds, such as impact loans and yen-based short-term lending from foreign banks in Japan. These trends, along with easier financial conditions, allowed a reduction in the dependence of securities companies on borrowings. On the other hand, bond dealer financing has increased very rapidly in recent years, reflecting the expansion of the secondary bond market. At the end of 1985, bond dealer financing stood at ¥800 milliard, an amount exceeding that of loans for margin transactions (¥606 milliard) (see Table 5.17).

TABLE 5.17   *Principal Accounts of Securities Finance Companies, by Year-end*

	1965 ¥100m.	1970 ¥100m.	1975 ¥100m.	1980 ¥100m.	1985 ¥100m.
Assets					
Cash and deposits	10	32	87	174	200
Loans	4,342	2,665	4,296	10,934	17,311
Loans on margin transactions	913	1,653	2,164	4,319	6,056
Loans on public and corporate bonds	—	—	1,325	4,151	8,002
Liabilities					
Borrowings	3,482	782	1,072	3,307	4,539
Call money	697	1,478	2,076	6,713	9,139
Guarantee money for margin transactions	34	5	296	58	51
Guarantee money for lent stocks	92	191	469	460	1,058
Deposits	3	131	278	330	196
Capital	34	34	48	48	63

Sources: BOJ, *Economic Statistics Monthly* and *Economic Statistics Annual.*

3. OTHER FINANCIAL INSTITUTIONS

a. Securities companies

(i) Overview

Under the Securities and Exchange Law (implemented in 1948), securities companies are defined to be financial institutions other than banks, trust banks, and other financial institutions determined by the Cabinet Order (i.e., the Enforcement Order of the Securities and Exchange Law). The securities companies are permitted to engage in the following types of business: (1)

trading, (2) performer for cross-transactions, intermediation, and agenting of trading, (3) performer for cross-transaction, intermediation, and agenting of trading entrusted with trading in securities markets, (4) underwriting, (5) sales to the public, and (6) agent for subscription or secondary distribution to the public. As discussed in Chapter 2, financial intermediaries such as banks were prohibited from engaging in securities business other than that for Government bonds, local government and public body bonds, and Government-guaranteed bonds, based on the principle of separation of banking and securities business in Article 65 of the Securities and Exchange Law. In addition, the securities investment trust business began on the basis of the Securities Investment Trust Law of 1951 and securities investment trust management companies were organized to handle the management of such trusts. Securities companies, however, handled the largest portion of the purchases and sales of securities for an investment trust, the sales of beneficiary certificates, and the payment of dividends and redemption funds. Thus the largest part of securities businesses in Japan today are carried out by the securities companies, and they play the central role in the Japanese securities markets. Moreover, the securities companies began to undertake intermediation of short-term funds with the expansion of short-term open money markets such as the *gensaki* market around the start of the 1970s. Thus, the securities companies are much larger than in the pre-war period, when the major share of their business was the management of transactions in equities.

The supervision and regulation of the securities industry was strengthened after the stock market depression of 1965. Partial revisions of the Securities and Exchange Law were made in May 1965, and these revisions required licensing of securities companies rather than registration (the shift to the licensing system was completed in April 1968) and also required a higher minimum level of capital for securities companies. At the end of 1985, there were 224 securities companies in Japan, 127 of which were full members of all eight Stock Exchanges in the country, and eight of which were broker companies that intermediated between the full members of the Exchanges. Eighty-nine of the companies were not members of exchanges. Of the members of the exchanges, however, four had overwhelmingly the largest shares of capital, employees, turnover, and securities investment trust business of their related firms. These were Nomura, Nikko, Yamaichi, and Daiwa. These firms were the pillars of the Japanese securities industry (see Table 5.18). In the environment of major changes in recent years of financial institution operations, the securities industry and, in particular, the major securities companies have been particularly active in diversifying, internationalizing, and mechanizing their operations.

Diversification has been pursued through several methods. Among these are the lending of funds to individual customers on collateral of public bonds, development of new financial products through a combination of investment

TABLE 5.18 *Scale of Securities Companies, 1984*[a,b]

	Big four companies	Other members of the Exchange	Non-members of the Exchange	Total
Capital (¥100m.)	2,616 (63·8)	1,414 (34·5)[c]	73 (1·8)	4,103 (100·0)
Branches	396 (18·4)	1,477 (68·5)	284 (13·2)	2,157 (100·0)
Employees	37,835 (38·7)	55,003 (56·2)	5,042 (5·2)	97,880 (100·0)
Securities trade (¥100m.)	5,154,798 (69·2)	2,240,112 (30·1)	56,107 (0·8)	7,451,017 (100·0)
Bonds	4,226,755 (74·7)	1,411,707 (25·0)	18,221 (0·3)	5,656,683 (100·0)
Equities	733,337 (47·4)	777,295 (50·2)	36,788 (2·4)	1,547,420 (100·0)
Underwriting, subscriptions and direct sales (¥100m.)	283,100 (65·3)	140,964 (32·5)	9,223 (2·1)	433,287 (100·0)
Securities safe-keeping deposits (¥100m.)	468,015 (63·0)	256,734 (34·6)	18,154 (2·4)	742,903 (100·0)

[a] The fiscal year begins in October of the year before that listed, and ends in September of the year listed.

[b] Based on 216 firms, excluding *Saitori* Member Securities (members acting as broker's broker on the floor), the Tokyo Rengo Securities, Nippon Kyoei Securities, Nippon Sogo Securities, Nippon Tento Securities, and the branches of foreign securities firms in Japan.

[c] Figures in parentheses are percentage shares.

Source: Ministry of Finance, *Okurasho Shokokenkyoku Nenpo* (Ministry of Finance Securities Bureau Yearbook).

trusts (e.g., medium-term Government bonds) with ordinary deposits, and entry into new fields of endeavour (such as establishment of mortgage securities companies and investment advisory firms). Because banks and other financial intermediaries began over-the-counter sales of and dealings in Government and public bonds, the competition between securities companies and these institutions intensified.

Internationalization has also been pursued by several means; the major and some intermediate-sized securities companies have established branches in foreign markets and are engaging either on their own account or through local subsidiaries in the promotion of securities investment in Japan by non-residents. They have also taken an active part in the underwriting of external bond issues by Japanese corporations, the subscription and sales of yen-denominated foreign bonds in Japan, and other international business. Euro-bond underwriting activities have grown conspicuously in recent years, bringing conflict between Japanese banks (bank affiliate securities companies) and Japanese securities companies abroad, and promoting the reduction of the barriers between the banking and securities businesses. The trend toward entry of foreign securities companies into Japan is also strengthening, and at the end of 1985 fourteen such companies had sixteen branches operating under licences received on the basis of the Law Concerning Foreign Securities Companies (implemented in 1971). There were also 118 representative offices of foreign securities companies.

Mechanization has been pursued actively by the securities industry. The largest companies, in particular, have created and expanded on-line systems for the purpose of improving the investment information services given to customers and remittance and settlement services. In the latter type of service, there have been several innovations. The securities companies have created a remittance service through a tie-up with the *sogo* banking industry. In addition, they provide a nation-wide service for the payment of medium-term Government bond funds, and for the automatic transfer and receipt of interest on public bonds through the nation-wide postal savings on-line system. There are also plans to diversify means of payment through unification of investment trusts such as medium-term Government bond funds with nation-wide regional bank card systems and other credit card systems. (Under this unified system, payment for purchases with credit cards could be made through automatic cancellation of medium-term Government bond funds; cashing services and card loans would also be possible.) In this trend toward mechanization of operations, there has been an increased tendency for medium-sized and small securities companies to use the computer systems of the larger securities companies, so that a reorganization within the securities industry focusing on the large companies is occurring because of mechanization and the development and handling of new types of products.

(ii) Operations

The main types of business for securities companies are specified in Clause 2 of Article 28 of the Securities and Exchange Law. These are listed as 'securities businesses', i.e., (1) dealer business, (2) broker business, (3) underwriter business, and (4) selling business. To engage in each of these types of business requires a licence from the Minister of Finance. The securities companies that have received business licences engage in all of these businesses concerning equities. Government bonds, local government bonds, Government-guaranteed bonds, bank debentures, industrial bonds, and beneficiary certificates for securities investment trusts. Reflecting the development of the bond markets in recent years, operations concerning the bond transactions have become the second pillar of the securities buisness along with operations in equities.

Securities companies are prohibited in principle from engaging in business outside of securities operations. However, business concerning securities is permitted so long as it is business that involves the securities industry and creates no problems of harming the public interest or investor protection within the securities business of the securities company in question. Thus, simultaneous operation of other businesses is permitted so long as approval of the Minister of Finance is received. There are six types of such 'tandem operation': (1) acting as agent for the receipt of funds for purchase of bonds and for payments related to principal and interests; (2) acting as agent for payments concerning the earnings, redemption, and partial cancellation of beneficiary certificates for securities investment trusts; (3) acting as agent, custodian, intermediary, or commissioned agent in the purchase of gold bullion; (4) lending collateralized by public bonds; (5) secondary market transactions in CDs; and (6) domestic sales of foreign certificates of deposit and commercial paper. Securities companies also act as safe-keeping deposits for securities on behalf of their clients, but such safe-keeping deposit operations do not require approval as tandem operations because of their character as a contingent business to securities transactions. Safe-keeping deposit operations include temporary holding until sale of a security that has been purchased and custody of a security until delivery (these depository operations also include the implementation of change of registration names on securities by proxy and the payment of interest or funds of redemption for securities on deposit).

With the approval of the Ministry of Finance, a securities company may also engage in so-called 'accumulated investment operations'. In such operations, a client pays instalments of funds to securities company on a regular basis, and the securities companies buys securities of equivalent value and then reinvests the interest and redemption funds from the securities so purchased. In addition, the securities companies that are permitted to engage in such operations are also permitted to handle accumulation savings accounts. Securities companies may also engage in foreign exchange operations within certain limits, to the extent that the foreign exchange operations accompany transactions of Japanese residents in foreign securities investment or of foreign investors in securities investment in Japan. Increasing amounts of foreign exchange transactions have been undertaken by securities companies owing to the start of sales of foreign CDs and commercial paper in domestic markets, to the abolition of the actual demand principle for forward exchange transactions (both of these changes occurred in April 1984), and the abolition of regulations on conversion of foreign funds into yen (in June 1984).

Let us now consider the main types of securities business as defined under the law, separating them into those concerning trading of securities (dealer business and broker business) and those concerning issue of securities (underwriting and selling).

(1) Trading operations. There are two types of trading activity carried out by securities companies. In dealing operations, the trades are made on own account, and the trading profits are the source of income. In brokering operations, the trades are carried out on behalf of individual clients either

over-the-counter or on the Stock Exchanges, and the commissions are the source of income. Almost all Japanese securities companies carry out both types of business simultaneously but trading in stocks is mostly brokering business on the floor of the Stock Exchanges, while trading in bonds is mostly over-the-counter dealing operations.

During the 1950s and 1960s, trading in equities was the largest share of the trading operations of securities companies, but in the early 1970s the development of the bond markets and the *gensaki* markets raised the share of bond trading. With the large-scale issues of Government bonds since 1975, the trading volume in bonds has exceeded that in equities.

The management fees paid by individual clients when carrying out securities transactions through securities companies are determined by each Stock Exchange according to the type of security involved and the value of the transaction.

(2) Securities issue business.   The types of issuing business carried out by securities companies are underwriting operations and selling operations. Underwriting is defined as (1) the acquisition of all or part of an issue of a security with the intention of later selling the acquired securities, and/or (2) the purchase of remaining amounts of a security issued should the issue not be fully subscribed. In contrast, selling operations are those in which the securities company manages the sales to general investors of a security being issued on behalf of the issuer, holders, or the underwriting securities company. In the case of selling operations, the securities company is under no obligation to purchase any amounts of the issue that remain unsold.

Long-term Government coupon bonds, Government-guaranteed bonds, and industrial bonds are usually issued through underwriting by securities companies or financial institutions such as banks. In the case of long-term Government bonds, underwriting and subscription are carried out by a syndicate composed of banks, insurance companies, and securities companies. The subscription share of the securities companies had been about 20 per cent on average since the late 1970s. For industrial bonds, underwriting by financial institutions such as banks is prohibited, so that the underwriting and subscription are usually handled by *ad hoc* syndicates composed of six regular members (including the big four securities companies) and others. In fact, however, the final absorption of these bonds is carried out primarily by banks.

For many years, the operations of securities companies in the bond issue market centred on underwriting business for electric power companies and selling operations for bank debentures. With the large-scale flotations of Government bonds since 1975, however, the composition has shifted toward underwriting business for Government bonds and selling operations of high-interest bond investment trusts that include Government bonds (for example, medium-term Government bond funds). Reflecting the internationalization of securities markets, there has also been an increase in underwriting activities accompanying the issue of Eurobonds by Japanese corporations (in particular, those in convertible debenture form) along with a diversification of related business.

Equity issues in earlier years concentrated on par-value issues or gratis issues to current stockholders or related parties. In recent years, however, there has been a rapid increase in market-price public issues of equities through subscription and underwriting by securities companies. These have now become part of the market.

From these types of business related to securities issue, the securities companies earn underwriting fees, subscription fees, and sales fees.

(iii) Recent developments

The earnings of securities companies come from three sources—trading profits, and dividends received through dealing operations, management fees through brokering operations, and underwriting, subscription, and sales

TABLE 5.19 *Profitability of Securities Companies[a]*

Fiscal year	No. of firms	Total Income (¥100m.)	Income from dealing (¥100m.)	Income from brokering (¥100m.)	Income from underwriting and selling (¥100m.)	Other income[b] (¥100m.)	Net income ¥100m.)
1965	444	1,538	149	594	206	589	Δ117[c]
1979	248	3,594	219	1,926	456	993	489
1975	236	6,349	778	2,695	1,304	1,572	396
1980	229	11,871	934	6,202	2,088	2,647	997
1981	227	14,071	1,173	7,765	2,167	2,966	1,329
1982	221	12,585	1,573	5,255	2,602	3,155	812
1983	218	17,294	2,171	9,011	2,542	3,570	1,631
1984	216	21,183	2,689	10,802	3,153	4,539	2,469

[a] Excludes *Saitori* Member Securities, Tokyo Rengo Securities, Nippon Kyoei Securities, Nippon Sogo Securities, Nippon Tento Securities, and the branches of foreign securities firms in Japan.

[b] 'Other' includes trust remuneration from medium-term Government bond funds, interest income on loans to customers for margin trading, etc.

[c] Δ indicates a deficit.

Source: Ministry of Finance, *Okurasho Shoken Kyoku Nenpo* (Ministry of Finance Securities Bureau Yearbook).

fees from underwriting and selling operations (see Table 5.19). The largest proportion (about 70 per cent) comes from fees on brokering, underwriting, and selling, and within this amount (about 50 per cent), brokerage management fees have a relatively high share.

Brokerage business income, which has such a large share in total income, is influenced heavily by movements of the stock market because the main source of such income is stock brokerage fees. As a result, there can be substantial movements in this income item from year to year, although recently it has in general been growing steadily. Income from dealer operations has also been growing steadily, supported by the growth of securities trading profits that accompany the expansion of over-the-counter transactions in bonds, due in turn to the large-scale Government bond flotations. Income from underwriting and selling operations has also been on an upward trend, particularly for the largest securities companies, due to the increased issues of all types of bond including Government bonds, market-price issues of equities, convertible debentures, and Eurobonds. Other types of income such as trust remuneration from medium-term Government bond funds have also been increasing.

These increases in the earnings of securities companies have strengthened the financial basis of the companies, and as a result the profitability of the big four securities companies is nearing the levels of the largest city banks. Even for medium- or small-sized securities companies, the increase of retained profits has raised income from own-account lending concerning margin trading (see section (g) above on securities finance companies), and this increase in income has made a significant contribution to improvement of their profitability (see Table 5.20 for the asset and liability composition of securities companies).

(iv) Regulation of securities companies

Securities companies are subject to various regulations both under the Securities and Exchange Laws and from other laws and regulations from the viewpoint of investor protection and appropriate management of the national economy. There are two such types of regulation, those concerning operations themselves and those concerning assets and accounting. For foreign securities companies operating in Japan, the underlying law (the Law Concerning Foreign Securities Companies), applies virtually all the various regulations concerning securities transactions that are applied to domestic securities companies. There are almost no differences *vis-à-vis* domestic securities companies regarding the regulations on operations, assets, or accounting.

(1) Regulations on operations. As discussed above, securities companies must be licensed by the Minister of Finance for each of the four types of securities business. In addition, other regulations on their day-to-day activity seek to ensure protection of investors and fair trading. There are three kinds of regulation on day-to-day activity. The first is regulation of joint operation of different types of securities business. For example, when a firm engages in both dealer and brokering businesses for securities of one company, it must clearly display its qualification as a licensed securities company and is prohibited from acting as agent for a connected party. For cases in which a company is acting as both broker and underwriter, there are restrictions on

TABLE 5.20   *Principal Accounts of Securities Companies,[a] end of 1985*

	¥100m.	%
Assets		
Cash and deposits	13,986	10·0
Short-term loans	2,609	1·9
Securities owned	24,246	17·3
Equities	(3,837)	(2·7)
Loans to customers for stocks bought on margin	29,496	21·0
Customers' securities	55,032	39·2
Investment securities	3,841	2·7
Other assets	11,093	7·9
TOTAL	140,303	100.0
Liabilities		
Short-term borrowings	36,222	25·8
From financial institutions	(23,853)	(17·0)
Deposits	5,355	3·8
Borrowings from securities finance companies on margin transactions	7,313	5·2
Payment to customers for stocks sold on margin	2,932	2·1
Borrowed securities	5,679	4·0
Funds under guarantee	50,172	35·8
Special allowances	1,676	1·2
Capital accounts	23,868	17·0
Capital	(4,768)	(3·4)
Other liabilities	7,086	5·1
TOTAL	140,303	100.0

[a] Based on 212 firms, excluding *Saitori* Member Securities, Tokyo Nippon Kyoei Securities, Nippon Sogo Securities, Nippon Tento Securities, and the branches of foreign securities companies in Japan.

Source: Japan Securities Dealers Association, *Shoken Gyoho* (Report on the Securities Industry).

credit provision by the underwriter and strict controls over use of information relating to some issue by the employees in the securities company who are connected with underwriting information. The second type of regulation concerns unfair trading practices. Examples include prohibition of solicitation through provision of conclusive judgements, loss guarantees, or special profits, and prohibition of fraudulent price formation. The third type of regulation concerns correction of unsound business practices. Examples include trading based on unconfirmed intentions of customers, excessive promotion of sales of any particular security, excessive promotion of sales of equities held by the securities company in question, and excessive competition in some implicit ways in underwriting. Any of these practices may become the object of an order of correction from the Minister of Finance. In addition, there are regulations mentioned above on tandem operations of the securities companies and prohibitions on outside undertakings by directors concerned with daily operations. Also, securities companies are forbidden from acting as trustee corporations in the subscription of corporate bonds because this is a type of business allocated to banks. This prohibition is based on the desire to separate the lines of business of securities companies and other financial institutions such as banks.

(2) Regulations on assets and accounting. Securities companies are required to obey the administrative measures ordered by the Minister of Finance concerning change or cessation of operations when problems arise concerning maintenance of the soundness of the financial condition of a firm. In addition, firms are required to provide reports and materials for reference concerning the state of their business and assets in accordance with the direction of the Minister of Finance, and are also required to permit on-site inspection. The Securities and Exchange Law lists three cases in which a securities company must obey the supervisory orders of the Ministry of Finance. The first is when the liability ratio (the ratio of total liabilities in money terms to net assets) exceeds a rate specified by order of the Ministry of Finance (currently ten times). The second is when borrowings of money or securities, lending or trustee assets, or securities and other asset holdings differ from the criteria of soundness determined by order of the Minister of Finance (for example, the limit of securities holdings is 40 per cent of net assets). The third is cases in which a correction of asset conditions is necessary (this would include cases in which net assets were lower than capital, operating income was insufficient, or bad assets were considerable).

In addition, securities companies are required to accumulate certain special reserves in order to maintain the soundness of their finance and to expand their retained earnings. Examples include profit reserves, trading loss reserves, and securities trading liability reserves.

b. Money market dealers

(i) Overview

As previously explained in Chapter 4, the money market dealers are active as specialized transaction intermediaries in the short-term money markets. The money market dealers are regulated under the Law Concerning the Regulation of Receiving of Capital Subscription, Deposits, and Interest on Deposits of 1954, just as are generalized money-lenders. Money market dealers, however, play an important role related to monetary policy, unlike money-lenders, and are directly under the supervision of the Minister of Finance. Currently, there are six money market dealers, Tokyo Tanshi,

Yamane Tanshi, Ueda Tanshi, Nippon Discount Tanshi, Yagi Tanshi, and Nagoya Tanshi.

(ii) Operations

For most financial institutions, the laws under which they are organized specify what types of business they may engage in, but this is not the case for money market dealers. However, the articles of the various companies specify the following types of operation.

(1) Call funds transactions. In the pre-war period, the call funds transactions of the money market dealers were mostly brokering, i.e., acting as intermediary in call transactions by bringing together lenders and borrowers. Currently, however, dealing is the chief type of business, i.e., transactions on own account of the money market dealers with either a borrower or a lender. However, this dealing is in fact closer to a type of brokering because the money market dealers are prohibited from holding a net position in call funds—in order to avoid transactions risks. In the uncollateralized call transactions introduced in July 1985, the money market dealers act purely as brokers.

(2) Bill trading transactions. Money market dealers act as intermediaries in bill market transactions by buying the bills of exchange (so-called 'cover bills' and reselling these bills to financial institutions with surplus funds, which bills are) issued by banks that are collateralized by the prime bills of corporations (so-called *gentegata*, underlying bills) and that name the money market dealers as payee. In this way, the individual transactions in bills are carried out on own account by the money market dealers, but, as in the case of call transactions, actual holdings on own account are kept within very strict limits in order to avoid risk. Thus, in fact, the largest proportion of transactions are broker-like transactions in which a buyer and a seller are matched.

(3) Transactions in Government bills. Money market dealers, like financial intermediaries such as banks, require the approval of the Minister of Finance in order to engage in securities operations. With approval of the Minister of Finance, the money market dealers engage in trading and intermediation in transactions involving Government bills (in fact, since May 1981, the money market dealers have sold Government bills into interbank markets that were purchased from the Bank of Japan). This has been a major factor in diversifying the business of money market dealers, along with their secondary handling of CDs.

(4) Intermediation of foreign exchange trading. In the foreign exchange market, those who carry out intermediation are known as foreign exchange brokers. As of March 1986, two of the money market dealers listed above acted as foreign exchange brokers, and there were six firms that acted exclusively as foreign exchange brokers, of which four were subsidiaries of money market dealers. Foreign exchange brokers do not trade on their own account, but instead are restricted to earning fees from both buyer and seller as transactions are concluded.

(5) Intermediation of dollar-call financing. The same companies mentioned above as foreign exchange brokers act as brokers in the dollar-call market.

(6) Trading transactions in CDs. Money market dealers may act either as intermediaries or as parties to transactions in CDs. They have functioned in this way since establishment of the CD market in May 1979, both at the stage of issue of CDs and in secondary transactions.

(7) Transactions in yen-denominated bankers' acceptances. With the establishment in June 1985 of an open market in yen-denominated bankers' acceptances in which the general public could participate, the money market dealers, together with other financial institutions, began to engage in trading and intermediation in transactions involving yen-denominated trade bills that were accepted by foreign exchange banks.

(8) Intermediation of interbank deposit transactions. With the liberalization of interest rates on large-scale time deposits in October 1985, there was a simultaneous liberalization of interbank interest rates on deposits of the same size and maturity. With this liberalization, money market dealers were permitted to carry out intermediation of such interbank transactions.

The principal accounts of money market dealers are shown in Table 5.21. As seen in the table, the amounts of bills bought currently exceed call lending and those bills purchased exceed call borrowing.

(iii) Relationship with the Bank of Japan

The Bank of Japan maintains a continuous close contact with the money market dealers in order to implement monetary policy, and provides guidance for their business activities. In ensuring the smooth functioning of the short-term money markets, the Bank of Japan carries out the following types of transaction with short funds companies.

(1) Current deposit transactions. Each money market dealer maintains a current deposit account at the Bank of Japan, and settlement of call and bill transactions are in principle made through current payment drafts on this account.

TABLE 5.21 *Principal Accounts of the Money Market Dealers,*[a] *by Year-end*

	1965		1970		1975		1980		1985	
	¥100m.	%	¥100m.	%	¥100m.	%	¥100m.	%	¥100m.	%
Assets										
Call loans	8,889	91·7	19,173	93·6	23,823	31·6	42,148	39·3	46,162	22·9
Bills bought	—	—	—	—	44,757	59·3	57,461	53·6	146,877	72·7
Securities	47	0·5	25	0·1	54	0·1	120	0·1	186	0·1
Cash and deposits	64	0·7	17	0·1	224	0·3	440	0·4	1,768	0·9
Other	690	7·1	1,274	6·2	6,587	8·7	7,034	6·6	6,989	3·5
TOTAL	9,690	100·0	20,489	100·0	75,445	100·0	107,203	100·0	201,982	100·0
Liabilities										
Call money	8,091	83·5	18,170	88·7	23,316	30·9	41,333	38·6	42,889	21·2
Bills sold	—	—	—	—	44,757	59·3	57,461	53·6	146,859	72·7
Borrowings	846	8·7	905	4·4	470	0·6	753	0·7	4,496	2·2
Capital	4	0·1	5	0·0	13	0·0	13	0·0	14	0·0
Other	749	7·7	1,409	6·9	6,889	9·2	7,643	7·1	7,724	3·8

[a] The balance sheet as shown here does not indicate broker activities such as intermediation in foreign exchange transactions or dollar call loan transactions.

Source: BOJ.

(2) Domestic exchange transactions. By utilizing exchange transactions between the head office and branches of the Bank of Japan, money market dealers not only may remit funds for their own inter-office accounts but also may carry out transactions in call funds and bill trading with financial institutions around the country. Through these payments, the markets in various parts of the country are tied together, and the efficiency of payment transfers is raised.

(3) Lending transactions. There are two types of lending by the Bank of Japan to the money market dealers, regular lending and lending related to margin transaction loans with securities finance companies. Regular lending is that which the Bank of Japan extends to the money market dealers when necessary because of conditions in the financial markets. Until recently, the money market dealers used the proceeds of such lending exclusively in the call market, but since March 1986 it has been possible to use these funds for the purchase of certificates of deposit. The latter type of lending, that concerning margin transactions, is in fact lending to the securities finance companies through the money market dealers. In such transactions, the securities finance companies borrow call money from the money market dealers in order to fund their own margin transactions, and a portion of these call-money borrowings are provided by the Bank of Japan to the money market dealers.

(4) Trading transactions in private bills and Government ordinary bills. Purchase of bills from financial institutions is one of the most important methods by which the Bank of Japan affects the short-term money markets. Such purchases were initiated in June 1972, and in principle are carried out with the money market dealers as the Bank of Japan's opposite party. In addition, the Bank of Japan uses the money market dealers to adjust the conditions in the financial markets through sales of Government bills and bills drawn for sale by the Bank of Japan (the former type of transaction was instituted in January 1966 and the latter in August 1971). In this sense, the Bank of Japan's market operations are carried out with all the participants in the markets, but through the money market dealers.

4. PUBLIC FINANCIAL INTERMEDIARIES

a. The fiscal investment and loan programme (FILP)

In addition to private-sector financial institutions, there exists a group of public financial intermediaries in Japan comprising the post office, the Trust Fund Bureau, and various financial institutions run by the Government. The function of these public financial institutions is to augment the operations of the private ones. Every year, the Government absorbs large quantities of funds through the publicly administered postal savings and other types of insurance and pension system and channels them into public financial intermediaries. These funds then become the principal resource for the Government's investment and loan activities, such as capitalization, lending, and underwriting of bonds of private-sector industries. These financial activities of the Government are called fiscal investments and loans. In general, the term 'fiscal investment and loan programme' (FILP) indicates the investment and lending activities of the Government that are covered in the allocation plan compiled every fiscal year.

Figure 5.3 is a diagram of FILP. As seen in the diagram, there are two types of source of funds for FILP, the so-called 'Government funds' comprising the Industrial Investment Special Account, the Trust Fund Bureau Fund, Postal Insurance Annuity Assets, and the so-called 'private funds' that are funds raised from Government-guaranteed bonds and Government-guaranteed borrowing. These funds are invested in capitalization, lending and, underrwriting of securities to various bodies that act in the public interest, such as special accounts of the Government, public corporations, public banks (such as the Japan Development Bank and the Export and Import Bank of Japan), public finance corporations, public bodies, local government and public bodies, and special public companies. These fiscal investment and loan activities of the Government have been managed in a comprehensive fashion under FILP since its inception in fiscal 1953.

FILP is determined together with the Government budget each fiscal year, through a process that is very similar. Until fiscal 1972, Diet approval was necessary for only a portion of FILP, i.e., the portion that was accounted for under the General Account of the budget and the special accounts within the budget such as lending and investment by Industrial Investment Special Account and the special accounts concerning Government-guaranteed bonds and loans. The largest portion of the funds, which came from Trust fund Bureau Funds and the Postal Life Insurance Annuity Assets, did not require approval from the Diet. After 1972, however, the scale of the FILP expanded, and its influence on the national economy became very great. From fiscal 1973, a new law was established in this regard, the Law Concerning Special Measures for Long-Term Investment of the Trust Fund Bureau Funds and Funds Accumulated from Postal Annuities and Postal Life Insurance Annuity (enacted in March 1973). Under the new law, the investment of the Trust Fund Bureau Funds or of Postal Insurance Annuity Assets for periods of over five years required that the Government obtain approval of the Diet for the amounts intended for each type of use under the general provisions of the budget for special account expenditures. As a result of this requirement, each element within FILP is listed in the budget at some point and is part of the budget plan that must be approved by the Diet.

FILP has an elastic clause built into it in order to enable the Government to react flexibly to changes in economic conditions that are difficult to foresee.

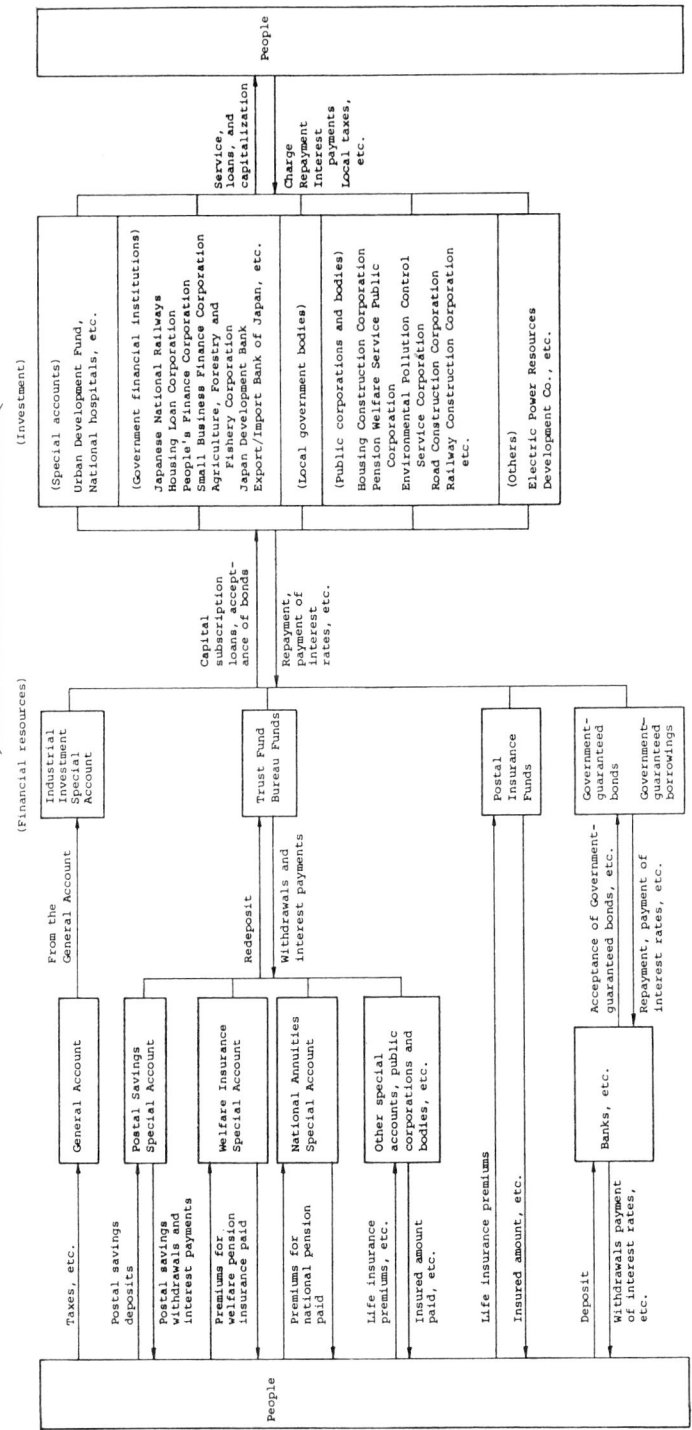

Fig. 5.3   *Fiscal Investment and Loans Program (FILP)*

For example, an amount of up to 50 per cent of the original programme amount may be added to the expected long-term investment funds from the Trust Fund Bureau and the Postal Life Insurance Annuity. In addition, carry-over of unused funds into the next fiscal year is permitted so long as the carry-over remains within one year. Another so-called 'elastic' clause allows a 50 per cent margin in the maximum amount of Government guarantees that may be granted.

The revenues and expenditures of FILP are shown in Table 5.22 and 5.23. On the funding side, the largest share comes from fiscal funds (88 per cent of the total in the FILP of fiscal 1985) and among these the share of Trust Fund Bureau monies is overwhelmingly the largest (78 per cent). In recent years, however, the shares of Government-guaranteed bonds and Government-guaranteed borrowing has risen, reflecting the depth of the insufficiency of fiscal funds. On the investment side, the majority of fiscal investment funds are supplied to the private sector either through banks, public finance corporations, or public bodies (which include Overseas Economic Co-operation Funds) or through institutions such as the *Shokochukin* Bank that are classifed as special corporations or investment and loan undertakings. In the 1985 FILP, about 62 per cent of fiscal investment and loans went to the private sector through such fiscal investment and loan institutions, while the rest went directly into capital formation by the public sector through public works based on fiscal investments and loans.

b. The function of fiscal investment and loans

At the heart of the character of the fiscal investment and loan programme is the fact that the largest portion of its funding depends on funds on which interest and principal must be repaid, such as postal savings, welfare pensions, and national pensions. As a result, the investments cannot ignore the aspect of profitability and must be in undertakings that promise a reasonable profit and that have a certainty of return and redemption. The second important point about fiscal investment and loan funds is that they are public funds raised through the credit of the state. As a result, their investment must be carried out in conformity with public goals such as the improvement of national welfare and the progress or development of society and economy. With these two basic characteristics, the fiscal investment and loan funds carry out a resource allocative function by travelling through two particular routes. The first route is supply of FILP funds to industrial undertakings such as the Japanese National Railways or the Public Housing Corporations and thereafter supply by these institutions of the goods and services they produce to the population. The second route is supply of FILP funds to financing institutions such as the Japan Development Bank or the People's Finance Corporation and the subsequent on-lending of such funds to private

TABLE 5.22 Sources of Funding for FILP, by Fiscal Year

	1965		1970		1975		1980		1984		1985	
	¥100m.	%	¥100m.	%	¥100m.	%	¥100m.	%	¥100m.	%	¥100m.	%
Trust Fund Bureau	11,872	66·8	27,913	73·5	98,002	86·4	199,389	85·9	216,701	79·4	200,290	77·5
Postal savings	(4,645)	(26·1)	(14,201)	(37·4)	(50,501)	(44·5)	(94,869)	(40·9)	(77,970)	(28·6)	(64,000)	(24·8)
Welfare or national pension funds	(3,697)	(20·9)	(10,243)	(27·0)	(21,321)	(18·8)	(46,604)	(20·1)	(51,988)	(19·1)	(39,500)	(15·3)
Assets of postal life insurance annuity	1,095	6·2	4,069	10·7	10,141	8·9	16,887	7·3	25,771	9·4	25,876	10·0
Industrial Investment Special Account	430	2·4	1,035	2·7	655	0·6	167	0·1	40	0·0	314	0·1
Other	—	—	—	—	—	—	—	—	—	—	—	—
Fiscal funds total	*13,397*	*75·4*	*33,017*	*86·9*	*108,798*	*95·9*	*216,443*	*93·3*	*242,512*	*88·9*	*226,480*	*87·6*
Government-guaranteed loans and bonds	4,367	24·6	4,973	13·1	4,639	4·1	15,666	6·7	30,325	11·1	32,100	12·4
TOTAL	17,764	100·0	37,990	100·0	113,437	100·0	232,109	100·0	272,837	100·0	258,580	100·0

Source: Ministry of Finance, *Zaisei Kinyu Tokei Geppo* (Fiscal Finance Statistics Monthly).

TABLE 5.23   *FILP Recipients, by Fiscal Year*

	1965		1970		1975		1980		1984 (estimate)		1985 (plan)	
	¥100m.	%	¥100m.	%	¥100m.	%	¥100m.	%	¥100m.	%	¥100m.	%
Special accounts	263	1·5	384	1·2	1,757	1·7	3,676	2·0	4,362	2·2	4,363	2·1
Public corporations	2,064	11·6	3,257	10·1	11,250	10·7	14,170	7·8	15,260	7·8	13,860	6·6
Banks	2,886	16·2	6,502	20·3	11,865	11·2	14,475	8·0	12,580	6·4	14,620	7·0
Public finance corporations	4,719	26·6	10,352	32·3	34,778	32·9	81,829	45·2	85,429	43·5	89,541	42·9
Public bodies, etc.	3,516	19·8	6,171	19·2	24,422	23·1	33,959	18·8	41,896	21·4	46,466	22·3
Local government bodies	3,764	21·2	4,968	15·5	20,482	19·4	31,017	17·1	34,989	17·8	37,980	18·2
Special corporations	552	3·1	393	1·2	1,056	1·0	1,910	1·1	1,680	0·9	1,750	0·8
Other	—	—	69	0·2	—	—	—	—	—	—	—	—
TOTAL	17,764	100·0	32,096	100·0	105,610	100·0	181,036	100·0	196,196	100·0	208,580	100·0

Source: Ministry of Finance, *Zaisei Kinyu Tokei Geppo* (Fiscal Finance Statistics Monthly) and *Zaisei Tokei* (Fiscal Statistics).

sector enterprises that, although socially beneficial, are not able to respond to needs with only private-sector financing for reasons such as a long period before funds can be recovered, high risk, or low profitability.

But FILP funds have not only a resource allocative function but also a business cycle adjustment function. That is, because of the flexible system of additions or carry-overs in the FILP budget, it is possible to either speed or slow the implementation of projects. Compared to the budget of the General Account, therefore, FILP funds come in a form that is easy to use for counter-cyclical policy because of their mobility and flexibility.

In the early post-war years, fiscal investment and loans emphasized recovery and promotion of basic industries such as steel, coal, electric power, and shipping, and did so through such institutions as the Reconstruction Finance Corporation (1946–9) and the USAID Counterpart Fund (1949–53). In the early 1950s, about 30 per cent of the fund-raising for plant and equipment investment of private industry came from fiscal investment and loans, and their character as a quantitative supplement to private funds became stronger. Thereafter, the various Government financial institutions were established. Nevertheless, major corporations began to rely on private financial institutions and capital markets in order to raise the largest portion of the funds they needed. As a result, the share of fiscal investment and loans in the fund-raising for plant and equipment investment by private industry fell precipitously. As a result, the object of fiscal investment and loans shifted toward industrial and other types of infrastructure, trade, and foreign economic assistance. Recently, the share of fiscal investment funds going to non-industrial infrastructure has risen to about 70 per cent (see Table 5.24).

The changes in fiscal investments and loans have of course reflected the changes in economic structure over the years, from economic recovery in the post-war period to high growth thereafter, and finally to the transition to lower in recent years. In order to realize stable economic development in the coming years, it is thought desirable that fiscal investments and loans concentrate on qualitative augmentation, fields into which private financial institutions cannot easily penetrate because of profitability problems due to the risk or earning power of the firms in these fields.

c. The funding for fiscal investments and loans

(i) Trust Fund Bureau 'funds'

The Trust Fund Bureau is an institution that receives postal savings deposits and deposits of excess funds and accumulated funds or various special accounts of the Government and used these monies to finance special corporations such as public bodies, Government financial institutions, and local government bodies. Thus, the Trust Fund Bureau plays the central role in fiscal investment and loans. The history of the Trust Fund Bureau goes back

TABLE 5.24 FILP Funds by Planned Use, by Fiscal Year[a]

	1965		1970		1975		1980		1984		1985	
	¥100m.	%	¥100m.	%	¥100m.	%	¥100m.	%	¥100m.	%	¥100m.	%
Livelihood infrastructure and welfare	8,561	52.8	20,179	56.3	59,724	64.1	130,568	71.8	147,151	69.7	145,662	69.8
Housing	2,259	13.9	6,896	19.3	19,966	21.4	47,619	26.2	52,895	25.1	52,893	25.4
Living environment	2,010	12.4	4,168	11.6	15,573	16.7	25,717	14.1	30,075	14.2	32,809	15.7
Health and welfare facilities	585	3.6	1,017	2.8	3,133	3.4	6,280	3.5	6,379	3.0	5,957	2.8
Education facilities	493	3.1	790	2.2	2,752	2.9	8,089	4.4	7,771	3.7	7,453	3.6
Small and medium business	2,045	12.6	5,523	15.4	14,505	15.6	34,004	18.7	39,683	18.8	37,644	18.0
Agriculture, forestry, and fisheries	1,169	7.2	1,785	5.0	3,795	4.1	8,859	4.9	10,348	4.9	8,906	4.3
Industrial infrastructure	5,164	31.9	9,792	27.4	23,452	25.2	35,565	19.6	44,784	21.2	45,738	21.9
Land management and reclamation	506	3.1	560	1.6	1,100	1.2	3,120	1.7	3,791	1.8	4,728	2.3
Roads	1,284	7.9	3,078	8.6	7,444	8.0	10,314	5.7	17,117	8.1	18,264	8.8
Transport and communications	2,250	13.9	4,723	13.2	11,849	12.7	17,437	9.6	18,876	8.9	17,634	8.4
Local development	1,124	7.0	1,431	4.0	3,059	3.3	4,694	2.6	5,000	2.4	5,112	2.4
Key industries	2,481	15.3	5,828	16.3	9,924	10.7	15,666	8.6	19,131	9.1	17,180	8.3
Industry and technology	1,262	7.8	2,028	5.7	2,764	3.0	5,473	3.0	6,203	3.0	6,033	2.9
Trade and economic co-operation	1,219	7.5	3,800	10.6	7,160	7.7	10,193	5.6	12,928	6.1	11,147	5.4
TOTAL	16,206	100.0	35,799	100.0	93,100	100.0	181,799	100.0	211,066	100.0	208,580	100.0

[a] The shares of fiscal funds in total industrial fund-raising of the private sector were as follows:

(in percent)

	1955	1960	1965	1970	1975	1980	1984
Total	14.4	7.5	8.9	8.0	11.8	12.7	5.8
of which Plant and equipment	32.3	13.0	16.8	12.4	19.2	23.9	19.2

Source: Ministry of Finance, Zaisei Kinyu Tokei Geppo (Fiscal Finance Statistics Monthly), and Showa 61-nendo Yosan oyobi Zaisei Toyushi Keikaku no

many years to the so-called 'Deposit Bureau' of the Ministry of Finance, but the Trust Fund Bureau Fund Law of 1951 established the Trust Fund Bureau in its present form, made major changes in the ways in which the funds could be invested, and created the basis for the current system.

The deposits in the Trust Fund Bureau come from several sources, some of which are required by law. First, all postal savings must be deposited with the Trust Fund Bureau except for those funds necessary for day-to-day payments to customers and lending to depositors. Secondly, the accumulated funds of special accounts of the government, i.e., surpluses from earlier fiscal years, must also be deposited with the Trust Fund Bureau, except for the Special Account for Post Office Life Insurance and Postal Annuity. Thirdly, the investment portions of surpluses of special accounts that must also be deposited with the Trust Fund Bureau, with the exception of the Government bonds held by the National Debt Consolidation Fund Special Account. Fourthly, it is also possible, though not required, for the Treasury surplus to be deposited with the Trust Fund Bureau as part of the investment of these funds. Fifthly, there is also the Trust Fund Bureau Special Account that was established in order to take care of the revenue on investments (yields in investment) by the Bureau and the expenditures of the Bureau (interest payments on deposits and administration costs). The surplus funds and accumulations from this special account also make up a portion of the funds of the Trust Fund Bureau but are not subject to the procedures of deposit. Sixthly and finally, among the funds that the Trust Fund Bureau may use as sources for the fiscal investment and loan program for each fiscal year are the redemption funds for investments made earlier and the draw-down of accumulated reserves.

Deposits in the Trust Fund Bureau must be for a minimum of one month and, depending on the length of deposit, interest rates must be between a minimum of an annual rate of 2 per cent (for deposits of more than one month but less than three) to a maximum of 6 per cent (for deposits of seven years or more). These interest rate limits are established by law; however, for deposits of seven years or more, a temporary procedure has been in effect since 1961 under which special interest over and above the legal interest is also paid (as of October 1985 this special interest rate was 0·8 percentage points extra). At the end of 1984, the total outstanding amount of funds available to the Trust Fund Bureau were ¥152bn.; the majority of these funds came from postal deposits and about 90 per cent of the total came from small-scale deposits of the populace, including not only postal savings deposits but also welfare pensions and national pensions (see Table 5.25). The maturity structure of deposits is very long, with the majority of funds having a maturity of more than seven years.

The investment of these funds is required to be carried out with methods that are profitable and certain of return, and in activities that will contribute to the improvement of public welfare. There are four major areas for use of

TABLE 5.25 *FILP Funds Outstanding by Source, by Fiscal Year-end*

	1965		1970		1975		1980		1984	
	¥100m.	%	¥100m.	%	¥100m.	%	¥100m.	%	¥100m.	%
Deposits of postal savings and postal transfer savings	26,732	52·9	76,757	52·5	241,986	56·5	605,082	60·5	928,848	60·9
Deposits of postal life insurance and postal annuity	898	1·8	3,501	2·4	10,921	2·5	18,499	1·8	23,599	1·5
Deposits of welfare pension insurance	14,061	27·8	43,435	29·7	120,976	28·3	275,424	27·5	434,336	28·6
Deposits of surplus of treasury accounts	—	—	—	—	—	—	—	—	—	—
Deposits of funds of national pension	1,885	3·7	7,172	4·9	17,982	4·2	23,596	2·4	24,869	1·6
Deposits of others	6,423	12·7	14,718	10·1	35,476	8·3	77,948	7·8	89,806	5·9
Total deposits	*49,999*	*98·9*	*145,583*	*99·5*	*427,341*	*99·8*	*1,000,549*	*100·0*	*1,498,458*	*98·6*
Other	540	1·1	715	0·5	755	0·2	404	0·0	21,050	1·4
TOTAL	50,539	100·0	146,297	100·0	428,096	100·0	1,000,953	100·0	1,519,510	100·0

Source: BOJ, *Economic Statistics Annual.*

these funds. The first is in Government or local government bonds or lending to local governments or to local public bodies. The second is purchase of bonds issued by Government-related institutions or special corporations such as public bodies or lending to such bodies. The third is providing loans or purchasing debentures of electric power resources development companies, and the fourth is purchase of bank debentures (but within certain limits).

Moreover, the investments must be deliberated on by the Trust Fund Advisory Council in order to ensure that they meet the policies and conditions for investment.[12]

The interest rate on lending from the Trust Fund Bureau is in principle identical to that on deposits at the Bureau with a maturity greater than seven years (including the special interest rate, 6·8 per cent in October 1985). When the Trust Fund Bureau underwrites bonds, the conditions are identical to those on Government guaranteed bonds or, for bank debentures, identical to those floated in the market-place.

Most lending and bond holdings are long-term investments (underwriting of Government bonds is excluded from the definition of fiscal investment and loans) of over five years that are included in FILP and require approval by the Diet. There are also some short-term investments of less than one year that are not included in FILP, as well as some intermediate investments of between one and five years. Among the short-term investments are purchases of Government bonds that are either redeemed or repaid within one year, and lending to special accounts of the Government that are repaid within the current fiscal year. In order to use Trust Fund Bureau funds in this way, it is sufficient that the Trust Advisory Council report to the succeeding year's Advisory Council the results of these investments in the 'Resolution Concerning Short-Term Investment of Trust Fund Bureau Funds'. For medium-term lending of between one and five years, approval of the Diet is not necessary, but submission for consideration to the Trust Fund Advisory Council is necessary.

The investment of Trust Fund Bureau monies is shown in Table 5.26. Lending accounted for 76 per cent of total investments at the end of fiscal 1984, in which lending to Government-related institutions and local governments and public bodies formed the largest part. Securities holdings comprise the other 24 per cent, in which holdings of long-term Government bonds were the most important element.

---

[12] The Trust Fund Advisory Council is an adjunct institution of the Prime Minster's Office and is composed of a maximum of seven persons of learning and experience appointed by the Prime Minister. In addition, there are some members just below the Advisory Council, who are a few specialists chosen from related ministeries or from persons of learning and experience, and six or fewer executive secretaries from related ministeries.

TABLE 5.26 *FILP Funds Outstanding by Investment, by Fiscal Year-end*

	1965		1970		1975		1980		1984	
	¥100m.	%	¥100m.	%	¥100m.	%	¥100m.	%	¥100m.	%
Securities										
Long-term Government bonds	887	1·8	11,125	7·6	29,855	7·0	116,991	11·7	296,007	19·5
Short-term Government bonds	4,112	8·1	6,030	4·1	12,335	2·9	36,217	3·6	3,827	0·3
Government-guaranteed bonds, etc.	2,694	5·3	19,112	13·1	33,526	7·8	38,896	3·9	57,998	3·8
Bank debentures	(557)	(1·1)	(2,981)	(2·0)	(9,588)	(2·2)	(11,544)	(1·2)	(18,476)	(1·2)
Total securities	*7,693*	*15·2*	*36,267*	*24·8*	*75,716*	*17·7*	*203,648*	*20·3*	*357,834*	*23·5*
Loans										
General and special accounts	1,985	3·9	5,046	3·4	26,801	6·3	108,943	10·9	160,254	10·5
Local government bodies	10,404	20·6	22,407	15·3	65,390	15·3	140,539	14·0	214,948	14·1
Government institutions	30,453	60·3	82,446	56·4	260,053	60·7	547,775	54·7	735,850	51·7
Total loans	*42,842*	*84·8*	*109,898*	*75·1*	*352,244*	*82·3*	*797,257*	*79·6*	*1,161,052*	*76·4*
Cash and others	4	0·0	132	0·1	136	0·0	45	0·0	623	0·0
TOTAL	50,539	100·0	146,297	100·0	428,096	100·0	1,000,953	100·0	1,519,510	100·0

Source: BOJ, *Economic Statistics Annual*.

(ii) Postal insurance funds

Postal insurance funds are the surpluses and accumulated profits generated from the closing of the books of the Special Account for Post Office Life Insurance and Postal Annuity. The Minister of Posts manages and oversees these funds, and this is the only exception to the general rule that Government monies are managed by the Trust Fund Bureau.

Almost all the postal insurance funds are accumulated profits from the postal life insurance system. Postal annuity funds were on a downward trend until the late 1970s because of the expansion of other types of pension system, and because of the emphasis placed by the post-war Ministry of Posts on the postal life insurance system. In recent years, however, as society has begun to age, the attractiveness of the postal annuity is beginning to be reconsidered. Nevertheless, at the end of fiscal 1984, 99 per cent of postal insurance funds were in the life insurance account and only 1 per cent in the annuity account. The life insurance funds used in FILP in every fiscal year are the sum of accumulated profits from the previous year (i.e., the previous year's surplus) and the funds from redemption of existing loans. The share of postal insurance funds in FILP funding follows in size that of Trust Fund Bureau monies and Government-guaranteed bonds.

Investment of postal insurance funds may be made in all areas in which the Trust Fund Bureau invests, but may also be made in certain other areas. These include lending to contract-holders in the postal life insurance system and postal annuity system, but also include high-yielding corporate debentures of electricity, gas, and railroad companies (i.e., issues by corporations with more than ¥4bn. in capital) for which the postal insurance system is in competition with private insurance companies. Moreover, in order to ensure the unified investment of postal insurance funds and Trust Fund Bureau funds, the investments of postal insurance funds must also undergo examination by the Trust Fund Advisory Council concerning investment policies and conditions, just as must the funds from the Trust Fund Bureau itself. The interest rate on lending is the same as that of the funds from the Trust Fund Bureau, i.e., 6·05 per cent p.a. as of March 1986.

At the end of fiscal 1984, the total amount of postal insurance funds outstanding had reached ¥26·1bn. Lending to local government bodies, public corporations, public bodies and public finance corporations accounted for 40 per cent of investments, while investment in securities such as bonds and local government bonds accounted for 49 per cent.

(iii) The Industrial Investment Special Account

The Industrial Investment Special Account was established in 1953 as a successor to the special account for counterpart funds from American aid. The purposes of this special account were economic reconstruction, industrial development, and trade promotion. At the end of fiscal 1984, the special account had ¥1·3bn. in capital. It has been a major source of funding for FILP in every fiscal year, and until 1980 relied on transfers from the General Account of the Government for the funds with which to respond to increasing demands for financing. In recent years, however, there have not been transfers from the General Account, and the contributions of the special account for industrial investment to FILP are therefore funded from interest earnings and principal repayments from the loans in the portfolio.

From the start of the fund until the end of fiscal 1955, the investment of funds by the Industrial Investment Special Account was concentrated in the supply of the financing necessary for trade promotion and expansion of basic industries. The funds were either lent or provided as capitalization to the Japan Development Bank, to the Export Import Bank of Japan, and to electric power resources development companies. After 1955, however, new objects for investment and loan were added—the public finance corporations, public bodies, and special corporations that were already receiving capitalization from the General Account. Since 1972, the Industrial Investment Special Account has ceased making new loans and has functioned as a special account that only provides capitalization.

In contrast to the fiscal investment and loan funds from such sources as the Trust Fund Bureau and the postal insurance funds that require debt-servicing, the capitalizations from the Industrial Investment Special Account are provided free of debt-servicing requirements in order to lower the financing costs of Government financial institutions and public bodies.

At the end of fiscal 1984, the total resources of the Industrial Investment Special Account stood at ¥1·8bn. These funds went as capitalization to twenty-two organizations including the Export Import Bank of Japan.

(iv) Government-guaranteed bonds and borrowings

When Government institutions, public corporations, or public bodies issue bonds or borrow long-term funds from private financial institutions, the Government will often guarantee the payment of interest and principal. These bonds or borrowings are called Government guaranteed bonds or borrowings. There are limits on the quantity of Government guarantees for funds raised in this way. It is required that the framework for the General Account budget establish guarantee limits for each institution, and these limits must be approved by the Diet. The proceeds of Government-guaranteed bonds and borrowings are included in the funds for fiscal investment and loans, despite the fact that they are borrowed from private instititions. This is considered appropriate because they correspond to funds that are managed by the Government in that they are fully backed by fiscal policy. In fact, the government guarantees the final payment of all interest and principal and for Government-guaranteed bonds, and the Government engages in negotiations with syndicates concerning the amounts of issue and terms of issue. The guarantee limits have also had elastic clauses since fiscal 1971. These were added in order to respond to unforeseeable changes in economic conditions, and are set at 50 per cent of the originally budgeted guarantee limit for each institution.

The interest rates on Government-guaranteed bonds are part of the long-term interest rate structure and are revised to reflect financial conditions. The subscriber's yields on Government-guaranteed bonds are usually set between those on Government bonds and publicly subscribed local government bonds, while the interest rates on Government-guaranteed loans are set at about the level of the long-term prime rate. Thus the fund-raising cost is less when Government-guaranteed bonds are used, and as a result, more than 90 per cent of Government-guaranteed funds are raised by using Government-guaranteed bonds.

Because of the insufficiency of fiscal funds from the Trust Fund Bureau and other sources in recent years (relative to the demands for fiscal investment and loans), the reliance on augmenting sources such as Government-guaranteed bonds and Government-guaranteed loans has been rising. This reliance rate was only 4 per cent in fiscal 1975, but rose to 7 per cent in fiscal 1980, was expected to be 11 per cent in fiscal 1984, and was planned to be 12 per cent in fiscal 1985.

d. Government financial institutions

The set of Government financial institutions comprises one institution that receives funds and over ten corporations that lend them. The fund-collecting institution is the post office, and the lending institutions comprise two banks and nine finance corporations. The two banks are the Japan Development Bank and the Export Import Bank of Japan, and the nine finance corporations are the People's Finance Corporation, the Housing Loan Corporation, the Agriculture, Forestry, and Fisheries Corporation, the Small Business Finance Corporation, the Hokkaido and Tohoku Development Corporation, the Japan Finance Corporation for Municipal Enterprises, the Small Business Credit Insurance Corporation, the Environmental Sanitation Business Finance Corporation, and the Okinawa Development Finance Corporation (until January 1985, there was also a Medical Care Facilities Corporation, but in that month it was merged with other social welfare institutions and began anew as the Social Welfare and Medical Care Facilities Corporation). The class of Government financial organizations also includes various public foundations and Government-related corporations and the Overseas Economic Co-operation Fund (foreign aid), all of which are public corporations capitalized in full by the Government.

The total funding of Government financial institutions (excluding certain special lending corporations) was ¥66bn. at the end of March 1985, equivalent to 18 per cent of the ¥363bn. of total financing granted by private financial institutions. The two Government banks provided 20 per cent of total Government funding, while the nine finance corporations provided 75 per cent. Funds channelled through the Trust Fund Bureau were the main source of funds for the Government financial institutions. Such borrowings from the Trust Fund Bureau were 79 per cent of total funding, while bond issues were 16 per cent and capitalization funding from the General Account and the special accounts such as the Industrial Investment Special Account were 5 per cent (see Table 5.27).

Simple explanations of the more important Government financial institutions follow.

(i) The post office

The post office was one of the first modern financial intermediaries in Japan. It began to take deposits in May 1875. The purposes of the postal saving system were to encourage thrift and savings among workers and to help stabilize the national welfare; but the system was also intended to aid in supplying one portion of industrial capital through the collection of small deposits. Originally nineteen post offices, eighteen in Tokyo and one in Yokohama, took deposits. Between then and now, some 24,000 post offices throughout the country have been established and currently carry out financial operations, not only deposit operations but also the handling of the Postal Life Insurance Annuity and Postal Annuity systems.

In line with the original intention of collecting small-scale deposits, the deposit operations of the post office are subject to the restriction that the maximum deposit for any single individual is ¥3m. Tax is not paid on these deposits (two other tranches of postal deposits are, however, permitted—¥0·5m. for instalment savings for housing purchase and ¥4·5m. for property accumulation savings). There are six types of postal deposit: (1) ordinary, (2) fixed-amount, (3) fixed-term, (4) instalment, (5) housing instalment, and (6) educational instalment deposits. Of these, fixed-amount deposits have a share of about 90 per cent. The deposit contract may be cancelled at any time after the deposits have been with the post office for six months or more, but, so long as there is no need for withdrawal, they may remain on deposit for up to ten years. The interest is compounded semi-annually so that the longer the period of deposit, the higher the rate of interest relative to the day on which the deposit was made. The housing instalment deposits and educational instalment deposits also have the special trait that loans at favourable rates from the Housing Finance Corporation and the People's Finance Corporation may be taken out for housing or education, respectively.

The post office has introduced many innovations over the years. Since 1973, it has made so-called 'double financing' loans (*yuyu* loans) that are based on fixed amount, fixed-term, or instalment deposits as collateral, and which must be below either 90 per cent of the deposited amount or ¥1m., whichever is lower. Automatic wage and salary deposit was introduced in March 1980, and cash card services using cash dispensers and automatic

TABLE 5.21 *Principal Accounts of Government Financial Institutions, end of March 1965*

| | Capital (¥100m.) | | | | Borrowing | | | | | Bonds (¥100m.) | Loans (¥100m.) |
	General account	Industrial investment special account	Other	Total	Trust fund bureau account	Postal life insurance and postal annuity	Industrial investment special account	Other	Total		
Banks											
Japan Development Bank[a]	—	2,340	—	2,340	62,396	—	—	241	62,637	3,442	73,726
Export–Import Bank of Japan	—	9,673	—	9,673	45,883	—	—	2,614	48,497	769	60,353
Total banks	—	*12,013*	—	*12,013*	*108,279*	—	—	*2,885*	*111,134*	*4,211*	*134,079*
Public finance corporations											
People's Finance Corp.	260	—	—	260	44,239	3,059	—	2,039	49,336	—	49,069
Housing Loan Corp.[b]	322	545	105	972	229,447	4,682	—	—	234,129	1,263	231,792
Agriculture, Forestry, and Fisheries Corp.[c]	499	1,118	65	1,682	47,045	2,388	—	—	49,434	—	50,507
Small Business Finance Corp.	220	92	—	312	39,248	3,455	—	—	42,703	8,322	52,054
Hokkaido and Tohoku Development Corp.	—	313	—	313	1,580	1,345	—	—	2,926	5,388	8,503
Japan Finance Corp. for Municipal Enterprises	119	—	119	—	—	—	—	—	—	89,256	88,742
Small Business Credit Insurance Corp.	3,675	58	—	3,734	—	—	—	—	—	—	3,040
Environmental Sanitation Business Finance Corp.	10	—	—	10	6,923	—	—	—	6,923	—	6,945
Okinawa Development Finance Corp.[d]	30	30	216	276	6,600	740	—	3	7,344	—	7,604
Total public finance corporations	*5,016*	*2,275*	*386*	*7,678*	*375,082*	*15,669*	—	*2,042*	*392,795*	*104,229*	*498,256*
Overseas Economic Co-operation Fund	14,402	—	—	14,402	17,001	—	—	618	17,619	600	30,554
TOTAL	19,418	14,288	386	34,093	500,362	15,669	—	5,515	521,544	109,040	662,889

[a] Loans and borrowing exclude foreign loans and borrowing.
[b] Other capital comprises ¥10bn. in capital counterpart transfer.
[c] Other capital comprises land improvement subsidies.
[d] Other capital includes carry-overs from the Ryukyu Development Finance Corporation.

Source: BOJ, *Economic Statistics Monthly.*

teller machines were introduced in 1980 and 1981. An integrated passbook was introduced in June 1981, which included in one passbook the accounts for ordinary postal deposits, fixed-amount postal deposits, and double financing loans. Automatic payment of public utilities charges was introduced in June 1982 and automatic receipt of interest and dividends on securities in July 1983. Particularly conspicuous has been the expansion of remittance and settlement services based on the completion of the nationwide Postal Savings on-line system in March 1984. Elements within this network include the joint postal savings card (introduced in July 1984) and the 'postal savings POS' concept. The total quantity of postal savings deposits has grown rather less rapidly in recent years since the introduction of new financial products by private financial institutions one after another (such as maturity-designated fixed-term deposits), new loan trusts (nicknamed 'Big') and new types of bank debenture ('Wide'). Nevertheless, during most of the post-war period, fixed-amount postal deposits, in particular, grew continuously at a higher rate than total deposits, and stood at ¥94bn. in March 1985, about the same level as the personal deposit balances of all banks in the country. Of these deposits, fixed-amount postal deposits account for about 90 per cent (see Table 5.28). Double financing loans were relatively small in outstanding amount, only ¥434 milliard in March 1985.

TABLE 5.28 *Postal Savings and Deposits of All Banks Outstanding*

Year (fiscal year-end)	Postal savings (A)			Deposits (B)		A/B (%)	A/C (%)
	Total (¥100m.)	Fixed-amount postal savings (¥100m.)	%	Deposits of all banks (¥100m.)	Deposits of individuals (C) (¥100m.)		
1965	27,025	15,461	57·2	215,201	70,256	12·6	38·5
1970	77,439	54,306	70·1	367,075	135,294	21·1	57·2
1975	245,626	196,488	80·0	959,166	380,648	25·6	64·5
1980	619,498	544,697	87·9	1,577,956	667,022	39·3	92·9
1981	695,628	615,289	88·5	1,749,157	743,241	39·8	93·6
1982	780,977	694,985	89·0	1,865,342	800,442	41·9	97·6
1983	862,932	773,377	89·6	2,012,935	854,255	42·9	101·0
1984	940,421	840,512	89·4	2,205,136	931,941	42·6	100·9

Sources: BOJ, *Economic Statistics Annual*, and Ministry of Posts and Telecommunications, *Yubin Tokei Nempo* (Postal Statistics Annual).

The determination of the deposit rates on postal savings is, as described in Chapter 4, carried out separately from that of private deposit rates. The Minister of Posts and Telecommunications is empowered to change the rates through Cabinet Order based on the Postal Savings Law after he had received a report from the Postal Services Advisory Council. As a result of this procedure, there have at times been difficulties because of a two-tiered structure of interest rate determination between the postal deposit rates and private deposit rates.

(ii) The Japan Development Bank

The Japan Development Bank was established in April 1951 to supply long-term funds in order to augment and promote financing by general financial institutions of industrial development and the economic development of society. The circumstances of its establishment were the abolition of the Reconstruction Finance Corporation and the USAID Counterpart fund that had played such an important role in the long-term financing during the post-war reconstruction period. In their place, the Japan Development Bank was founded as a Government financial institution for the supply of industrial equipment funds. As of March 1985, the capital of the institution was ¥234 milliard (all of which were Government capitalization funds). Additional resources are provided through Government borrowings and foreign bond issues up to a limit of ten times the total of capital plus reserves.

The Japan Development Bank acts through its main office in Tokyo along with seven branches in major cities of the country, two other domestic offices, and four foreign representative offices. The main activities of the Bank are lending development funds, liability guarantees, providing capitalization, and miscellaneous activities. Development lending is concentrated on lending of funds that would be difficult to obtain from private financial institutions for certain public purposes. Among these are the acquisition or improvement of equipment, and land reclamation on construction or improvement of facilities related to existing renewal schemes in cities and towns, that would contribute to the economic development of society. Owing to a legal revision of 1985, it also became possible to lend funds necessary for the research and development of high technology that would contribute to the economic development of society and industrial improvement. The purpose of this change was to support with 'system finance' the response to new conditions of recent years in which the development of technology has become more important.

The maturity of Japan Development Bank loans is in principle between one and ten years but may go as high as thirty years if necessary. The standard interest rate reflects general financial conditions and changes corresponding to the lending rates of banks. In March 1986, the rate was 6·4 per cent, the same level as the long-term prime rate. Many of the Japan Development Bank's loans take the form of joint lending with private banks. Liability guarantees are those which guarantee payments of funds necessary for development projects. Currently, these are limited to payment guarantees for foreign currency borrowings from such institutions as the Export Import Bank of the United States. The basic fee for guarantees is currently 0·3 per cent per year.

Capitalization funding by the Japan Development Bank was limited for many years to construction enterprises for large-scale industrial parks. But, as with the lending function described above, the legal revision of 1985 expanded the capitalization function of the Bank and allowed capitalization spending in undertakings that contributed to the economic development of society and the improvement of industry. The intent was to augment and provide incentives for the private sector through capitalization by the Bank in new fields such as research and development of technology and urban renewal. Such activities were viewed as a practical application of the power of the private sector.

The miscellaneous activities of the Bank have at times included subscription of corporate debentures that are floated for raising development funds or for redemptions when securities companies have difficulty underwriting or providing subscription services for such bonds. The Bank has also at times lent funds necessary for repayment of development borrowings and has repaid borrowings on behalf of others. Currently, however, the Bank is not engaged in such activities.

At the end of 1985, the Japan Development Bank had ¥7·6bn. of loans outstanding, about the level of a medium-sized city bank. Loans focused on basic industries such as electric power, shipping, and mining when the Bank was first established, but thereafter, reflecting the changes in the industrial structure of the country, the composition of loans gradually diversified. By category of industry as of the end of 1985, the share of electricity, gas, heat supply, and water works had continued its expansion to 44 per cent of the total, reflecting the active attitude of the Bank toward energy resource related lending. On the other hand, lending to transport and communications had fallen from the 30–40 per cent level of the decade starting in 1965 to about 23 per cent.

(iii) The Export Import Bank of Japan

The Export Import Bank of Japan was originally established in December of 1950 in the form of the Export Bank of Japan, whose purpose was to provide long-term funding for export promotion on the basis of the Export Bank of Japan Law of the time. In 1952, however, its operations expanded into import finance, and its name was changed to the Export Import Bank of Japan. The purposes set out at the time of this revision were to supplement and augment financing related to the exports, imports, and foreign investment carried out by private financial institutions, for the purpose of promoting economic exchange, primarily through trade, between Japan and foreign countries by means of financial aid.

Thereafter, the business activities of the Export Import Bank expanded gradually to foreign investment finance in 1953, to development project finance for foreign governments in 1957, and to direct loans in 1972. In July of 1975, a clarification of the division of labour between the Export Import Bank and the Overseas Economic Co-operation Fund (see below) was carried out.

The capital of the Export Import Bank of Japan stood at ¥967 milliard at the end of March 1985, all of which was provided by the Industrial Investment

Special Account. Other funding comes from borrowings from the Government which must remain within the limit of four times of the total of capital plus reserves. These borrowings amounted to ¥4·8bn. at the end of March 1985; ¥4·6bn. came from the Trust Fund Bureau fund, ¥240 milliard from the Foreign Exchange Fund Special Account, and ¥22 milliard from the General Account.

The Export Import Bank has its main office in Tokyo and one branch in Osaka in addition to fifteen representative offices abroad. The main activities of the Bank are domestic lending, direct loans, and liability guarantees. Domestic lending of the Export Import Bank goes to domestic firms for three purposes. The first is financing for exports and technology supply, i.e., lending of the funds necessary for export of equipment produced in Japan or for supply of technology to foreign countries. The second is import finance, i.e., lending of the funds necessary for import of particularly important materials. The third is finance of foreign investment and foreign undertakings, i.e., lending of funds necessary for foreign investment or for direct undertakings abroad. As part of the legal revisions of 1985, the Bank was empowered to make direct lending to foreign corporations that were tied to domestic corporations through their capital (hitherto, in principle, lending had to be channelled through domestic corporations). Direct loans by the Export Import Bank take the form of loans to foreign governments, foreign banks, and foreign corporations. There are several such types of lending. One is tied loans, i.e., lending of funds necessary for the import of machinery and equipment from Japan. Another is untied loans, i.e., lending of industrial funds or import funds that are not tied to any particular transactions with Japan. A third is investment financing, i.e., providing funds necessary for capitalization of joint ventures with Japanese corporations. A fourth is refinancing, i.e., provision of funds necessary in cases where foreign governments are unable to make payments of obligations to Japan because of such factors as deterioration of their balance of payments. The Export Import Bank also carries out several types of liability guarantee. These include guarantee of funds provided by financial institutions for domestic lending and the reguarantee of lending guarantees undertaken in place of lending for foreign investments. In addition, the Bank also guarantees the funds provided by financial institutions under tied or untied loans that are made jointly with the Export Import Bank. The Bank's guarantee powers were expanded in the legal revisions of 1985 with the intent of facilitating foreign direct loans by encouraging private-sector activity in this area. The Export Import Bank is empowered under the new revisions to guarantee direct foreign lending made by private financial institutions even when the Export Import Bank is not a partner in the loan.

Lending by the Export Import Bank is in principle carried out as joint financing with private banks. In these cases, the share of the Export Import Bank is limited to 70 per cent of the total loan. The interest rates on Export

Import Bank loans were between 6 per cent and 9·4 per cent at the end of March 1986 and were decided on a case-by-case basis for direct loans. Maturities are in principle between six months and five years for export, import, and investment financing but are determined on a case-by-case basis for direct loans. The fee for guarantee of liabilities is required to be more than 0·5 per cent per year, but for guarantees related to foreign activities, the fee is required to be above 0·3 per cent per year.

The composition of loans of the Export Import Bank as of the end of March 1985 showed a large share for export financing, primarily the deferred payment for plant exports. (The share for export financing was 35 per cent, including financing for technology supply at the end of March 1985.) Policy considerations concerning aid to developing countries and international co-operation have been strengthening recently, so that the share of funding going to import and investment finance has reached 34 per cent and that going to direct loans, 32 per cent. The geographical distribution of lending showed that Asia took the largest portion at 46 per cent, Europe the second largest at 16 per cent, and Latin America followed with 15 per cent. The increased concern in recent years with ensuring a stable supply of resources has led to an increase in funding of resource development projects; such projects took 22 per cent of the total of ¥780 milliard in accumulated financing approved during fiscal 1984.

(iv) The Overseas Economic Co-operation Fund

The Overseas Economic Co-operation Fund was established in March 1961 on the basis of the Overseas Economic Co-operation Fund Law. The purpose of the Fund was

to promote overseas economic co-operation and to contribute to the stabilization of economies and development of industry in Southeast Asia and other overseas areas currently in the midst of economic development. This is to be done through operations that are necessary to facilitate the supply of funds when such provision of funds would be difficult through general financial institutions or through the Export Import Bank of Japan.

Until that time, funds for economic aid had been provided to Southeast Asia and the other areas indirectly through deferred credits from the Export Import Bank of Japan. But around 1960, a more active stance toward economic co-operation became necessary for Japan, and so the OECF was established as a separate entity.

The capital for the OECF came at first from the Southeast Asia Development Co-operation Fund that had been established at the time by the Export Import Bank. This funding amounted to ¥5·4bn., composed of capitalization funding from the General Account and accumulation of profits of the above-mentioned Fund. Since then the General Account has added more in capital contributions, so that total capital stood at ¥1·4bn. by March 1985.

Additional funding comes from ¥1·8bn. of borrowings (¥1·7 milliard from the Trust Fund Bureau Fund) and ¥60 milliard in bonds floated by the OECF.

The main operations of the OECF are lending for development projects, lending for development research, lending for economic stabilization and capitalization. Lending for development projects constitutes the lending of funds to undertakings that are recognized to be essential for the contribution to development of industries in countries in the process of development, and that will promote economic exchange with Japan. Lending for development research is the provision of funds necessary for research in the preparation of a development project or experimental implementation of such projects. Lending for economic stabilization is the provision of funds necessary for import of materials that are recognized to be essential for the stability of a country. These funds are provided to the government of the developing country, including government-related institutions. The OECF also carries out capitalization of certain projects. Such capitalizations are limited to cases in which there are special circumstances in which smooth achieve of goals for the development project cannot be expected under any loan.

There has arisen at times some overlap in the activities of the OECF and the Export Import Bank because of the difficulty of clearly separating the loans by OECF for the purpose of economic co-operation or aid from the foreign investment by the Export Import Bank for the purposes of trade promotion. As a result of this overlap, a reform was carried out in July 1975. Under this reform, the OECF was made responsible in principle for the loans to governments for the purposes of economic co-operation, while the Export Import Bank was made responsible in principle for lending to Japanese citizens or Japanese corporations.

The terms for lending by the OECF are specified in its business code: an interest rate of 3·5 per cent or more and maturity of under twenty years. The actual amount of lending by the OECF has risen very sharply since direct loans were started in fiscal 1965, and by March 1985, the accumulated financing provided by the OECF since its inception had reached ¥5·3bn., of which 93 per cent or ¥4·9bn. was direct loans.

5. OTHER INSTITUTIONS

The progress of financial liberalization and the diversification of the needs of corporations and individuals has brought a new industry into existence, the industry of selling information related to finance to enable financial transactions to be effected more smoothly. Though the institutions in this industry are not financial institutions *per se*, they are gathered around financial institutions and have very close relations with them. Further development of this industry is predicted, and the financial institutions themselves have begun to enter and to compete in these industries through the formation of subsidiaries. This has been done in order to attract more customers and to facilitate their other activities. Let us briefly describe two typical industries based on financial information, investment advisory companies, and bond-rating organizations.

a. Investment advisory companies

An investment advisory company is a company that earns fees from supplying investment information and reference information to clients (investors), from giving investment advice, from managing assets, or from other services.

For many years there existed no basic law concerning the investment advisory industry in Japan, and firms were free to operate in investment advice except in the case of investment advice concerning securities transactions. Total discretion investment business, however—in which complete discretion for investment sales, choice of stocks, etc., was left to the securities company—was forbidden by Article 127 of the Securities and Exchange Law and the administrative guidance based upon it (Article 127 contains provisions concerning discretionary accounts for transactions in securities; the total discretion investment business was born of such discretionary accounts).

Both securities companies (through affiliated companies) and trust banks began to engage in investment advisory business in the early 1960s and so into the 1970s. During these years, there also emerged specialized investment advisory companies that engaged in funds management for their clients. Since 1975, many independent investment advisory companies have been founded as the need for an investment advisory industry has grown, reflecting the increase of individual and corporate financial assets and the diversification and internationalization of the securities industry. The core of the industry was the group of investment advisory companies related to the securities companies (nine companies) and the economic research institutes (four companies). But in addition, there were about 300–350 so-called 'city' investment advisory firms, of which 140 were registered corporations (most with capital of under ¥10m.), the remainder being non-registered or individual firms. In part because of the lack of legal regulation, there were not a few operators with whom unceasing trouble occurred among clients, particularly among the city investment advisers. Despite the increasing needs for investment advice that came with accumulation of financial assets, one cannot necessarily say that there was a smooth development of trust on the part of investors in the general public toward the investment advisory industry. This lack of trust, along with the difficulties between some firms and their clients, was one factor preventing healthy growth of the industry.

Because of these difficulties, a report in November 1985 from the Securities and Exchange Advisory Council proposed that new law relating to the investment advisory business should be established as quickly as possible in the investment advisory industry that concerned securities. The proposal was based on the notions that a balance must be struck between investor protection and the principle of self-responsibility on the part of the investor, but also that excessive regulation must be avoided. The proposal recommended a system of approval for firms that wish to engage in the much-disputed total discretion investment advisory business because of the similarities between this business and the trust business. In addition, the proposal also pointed to a response that limited itself to important points such as a registration system for firms starting in the business and very thorough disclosure requirements. On the basis of this proposal, a law was passed in May 1986, the Law Concerning Regulation of Investment Advisory Industries Related to Securities.

With an eye to the increased needs for investment advisory services and the potential for laws concerning it, the city banks, from around 1985, began to establish investment advisory affiliated companies one after another, in hopes of entering the pension trust business through the use of total discretion accounts. One purpose of the entry of foreign banks into the trust business is also thought to have been this same desire. But life insurance companies and trust banks as well have become active in establishing investment advisory companies in order to respond to the needs of individuals and corporations for efficient asset management.

There are no reliable figures on the total contracted amount of assets managed by the investment advisory companies, but partial data are available. For example, the contracted amount of assets managed by the investment advisory companies related to securities companies stood at about ¥ 4·5bn. in September 1985, an increase of about ten times in the four years until that date (the largest portion of this is said to be the assets of foreign investors). The growth potential in this industry appears to be high and hence the competition is becoming more fierce because of entry of new firms as described above.

b. Bond-rating organizations

Bond-rating organizations carry out rankings (AAA, AA, etc.) of the bonds issued by corporations and others according to the rating organization's general judgement concerning the trend of profits of the corporation or other institution, the state of management, and prospects. These institutions then provide this information concerning the certainty and safety of payment of interest and principal to investors.

For many years, no particular need was felt for third-party rating of bonds and only experimental ratings were carried out by a very limited number of organizations. This situation occurred because bonds were based upon collateral, so that the Bond Issue Committee (*Kisaikai*) selected which issues were to come to market and determined the amounts of issue and the conditions of issue.[13]

However, the necessity for bond-rating organizations in Japan has grown very rapidly owing to the internationalization of financial and capital markets. For example, the major relaxation of issue conditions on Euro-yen bonds that occurred as a result of the May 1984 report of the Japan–US Yen–Dollar Committee brought out the possibility of changing the issue criteria to judgement by bond-rating organizations at some time in the future. In addition, by means of deregulation of the domestic issue market, expansion of number of investors, and diversification of investment instruments, an expansion of the issue of non-collateralized bonds is foreseen, along with the easing of the principle of collateralization. At the same time, an increase is foreseen in the issue of bonds by corporations relatively unknown to investors. Thus, from the viewpoint of investor protection, the need for bond-rating has grown, because it is a means of providing investors with information that clearly expresses the creditworthiness of corporations.

As a result of these developments, three bond-rating organizations have been established in Japan recently. These are the Japan Bond Research Institute, which was originally established as an internal division of the *Nippon Keizai Shinbun* Corporation in April 1979 but was then reorganized into an independent corporation with capital of ¥100m. in April 1985, the Japan Credit Rating Agency Ltd., which was established with capital of ¥2·9 milliard in April 1985, and the Nippon Investors' Service, which was established with capital of ¥5·8 milliard in April 1985. These three rating organizations not only carry out ratings of domestic bonds and yen-denominated external bonds, but also carry out analysis and research concerning both foreign and domestic financial, economic, and corporate information. Because of their recent establishment, however, these companies are not yet at the stage in which they are making comparative ratings of equivalent value or of selling such information.

III. The Payments Mechanism

1. OVERVIEW

Almost all of economic transactions carried out by the various economic entities in the economy—Governments, corporations, households, etc.—are settled through cash currency in the first place, but also by cheques, bills, credit cards, exchange, account transfers, and other such methods. With the exception of cash currency, all of the above methods are based on the existence of settlement accounts such as current or ordinary accounts at banks. Thus the

---

[13] The Bond Issue Committee is composed of the trustee banks and four major securities companies and certain other parties. For a full description, see above, ch. 4.

various means of settlement boil down to either cash currency or settlement accounts.

As mentioned earlier, cash currency is supplied solely by the single bank of issue in Japan, the Bank of Japan. On the other hand, settlements accounts are provided by the private depository financial institutions, foremost among which are ordinary banks.

The term 'payments mechanism' is defined as referring to the organization that organically ties together the financial institutions that supply means of settlement. In Japan, the payments mechanism may be thought of as composed of the Bank of Japan plus the various types of private depository financial institution, all acting together as a unit.[14] The Bank of Japan plays an axial role in the payments mechanism as the final institution of settlement. This is because the balance of transactions among the financial institutions is settled finally through transfers of current deposit accounts at the Bank of Japan.

With the rapid development of computer and telecommunications technology, however, several changes have occurred within the payments mechanism of Japan. First, there has been a decline in the use of cash currency, which is the primary means of settlement, because of the spread of account transfers and credit cards. The use of settlement accounts has been reduced because of the emergence of new financial products (such as *sogo* accounts) that mix the characteristics of settlement accounts and investment accounts. Secondly, there has been rapid advance in the mechanization and automation of payments operations and systems, as seen in the spread of cash dispensers and automatic teller machines or in the spread of on-line computer systems for financial institution business (see Table 5.29). Thirdly, the settlements network has rapidly broadened its scope and become more integrated, because of the joint supply of on-line cash dispensers among financial institutions, the expansion of the Data Telecommunications Systems of All Banks in Japan, and the conversion of financial operations of the post office to an on-line, nation-wide computer network. For example, since 1980, various financial institutions have linked their own generalized computer systems with those of other banks and have created systems for conversion of deposits to cash by use of cash dispensers and automatic teller machines; thus the banks have created a system under which cash may be withdrawn from machines belonging to other banks so long as the machines are within the same system (as of March 1986, there were five such systems in existence, with 609 participating financial institutions).

---

[14] The post office may also be considered part of the payments mechanism because of recent expansion of its funds settlement functions that are similar to those performed by private depository financial institutions. For example, the post office has begun a nationwide on-line system (in Mar. 1984), automatic salary deposit schemes (in Mar. 1980), automatic payment of public utilities charges (in June 1982), and automatic receipt services for interest and dividends on securities (in July 1983). In addition, the post office supplies a unique settlement service called postal money order.

TABLE 5.29 *Cash Dispensers and Automatic Teller Machines, end September 198*

	No. of institutions	No. of cash dispensers and automatic tellers	No. of automatic tellers	No. of branches with such machinery (A)	Total no. of branches (B)	Diffusion rate (A/B) (%)
All banks	87	26,727	15,219	10,038	10,292	97·5
City banks	13	12,733	8,250	3,035	3,040	99·8
Regional banks	64	13,357	6,386	6,579	6,828	96·4
Trust banks	7	571	517	360	360	100·0
Long-term credit banks	3	66	66	64	64	100·0
Sogo banks	69	6,047	2,448	4,134	4,279	96·6
Shinkin banks	456	8,499	5,515	6,577	6,972	94·3
Credit co-operatives	449	1,226	469	1,192	2,816	42·3
Agricultural co-operatives[a]	4,323	6,037	3,147	5,762	15,762	36·6
Fishery co-operatives	1,718	1	0	1	2,175	0·0
Labour credit association	47	669	443	520	584	89·0
Subtotal	*7,149*	*49,206*	*27,241*	*28,224*	*42,880*	*65·8*
Post Office[b]	1	3,699	2,809	3,699	22,912	16·1

[a] Includes machines of prefectural federations.
[b] Figures for the post office are for end October 1985.

Sources: Financial organizations for each type of institution.

In the future, changes such as those described above are expected to accelerate even further. For example, it is currently planned that transactions between the Bank of Japan and client financial institutions will be computerized. In addition, there will be a gradual development of computerized networks between banks and their external customers, so-called 'firm banking' and 'home banking' [2].

As a result of the further use of data telecommunications for financial transactions, it is expected that the settlements function provided by financial institutions will expand in the future, and that there will be a further increase in the efficiency of the payments mechanism as a whole. As a result, the convenience of making settlements will increase substantially. On the other hand, the risks of accidents with computer systems and also the system risk among financial institutions that accompanies the huge increase of funds flows is also expected to rise (for a description of system risk, see Chapter 2).

The continued maintenance of a safe financial system therefore raises several important problems concerning the payments mechanism. Among these problems are not only those mentioned above, but also that of ensuring the safety of the system as a whole through the sound management of the individual financial institutions that comprise the system.

Let us now outline the important settlement systems that compose the payments mechanism in Japan.

2. OUTLINE OF THE VARIOUS SETTLEMENT SYSTEMS

a. The bill-clearing system

Bill-clearing is the system under which financial institutions of a specified area come together at a specified place, at a specified time every day in order to exchange cheques payable at other institutions along with bills, bond coupons, postal money order certificates, dividend receipts, or other such instruments. The place at which these exchanges occur is called the clearing house. As of December 1985, there were 184 clearing houses in Japan designated by the Minister of Justice. These were managed either as associate institutions of the Bankers' Associations of the various regions or as independent corporations. The exchanges and settlements at the clearing houses include not only city banks, regional banks, trust banks, and long-term credit banks, but also *sogo* banks, *shinkin* banks, credit co-operatives, and other institutions either as direct participants or as participants through correspondents with which they have dealings. In addition, the head office and every branch of the Bank of Japan and important post offices participate as members of clearing houses in the appropriate regions and collect the receipts of banks in the market along with budgetary revenue, rediscounted bills, exchange of government cheques and postal money order certificates. The clearing balance for the individual banks is normally settled through transfers among current deposits of the banks at the Bank of Japan. For areas where the Bank of Japan does not have branches, settlements are carried out through interbank deposits at specified banks.

In recent years, the use of magnetic ink character recognition (MICR) has enabled a mechanization of clearing operations so that the burden of such operations has been tremendously reduced compared to earlier years.

In order to maintain the soundness of credit transactions, the clearing houses have implemented the suspension of transactions system. Because the cheques and bills brought to the clearing house are viewed as legally binding payment obligations, the issuer of a bill or cheque that is dishonoured because of insufficient funds or for other reasons is subject to the posting of a notice of failure to collect. Those who issue dishonoured bills again within six months are subject to a two-year prohibition from current transactions and lending transactions with member financial institutions of the clearing house.

b. The domestic exchange settlement system

While the bill-clearing system is the system of settlement for bills and cheques for the financial institutions of a specified area, the domestic exchange system is a nation-wide system that settles the net positions among banks participating in the domestic exchange operations of lending and borrowing between the Bank of Japan and the financial institutions. The Bank of Japan is the settlement institution for this system.

When an exchange transaction takes place between financial institutions, the Bank of Japan settles the exchange balance that has occurred between the bank of the payer and the bank of the payee through the exchange settlement accounts of the two institutions concerned. As a result, the financial institutions are able to concentrate the settlement of their exchange balances at the Bank of Japan. Thus the system plays an important role in the rationalization of financial institution operations and in the improvement of efficiency of funds transfer.

For institutions such as *shinkin* banks, Credit Federations of Agricultural Co-operatives, or Credit Federations of Fishery Co-operatives that have no exchange settlement transactions with the Bank of Japan, their respective central financial institutions such as the *Zenshinren* Bank or the *Norinchukin* Bank act on their behalf. The exchange settlements of these central institutions with the Bank of Japan include their own exchange balances plus those of the umbrella financial institutions (this sytem is called the proxy settlement system and was initiated in February 1979).

The exchange transactions among financial institutions are carried out through the Data Telecommunication System of All Banks in Japan that was completed in April 1973. This system, also called the *Zengin* system, ties the member financial institutions through telecommunication lines with a centre established in Tokyo.

The centre of the *Zengin* system not only transmits the notice of exchange from the paying bank to the payee bank but also tabulates the various exchange transactions of the day on a computer and calculates the net balances on a institution-by-institution basis for the members. These results are then transmitted on the same day to the member institutions and on the next business day, the date of settlement, to the head office of the Bank of Japan. On receipt of this transmission, the Bank of Japan then carries out settlement of the exchange balances of the financial institutions at the time of settlement (1300 hours for week days and 1130 hours for Saturdays), through head office and its eight settlement branches.

The Data Telecommunications system of all Banks in Japan has grown over the years. Its original members were all banks and the *Shokochukin* Bank, but the *sogo* banks, the *shinkin* banks, and the *Norinchukin* Bank joined in February 1979. Credit co-operatives, labour credit associations, and agricultural co-operatives joined in August 1984. In addition, certain foreign banks are also members. At the end of 1985, the system included 5,435 institutions with 41,220 places of business. During the course of 1984, the system handled 340 million individual transactions with a value of about ¥577bn.

c. Other payments systems

(i) Magnetic tape exchange systems of bankers' associations

The Tokyo Bankers' Association began a magnetic tape exchange system in 1973 in order to deal rapidly and efficiently with the clerical work relating to the large number of transactions among its banks.

In the magnetic tape exchange system, the paying financial institutions bring a magnetic tape with the payments data encoded to the Bankers' Association on or before a specified date (currently four types of payment are included in the system—wages and salaries, pension payments, stock dividends, and loan trust beneficiary certificate distributions). The computer of the Bankers' Association then sorts the payments according to payee financial institution and records the payments on other magnetic tapes for the various payee banks. The latter than take these tapes to their own bank computers and transfer the funds to the final recipients' accounts. By December 1985, the system of the Tokyo Bankers' Association had 105 participating financial institutions. During the course of 1984, it handled 30m. transactions with a value of about ¥6bn. The Osaka Bankers' Association also operates a similar system for the transfer of wages and salaries.

(ii) The yen-based settlement system for foreign exchange

The yen-based system of settlement for foreign exchange (started in October 1984) is operated by the Tokyo Bankers' Association for the purpose of rapid and efficient settlement in yen funds of transactions connected with foreign exchange dealings among banks.

Under this system, the member banks exchange payment instructions on the floor of the Exchange but also tabulate received/paid funds and the net payments and make settlements through current deposit accounts at the Bank of Japan. As of December 1985, there were seventy-five member banks (of which forty-four were foreign banks), and during the course of 1984 the total amount settled was ¥1,341bn.

(iii) The Society for World-wide Interbank Financial Telecommunication (SWIFT)

The SWIFT system is an international data telecommunication system, and is managed as a non-profit corporation with its centre in Brussels. SWIFT handles the details of instructions concerning international transactions among banks in matters of client remittances, foreign exchange trading, documentary bills, letters of credit, and other such instruments. The system works through a network of computers and telecommunications lines. The final settlement of the transactions in the system is carried out either through bilateral transactions among correspondent banks or through the yen-based foreign exchange settlement system. As of December 1985, these were 1,286 members from fifty-eight countries. Of these, 111 were from Japan, including forty-six foreign banks. During the course of 1984, the system transmitted 3·6m. notifications and received 4·3m.

6

The Bank of Japan and Monetary Policy

I. Purposes, functions, and organization of the Bank of Japan

1. THE PURPOSES OF THE BANK OF JAPAN

THE Bank of Japan was founded in October 1882 as the nation's central bank, but was reorganized in February 1942 under the Bank of Japan Law, which is still in force. Because the Bank of Japan Law was established during the Second World War there have been several discussions in the post-war period concerning revisions. Apart, however, from the new establishment of the Policy Board as the highest body of decision within the Bank, in June 1949, no important reforms have taken place.

Article 1 of the Bank of Japan Law determines the following purposes for the Bank of Japan:

The Bank of Japan has for its object the regulation of the currency, the control and facilitation of credit and finance, and the maintenance and fostering of the credit system, pursuant to the national policy, in order that the general economic activities of the nation might adequately be enhanced.

The mode of expression is out of tune with current conditions because the Law was written forty-four years ago under wartime conditions; today the latter part of the statement may be taken to mean 'to foster the stable development of the Japanese economy'.

The former parts of the statement may be interpreted as meaning that the objectives of the operations of the Bank of Japan are to foster stability in the value of the currency and to maintain orderly credit conditions. Maintaining a stable currency is the essential purpose of a central bank, which is the issuer of currency. This stability is most essential for the development of the national economy. At the same time, an important precondition for stability is the maintenance of orderly credit conditions, considering the fact that major swings in credit conditions in the past have occurred at times when the economy was fluctuating violently. The Bank of Japan is in continuous contact with financial markets through its everyday operations. This contact helps to foster currency stability and the maintenance of orderly credit conditions, and thus contributes to the stable development of the Japanese economy.

305

2. THE FUNCTIONS OF THE BANK OF JAPAN

The functions of the Bank of Japan do not differ particularly from those of the other central banks; that is, there are four major functions: (1) the function of a bank of issue for the currency; (2) the function of being of a bank of banks (or more precisely a bank for financial institutions); (3) the function as a bank between the Government and the private sector; and (4) the function of operating a monetary policy through the other three functions. The first three functions will be dealt with in detail in this section and the fourth in the next section.

Over the years the Bank of Japan has gradually mechanized its operations in order to perform these functions. In recent years, in response to the rapid and wide development of data telecommunications, computer systems have been developed not only for inter-office telecommunications of the Bank of Japan itself but also for financial transactions between the Bank of Japan and its clients (the 'Bank of Japan On-line-Network system').

a. The Bank of Japan as a bank of issue

Based on Article 29 of the Bank of Japan Law, the Bank of Japan is the sole bank of issue in Japan, and the Bank of Japan notes that its issues have an unlimited circulation for all transactions both public and private (see Table 6.1 for a summary balance sheet of the Bank of Japan). The system of banknote issue is the so-called 'elastic maximum issue limit' system. This system was instituted in March 1941 by the Law Concerning Temporary Special Treatment of the Convertible Banknote Act. In 1942 this system became permanent under Article 30 of the Bank of Japan Law. The main provisions of the system are as follows:

(*a*) Concerning the issue of banknotes, the Bank of Japan Law (Article 29) determines that 'the Bank of Japan is authorized to issue banknotes' but does not prescribe responsibilities concerning convertibility.

(*b*) The maximum issue limit for banknotes is determined by the Minister of Finance after consultation with the Cabinet Council. Since 8 December 1984 the limit has been ¥23·9bn.

(*c*) When the Bank of Japan believes it to be necessary, issues of banknotes above the limit may be made (so-called 'excess issues'), but continuation of excess issue for longer than fifteen days requires approval by the Minister of Finance. Moreover, for excess issues exceeding sixteen days, the Bank of Japan must pay an issuing tax at a rate determined by the Minister of Finance. Currently, the excess issue tax is 3 per cent per year.

(*d*) Issues of banknotes by the Bank of Japan must be backed by assets of equivalent value. The assets eligible for holding by the Bank of Japan include bills such as commercial bills, loans, Government bonds or other bonds, foreign exchange, and gold and silver bullion. For assets other than gold and

TABLE 6.1 *Principal Accounts of the Bank of Japan, by Year-end*

	1965 ¥100m.	%	1970 ¥100m.	%	1975 ¥100m.	%	1980 ¥100m.	%	1985 ¥100m.	%
Assets										
Gold bullion	309	1·0	308	0·5	308	0·2	1,405	0·6	1,404	0·5
Bills discounted	1,942	6·1	4,086	6·4	974	0·6	2,270	0·9	1,982	0·6
Loans	14,334	45·5	19,447	30·2	16,798	10·8	21,020	8·7	42,585	13·7
Bills bought	—	—	—	—	23,237	14·9	32,000	13·3	52,932	17·0
Government bonds	9,300	29·5	23,813	37·0	73,945	47·3	158,351	65·7	172,786	55·5
Other securities	1,571	5·0	4,432	6·9	3,008	1·9	318	0·1	0	0·0
Foreign assets	3,713	11·8	11,232	17·5	35,060	22·4	21,893	9·1	34,280	11·0
Other	357	1·1	970	1·5	2,901	1·9	3,788	1·6	5,238	1·7
TOTAL ASSETS	31,529	100·0	64,291	100·0	156,235	100·0	241,046	100·0	311,207	100·0
Liabilities and net worth										
Banknotes issued	25,638	81·3	55,560	86·4	126,171	80·8	193,473	80·3	254,743	81·8
Deposits of financial institutions	885	2·8	2,983	4·6	15,516	9·9	26,443	11·0	26,799	8·6
Government deposits	621	2·0	428	0·7	1,387	0·9	1,257	0·5	2,080	0·7
Reserves and surpluses	1,985	6·3	4,096	6·4	9,614	6·1	13,171	5·5	21,685	7·0
Capital	1	0·0	1	0·0	1	0·0	1	0·0	1	0·0
Other	2,397	7·6	1,219	1·9	3,544	2·3	6,701	2·8	5,899	1·9

Source: BOJ, *Economic Statistics Annual.*

silver bullion or foreign exchange, the Minister of Finance determines holding limits on an asset-by-asset basis. Other than this provision, however, silver and gold bullion and foreign exchange are treated identically with other assets, and there exists no special specie reserve under the current system.

There are nine types of Bank of Japan note, in denominations of ¥10,000, ¥5,000, ¥1,000, ¥500, ¥50, ¥10, ¥5, and ¥1. For denominations of ¥100 and less, however, the Bank of Japan currently only accepts these notes in payment, having suspended payment of them to others. On 1 November 1984, the designs for the ¥10,000, ¥5,000, and ¥1,000 notes were changed, and by the end of 1985 the replacement of the old notes with the new notes was virtually complete. The Government also issues subsidiary coins through the Bank of Japan in denominations of ¥500, ¥100, ¥50, ¥10, ¥5 and ¥1. The share of subsidiary coin in total notes and coin outstanding, however, is only about 6 per cent (as of the end of 1985).

b. The Bank of Japan as a bank for financial institutions

The Bank of Japan leaves deposit business and lending transactions with the corporations and individuals of the general public to financial institutions in the market, and concentrates instead on being a 'bank of banks', i.e., carrying out transactions exclusively with commercial financial institutions (with the exception of transactions with the Government described below). The Bank of Japan currently has transactions relationships with virtually all of the important financial institutions, that is, city banks, regional banks, long-term credit banks, trust banks, foreign banks, *sogo* banks, *shinkin* banks, the *Zenshinren* Bank, the National Federation of Credit Co-operatives, the *Shokochukin* Bank, the *Norinchukin* Bank, the securities companies, the securities finance companies, the money market dealers and others. The important types of transaction which the Bank of Japan carries out with these institutions as a 'bank of banks' are as follows.

(i) Current deposit transactions

The Bank of Japan accepts current deposits from client financial institutions. These current deposits, like the current deposits accepted by commercial financial institutions, earn no interest. There are used for settlement of clearing transactions balances, remittances of funds, call money transactions, and other transactions among financial institutions. In addition, all transactions of financial institutions with the Bank of Japan, for example, payments related to securities trading or to Bank of Japan lending, pass through these current deposit accounts. The reserve deposits kept under the reserve requirement system (described below) and also kept in these accounts.

(ii) Lending transactions

The Bank of Japan also carries out lending on bills and discount of bills with financial institutions (clients eligible for lending transactions are somewhat narrower in scope than those who have current deposits).

Bill-discounting by the Bank of Japan is the rediscount of bills that have already been discounted by a financial institution for the clients of that institution. Bank of Japan bill-discount operations are carried out only for bills that have been designated as acceptable for rediscount and not for all commercial bills. A commercial bill is a promissory note or bill of exchange issued for the purpose of settlement of payment of goods that have been sold. Such bills designate the buyer as the issuer of the bill or as the payer of the bill. Among the conditions required for the bill to qualify for rediscount by the Bank of Japan are that the bill must mature within three months of the date of rediscount, and that the bill must be endorsed by one or more persons of a certain creditworthiness in addition to the original debtor. Such rediscounts of commercial bills have traditionally been viewed as the basic form of Bank of Japan lending.

Loans on bills by the Bank of Japan are loans made directly to financial institutions and are collateralized by bills or securities that have been recognized as a qualified collateral by the Bank of Japan. Types of qualified collateral currently include Government bonds, Government bills, Government-guaranteed bonds, financial debentures, and certain local government bonds or corporate debentures and bills that the Bank of Japan has recognized as appropriate.

The rates of interest on Bank of Japan discounts and loans are publicly posted rates and are known as official discount rates. The discount rates of the Bank of Japan are determined by the type of loan or discount in question, and there are currently two types. When the term 'official discount rate' is used, however, it generally refers to the discount rate on commercial bill rediscounts. As of 21 April 1986, the official discount rates of the Bank of Japan were 3·5 per cent for discount of commercial bills or for lending collateralized by Government bonds, designated securities, or bills similar to commercial bills, and 3·75 per cent for lending collateralized by other assets.

In addition, a separate lending system was created in March 1981. Under this system, loans on bills at a basic interest rate determined separately from the official discount rate may be carried out in circumstances in which it is necessary for appropriate management of financial markets.

(iii) Purchase and sale of securities and bills

The Bank of Japan also trades in bills and securities such as Government bonds with financial institutions when such transactions are necessary. Trading in both long-term Government bonds and short-term Government bills has been carried out, but currently such transactions concentrate on the purchase of long-term bonds. The trading of bills is also of two types, trading of bills held by commercial financial institutions (bills purchased) and the sale of bills issued by the Bank of Japan (bills sold). Transactions in securities and bills are an important means of adjusting financial markets and have recently become even more important. These matters will be treated in detail below.

(iv) Other types of transaction

Trading in bullion is a type of business peculiar to the Bank of Japan. Such trading was extremely important under the gold standard system for the concentration, increase, and management of specie reserves. With the move to managed currency system during the Second World War, however, gold production was concentrated in the hands of the Government, and bullion trading lost its practical relevance for the Bank of Japan. In the post-war period, the Bank of Japan has traded bullion with Government and has also acted as agent for the Government in trading with the public through the Precious Metals Special Account. But this special account was abolished at the end of fiscal 1977, and currently no bullion transactions are carried out through the Bank of Japan.

Foreign exchange trading is one of the important functions of a central bank, and the Bank of Japan carries out such trading when it is thought to be necessary. In the post-war period the Bank of Japan carried out transactions only with the Government, and transactions with the public, such as intervention in the foreign exchange market, were been carried out by the Foreign Exchange Fund Special Account transactions of the Ministry of Finance, using the Bank of Japan as agent. In addition, the Bank of Japan carries out foreign exchange trading on behalf of foreign central banks and international institutions in order to promote international financial co-operation.

The Bank of Japan is also the settlement institution for the exchange settlement mechanism. The exchange settlement system is a system for the settlement of transactions among banks, and works through exchange settlement accounts at the Bank of Japan. Private financial institutions that carry out domestic exchange operations convert the balances that arise from their transactions with the other banks due to collection of bills and remittances from various parts of the country into balances with the Bank of Japan. These balances are then settled by the central bank.

The Bank of Japan also acts as the central institution for the Government bond book-entry system started in February 1980 in order to facilitate secondary transactions in Goverment bonds. The purpose of this System is to contribute to the development of a sound secondary market in Government bonds by rationalizing delivery and custody. Under this system, banks, securities companies, and other participants entrust Government bonds to the Bank of Japan and the Bank of Japan carries out the transactions in bonds through deposit transfer book entries managed by the Bank of Japan and the participants.

c. The Bank of Japan as the bank intermediating between the Government and the private sector

The Bank of Japan carries out both deposits and lending transactions with the Government but also acts as agent for part of the Government's business with the public in treasury, Government bond, and foreign exchange business. These activities by the Bank of Japan are based on various laws.

(i) Government deposits

The Bank of Japan carries out the payments operations of the Treasury, and all payments are made through balances of Goverment deposits at the Bank of Japan (with the exception of intra-treasury payments). Thus all receipts of the Government, including tax receipts and others, are entered into the Government's deposits at the Bank of Japan, and all payments by the Government are made with Government cheques drawn on the Bank of Japan.

(ii) Extension of credit to the Government

The Bank of Japan Law determines that the Bank of Japan may carry out uncollateralized lending to the Government and may underwrite or subscribe to Government bonds; thus there are no limits on credit to the Government which the Bank of Japan may grant. These provisions reflect the wartime origins of the Bank of Japan Law. The Finance Law of 1947, however, prohibits in principle the underwriting by the Bank of Japan of long-term bonds of maturity greater than one year or loans by the Bank of Japan of greater than one year. These provisions were made on the principle of ensuring sound finance for the Government, and are included in Article 5 of the Finance Law. Indeed, since 1948, there have been no underwritings of long-term Government bonds by the Bank of Japan and no long-term lendings to the Government. For short-term cash management of the Government, however, the Bank of Japan has provided credit in the form of underwriting of Government bills. In principle, such Government bills are to be subscribed in the market-place. In practice, however, the interest rates on them are rather low, and the portion absorbed in the market is extremely small. As a result, the Bank of Japan is the underwriter for the largest portion. In 1985, the issue of short-term Government bonds of maturity less than six months began, in order to facilitate roll-over of Government bonds then coming due; because these short-term Government bonds differ in character from Government bills, however, the Bank of Japan is prohibited from underwriting them.

(iii) Business delegated by law and ordinance

Various laws prescribe certain types of business for the Bank of Japan to carry out as agent for the Government.

(1) Treasury business. The Bank of Japan law prescribes that the Bank of Japan is to carry out the business of the Treasury. The scope of this business is not limited to the payment and receipt of funds into Government deposits at the Bank of Japan. It extends to carrying out other types of calculation and also to payments concerning and custody of securities either held by the Government or in the custody of the Government. Thus the Treasury business of the Bank of Japan are huge in scale, and are dealt with not only at the head office and branches of the Bank of Japan but also through the establishment of a system of Treasury agencies and revenue agencies. In addition, a portion of the Treasury business is entrusted to banks and other commercial financial institutions.

(2) Government bond business. The Bank of Japan acts as agent for the Government in all the clerical operations concerning Government bonds such as the issue, redemption, interest payments, and registration of the securities. A system of agencies has been established to deal with Government bond business. This system includes the Treasury agencies described above and has placed agencies for Government bonds nation-wide in order primarily to handle the payments of interest and principal on Government bonds.

(3) Foreign exchange business. The Government's holding of foreign exchange are currently managed in the Foreign Exchange Fund Special Account. The Bank of Japan, on the basis of the Foreign Exchange Fund Special Account Law, currently carries out the clerical work concerning payments in yen funds and foreign exchange funds through this special account, by acting as agent for the Ministry of Finance. Because the trading in foreign exchange with authorized foreign exchange banks involves foreign exchange market-smoothing operations, the Bank of Japan intervenes in the foreign exchange market in its capacity as agent for the Minister of Finance. As the institution managing foreign exchange for Japan, the Bank of Japan plays an important role in its responsibilities for carrying out this type of business. Under the Foreign Exchange and Foreign Trade Control Law, the Bank of Japan acted as agent in the management of foreign exchange trade and foreign funds for the Government. Since the revision of the above Law in December 1980, however, the level of such business has been reduced as a result of the liberalization of foreign exchange control.

3. ORGANIZATION OF THE BANK OF JAPAN

The Bank of Japan is a special corporation organized under the Bank of Japan Law. Because the Bank of Japan Law was enacted in 1942, during the war, several attempts at reform have been made in the post-war period, but, as noted above, the only important one has been the establishment of the Policy Board under the revision of the Law in 1949.

a. Capital

The Bank of Japan is capitalized at ¥100m., of which ¥55m. is contributed by the Government and ¥45m. by the private sector. Dividends are limited to a total of 5 per cent per annum for contributors, and there is no annual meeting of stockholders as with most corporations. Management participation is not permitted. The surpluses from operations during any business period are paid into the Treasury, with the exception of dividends and reserve accumulation.

b. The Policy Board of the Bank of Japan

The Policy Board is the highest decision-making body of the Bank of Japan. Its duties are the operation of the business of the Bank of Japan, currency regulation, credit control and the administration of other monetary policies so as to meet the needs of the economy. The specific areas in which the Policy Board has jurisdiction are rather broad and extend to all the major policy instruments such as official discount rates, open-market operations, and reserve requirements, and also include regulation of main market interest rates. For reserve requirements, however, the setting, change, or abolition of reserve ratios requires the approval of the Minister of Finance. Also, the setting, change, or abolition of maximum limits for market interest rates is carried out by the Bank only after proposals by the Minister of Finance and deliberation by the Interest Adjustment Council.

The Policy Board is composed of seven persons, the Governor of the Bank of Japan, two representatives of the Government (one representative each from the Ministry of Finance and the Economic Planning Agency), and four appointed representatives (one person of outstanding experience and knowledge each as representatives of the city banks, the regional banks, commerce and industry, and agriculture). Of these seven, the two representatives of Government do not have voting power, so that decisions are taken by majority vote of the Governor and the appointed members. The appointed members are selected by the Cabinet and approved by both houses of the Diet for terms of four years, with reappointment possible. The Chairman of the Policy Board is elected by vote of the members with voting rights, but as a matter of custom the Governor is selected.

c. The executive

The officers of the Bank of Japan are the Governor, the Vice-Governor, three or more Executive Directors (currently seven), two or more Auditors (currently five) and a number of Advisers. The Governor represents the Bank of Japan and conducts the operations of the Bank in accordance with the policies decided by the Policy Board. The Vice-Governor and the Executive Directors aid the Governor in conduct of the Bank's business, while Auditors inspect the business of the Bank. The Advisers may express to the Governor their views on matters of importance concerning the business of the Bank. The Governor and the Vice-Governor are appointed by the Cabinet, while the Executive Directors are appointed by the Minister of Finance from among persons recommended by the Governor. The Auditors and the Advisers are appointed by the Ministry of Finance. The Governor and the Vice-Governor serve five-year terms, the Executive Directors four-year terms, the Auditors three-year terms and Advisers two-year terms, with reappointment possible. The head office of the Bank of Japan is in Tokyo, and there are thirty-three branches and twelve offices in important cities throughout the country. The Bank also has representative offices in London and New York with three individual representatives in other cities abroad. These offices and representatives carry out liaison with foreign central banks and research on foreign conditions.

d. Relationship with the Government

Under current laws, the Bank of Japan is under the rather broad control of the Government. Not only are there detailed provisions concerning individual types of activity, but the Minister of Finance has general powers of order over operations and supervision, along with the right to appoint and dismiss directors. This situation strongly reflects the wartime character of the laws. In fact, however, the Government and the Bank of Japan maintain close contact and co-operation on a regular basis, and the powers of order have never in fact been used. In reality, the management of monetary policy is carried out under the responsibility of the Bank of Japan from an independent point of view.

Between 1957 and 1960 the Committee for Financial System Research (an advisory body of the Minister of Finance) discussed a revision of the Bank of Japan Law. During these discussions the biggest issue was how to specify the independence of the Bank of Japan. On this matter the Committee could not come to a unified conclusion. The result was a report with two plans, plan A and plan B, for cases of disagreement. In cases in which the Minister of Finance believed that there were fears that the policies of the Bank of Japan would cause barriers to achievement of Government policy and in which agreement could not be reached on these matters by the Minister of

Finance and the Governor of the Bank, plan A called for the Minister to give direct instructions to the Bank. Plan B called for a request by the Minister for the Policy Committee to postpone decisions for a certain length of time, after which the Policy Board would resume its decision-making as usual. No conclusion about how to deal with such cases was arrived at, and the problem remains unresolved even today.

II. *Objectives and instruments of monetary policy*

1. THE OBJECTIVES OF MONETARY POLICY

Let us first describe the objectives of monetary policy, and then describe the instruments that the Bank of Japan uses to implement policy.

Among the final objectives of monetary policy, the most important is price stability, but in addition it is common to list as objectives the support of economic growth or stable employment, and equilibrium in the balance of payments.

There are times when it is possible for the central bank to pursue all three of these objectives simultaneously. The problems arise, however, when there are trade-offs among the objectives. The historical experience of both Japan and other nations has shown the two greatest problems as the 'stability versus growth' dilemma and the 'domestic versus foreign' dilemma. In the former, the problem is whether to view price stability or employment support (i.e., economic growth) as more important. In the latter, the question is whether to view the domestic objective of price stability or the international objective of balance of payments equilibrium as more important.

In the case of Japan there were no serious trade-offs among the three objectives until about 1968. This was because price stability was a precondition for equilibrium in the balance of payments and because, under the Bretton Woods system, equilibrium in the balance of payments was a precondition for the maintenance of growth. In 1969, however, monetary policy confronted the two types of trade-offs mentioned above, because inflation began while the balance of payments was in surplus. At that time, the Bank of Japan chose price stability and tightened monetary policy. As a result economic growth slowed, and the surplus in the balance of payments expanded even further, leading to the revaluation of the yen in December 1971. Thereafter, there occurred several instances in which a resolution of this dilemma, in more serious depth, was necessary. Between 1969 and 1973, monetary policy could not decide on the chief objectives: in the earlier period, price stability was seen as being important, whereas the later period saw instead an emphasis on growth and balance of payments equilibrium. The result was the violent inflation and deficits in the balance of payments that accompanied the first oil crisis, and the experience of the deep recession after the crisis [4].

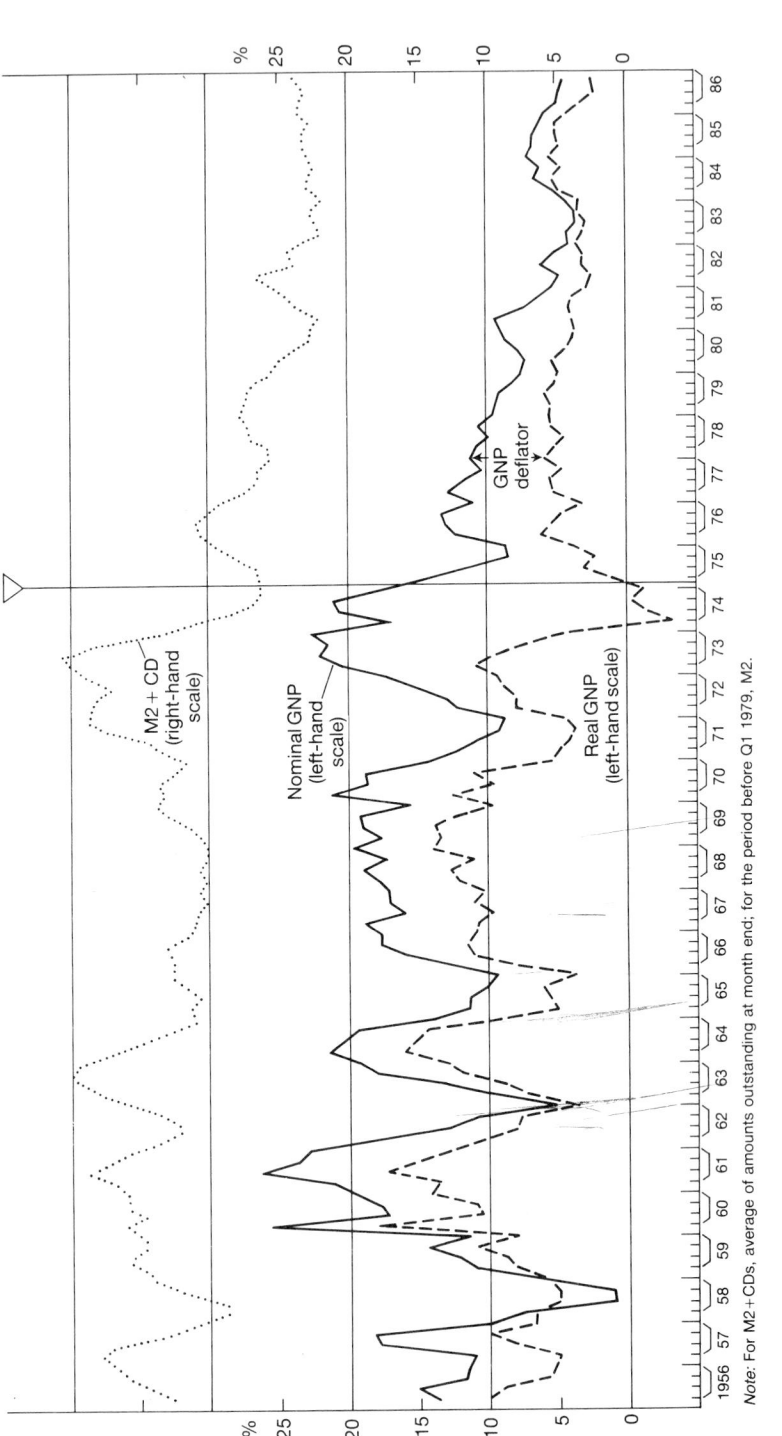

Figure 6.1 *Money Supply and GNP in Japan (percent change from same period of previous year)*
Note: For M2 + CDs, average of amounts outstanding at month-end; for the period before Q1 1979, M2.

Reflecting on this experience, the Bank of Japan strengthened its view that price stability was indeed a precondition for the maintenance of employment and growth, at least over the medium term. In addition, the shift from the fixed exchange rate system to the floating exchange rate system in February 1973 meant that equilibrium in the balance of payments was in principle left to the automatic equilibrating power of the foreign exchange market. This left the central bank of each country in a position to take responsibility for the stabilization of domestic prices. Since 1975, the Bank of Japan has recognized this position and has carried out a monetary policy with the primary objective of a stable value for the currency. A problem arose, however, in the first half of the 1980s, when the world experienced the divergence of exchange rates from purchasing power parity even in the medium term, and even within the flexible exchange rate system. Thus there could be cases in which external equilibrium was not fully established in the balance of payments. The Bank of Japan, even though maintaining the primary importance of price stability, operated a flexible monetary policy, paying some attention to the exchange markets in such cases.

2. THE INSTRUMENTS OF MONETARY POLICY

The usual instruments of monetary policy for a central bank are lending policy (including changes in the official discount rate), open-market operations, and changes in reserve requirements. During Japan's high growth period the most important role in monetary policy was played by changes in lending policy at the Bank of Japan. In addition, so-called 'window guidance', that is, credit controls on increases in loans by city banks, played a supplementary role. These various instruments of monetary policy were effective because the over-borrowing by corporations and the over-loan situation of financial institutions. On the other hand, one result of policy operations that focused on lending was that the commercial banks, and particularly city banks, came to depend excessively on borrowings from the Bank of Japan. In response, the Bank of Japan introduced the so-called 'new scheme for monetary control' in 1962. Under this new formula the money required to accommodate economic growth (so-called 'growth money') would be supplied through purchase of securities rather than through lending. Other instruments have developed over the years, with the establishment of separate bill market operations by the Bank of Japan, began after 1972, and Government bill operations, begun after 1981, though on a limited scale. Thus the role of market operations in securities and bills in the implementation of monetary policy has gradually become greater.

Nevertheless, there still remain barriers to the use of open-market operations in the original sense of the term, that is, flexible operations in open markets in which non-financial institutions are participants. In order to ensure the effectiveness of monetary policy under a regime of financial liberalization, it will be necessary to use open-market operations on a day-to-day basis. Thus it has become even more important to create markets in which such thoroughgoing open-market operations are possible (for example, a market in Government bills, that is, TBs). Let us next outline the major policy instruments.

a. Lending policy

The Bank of Japan carries out its day-to-day monetary adjustments through changes in its lending policy towards private financial institutions at the lending window. These day-to-day changes occur after the basic stance of monetary policy has been clarified through official discount rate changes. The quantity of lending is subject to an upper limit under the credit ceiling system. For lending not subject to the official discount rate, there exists the special lending facility with interest rates that are established separately.

(i) The official discount rate

Changes in the official discount rate have an influence on the cost of raising funds of financial institutions, not only directly, through the higher-cost lending by the Bank of Japan, but also indirectly, through movements in the interest rates in the short-term money markets. Private financial institutions change their attitudes toward lending and securities investment in response to such changes in interest costs, and such movements on the part of financial institutions change the money supply. In turn, the effects spread to the economic activities of corporations and individuals. This series of effects is called the 'cost effects' of discount rate operations. In addition, however, discount rate operations have 'announcement effects'—those effects on the behaviour of financial institutions, corporations, and individuals based on their expectations of how, in the light of experience in the past, the economy will be affected by changes in the discount rate. For example, in the past, when the discount rate was raised, the increase indicated a restrictive attitude towards the business cycle; thus, one might expect market movements due to psychological effects of cautious attitudes toward production and investment on the part of firms before the actual spread of the cost effects of the discount rate increase.

(ii) Stances on lendings

Day-to-day lending policy is carried out within the framework of discount rate operations. Lending by the Bank of Japan to the private financial institutions is not carried out passively according to the demand for borrowing for which the banks are prepared to pay the discount rate. Rather, the quantity of lending is adjusted within overall limits in order to affect the liquidity position of the private financial institutions. These changes in the policy of the Bank of Japan toward lending, and the consequent changes in the liquidity positions of banks, affect the attitude of the financial institutions toward lending and securities investment, and also affect their attitudes toward borrowing and lending in the interbank markets. The attitude changes also bring changes in the interest rates in short-term money markets, the yields in securities markets, and the lending rates of banks, along with changes in quantities of credit granted. Such changes all affect the money supply and are called 'liquidity effects'.

(iii) The special lending facility

In March 1981, the Bank of Japan introduced a special lending formula with an interest rate determined separately from the official discount rate. This facility was to be used as a means for financial adjustment in cases where it was needed for appropriate management of money markets. An example might be the flexible response in cases in which disruptive influences were felt in the foreign exchange markets on account of active short-term capital flows generated by changes in foreign interest rates. So far no use has been made of the special lending facilities, and no interest rates for them have been set; but if the use of this facility were in fact to become necessary, the lending would be carried out flexibly, along with determination and changes in interest rates in response to movement of foreign interest rates and domestic market trends.

(iv) The credit ceiling

In order to reduce the dependence on Bank of Japan lending by client financial institutions, the Bank of Japan has established a maximum limit on lendings for city banks with high dependence on such loans.

The credit ceiling system was introduced in November 1962 with the intention of preventing excesses of the so-called 'over-loan' situation, in which city banks in particular came to depend very highly, even in normal times, on large amounts of Bank of Japan lending. The credit ceiling system was part of the normalization of financial conditions under the new scheme for monetary control and is currently applied to ten city banks. Under this system, the Bank of Japan establishes credit ceilings on a quarterly basis for each of the banks and in principle does not lend above these limits. In cases where lending above the maximum is unavoidable, it is made for periods of less than two weeks, and an interest rate 4 percentage points above the discount rate is applied to the loans.

b. Securities and bills operations

In the original sense of the term, 'open-market operations' are activities of a central bank in the open market in which it trades flexibly in securities and bills. Through these operations the central bank directly changes the cash reserves of private banks and indirectly changes interest rates, thus effecting changes in credit activities in terms of both quantity and price, and adjustments in the money supply. When trading is with economic entities other than private banks, the money supply is affected directly. Such operations are called open-market operations because the central bank goes into open markets to trade.

In Japan the history of securities trading by the Bank of Japan is relatively old, going back into the pre-war period. Because the open markets were underdeveloped, however, such operations were originally limited to exceptional cases of supplementary augmentation of lending. In November 1962, however, the Bank of Japan sought to make more flexible use of securities operations along with the introduction of the credit ceiling system described above. The purpose of these moves was twofold: to diversify the set of monetary adjustment instruments and to normalize the financial markets. Through these securities operations the Bank of Japan sought to supply the currency necessary for economic growth instead of supplying such funds through Bank of Japan lending. Originally the bond-trading operations were bilateral trades with financial institutions at fixed rates and with repurchase agreements attached. With the reopening of the bond market in February 1966, however, the system was changed to its current method of sale at market price without repurchase agreement. The system was augmented in June 1972 when active operations of bills commenced.

As things stand presently, however, the open-market operations in Japan do not take the form of open-market operations in the original sense of the term, because corporations and other non-financial institutions do not participate. Thus, Japan's open-market operations do not have the direct effect of changing the money supply. Even the market sales of Government bills, which were begun again in 1981 by the Bank of Japan, continue to be rather exceptional. Let us consider these types of operation one by one.

(i) Securities operations

Since February 1966, the Bank of Japan has carried out purchases of Government-guaranteed bonds at market prices (so-called 'unconditional' operations), replacing the bond purchases with repurchase agreements at non-market prices that had been carried out before then. At that time, the counterparts in transactions were expanded from a group consisting only of banks, long-term credit banks, foreign exchange banks, *sogo* banks, and the Federation of Credit Co-operatives to include the securities companies that had current deposits at the Bank of Japan. In this way, the road was opened for financial adjustments through the securities markets. In January 1967, the securities eligible for such operations were expanded to Government bonds, and the *Norinchukin* Bank also became eligible for such transactions. After August 1972 the Bank of Japan also began to carry out sales of its own holdings of securities when necessary for financial adjustments. (The eligible securities and eligible partners for such transactions were the same as in the case of securities purchases.)

After 1975 there were major developments in the use of securities purchase operations. Prior to December 1977 the amounts of securities operations were determined by the Bank of Japan and were carried out in bilateral transactions with financial institutions. Thereafter, however, the basis for transactions changed to the amounts desired by the financial institutions. After June 1978 a system of bidding for bonds was introduced to replace the system of using the prices for bonds listed on the Exchange. This change was made in order to improve the functioning of interest rates and to facilitate the use of securities operations. (At this same time some *shinkin* banks were added to the list of eligible transactors for securities transactions with the Bank of Japan.) With the mechanization of the bookkeeping tasks concerning the bid calculations for Government bond operations, the Bank of Japan decided to make its securities operations more flexible in May 1979, in conjunction with the move towards interest rate liberalization. So-called 'quick' operations were introduced in June 1979; in these operations, the purchases are not concentrated within a single day but are rather carried out in smaller amounts on several days. Also, the amounts sold are determined on the day of the bid and notified to the purchaser. After these changes were introduced, the flexibility of such operations increased substantially.

(ii) Bills operations

(1) Purchase of private bills.   Responding to an increase in the seasonal imbalances of funds, the Bank of Japan decided to purchase prime bills from the financial institutions in June 1972. The intention was to diversify the methods of financial adjustment, with resale of bills also permitted, and such operations were called bills operations. Until about 1975, purchases of private bills were made directly with client financial institutions, but currently such purchases are made through the money market dealers from the bill market. The bills eligible for such trading are bills issued by non-financial institutions (for example domestic corporate bill issues) that are recognized to be of high creditworthiness. In addition, the bills of exchange issued by financial institutions that have current deposit accounts at the Bank of Japan and that participate in the bill market are also eligible ('cover bills' with less than three months' maturity). The rate of interest on such transactions is based on market rates.

(2) The system for sale of bills drawn by the Bank of Japan.   The system for sale of bills drawn by the Bank of Japan was introduced as a means of absorbing funds from the market, and was meant to augment the sales of Government bills by the Bank of Japan to the short funds companies. The bill sales system was introduced in August 1971 to enable a smooth adjustment of monetary conditions in response to the surplus of funds in the financial markets that had been generated at that time by the surplus in the balance

of payments and the inflows of foreign exchange. In such operations, bills of exchange of less than three months of maturity are issued with the Bank of Japan as issuer and payor (acceptor) and then sold through the short funds companies either in the call market or in the bill market (when necessary, direct sales to client financial institutions may be made). The interest rates applying to such bill sales are based on the interest rates in either the call market or the bill market.

(iii) Sales of Government bills (TBs)

The Bank of Japan decided to sell Government bills in its portfolio to the money market dealers in January 1966, for the purpose of smoothing as far as possible the seasonal fluctuations of funds demand and supply and thus contributing to the adjustment of market conditions. But certain conventions applied to such cases. The effective yield to the money market dealers was to be around that of market interest rates. In addition, there were to be agreements for repurchase on the day of redemption according to the instructions from the Bank of Japan. Such operations, however, were not carried out after November 1972, in part because of the introduction of bill operations.

But in May 1981 the Bank of Japan reopened its sales of Government bills as a means of absorbing funds during periods of excess liquidity. This was the first time since the end of the Second World War that the Bank of Japan had engaged in an open-market operation in the true sense of the term. In cases before 1981, the bills were sold only to money market dealers without a requirement for resale (the money market dealers used the bills as collateral for call-market transactions). For sales since 1981, however, resale of the bills by money market dealers to financial institutions has been permitted, and the financial institutions have then resold the bills to corporations. At first, such sales of Government bills were limited to periods of excess liquidity, but in 1985 they were also used in a period of tight liquidity so that the duration for which Government bills were held in the financial institutions became longer. Nevertheless, a large-scale market in Government bills that could act as the centre of an open money market does not yet exist.

c. Reserve ratio operations

The reserve deposit requirement system is a system under which commercial financial institutions are required to deposit in non-interest bearing accounts at the Bank of Japan amounts in certain proportions to their deposits and other liabilities (these proportions are called 'reserve ratios'). This system was introduced in 1958 under the Law Concerning the Reserve Deposit Requirement System, and reserve ratios were established for each of the financial institutions for the first time in September 1959 (for the reserve ratios as of June 1986, see Table 6.2).[1]

The reserve deposit requirement system was originally applied only to banks, long-term credit banks, and the specialized foreign exchange bank (the Bank of Tokyo). But, as will be described below, the system was later expanded to other financial institutions and other types of financial liability. During periods of financial tightening, and subsequent loosening or relaxation until around 1980, reserve requirements were changed relatively frequently and thus were a powerful policy instrument for the adjustment of the liquidity position of financial institutions, together with lending policy and securities and bills operations.

A short history of the changes in the reserve deposit requirement system shows that it has expanded over time. After the establishment of reserve ratios in September 1959, the system was expanded to include reserve requirements for *sogo* banks and *shinkin* banks that had deposits exceeding ¥20 milliard. In September 1969, the *Norinchukin* Bank was included in the system.

A reform of the system was carried out in May 1972, along the lines of a report by the Committee for Financial System Research ('Report Concerning Utilization of the Reserve Deposit Requirement System' of December 1971). The purpose of the reforms was to respond to the changes in the financial environment accompanying the progress towards internationalization and to promote the more efficient management of monetary policy. Under the

---

[1] The outlines of the reserve deposit system as it currently operates are as follows:

1. Applicability: banks (including foreign banks in Japan), long-term credit banks, and foreign exchange banks; in addition, *sogo* banks and *shinkin* banks with deposits of more than ¥120 milliard are required to participate (however, for *sogo* banks and *shinkin* banks with deposits between ¥120 milliard and ¥160 milliard no reserve ratios have been established). In addition the *Norinchukin* Bank is required to participate.

2. Types of liability subject to reserve requirements: (*a*) time deposits, CDs, and other deposits (including instalment savings but excluding foreign currency deposits at authorized foreign exchange banks and non-resident yen deposits); (*b*) debentures issued by long-term credit banks and the foreign exchange bank; (*c*) money trusts with contracts under which deficiencies of principal are recouped (including loan trusts); (*d*) the liabilities in Japanese currency of authorized foreign exchange banks to non-residents (excluding those covered under items (*b*) and (*c*) above and guaranteed liabilities); (*e*) all foreign currency liability accounts of non-residents with authorized foreign exchange banks (excluding guaranteed liabilities) and foreign currency deposits from residents (excluding deposits in the name of the Minister of Finance).

3. Maximum reserve ratio: 20 per cent (however, for items 2 (*d*) and 2 (*e*) above the maximum is 100 per cent).

4. Types of reserve ratio: (reserve requirements may be established, changed or abolished): (*a*) for the outstanding balance of eligible liabilities or against increases in such liabilities or against both; (*b*) for different types of applicable liability or different types of applicable institution.

5. Reserve deposits: institutions subject to reserve requirements are required to maintain deposits at the Bank of Japan in amounts equivalent to the fixed proportion of their deposits or liabilities when the reserve rations are established.

6. Penalties: in cases when institutions subject to reserve requirements fail to maintain the reserve deposits as specified, a penalty is to be paid to the Bank of Japan in the amount of the insufficiency times 3·5 per cent above the Bank of Japan's bill discount rate. This penalty payment is then transferred from the Bank of Japan to the Government.

TABLE 6.2   *Required Reserve Ratios (June 1986)*

	Time deposits or CDs (%)	Other deposits (%)
On levels of deposits outstanding		
On banks, long-term credit banks, and foreign exchange banks		
On amounts above ¥3·3bn.	1·625	2·5
On amounts from ¥1bn. to ¥3·3bn.	0·625	1·25
On amounts below ¥1bn.	0·125	0·25
Sogo and *shinkin* banks		
On amounts above ¥1·0bn.	0·125	0·25
On amounts from ¥160 to ¥1bn.	0·125	0·25
The *Norinchukin* Bank	0·125	0·25
On the levels of securities outstanding		
On long-term credit banks and foreign exchange banks	0·125	
On money trusts (including loan trusts), principal outstanding	0·125	
On foreign currency deposits, etc		
On foreign currency liabilities to non-residents	0·25	
On foreign currency liabilities to residents		
Time deposits	0·375	
Other deposits	0·5	
On yen-liabilities to non-residents	0·25	

reforms, there was an expansion of the range of institutions to which the system applied (to include life insurance companies) and of the type of account to which it applied (to include financial debentures, the principal of trusts, and liabilities to non-residents). In addition, the maximum reserve ratio was raised from 10 per cent to 20 per cent, and the limit for reserve requirements on foreign currency and non-resident liabilities was set at 100 per cent. Also, a system of reserve requirements on increases in liabilities was introduced. In January 1973, as a result of these legal changes, reserve ratios were established on financial debentures and on the principal of money trusts for which a contract existed to recoup deficiencies of principal (including loan trusts). In November 1976, the Ministry of Finance Notification designating the limits of reserve requirements for foreign currency liabilities was published, and after June 1977 the actual reserve ratios on the outstanding amounts of liabilities such as foreign currency deposits and non-resident free yen deposits were established. (The requirements on the latter were revised in December 1980 to apply to non-resident yen deposits.) Between June 1972 and September 1974 and between November 1977 and February 1979, reserve requirements were placed against increases in the liabilities of non-resident free yen deposit accounts.

In April 1979, with the creation of CDs, the Enforcement Order of the Law Concerning Reserve Deposit Requirement System was revised, and reserve ratios were established for CDs.

Another legal revision was carried out in May 1986, for the purpose of introducing a progressive schedule of reserve ratios. This was done in order to respond to the progress in financial liberalization and to ensure the effectiveness of monetary policy. The new system was implemented in July. Under the progressive ratio system, tranches are established according to the outstanding amounts in the accounts that are subject to reserve requirements, and higher reserve ratios are applied to the higher tranches. Under the previous system of reserve ratios, the ratios themselves applied to the total amounts of deposits in financial institutions (and not just the higher tranches) so that there could be severe increases in the burden of reserve requirements as the institution became larger. Under the progressive reserve ratio system, the higher reserve ratios apply only to the higher tranches, so that the burden of rapid increases in required reserves is eased. This reform will make it possible to use the reserve requirement system more flexibly.

d. Guidance on bank lending

During its day-to-day contact through deposit and lending transactions with client financial institutions, the Bank of Japan receives various types of information concerning the plans and actual developments of the funds and lending positions of these institutions. Using this information, the Bank of Japan provides guidance to the financial institutions to keep the increase in their lending to clients within limits that the Bank of Japan feels to be appropriate. Such guidance is particularly important in times of tight money and for lending by major institutions such as city banks. This type of guidance is in general called 'window guidance', and the type of guidance is changed from time to time according to financial conditions. Reflecting these conditions, the guidance sometimes takes the form of regulation of increases in loans and sometimes the form of guidance of overall positions.

For example, during each of the tight money periods between 1957 and around 1963, the Bank of Japan gave directives to keep lending by financial institutions within specified limits on a monthly basis, in order to prevent borrowings from the Bank of Japan from rising too much. This guidance was carried out primarily *vis-à-vis* city banks that had high levels of Bank of Japan borrowings. In the tight money period of 1964 there were directives to control the increases in lending on a quarterly basis, and the objects of such guidance were expanded from city banks and long-term credit banks to include trust banks (the banking accounts thereof) and regional banks. In the tight money period of 1967, the institutions subject to guidance were again expanded to include the larger *sogo* banks. In the tight money period following January 1973, the extent of guidance was expanded further to include the larger *shinkin* banks and the larger foreign banks in Japan, that is, almost all the Bank of Japan's client financial institutions. In addition, there was guidance concerning not only the restraint of overall lending but on lending to trading companies, and also guidance concerning restraint of securities investment.

After 1975, the period of tight money was gradually relaxed, and from July 1977 a new formula was introduced under which the voluntary lending plans of the various financial institutions were essentially accepted within the window guidance framework; the framework itself, however, was maintained in order to continue appropriate management of the money supply. In 1979, a strict guidance was implemented that was similar to that in previous periods of tightening; but in the second half of 1980 this guidance was gradually eased along with the change of policies. Since early 1982, the lending programmes of the individual financial institutions have been accepted completely.

Over-the-counter guidance is a form of moral persuasion based on cooperation of the Bank of Japan's client financial institutions; but because it is a form of moral suasion one cannot deny that so-called 'off-the-record lending' occurred, particularly in periods of change from easy to tight money. Guidance does, however, appear to have been followed in general. In this sense it has been a powerful instrument supporting the effectiveness of monetary policy. But if strong window advice is continued for long periods, there emerge disequilibria among financial institutions between those that are subject to controls and those that are not. In addition, the lending shares within one type of financial institution tend to become fixed. Thus window guidance is, in the final analysis, only a supplementary method of monetary policy supporting discount rate changes, securities and bills, operations, and reserve ratio changes, and is used primarily during periods of tight money. As liberalization of the financial structure and internationalization continue, as the effectiveness of monetary policy working through interest rates grows, and as the diversification of sources of funding for corporations progresses, the role of window guidance is expected to decline gradually.

III. The effectiveness of monetary policy

1. THE OPERATING TARGETS OF MONETARY POLICY

The channels of transmission between the policy instruments of the central bank and the final objectives are very long, and much time is required before effects become noticeable. Therefore the central bank must pay attention to monetary variables in the middle of this transmission channel, and must carry out monetary policy by making judgements from time to time about the effects of policy on these intermediate variables. Such variables are known formally as the operating targets of monetary policy. There is a further distinction among the operating targets between those financial variables that are close at hand for the central bank (known as operating variables) and those which are closer to final objectives (know as intermediate objectives). Because the operating variables are close to the central bank, they are affected directly by policy instruments. But precisely because they are easy to control, their relationship with policy objectives is somewhat unstable. In contrast, the intermediate objectives are rather farther from the control of the central bank and are only indirectly affected by the policy instruments. On the other hand, their relationships with policy objectives such as the price level are relatively stable.

Thus the transmission mechanism for monetary policy goes from policy instruments to operating variables, next to intermediate objectives, and then to final objectives. The Bank of Japan conducts its financial adjustments paying attention to the interest rate movements in the interbank markets as its operating variables. Continuous attention is paid to the intermediate objective, increases in lending, particularly the increases in lending by city banks (compared to the same period of the previous year). There are two reasons for these choices.

First, because Japan's interest rate regulations of the post-war period kept many interest rates at low levels, there were few interest rates that reflected demand and supply conditions in the financial markets clearly and hence few that could be used as intermediate objectives. Deposit rates and bond issue conditions were extremely inflexible, and even the particularly important lending rates such as short- and long-term prime rate were subject to regulation—and also were determined inflexibly on the basis of fund-raising costs. As a result, these interest rates lacked flexibility (of course, effective lending interest rates that accounted for compensating balances could move flexibly, but these were difficult to observe). The *gensaki* market and the secondary bond market did develop gradually over the years, but even these markets remained shallow until the late 1960s and did not precisely reflect conditions of demand and supply in the financial markets. It was well known that the *gensaki* rate became extremely high in periods of tight money. In this environment, only the interbank market interest rates could fluctuate freely, and thus, although they were at the level of operating variables, they could not help but become intermediate objectives.

Second was the almost complete dependence of investment activity on bank borrowing because of the situation of so-called 'over-borrowing' by corporations during the high growth period with its investment and export-based growth. Thus the increase in bank lending was a leading indicator of corporate investment activity, so that the increase in bank loans could function as an appropriate intermediate objective during the high growth period because corporate investment was the motive force behind growth. In addition, because the shares of banks in lending did not change very much over the short term, the loan increases by city banks could be used as a representative indicator but were also an indicator that had a short reporting lag.

2. INTERMEDIATE OBJECTIVES: MONEY-FOCUSED MONETARY POLICY

a. The change to money-focused monetary policy and its background

The Bank of Japan published an article entitled 'The Importance of the Money Supply in Japan' in its monthly report of July 1975. In this article the importance of the money supply in monetary management was emphasized [6]. A portion of the article read as follows:

In order to achieve price stability and to strive for the appropriate development of the economy, it will be necessary to pay sufficient attention in the future to the movements of M2 in the management of monetary policy.... In the actual management of policy, the growth rate of the money supply should be kept stable in cases when it is judged that no particularly large economic problems loom, and in cases when problems do loom the reasons for these problems should be analysed and a realistic monetary policy attitude should be adopted which continuously reconsiders policy management in the direction of correcting future growth rates of the money supply.... Money-focused monetary policy in no way implies decreased importance for interest rate policy. Rather, in order to achieve effectiveness in quantitative adjustments it is absolutely necessary that interest rate policy be managed in a form that is consistent with the underlying tenor of quantitative adjustment policy.

The purpose of this article was to give the money supply a place as an intermediate objective. On the basis of these ideas, a change in monetary management occurred in Japan, beginning in July 1978. Since that time, the Bank of Japan has made it a rule to announce, at the beginning of every quarter, an estimated value for the growth rate of the average outstanding balance, of the money supply relative to the same period in the previous year. This estimated value is called a forecast and applies to the current quarter. Originally, the definition of the money supply used was M2, but the definition was changed to M2 + CDs when the latter began to be issued. The reasons for the change to money-focused policy were several changes in the circumstances of the Japanese economy [46].

The first change of circumstance was the increased difficulty in distinguishing just exactly what information interest rate movements were giving about the effectiveness of monetary policy. This difficulty emerged because of the gradual acceleration of inflation in the second half of the 1960s followed by the intensified world-wide inflation after the first oil crisis and the chronic inflation thereafter. For example, when interest rates rise, it is not possible to judge conclusively whether this rise has occurred because of high inflationary expectations, because of the increase in money demand generated by overheating of the business cycle, or because of a decrease in money supply as the effects of tighter monetary policy permeate through the economy [33]. If either of the former two reasons is correct, then there is a need to tighten monetary policy further; but if the latter is correct there is no such need. An indicator that does not allow such judgements is inappropriate as an intermediate objective. And, in fact, in several countries, the former two reasons and the latter reason were confused, inviting delays in monetary tightening and intensification of inflation.

The second change of circumstance leading to the shift to money-focused monetary policy was Japan's experience during the early 1970s. As a result of the excess money supply growth during 1971–2 (the peak money supply growth rates for M1 and M2 were about 30 per cent over the same period of the previous year), consumer price inflation rose to double-figure levels from 1973 to 1975. In order to overcome this inflation, a long and painful adjustment process, lasting until 1977, was unavoidable.

The third change of circumstance was the reduction in the funds deficit of the corporate sector, reflecting the downward kink in economic growth, and the expansion of the funds deficit of the public sector (i.e., the large-scale flotation of Government bonds). As a result, the channels of creation of the money supply were no longer limited to increases in lending to the private sector but also now included the substantial channel of Government bond underwriting by the banks. (In this case as well, of course, the total supply of money in the final analysis is the determined by the Bank of Japan's attitude toward supply of base money—see Chapter 4.) The supply of money that accompanies bank underwriting of Government bonds was accumulated as currency balances in the own funds of the corporate sector, that is, effected an increase in corporate liquidity, and thus became the financial support of the expenditure activities of corporations. Thus the money stock became a buffer between the credit flows, such as increases in lending to the private sector, and aggregate expenditure activities. Increases in lending did not necessarily coincide with high levels of cash holdings or with an extension of expenditure. In a sense, the use of increases in loans as an intermediate objective implicitly used the increase in the money supply as an intermediate objective; but after 1975 it became necessary to use the money supply itself as the intermediate objective.

b. The method of monetary targeting

The use of the money supply as the intermediate objective of monetary policy in Japan began only after 1975 and involved certain practical problems. These included (1) which monetary aggregate to use as the main intermediate objective; (2) what period of time to use for the achievement of the intermediate objective; and (3) whether to announce the intermediate objective.

(i) Choice of monetary indicator

As seen in Chapter 3, there are several types of statistical indicator of the money supply. Normally, the monetary indicators used as intermediate objectives for monetary policy are, in order of increasing coverage, base money, narrow money (M1), and broad money (the latter might include M2, M3, or a proxy variable for the latter known as 'central bank money')[2] The choice of which monetary indicator to emphasize is essentially an empirical one. The Bank of Japan emphasizes an indicator that falls in the category of broad money, that is, M2 + CDs.

One reason for this choice is that M2 + CDs has the closest relationship with income and expenditure, in the sense that it is a leading indicator that affects the latter two variables in the future. Though M1 has a closer relationship with income and expenditure in the current period, the movements of M1 reflect only the changes in income and expenditure that are already being realized. For a central bank, however, the most important factor is to control a monetary indicator that has the closest relationship with the potential movements of income and expenditure in the future. Currently, the results of empirical analysis indicate that M2 + CDs has a closer causal relationship with money and expenditure in the future than does M1 [35].

A second reason for using M2 + CDs is its superior controllability. There are rather strict limits on the ability to exert a short-term control over base money and M1 because of their close relationships with current income and expenditure. This is because it is difficult to control the short-term shifts of funds between a currency and M1 or between M1 and time deposits. With respects to M2 + CDs, however, such shifts are only compositional shifts within the definition, so that control of the total amount of credit granted by banks allows control even in the short run of the total amount of M2 + CDs.

In addition, the statistics on M2 + CDs have a high degree of reliability, but are not inferior to base money or M1 with respect to reporting lags.

(ii) The period over which control is exerted

The problem of the period over which to achieve control of the intermediate target is related to the problem of which indicator to choose. The Bank of Japan makes an announcement in the first month of each quarter of an

[2] Central bank money is a weighted average of currency and reserve requirements held against the components of broad money.

estimated value for the current quarter of the increase of M2 + CDs versus the same period of the previous year. In this sense, the annual rate of increase is the focus of attention. This is done because the influence of M2 + CDs on the current values of income, expenditure, and prices are derived from the course of M2 + CDs over approximately the previous two years. Thus it is thought important to exert appropriate control over the value of the quantity of money measured over a period of a year or more rather than over a short period [46].

(iii) Determination and announcement of the intermediate objective

Monetary policy in Japan focuses on M2 + CDs but does not determine 'targets' in the strict sense of the word. Only 'forecasts' are announced. However, the policy actions of the Bank of Japan itself are included in the determination of these forecasts, and in this sense the forecasts represent increases in the money supply that the Bank of Japan is willing to permit. The Bank of Japan pays continuously close attention to the effects that the trends of money supply growth will have on future income, expenditure, and prices. In cases when undesirable effects are judged to be possible, policy actions are carried out without delay. At such times the forecasts include the changes in policy action and move gradually in the desirable direction. Indeed, a comparison of the forecasts announced by the Bank of Japan and the actual growth rates of M2 + CDs shows that the forecasts are very close to actual growth; during this period, the movements of the price level were in general stable [32].

3. THE CONTROLLABILITY OF MONEY AND OPERATING VARIABLES

a. Interbank interest rates as operating variables

As described above, operating variables are policy variables that are close at hand for use in controlling the intermediate objectives. The operating variables for Japan have always been interbank interest rates (the call rate and the bill rate), from the high growth period into the present [44], [45].

The ability of the Bank of Japan to control interbank interest rates as a means of day-to-day monetary adjustment is based on its ability to affect demand and supply conditions for funds in the interbank market through lending policy and bill operations. At a more basic level, the Bank of Japan's ability to control rates is based on its ability to affect the path along which reserves are accumulated. Under the reserve requirement system in Japan, required reserve levels are based on the average deposits over the period of one calendar month, but the reserves must be accumulated (in Bank of Japan deposits) from the sixteenth of this calendar month to the fifteenth of the succeeding calendar month. It is the average level of required reserves during the period from the sixteenth of one month to the fifteenth of the next that counts in calculating compliance with the reserve requirements, but the amount outstanding of reserve deposits may fluctuate from day to day. If, however, repayment of Bank of Japan loans or other factors causes financial adjustments in the market such that the quantity of reserve deposits continues for several days to be less than required reserves, then the so-called 'reserves accumulation path' gradually falls behind schedule. As a result, the financial institutions will begin to look for funding in the interbank market in order to raise their reserves accumulation, and the demand-supply balance will gradually become more strained and raise interbank market interest rates. Of course, if financial adjustments were carried out so that on a given day the reserve deposits for the banking system as a whole become negative, then somewhere in the system a bank would have fallen into default, and credit conditions would have become disorderly. (In order to avoid such conditions the Bank of Japan of course acts as lender of last resort.) Even without forcing reserves to such a low level, however, a delay in the reserve accumulation path can cause interest rates in the market to rise gradually. It is also possible, in contrast, for the Bank of Japan to accelerate the reserve accumulation path through the supply of lump sums for purchase of bills. In such cases the demand-supply situation in the interbank markets gradually becomes easier and interest rates begin to fall [53], [54].

b. Influence of interbank market interest rates on the money supply

Let us next consider the process by which the operating variables affect the intermediate objective of the money supply.

Changes in the interbank market rates affect the money supply primarily through three channels of influence: (1) effects on the bank's portfolio selection, (2) financial disintermediation, and (3) effects of the interest rate fluctuations on private expenditure. The first of these was the traditional transmission channel during the high growth period, while the second and third are channels that have opened since the development of open markets and the more flexible movements of interest rates in these markets. Let us consider the transmission of effects through each of these three channels in the case of an increase in interbank interest rates owing to a tightening of monetary policy.

First come the effects of the interest rate increase on the bank's portfolio selection. Although interest rates on loans in Japan are free interest rates, they tend to be inflexible because of the *de facto* link between prime rates and the official discount rate, because of inflexible fund-raising costs reflecting regulation of deposit rates, and because of the difficulty of sudden changes of interest rates out of consideration of long-term customer relationships with clients in bilateral lending transactions. In addition, the subscriber's yield on bonds were for a long period *de facto* regulated and inflexible.

Because lending rates and bond subscriber's yields were inflexible compared with interbank interest rates, large differentials between the interbank rates and the official discount rate would cause banks and other financial institutions to reduce their lending and absorption of bonds and to increase their lending in the interbank markets or at least to repay what they had borrowed in the interbank markets (the resultant easing of the demand–supply balance in the interbank markets would be absorbed without delay by further Bank of Japan monetary adjustments) [18], [22], [44]. As a result, provision of credit to the private sector was reduced, and the availability of credit fell simultaneously, leading to a reduction in expenditure activity. This is nothing other than a reduction in spending due to a fall in the money supply. The Bank of Japan's guidance on the increases of loans to the private sector by banks supplemented these policies and had the effect of quickening the speed of asset adjustment by banks.

High interbank interest rates could also cause financial dis-intermediation. Because the interest rate on deposits offered by banks were subject to regulation, the deposit rates came to be relatively low in comparison to free rates in the open markets that had arbitrage relationships with the higher interbank market interest rates. The result was that the non-bank sector shifted its assets from deposits to the free markets. As a result, banks found it difficult to gather funds and reduced their provision of credit. This process is known as financial disintermediation and reduces the money supply. If the customers who are no longer able to get bank credit are able to raise equivalent amounts from the open markets, then there is no tightening of financial conditions; however, in fact, monetary conditions do tighten because small and medium-sized businesses and individuals cannot issue securities in these markets.

The third effect of increased interbank interest rates is their influence on private expenditure. Increases in interbank money market interest rates invite increases in open market interest rates such as the *gensaki*, CD, and secondary bond markets through interest rate arbitrage; the pressure from interest rate increases eventually reaches even the inflexible lending rates and bond subscription rate. These increases constitute improvements in investment yields for sectors of the economy with surplus funds, and also constitute increases in fund-raising costs for deficit sectors. In other words, the opportunity cost of investment rises for surplus sectors while the borrowing cost of investment rises for deficit sectors. Both these changes tend to reduce investment activity and thus income. As a result, demand for money falls and the money supply is reduced.

The relative importance of these three channels of transmission of effects differs according to the character of interest rates in a financial system. For example, as lending rates and bond subscriber rates become more flexible, then the first channel becomes weaker and the third becomes stronger. If deposit rates become more flexible, then the second channel becomes weaker and the third channel becomes stronger. In all cases, however, influence over interbank interest rates ensures the controllability of the money supply [35].

4. MONEY SUPPLY MOVEMENTS AND THE JAPANESE ECONOMY

Now that we have considered the management of monetary policy in recent years and the channels through which the effects of policy flow, let us next examine what the effects of monetary policy conducted in this way actually were.

Figure 6.1 compares the movements of money supply, nominal GNP, and real GNP for the periods before and after 1975 when the money-focused monetary policy began to operate. The period after 1975 has four characteristics. First, the growth rate of the money supply versus the same period of the previous year has been declining, and the variations have been within 5 per cent around the trend. Secondly, the growth rates of nominal GNP have also been declining and their variability has also fallen. Thirdly, the growth rate of real GNP has been at about the 5 per cent level, with the exception of the 1981–3 period in which there was a simultaneous world-wide recession. Fourthly, as a result of these three previous factors, the inflation rate has also been falling, and in recent years has been contained within 1 to 2 per cent (as measured by the GNP deflactor).

These movements of macro-economic indicators contrast clearly with those in the period up to 1974. In the earlier period, the growth rate of money supply ranged between 15 to 25 per cent, a very wide band. As a result, growth rates of nominal GNP also fluctuated widely, as did the growth rates of real GNP. In addition, the average growth rate of the GNP deflator was as high as 6 per cent.

One reason for the difference of performance of these indicators after 1975 is surely to be found in the policy which sought stable control of the money supply while simultaneously working through interest rates [14]. This performance is particularly interesting in light of the many large shocks that occurred during this period, such as reactions to the unfamiliar floating exchange rate system, the second oil crisis, the world-wide inflation and subsequent simultaneous recession, and the deepening of the debt crisis. The Japanese economy was able to achieve a stable performance in this environment even though the economies of many advanced countries were destabilized.

IV. Monetary policy and changes in the financial environment

As described in Chapter 2, there is every expectation that the liberalization and internationalization of the Japanese financial system will continue along with the appearance of various financial innovations such as new financial markets, new assets, and new methods of trading. Let us now consider changes in the management of monetary policy and its effectiveness in the face of these changes in the financial environment.

1. FINANCIAL LIBERALIZATION AND MONETARY POLICY

a. Financial liberalization and money supply control

The major motive forces behind the development of financial liberalization in Japan have been large-scale flotations of Government bonds since 1975 and the simultaneous development of open financial markets with free interest rates and of new financial assets in this environment. Let us first consider the relationship between the financial innovations that accompanied the large-scale bond flotations and control of the money supply [13].

(i) Government bond issue and the money supply

Since the large-scale flotation of Government bonds has continued unavoidably since 1975, the problems that accompany such large-scale flotations, and in particular worries about inflation, have been very much in the public awareness. The great inflation that started with the large-scale bond issues under Finance Minister Takahashi in the 1930s remains very much in memory, and there have been also been analogies to the price explosion after the excess liquidity created by the large inflows of foreign exchange in the early 1970s.

For these reasons, the switch to easy monetary policy during 1975–8 was accompanied by frequent debates concerning the danger of excess liquidity that might accompany large-scale issues of Government bonds. Such debates flared up whenever the growth of the money supply rose even slightly and when the fiscal authorities began to stress their programme of fiscal reconstruction around 1980. The fiscal authorities continuously mentioned the worries of inflation as one of the dangers of large-scale bond flotations. For example, the Ministry of Finance report 'Considering Fiscal Reconstruction' (August 1980) listed four reasons why large-scale Government bond flotations—that is, fiscal deficits—were undesirable. These were (1) the increase in bond costs that would be required for interest payments and redemption of public bonds, (2) pressure on private fund demand and worries about fiscal inflation, (3) the burden on future generations from public bonds and particularly deficit bonds, and (4) the loss of fiscal discipline that would accompany the decline in cost consciousness.

But such worries would not necessarily be borne out in every case. This is because the link between accumulated Government debts and increases in the money supply, and hence increases in inflation, would be determined by the method of issuing Government bonds and the attitude on the part of the Bank of Japan based on this method of issue.

Commercial financial institutions, and not the Bank of Japan, underwrite and absorb the largest portion of Government bond issues in Japan today. Let us examine this process in some detail. Say that Government bonds are issued through underwriting by a commercial bank (an institution supplying money) and that the proceeds of this issue are used for the purchase of goods and services from the private non-banking sector. At the initial instant of flotation the reserves held by the bank will decrease by an amount equivalent to the proceeds of the bond issue that is exactly the same as the increase in the value of the bonds held (if bank reserves were in equilibrium before the bond underwriting, then reserves will be sufficient). At this stage the cash and deposit position of the private non-banking sector has not changed, and therefore the money supply has not moved. The second stage is reached when the proceeds of the bond issue are used to purchase goods and services. The payments for these goods and services provided by the private non-banking sector are held in the form of cash or bank deposits (that is, increases in the money supply). For the banks, these movements of the private non-banking sector are reflected as increases in reserves on the asset side and increases in deposits on the liability side. Comparing the initial state to the second state, the reserve position of the banks has returned to its situation before the bond flotation, while the money supply has increased by an amount equivalent to the bond flotation. That is, reserves are unchanged but the money supply has increased. Therefore, a situation of insufficient reserves has occurred.

In this theoretical exercise, the underwriting of bonds by the commercial banks led to an increase in the money supply, but in the previous section we saw that in fact the increases in the money supply since 1975 have been on a gradual downward trend. Because the Bank of Japan did not passively supply base money to counter the occurrence of inadequate reserves, the commercial banks were forced to reduce their provision of credit through such measures as reducing their lending or sales of bonds, and thus had no choice but to return the money supply to its original level. In this sense, the control of the money supply in the final analysis depended on the attitude of the Bank of Japan toward supply of base money.

From the viewpoint of money supply control, the liberalization of sales of Government bonds by commercial banks in April 1977 was an epoch-making measure. This is because the liberalization allowed the banks to respond with voluntary sales of bonds to the worsening of their position that accompanied the Bank of Japan's refusal to supply more base money. As a result, there was a lessening of the danger that the Bank of Japan would passively supply base money and thus permit the increases in the money supply that accompany bank underwriting of Government bonds.

After this liberalization, the commercial banks became more active in their sales of Government bonds, and these bonds, which had now become more liquid, were in large part absorbed by corporations and others in the private non-banking sector. This was possible because corporations faced a new financial situation in which the degree of their net demand for funds had fallen with the shift toward lower economic growth, and in which they could diversify the investments of their own funds without so much consideration of their long-term client relationships with banks. Corporate purchases of outstanding Government bonds were identical to the case of individual purchase of such bonds, at least as far as their effect on the money supply is concerned.

Thus the large-scale flotations of Government bonds that took place after 1975 were in the final analysis, to a large extent, absorbed by individuals and corporations in the private non-banking sector. Thus the *a priori* potential for money supply increases due to flotation through banks was thus counter-acted *a posteriori*.

(ii) Financial innovation and money supply

Financial innovation in Japan may be characterized, if somewhat boldly, as having two basic types of innovation. The first were innovations that helped to economize the use of settlements account assets (currency and demand deposits) having either interest rates of zero or interest rates regulated at low levels. Examples would include economization on the use of currency through the spread of automatic salary deposit, cash dispensers, and automatic teller machines, and economization of ordinary deposits through creation of *sogo* (integrated) accounts. A second type of innovation created safe investment account assets that paid market interest rates (or, in other words, raised the rate of return on safe investment account assets). Examples include the creation of CDs, MMCs, and medium-term Government bond funds.

The development of financial innovations that absorbed funds into the open markets at first led to financial dis-intermediation and reduced the money supply. Also important was the development of new types of financial product that used Government bonds (for example, medium-term bond funds, Government bond time deposit accounts, and public bond *sogo* (integrated) accounts), all of which made it easier not only for corporations but also for individuals to hold Government bonds. The outflow of funds into the open markets from the financial intermediary institutions led to a reduction of the lending power of the intermediaries. In addition, the development of new products such as the medium-term bond funds occurred in a form that increased the absorption of Government bonds by individuals.

But in considering financial innovation from a longer-term perspective, other effects must be considered. First is the change in the nature of the money supply indicators that are the intermediate objectives of monetary policy. With the development of financial innovations that allow econ-omization of currency and deposit money, the growth rate of M1 will decline, and its variations will gradually become smaller; as a result, it may lose its meaning as an indicator of the amount of transactions. Moreover, if the new financial products brought by financial innovation function either as currency or quasi-money, then the definition of the money supply will have to be reconsidered.

The second, longer-term problem with financial innovation is the change in the demand function for broad money. As a result of financial innovations, there will be an increase in the share of assets within M2 or M3 that reflect market interest rates, and as a result M2 and M3 themselves will become gradually less sensitive to movements in the market interest rates. Moreover, an increase in the growth rates of M2 and M3 may be expected because asset selection for investment motives will increase its concentration on high-yielding safe assets that are included in M2 and M3.

As a result of these changes in money demand, several problems will arise in the use of the definition of M2 and M3 as intermediate objectives for monetary policy. First is the possibility that it will become more difficult to control M2 and M3 from the supply side through movements of market interest rates as has been done in the past (that is, it will be more difficult to cause financial dis-intermediation). There is also the possibility that M2 and M3 will begin to move simultaneously with transactions in the economy and that they will lose their function as leading indicators of policy objectives such as nominal GNP and prices. Nevertheless, interest movements will continue to influence expenditure through their influences on the demand side, and, in addition, money supply will continue to be important in the management of monetary policy because of its role as a coincident indicator of high reliability and short reporting lag between its own movements and indicators of the economy in general, such as nominal GNP and prices.

Of course, financial innovation in Japan has not been so rapid or dramatic that it has necessitated an immediate reconsideration of money supply [42]. Nor has innovation been so sudden that it has immediately reduced the controllability of the monetary aggregates. Indeed, shifts in the money demand function have so far been limited to those that could be captured through certain types of special factor within the year-by-year growth rates of the money supply. In the future, too, various processes of change will accompany financial innovation, and it will be possible to respond to inno-vation by broadening the definition of the money supply; in addition, it will be possible to use 'Divisia' money supply definitions that attach weight to assets according to their degrees of moneyness [21].

The important point is this: if economic stability is to be maintained through appropriate management of monetary policy, then it is necessary to minimize the difficulties concerning the money-focused monetary policy. So long as the economy is stable, financial liberalization will proceed gradually without abrupt liberalization of interest rate regulations or abrupt change of the lines of demarcation between types of business arising from wild fluct-uations of free interest rates. Without such abrupt changes, the shifts in the money demand function and changes in the character of money supply will proceed at a deliberate tempo that can be understood as it occurs. Moreover, so long as income moves in a stable manner, it will be easy to forecast interest rates and expected inflation rates that affect the money demand function, and therefore it will be easier to estimate an appropriate money supply.

b. Financial liberalization and the effectiveness of monetary policy

Section III above showed that there are three channels through which the effects of monetary policy are transmitted (1) effects on the bank's portfolio selection, (2) financial dis-intermediation, and (3) effects of interest rate fluctuations on private expenditure. And, as also explained, the first route of transmission depends on the inflexibility of bank lending rates while the second depends on the inflexibility of interest rates on bank liabilities such as deposits.

The relative importance of these three transmission channels will change as interest rate regulations are gradually abolished. As lending rates become more flexible, and as a larger portion of the money supply falls into categories that fluctuate with market interest rates, there will be a weakening of the policy effects through the first and second transmission channels and a strengthening of the interest rate effects through the third channel. Under financial liberalization, the effectiveness of monetary policy will be maintained through the third transmission channel. The reason is that both the borrowing cost of expenditure activity for economic agents that are in funds deficit (interest paid) and the opportunity cost of expenditure activity for economic agents that are in funds surplus (the interest received as a measure of opportunity cost) will move much more than in the past. Not only will the interest rates in open markets that are expanding become more flexible, but also the interest rates on lending and deposits of banks will become more flexible. This means that the influence of monetary policy on the money supply will act through demand-side factors rather than through supply-side factors such as financial dis-intermediation. Of course, the effectiveness of the transmission of monetary policy through this channel depends on a sufficiently high-interest elasticity of expenditure by private sectors. On this point, various statistical investigations carried out recently have shown that the effects of real interest rates on real total expenditure in Japan are fairly high [35].

Put another way, ensuring the effectiveness of monetary policy in a liberalized financial world means that it is important to strengthen the transmission of policy effects through the third transmission channel. As open markets expand, both at home and abroad, and as increases continue in the quantities of free interest rate assets, maintaining the money supply at an appropriate level will require further use of adjustment of interest rates in the short-term financial markets. Thus, an urgent task for Japan is to nurture not only the interbank markets but also open markets and particularly the market for Government bills (TBs).

2. FINANCIAL INTERNATIONALIZATION AND MONETARY POLICY

a. Capital movements and money supply control

International financial transactions were almost completely liberalized for Japanese residents with the revision of the Foreign Exchange and Foreign Trade Control Law in December 1980, the abolition of yen conversion quotas in June 1984, and other such measures. In addition, relaxation of controls concerning Euro-yen transactions have continued since June 1984. How then has the domestic money supply been affected by the more lively capital flows that have accompanied the relaxation of regulations?

Let us first consider the flow of foreign currencies. To put the conclusion first, the flow of foreign currencies has no effect on the domestic money supply so long as the monetary authorities do not intervene in the foreign exchange market. For example, when foreign currency flows into Japan, the foreign exchange inflows must be converted into Japanese yen if they are to be used in domestic transactions; thus, when the counterpart to the transaction is in the non-bank sector, the foreign currency inflow means only that the holders of the money supply have changed, not only the total quantity of money has changed. If the counterpart to the foreign exchange transaction is in the banking sector, then in the first instance the money supply does rise along with the purchase of the foreign currency, but there also occurs an insufficiency of reserves and so, as long as the Bank of Japan does not supply extra base money, the banking sector as a whole must either call in loans or sell securities in an amount equivalent to the foreign currency inflow, and thus the money supply will return to its original level. In the short run, the exchange rate and interest rates will probably change but the effects on the domestic economy are likely to be only transitional and small in scale. In the absence of excessive intervention in the foreign exchange markets, the effectiveness of monetary policy will be maintained even in the face or more vigorous capital flows.

The case of more vigorous Euro-yen transactions is fundamentally the same. No matter whether yen deposits are domestic deposits or Euro-deposits, the payment reserves behind these yen will remain in Japan; that is, the payment reserves behind Euro-yen deposits will exist in Japan through yen-denominated claims on domestic banks. So long as the Eurobank does not bring payments reserves against yen into Japan, the bank cannot simultaneously increase its lending and deposits in Euro-yen. Moreover, the total supply of yen base money determines the total quantity of payment reserves against yen-dominated deposits as a whole, including Euro-yen. Thus, the interest rates in the Euromarket are determined within the same framework as are the interest rates in the markets for domestic payment reserves that are controlled by the sole supplier of such reserves (the Bank of Japan). Euro-yen rates, therefore, are affected by domestic short-term yen interest rates through arbitrage. From the viewpoint of monetary control, the Euromarkets are in essence not different from domestic open markets such as the *gensaki* market and the CD market. The only difference is that the Euromarkets are located abroad.

In passing, it should be noted that Euro-yen interest rates and *gensaki* interest rates have been extremely closely related since the easing of controls on capital inflows and the approval for non-resident participation in *gensaki* markets in 1979. Indeed, the arbitrage has been almost perfect since the abolition of yen conversion quotas in 1984 (see Figure 6.2).

Nevertheless, certain problems remain concerning control of the money supply. The first concerns deposit reserve ratios and the second concerns definitions of monetary indicators.

First, on the matter of deposit reserve ratios, in a situation in which reserve ratios are not levied on the yen liabilities of domestic banks *via-à-vis* Eurobanks, a shift of deposits of the non-banking sector from domestic banks to Eurobanks will, immediately after the shift, lead to the occurrence of excess reserves. This is because the composition of liabilities of the domestic bank has shifted from deposits on which reserves are levied to claims on a Eurobank on which reserve ratios are not levied. (The claims on the Eurobank are listed as either interbank accounts or deposits of correspondent banks.) When the domestic bank uses the fund resulting from its liability to the Eurobank in order to increase its lending, then there is an increase in the quantity of yen-denominated money if one combines the domestic banking sector and the Eurobanking sector. If the same reserve ratio were applied to the liabilities of domestic banks to Eurobanks, then such situations would in part be prevented. However, if the Eurobank does not keep 100 per cent reserves against its Euro-yen deposits (its claims on the domestic bank) and uses these reserves to lend directly on the domestic non-bank sector and thus creates Euro-yen deposits, then there will be an increase in the total of yen deposits in the domestic and Euromarkets, that is, an increase in the total money supply. In order to prevent such increases, it would be necessary to levy direct reserve requirements on the yen deposits or yen lending of Euro-banks; in reality it is difficult to gain the co-operation of the countries concerned, so that the present situation is one of each country reacting individually.

The domestic reserve ratios in Japan (for the time deposits and CDs of very large banks with over ¥3·3bn. in deposits) were 1·6 to 5 per cent as of the end of June 1986, while the reserve ratios on yen account liabilities to non-residents including Eurobanks was 0·25 per cent.

The second problem is whether to include Euro-yen in the money supply statistics, and this problem is somewhat technical in nature. If large shifts were to occur between Euro-yen deposits and domestic yen deposits, then it would be only natural for there to be differences between the calculation of a domestic money supply that included only domestic yen deposits and the

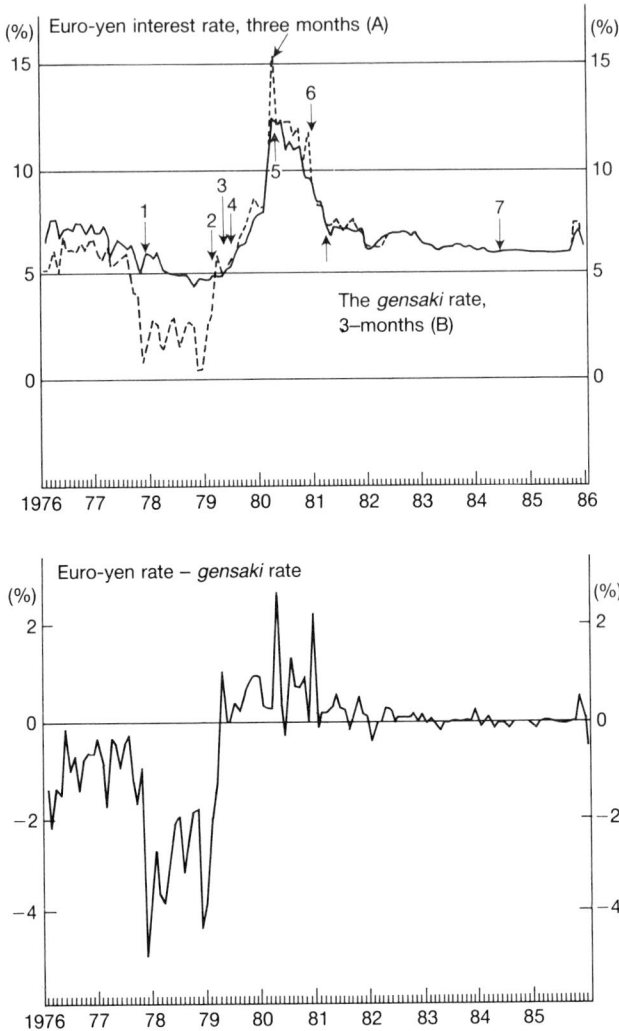

Figure 6.2   *Euro-Yen Interest Rates and Domestic Interest Rates (in per cent)*

1. November 1977: Measures to regulate short-term fund flows (50 per cent, reserve requirement on increases in free-yen deposits; raised to 100 per cent in March 1978).
2. February 1979: Abolition of regulations on acquisition of domestic securities by non-residents.
3. May 1979: Abolition of prohibition on *gensaki* transactions by non-residents.
4. June 1979: Abolition of prohibition on introduction of short-term impact loans.
5. March 1980: Liberalization of interest rates on free-yen deposits of foreign governments.
6. December 1980: Revision of the Foreign Exchange and Foreign Trade Control Law.
7. June 1984: Abolition of yen conversion quotas.

total yen money supply that also included Euro-yen deposits. There are six important factors to consider when defining the money stock of a nation in a situation of strengthening international financial relationships. These are the types of financial institution, the location of the financial institutions, the types of liability of financial institutions, the types of currency of denomination, the types of asset-holder, and the location of the asset-holders.

The determination of which types of Euro-yen to include in money statistics according to these attributes is an extremely difficult empirical problem. This determination can only be made after considering several important factors. Apart from the practical problems of obtaining the data in a timely manner, there are more fundamental problems such as the stability of the relationship between these data and economic indicators, and the controllability of these Euro-deposits by the Bank of Japan. As of now, the Euro-yen holdings of resident financial institutions that could be included in money supply statistics are quite small (at the end of 1983, $940m. or only 0.1 per cent of M2 + CDs); thus it would not at present appear meaningful to carry out quantitative empirical analysis.

Moreover, the majority of Euro-yen deposits are time deposits, and there are almost no cases in which final settlement of domestic transactions is carried out in the Euromarkets; including such deposits in M1 would not be appropriate. However, the ease of conversion of such Euro-deposits into deposits that can be used for domestic settlement is hardly different from that of financial assets that are included in quasi-money. Thus, when the holding of Euro-yen deposits is largely deregulated or liberalized, it will be necessary to consider including these deposits in the definition of broad money. There will remain difficulties in obtaining data for the calculation of deposits placed with foreign banks, and hence it may be better to include such deposits in M3 rather than M2.

b. Foreign exchange market fluctuations and the conduct of monetary policy

Another important point concerning the internationalization of the financial structure is the effect that fluctuations of the foreign exchange market have on the management of monetary policy. Since the shift to the floating-rate system in 1973, the foreign exchange market has moved very flexibly. At the time of the shift to floating rates, it was believed, particularly in the academic world, that monetary policy would be more independent under the floating-rate system than it had been under the fixed-rate system.

But looking back on more than ten years of experience under the floating exchange rate system, it would be difficult to say that floating rates have functioned as adequately as was expected. The first problem has been that the short-term price elasticity of export and import quantities has been rather low, so that, with so-called 'J-curve effects' (terms-of-trade effects), recovery of equilibrium in current account balances has required very long periods of time [27]. As a result, the foreign exchange market has had a tendency repeatedly to overshoot the levels of exchange rates that correspond to equilibrium. The second problem has been that the foreign exchange markets have diverged from the levels corresponding to purchasing-power parity not only in the short term but in the medium term as well. As a result, disequilibria in the current account have continued in the medium term and have stimulated protectionism. The medium-term divergences of exchange rates from purchasing-power parity have had several causes, including the continuation of real interest rate differentials among the major countries due to asymmetries in policy mixes, the reduction in risk premiums due to enhanced substitutability among currencies that has in turn accompanied financial internationalization, and the reduction in the ability of the exchange markets to restore equilibrium because of the accumulation of disequilibria in the current account.

Because of these problems with the floating rate system, it is not practically possible for central banks to focus solely on the achievements of domestic equilibrium even though the final objectives in the conduct of monetary policy are the stability of domestic output and prices. Cautious consideration must also be given to the fluctuations in the foreign exchange market caused by disequilibria in the current account, and also to the movements of real interest rate differentials among countries that have caused the disequilibria in the current accounts.

BIBLIOGRAPHY

[1] ANDO, ALBERT, HIDE KAZU, ROGER FARMER, and YOSHIO SUZUKI, eds., *Monetary Policy in Our Times* (The Proceedings of the First International Conference, Massachusetts Institute of Technology, Spring 1985).

[2] Bank for International Settlements, *Payment Systems in Eleven Developed Countries*, (Basle, February 1985).

[3] Bank of Japan, 'Characteristics of Interest Rate Fluctuations amidst Deregulations and Internationalization of Financing', (Special Paper 126, Tokyo, Bank of Japan Research and Statistics Department, October 1985).

[4] —— *Nippon Ginko Hyakunenshi* (Centennial History of the Bank of Japan; Tokyo).

[5] —— 'Recent Changes in Financial Asset Preference by Households' (Special Paper 119, Tokyo, Bank of Japan Research and Statistics Department, April 1985).

[6] —— 'Role of the Money Supply in the Japanese Economy', (Special Paper 60, Tokyo, Bank of Japan Research and Statistics Department, October 1975).

[7] —— 'Stepped-up Capital Movements In and Out of Japan and their Effect on the Japanese Financial Market' (Special Paper 112, Tokyo, Bank of Japan Research and Statistics Department, March 1986).

[8] —— 'Structural Changes in the Secondary Market for Bonds and Recent Trends in Yields on Long-term Bonds' (Special Paper 132, Tokyo, Bank of Japan Research and Statistics Department, March 1986).

[9] —— *Money and Banking in Japan*, ed. L. S. Pressnell Japan (1973).

[10] CARGILL, THOMAS F., 'A U.S. Perspective on Japanese Financial Liberalization', *Monetary and Economic Studies, 3.1 (1985)* (Tokyo, Bank of Japan Institute for Monetary and Economic Studies).

[11] DOTSEY, MICHAEL, 'Japanese Monetary Policy, A Comparative Analysis', *Monetary and Economic Studies*, 4.2 (1986) (Tokyo, Bank of Japan Institute for Monetary and Economic Studies).

[12] Federal Reserve System, *'The Federal Reserve System—Purposes and Functions'* USA (1984).

[13] FELDMAN, ROBERT ALAN *'Japanese Financial Markets: Deficits, Dilemmas and Deregulation'* (Cambridge, Mass., 1986).

[14] FRIEDMAN, MILTON, 'Monetarism in Rhetoric and Practice' (included in [1]).

[15] FUKAO, MITSUHIRO AND TAKASHI OKUBO, 'International Linkage of Interest Rates: The Case of Japan and the United States' (Discussion Paper 13, Tokyo, Bank of Japan Monetary and Economic Studies Department, June 1982).

[16] FUKUI, TOSHIHIKO, 'Recent Developments of the Short-term Money Market in Japan and Changes in Monetary Control Techniques and Procedures by the Bank of Japan' (Special Paper 130, Tokyo, Bank of Japan Research and Statistics Department, January 1986).

[17] HASUI, AKIHIRO, 'Ginko no Kenzensei to Koteki Kisei Kantoku' (Sound Banking and Supervision by Monetary Authorities), *Kin'yu Kenkyu* 5.2 (1986) (Tokyo, Bank of Japan Institute for Monetary and Economic Studies).

[18] HORIUCHI, AKIYOSHI, *'Nihon no Kin'yu Seisaku—Kin'yu Mekanizumu no Jissho Bunseki',* (Monetary Policy in Japan), (Tokyo, Toyo Keizai Shinpo Sha, 1980).

[19] HORIYE, YASUHIRO, 'Saving Behaviour of Japanese Households', *Monetary and Economic Studies* 3.3 (1985) (Tokyo, Bank of Japan Institute for Monetary and Economic Studies).

[20] IKEO, KAZUHITO, *'Nihon no Kin'yushi jo to Soshiki'* (Financial Markets and Organizations in Japan) (Tokyo, Toyo Keizai Shinpo Sha, 1985).

[21] ISHIDA, KAZUHIKO, 'Divisia Monetary Aggregates and Demand for Money: A Japanese Case', *Monetary and Economic Studies*, 2.1 (1984) (Tokyo, Bank of Japan Institute for Monetary and Economic Studies).

[22] IWATA, KAZUMASA AND HAMADA KOICHI, *Kin'yu Seisaku to Ginko Kodo* (Monetary Policy and Bank Behaviour) Tokyo, Toyo Keizai Shinpo Sha, 1980).

[23] KASUYA, MUNEHISA, 'Economies of Scope: Theory and Applications to Banking', *Monetary and Economic Studies*, 4.2 (1986) (Tokyo, Bank of Japan Institute for Monetary and Economic Studies).

[24] KATOH, TOSHIHIKO, *Honpo Ginko Shiron* (A History of Banks in Japan) (Tokyo University Press, 1957).

[25] KINOSHITA, MASATOSHI, 'Bank Management and Financial Order in the Phase of Liberalization and Internationalization of Financial Markets', *Monetary and Economic Studies*, 3.2 (1985) (Tokyo, Bank of Japan Institute for Monetary and Economic Studies).

[26] —— 'Wagakuni no Yutanpo Gensoku no Hyoka to Kongo no Arikata—Shasai Hakko wo Chushin ni' (The Principle of Bond Collateral Requirements in Japan: A Current Appraisal and Future Prospects), *Kin'yu Kenkyu* 3.3 (1984) (Tokyo, Bank of Japan Institute for Monetary and Economic Studies).

[27] KOMIYA, RYUTARO AND MIYAKO SUDA, *Gendai Kokusai Kin'yuron* (Modern International Monetary Theory) (Tokyo, Nikon Keizai Shinbun Sha, 1983).

[28] KURODA, AKIO AND TAKASHI OKUBO, 'An Empirical Investigation of the Term Structure of Japanese Government Bond Yields: An Analysis Using a Bivariate Time-Series Model' (Discussion Paper 11, Tokyo, Bank of Japan Monetary and Economic Studies Department, January 1982).

[29] —— 'On the Determination of Yields in Japanese Secondary Bond Market: An Expectations Theory Approach' (Discussion Paper 7, Tokyo, Bank of Japan Monetary and Economic Studies Department, August 1981).

[30] KURODA, AKIO, 'Expected Inflation Rates and the Term Structure of Interest Rates', *Monetary and Economic Studies*, 1.1 (1983) (Tokyo, Bank of Japan Institute for Monetary and Economic Studies).

[31] KURODA, IWAO, 'Mechanism of Bank-Loan Rates Determination in Japan: Re-Examination of the Traditional Theory and a New View' (Discussion Paper 2, Tokyo, Bank of Japan Special Economic Studies Department, October 1980).

[32] MELTZER, ALLAN H., 'Variability of Prices, Output and Money Under Fixed and Fluctuating Exchange Rates: An Empirical Study of Monetary Regimes in

Japan and United States', *Monetary and Economic Studies*, 3.3 (1985) (Tokyo, Bank of Japan Institute for Monetary and Economic Studies).

[33] NARIKAWA, RYOSUKE, 'Manee Sapurai to Kinri no Kankei ni tsuite' (On the Relationship between the Money Supply and Interest Rates), *Kin'yu Kenkyu Shiryo*, 13 (Tokyo, Bank of Japan Monetary and Economic Studies Department, June 1982).

[34] OHTA, TSUTOMU, 'Kin'yu Jiyuka Shinten no moto de no Shin'yo Chitsujo Iji no Shomondai' (Stability of the Monetary System and the Transition to the Regime of Deregulated Interest Rates), *Kin'yu Kenkyu* 3.1 (1984) (Tokyo, Bank of Japan Institute for Monetary and Economic Studies).

[35] OKUBO, TAKASHI, 'Money, Interest, Income and Prices', *Monetary and Economic Studies*, 1.2 (1983) (Tokyo, Bank of Japan Institute for monetary and Economic Studies).

[36] PATRICK, HUGH T., *Monetary Policy and Central Banking in Contemporary Japan* (Series in Monetary and International Economics 5, University of Bombay, 1962).

[37] ROYAMA, SHOICHI, 'Wagakuni no Kin'yu Mekanizumu' (The Monetary Mechanisn in Japan), in Takuji Shimano and Hamado Koichi, eds., *Nihon no Kin'yu* (Finance in Japan) (Tokyo, Iwanami Shoten, 1971).

[38] —— *Nihon no Kin'yu Shisutemu* (The Financial System in Japan) (Tokyo, Toyo Keizai Shinpo Sha, 1985).

[39] SHINOHARA, MIYOHEI, *Industrial Growth, Trade and Dynamic Patterns in the Japanese Economy* (University of Tokyo Press, 1982).

[40] SUZUKI, TAKEO AND ICHIRO KAWAMOTO, *Shoken Torihiki Hou* (The Securities Exchange Law) (Tokyo, Yuhikaku, 1984).

[41] SUZUKI, YOSHIO, 'Changes in Financial Asset Selection and the Development of Financial Markets in Japan', *Monetary and Economic Studies*, 1.2 (1983) (Tokyo, Bank of Japan Institute for Monetary and Economic Studies).

[42] —— 'Financial Innovation and Monetary Policy in Japan', *Monetary and Economic Studies*, 2.1 (1984) (Tokyo, Bank of Japan Institute for Monetary and Economic Studies).

[43] —— *Kin'yu Jiyuka to Kin'yu Seisaku* (Financial Liberalization and Monetary Policy) (Tokyo, Toyo Keizai Shinpo Sha, 1985).

[44] —— *Kin'yu Seisaku no Koka—Ginko Kodo no Riron to Keisoku* (The Effects of Monetary Policy—Theory and Estimation of Bank Behaviour) (Tokyo, Toyo Keizai Shinpo Sha, 1966).

[45] —— *Money and Banking in Contemporary Japan* (New Haven, Conn., Yale University Press, 1980).

[46] —— *Money, Finance, and Macroeconomic Performance in Japan* (New Haven, Conn., Yale University Press, 1986).

[47] —— *Nihon Keizai to Kin'yu—Sono Tenkan to Tekio* (Finance and the Japanese Economy: Change and Adaptation) (Tokyo, Toyo Keizai Shinpo Sha, 1981).

[48] SUZUKI, YOSHIO and HIROSHI YOMO, eds., *Financial Innovation and Monetary Policy: Asia and the West* (Proceedings of the Second International Conference, University of Tokyo Press, 1986).

[49] TACHI, RYUICHIRO, *Kin'yu Seisaku no Riron* (Theory of Monetary Policy) (University of Tokyo Press, 1982).

[50] TERANISHI, JURO, *Nihon no Keizai Hatten to Kin'yu* (Finance and Economic

Development in Japan) (Tokyo, Iwanami Shoten, 1982).

[51] TOBIN, JAMES, 'Financial Innovation and Deregulation in Perspective', *Monetary and Economic Studies*, 3.2 (1985) (Tokyo, Bank of Japan Institute for Monetary and Economic Studies).

[52] WAKITA, YASUHIRO, 'Good Customer relationship to Ginko Kodo' (Banking Behaviour and Good Customer Relationship), *Kin'yu Kenkyu Shiryo* 7 (Tokyo, Bank of Japan Special Economic Studies Department).

[53] YAMAMOTO, KANOH, 'Wagakuni ni okeru Manee Sapurai Kontororu no Mekanizumu ni tsuite' (On the Mechanism of Controlling the Money Supply in Japan), *Kin'yu Kenkyu Shiryo* 5 (Tokyo, Bank of Japan Special Economic Studies Department, May 1980).

[54] YASUDA, TAKASHI, 'Supply of Legal Reserves and the Short-term Money Market Rates: A Theoretical Framework' (Discussion Paper 6, Tokyo Bank of Japan Monetary and Economic Studies Department, June 1981).

[55] YUMOTO, MASASHI, KINZO SHIMA, HAJIME KOIKE, and HIROO TAGUCHI, 'Financial Innovation in Major Industrial Countries' (included in [48]).

STATISTICS

[56] Bank of Japan, *Economic Statistics Annual* (Tokyo, Research and Statistics Department).

[57] —— *Economic Statistics Monthly* (Tokyo, Research and Statistics Department).

[58] —— *Financial Statements of Principal Enterprises* (Tokyo, Research and Statistics Department).

[59] —— 'Flow of Funds Accounts in Japan' (Tokyo, Research and Statistics Department).

[60] BOND UNDERWRITERS' ASSOCIATION OF JAPAN, *Bond Review*, Japan.

[61] Economic Planning Agency, *Annual Report on National Accounts*.

[62] Federation of Bankers' Associations of Japan, *Analysis of Financial Statements to All Banks* (Tokyo (half-yearly)).

INDEX